Lean Foundations

An action guide for leaders in manufacturing to enhance workplace happiness, improve operational performance, and provide a platform for Lean.

by **Kane Marshall**

ISBN 978 1 9161692 0 3

First published August 2019

Acknowledgements

This book, as you might expect, has been written following quite a long and difficult process of learning and reflection. It's also come about thanks to the efforts and support of lots of other people.

First of all, there are the committed and passionate professionals that I have had the great privilege to work with throughout my career. Many have been subjected to my mistakes, but hopefully these are far outweighed by our shared successes. To all of those people, who are far too numerous to mention by name here, I offer my sincere thanks, and where appropriate my apologies.

Second, some of those professionals, of course, stand out more than others, and have become friends that have offered advice and support as I have endeavoured to write down what we have learned together. Thank you to Mark Hudman, Robbie Phelps, Andy Steele, and Ian Boyle for keeping me on the right track when needed. Your passion and enthusiasm have reminded me of why we work the way we do.

Third, I'd like to thank Jo Watson, who has edited early parts of the book, and has given me the confidence to believe that I can actually write. If you're an aspiring writer and are looking for a little support on your journey, I can certainly recommend that you seek her out.

Fourth, I'd like to thank the various leaders, managers and mentors that have supported me on my leadership journey. Fiona Cameron is a coach and mentor extraordinaire who has challenged my thoughts, nurtured my humility, and encouraged my learning more than I ever thought possible. And, Nemanja Mijic, Matt Dhillon, Jonathan Davies, Steve Spence, Joerg Lichtenberg, Chris Trevithick, Pat Salter, Martin Hands, George Marinos, and John Arnold have all contributed to my understanding of Lean, and my approach to leadership.

Fifth, a special thanks go to my mum and dad for being so supportive and behind me every step of the way. My mum in particular has read every page, more than once, and has never wavered in her encouragement. Thanks to both of you for believing in me.

And finally, my greatest thanks have to go to my wife Sarah, and our two amazing boys William and Thomas. Despite being gainfully unemployed for the last seven months, and therefore forcing us to stare down the barrel of financial insecurity, your faith in me has never faltered. You have engaged with every debate, have grammar and spell-checked every word (as any good teacher should), have lifted me through every crisis in confidence, and have put up with my long hours at the computer. Our life together is my greatest adventure, and I know that I'm one hell of a lucky guy.

Testimonials

These are genuine testimonials from people that it's been my privilege to work with as I have developed the *Lean Foundations™* approach. Hopefully, once you have read the book, you'll understand why they feel the way they do…

"…*Lean Foundations™*! Gives you the power to change everything…. the belief that people care, the support from all levels, the confidence to grow as a person, the sense of purpose and the pure pride of being part of a successful team. I found with these qualities any company can be the best…" *Sally - Purchasing*

"…After an initial period of uncertainty, where I worried about many things, including about exactly what was expected of me, whether we were working on the right things, and whether I could trust my manager and my peers, I soon began to feel increasingly comfortable on our *Lean Foundations™* journey. Within a couple of weeks of meetings in an open and honest forum I began to develop a clear understanding of what was expected of me as an individual and why my contribution was important to both the team and the business. Collectively, the team agreed and executed a clear plan of goals and business improvement. This was supported by my manager who through coaching, mentoring and sponsorship, developed a palpable team approach. For me, this has led to an improvement in my own engagement with the business, a true feeling of empowerment, and a feeling of being genuinely valued and appreciated…"
Hadrian – Trade Compliance

"… Starting our *Lean Foundations™* journey in a major tier one automotive JIT plant seemed like an impossible task. The only way we knew how to operate was with constant fire-fighting every day, and we were frightened of change. But, as we have progressed on our journey, and have implemented the various processes and techniques, we've seen that we are gaining control, and have realised that there is another way. We have started to feel that we are no longer alone, and that we are a team who believe in each other. Following the *Lean Foundations™* approach has made our working day more exciting, interesting and enjoyable, and has given us the feeling that together we can achieve anything. Getting up for work is now something we look forward to…" *Wayne - Production*

"… *Lean Foundations™* brought clarity to what was a very busy and confused situation. After every meeting and review, we all felt involved and had a clear path to achieving our goals and objectives. With clear guidance, teams were able to flourish, feeling empowered to solve the most difficult and long-standing problems…" *Darren – Manufacturing Engineering*

"… What has struck me most on my *Lean Foundations™* journey is the open communication between all levels of the organisation, with everyone made to feel involved and a key part of making the business successful. All functions are aligned through the use of A3's and the 'X-Matrix', and the MDI boards help to drive performance whilst empowering people. I feel empowered, and feel that I'm working in a place without blame or fear of retribution. People believe that the management team has faith in them to collect data, problem-solve, and make decisions to do what is best for the business. Our Facilities & Maintenance team is now organised and efficient and is focused on providing a good service to the factory…" *Andy – Facilities & Maintenance*

"… *Lean Foundations™* gives you the opportunity to become a team player instead of trying to achieve everything by yourself. It brings everyone together as a powerful 'organism' which is designed to succeed in reducing waste and improving performance. It makes you feel valued, gives you purpose and direction, and most importantly, gives you a sense of fulfilment…" *Kinga - Quality*

"… *Lean Foundations™* helps to bring everyone together and gets people pulling in the same direction. It makes me feel that my opinion matters, that I'm trusted, that my contribution is valued, and has given me the confidence to grow as a person both at work and in my personal life…" *Anita – Purchasing*

"… Introducing *Lean Foundations™* enabled our teams to become better at identifying problems and finding relevant and workable solutions. They became more engaged in the process and confident to change when things weren't working. And our performance improved, with absence levels falling, employee turnover improving, and our engagement levels increasing…" *Steph - HR*

"… For me, the best part of our *Lean Foundations™* journey is the voice it has given to everyone in our team. We're tapping into the best resource available, our people, and we're giving them the opportunity to speak up and voice their opinions whilst asking them to be responsible and accountable. We're bringing people together from all departments to work as a team, and we're focussing on solving problems so that we can stop fire-fighting and start enjoying our jobs…" *Marko - Production*

"… Once we started our *Lean Foundations™* journey, we saw a great level of enthusiasm and passion throughout. Everyone knew where we were, where we wanted to be, and what we had to do to get there. With a great mentor, the right tools, and driven by a commitment to continuous improvement, we saw positive results week after week. We became efficient, and more open to change, both as individuals and as a team. Most importantly, I felt empowered, gaining a high level of control and confidence…" *Matt – Logistics*

"… After implementing *Lean Foundations™*, and introducing processes like the MDI meetings and the Improvement Plans, we've seen a noticeable increase in the sense of passion and pride. Team members now have the drive to perform and continuously improve their environment and procedures, and we all feel part of a team…" *Helen - Planning*

"... Introducing the *Lean Foundations™* approach has been really interesting. It's given everyone the opportunity to be involved, and has made the everything in the manufacturing team really transparent. It's also meant that if one discipline is struggling, another part of the team has understood and have stepped in to help..." *Garry - Production*

"… The *Lean Foundations™* approach has really helped me, as EHS Officer, embed a structured management system with defined procedures and processes. It's been fundamental in changing the Health & Safety culture in the factory from a reactive to a proactive mindset. There is a clear vision with common goals and objectives, and Health & Safety is embraced by all departments. We're now accredited to OHSAS 18001 because of the work of everyone in the team…" *Paul – Health & Safety*

"… In my early years as a Lean facilitator I was constantly frustrated with my ability to influence the sustainability of process improvements. The use of the *Lean Foundations™* approach changed all that. With a new leader in place, a strategic vision and plan was cascaded throughout the business which aligned all functions on the same journey. Every employee was included as part of a team with their own targets and objectives, and the MDI process was introduced to drive performance in Safety, Quality, Delivery and Cost. Managers now had the tool to become leaders and to support their team. They were at last able to listen to the problems that mattered, and worked together to solve them. Teams matured, problem-solving improved and the morale and well-being of the employees increased dramatically. It takes time, but if you're patient and believe, it can happen…" *Mark – Continuous Improvement*

"… My *Lean Foundations™* journey was very simple. It gave me the ability to be part of a team with a common goal through communication with one message. The sense of empowerment to achieve with everybody's contribution is a must in my working world…" *Mark - Engineering*

"… Following the *Lean Foundations™* approach has changed the way I think and the way I work. It is profoundly inspiring, and has supported my personal improvement, whilst at the same time has helped our organisation realise its potential. The approach is easy to follow, and directs you to become the architect of your own successful future. The totality of its vision is truly awesome, and the book is a must read for anyone looking to improve their organisation…" *Robbie - Quality*

"…I have experienced, first hand, how powerful and effective the *Lean Foundations™* approach is. Admitting when things are wrong, and applying a structured methodology to fixing issues, promotes a focussed, team oriented, problem-solving culture that is fun to be part of. A refreshing change to the 'sticking-plaster' approach used in a lot of companies I have worked for…" *Jim – Manufacturing Engineering*

"… Applying the *Lean Foundations™* approach has been one of the most empowering leadership and management journeys that I have ever been on. The leadership style that it promotes is designed to empower people and has helped everyone to understand their true worth. And the management theories and tools that the approach shares have proved to be a truly unstoppable force, driving us all towards a common goal of improvement whilst actually enjoying ourselves in the process. Everything we've learned is still in place today, and is continuing to help us to move forward…" *Ian - Operations*

Contents

introduction

This book is born from a desire to support the achievement of three inter-related aspirations.

The first is to make going to work in a manufacturing environment a more enjoyable and fulfilling experience for everyone involved.

Building workplace happiness has become my focus as I have progressed as an Operations leader in various manufacturing facilities over the last 20+ years. It's possible that this originates from having spent more time *not* enjoying work than I care to remember, and as a leader I feel a responsibility to protect the people that I represent from going through the same experience themselves. I have certainly suffered those feelings of frustration, mis-trust, under appreciation and stress that no doubt many others have done in the workplace. Like them, I wish to derive a sense of fulfilment and pleasure from going to the place where I spend the majority of my waking life. I want to feel successful, appreciated, involved and trusted. I want to belong, and to feel that I'm contributing, just as everyone else does. The fact that so many of us have not been able to achieve this consistently enough in our working lives, and as a result no doubt carry a significant emotional burden into our personal lives, is surely a cause for concern. As a leader, I feel the responsibility to create an environment that addresses this problem for the people that I represent. What I have learned is that it *can* be done. There *is* a positive alternative.

The second aspiration is to develop a method for delivering stable and effective operational performance in a manufacturing facility.

My experience has shown that, all too often, operational performance in manufacturing facilities is poor and/or unstable. The small number of consistently high performing exemplars are unfortunately the exception that proves the rule. If you work in a manufacturing facility, it's likely that you're facing daily challenges with your most basic operational performance requirements. As a result, you won't be meeting the Safety, Quality, Delivery and Cost needs of your employees, customers, or stakeholders. Like you, I've received those late-night phone calls from short-tempered customers challenging me over missed deliveries or quality failures. I've joined those conference calls to try and explain high scrap, overtime and freight costs above budget. Worst of all, I've made the stomach-churning dash to a colleague's side after they have been injured in an accident. Each of those scenarios plays out daily in the manufacturing world.

You might think that as an operational leader, my primary objective would be to ensure that my manufacturing facility performs well so that it can be successful. After all, a business needs to be successful in order to survive; and if you don't survive, the aspiration of workplace happiness becomes somewhat unachievable, if not irrelevant. However, I believe that workplace happiness is an essential part of building an organisation that performs well. Creating a working environment that is more enjoyable and more fulfilling results in it being more successful by default. It's a logical cause and effect relationship that I have seen to be correct on numerous occasions. The fact that operational performance is often prioritised far in excess of workplace happiness is obvious and has become the norm, but it seems to be something that no one

2

really wants to talk about. All too often we give up on the idea of enjoying our job, because instead we've simply got to make it work. My research tells me that you *can* bring these complimentary ideas together to deliver even greater results. There *is* a better way.

The third aspiration is to create the platform within a manufacturing facility that enables the practice of Lean to 'stick', so that it can be utilised to lift workplace happiness and drive operational performance towards excellence.

If you work in manufacturing, Lean is something that you are more likely to have had a negative experience of than positive. An unfortunate state of affairs but very true. I know from bitter experience that Lean is often used as a weapon; as a means of cutting costs ruthlessly and without thought for consequence. It can be wielded as the blunt instrument of ill-considered change, and as a result fails to meet its true potential. I also know that Lean can have moments of success that tease at greater achievements, but fall short on delivering over time. Small teams can deliver specific improvements that spark enthusiasm for change, but the fire never really catches, the enthusiasm fails to spread, and the spark eventually dies. All too rarely will Lean manage to embed itself. But when it does the results can be dramatic and only serve to enhance workplace happiness and operational performance; taking both to the best in class levels that all but a few attain. The opportunity to create something truly worthwhile through Lean *does* exist. I believe that there *is* a way to enable it.

Over the last 20 years I have developed an approach; a methodology for leading a manufacturing facility that I believe meets these three aspirations. I call it *Lean Foundations*™. This approach, delivered through the application of a carefully developed 8-Step model, is a genuinely effective change programme that builds the foundations that improve operational performance, enhance workplace happiness, and enables Lean practice to take root. It must be implemented with real passion and commitment, and all 8-Steps need to be followed to achieve complete success. There is a logical sequence in which they must be addressed, but work has to be completed on each component progressively and in conjunction with one another. Alongside this, the day job still has to happen, and goods need to be manufactured and shipped out of the door. It's a challenge, but isn't everything that is worthwhile?

I have seen, on numerous occasions, that when applied correctly, the *Lean Foundations*™ approach really delivers. Operational metrics improve and are consistent. Employee engagement and happiness reach new heights. Lean culture is embraced and the use of tools and philosophies begin to stick. Once that happens, the passion for improvement and change becomes unstoppable.

What follows here is a practical guide for implementation of the *Lean Foundations*™ approach for leaders of manufacturing facilities. In sharing it, I hope to add some small value to the manufacturing community. Much of what is included here may also add value for people who are managers of individual functions within a manufacturing facility (it's how I started after all), but of course it's likely to have less of an overall impact in these cases. I also hope that there may be relevance to sectors other than just manufacturing, and that some of the tools, structures and methodologies defined will simply need minor adjustments to suit their application.

I have endeavoured to present the *Lean Foundations*™ approach in a way that is engaging and easy to read; like a conversation between two fellow professionals. I hope I have been successful in sharing it in this way.

There are areas of the book that discuss the ideas and concepts that underpin *Lean Foundations*™, and there are parts that describe practical activities and methodologies for implementation. When describing these I aim to do so from the perspective of a mentor and coach; someone who is introducing ideas for you to potentially utilise on your own *Lean Foundations*™ journey, and subsequently guiding you through the process of their application. In each case, please feel free to choose the elements that work for you, and discard the elements that don't.

I'll be drawing on my own experiences and understanding, whilst including significant references to the opinions and concepts of the published professionals that I have sought guidance and understanding from in their many and varied books. This book stands on the shoulders of these giants and I thank them for that. Where quantitative data is appropriate and relevant I have endeavoured to include it, but the bulk of the approach is based on my qualitative experiences and observations, which I hope are no less valuable.

Most importantly in all of this, I hope that you enjoy reading *Lean Foundations*™, and that you find the book useful in navigating your own way to meeting the aspirations of workplace happiness, operational performance and preparation for Lean, whether that's in leadership within manufacturing, or in some other context or industry.

finding the way

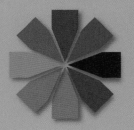

I'm sure that, like me, you've heard the phrase 'good is the enemy of great'. I have to say, it's not a phrase I'm completely comfortable with. It's not that I necessarily disagree with the sentiment, it's just that I believe that it can encourage the wrong kind of behaviour. For me, it suggests that we should be striving to achieve great at the expense of good. Whereas instead, I believe that good is something to be achieved on the pathway to greatness. I believe that being classed as good is an achievement in itself, and that it's a milestone that shows that we're moving in the right direction towards greatness. The same applies when striving to achieve operational excellence in a manufacturing facility, or in any other organisation for that matter. If your facility can't perform well, and isn't good; it's not going to achieve excellence, and be great. All too often, organisations jump straight into trying to be great, without having achieved a level of being good first.

Whenever I have visited a manufacturing facility for the first time, whether as its leader, a functional manager, a customer, a supplier, a consultant, or just as a visitor; I almost always notice the same thing… It has problems. I'm not talking about minor day to day issues that you would expect to see in any working environment. I'm talking about fundamental problems that are affecting the very fabric of the manufacturing operation. As a consequence, that manufacturing facility in question isn't performing well, and clearly hasn't achieved a level of good. And yet, it's quite possible that it has some kind of Lean operational excellence programme running, and is trying its hardest to be great.

Because it's my natural instinct to 'fix' things (I'm hard wired that way), my brain automatically looks for ways to understand the problems that stop a facility from being good, and to find a solution to remedy them. In doing so, I've come to recognise that at their heart most typical manufacturing facilities suffer from the same three core problems.

- *Workplace happiness is poor* - Job satisfaction and Employee Engagement are low. A sense of fulfilment and purpose is rarely achieved by many. Levels of stress and anxiety can be unacceptably high. Absenteeism and high staff turnover are a common feature. Occupational health support is a necessity, not a benefit.
- *Operational performance is poor* - Core metrics around safety, delivery, lead time, customer quality, labour efficiency, overhead costs, inventory and more are often far below expected levels. Good performance is sporadic and unexpected. Poor performance can be frequent and often not adequately understood or explained. As a consequence, nobody has the time or inclination to introduce or sustain improvement.
- *The utilisation of lean is failing* - Supposed solutions haven't worked and organisations are not experiencing the total business improvements previously expected. Whether insisted on from above, or driven by small local teams in individual activities, tangible and consistent improvements to the core metrics are elusive. Cost savings are required and often reported as achieved, but are fragile and in no

way permanent. The holy grail of achieving Toyota-like performance seems nothing more than a distant dream.

I would take a guess that if you work in manufacturing, whether in a leadership role or not, then the description of these three core problems will resonate with you. You might shout a small 'Hallelujah' that your daily experiences are at last being recognised. To make you cheer even more loudly, there is data out there that reinforces the point.

On research into employee engagement, for example, the numbers are alarming. In Gallup's 2017 State of the American Workplace report, manufacturing employees list as being the least engaged occupation, with just 25% of employees identifying as engaged against a national average of 33% for all industry sectors. In the UK, a 2018 report by the Workforce Institute at Kronos by Coleman Parks reported that just 35% of UK manufacturers have strong employee engagement (Allan, 2018). Not great – or even good - reading.

Operational performance results aren't any better. Industry Week magazine in the US undertakes an annual 'Best Plants' award, and reports a number of Key Performance Indicators from the winners and finalists of that award each year. In 2017, they reported that for 2012 to 2016, these 'Best Plant' candidates were achieving performance such as 95.4% average First Pass Yield, 91.9% average Supplier On-time delivery, and average Inventory days of 36.5. Hardly numbers that you would expect from facilities chasing operational excellence, and certainly nothing in comparison to the kinds of numbers we know that the likes of Toyota, Nissan and Honda achieve.

Lean implementation numbers are possibly the most confidence sapping of all. There are a great many journal articles available which address the issues around the success of Lean implementation. Referencing just a few provide statistics like 60% of Six Sigma initiatives failing to achieve desired results (Angel & Pritchard, 2008), and that only 10% of UK organisations are successful in their Lean implementation efforts (Bhasin, 2012). I'm sure that these are not the kind of results that the Lean community at large would be hoping to achieve.

As someone who has been responsible for trying to solve these three core problems in a variety of manufacturing environments, I have asked myself a couple of fairly obvious questions…

'Why is this true?' And, 'How can I fix it?'

Why is it so?

I have managed and lead numerous manufacturing facilities, and have shaped my answers to both questions through trial and error, and through responding to the various successes and failures of working with hundreds of manufacturing professionals. I have bought and read more 'management' books than I can now safely store, and have incorporated many of the ideas that they contain into my own belief systems and working processes. Mentors have shaped my thinking, along with colleagues, line managers and friends. I have made more mistakes than I would care to remember, but have endeavoured to learn from as many of them as possible. This process of constant learning and reflection has led me to a couple of important conclusions.

First, I believe that many manufacturing organisations are structured and function in such a way that they negatively impact the performance and capability of their employees. They do so by restricting and even reducing what Alfie Kohn in his book '*Punished by Rewards*', and Dan Pink in his book '*Drive*', call our intrinsic motivators. As a result of how they operate, and how they are organised, they adversely impact every team member's internal professional desires: to have a sense of purpose, to be part of a team, to work autonomously and with accountability, and to be successful and improve both personally and as part of a group. In having this negative impact, manufacturing organisations are failing to utilise their greatest asset to its greatest potential - their people.

Second, I believe that there are three common but critical factors which cause this impact. I believe that many manufacturing facilities...

- *lack the characteristics of a healthy organisation and effective teamwork,*
- *fail to engage empowered front-line team members,* and
- *lack a well-functioning management system.*

For me, it's these three factors which impact every individual's intrinsic motivators, and which therefore result in poor workplace happiness, poor operational performance, and an inability to utilise Lean. It's these three factors that are the bedrock of being defined as good, and which enable a facility to operate well. It's these three factors which establish the solid foundations upon which operational excellence is built, and which make it possible to be great. And, it's these three factors upon which Lean practice and process takes root, and whose absence causes Lean programmes to wither and fail. If we look at each of these factors in turn, we can perhaps understand why this is the case.

A healthy organisation embraces teamwork and rejects internal politics. It focuses on creating alignment, on enabling individuals to express themselves without fear of retribution, and on driving performance. Without organisational health, teamwork is a myth and silo's and politics reign. Confusion and misalignment, alongside finger pointing and blame, lead to conflicting priorities that lead to waste, impact on performance, and create an unhappy workplace that employees chose to leave or suffer in silence.

The engagement of empowered front-line team members takes advantage of the ideas, capabilities and potential of all team members. In doing so it galvanises real feelings of autonomy, ownership and accountability across the entire organisation. It's the energy that fuels the process of improvement, for both the individual and the group, whilst simultaneously enhancing the working lives of every person present.

Without the engagement of empowered front-line team members, individuals pass problems up the management chain for solution, trust is lost and conflict rises, poor performance becomes someone else's problem, and change is resisted. Most importantly, team members lose the enthusiasm and desire to be involved and to develop. They choose to leave their brain at the door when they arrive, ready to be picked up again on their way home.

A well-functioning management system is built on a clear organisation structure that clarifies responsibilities, is supported by well-designed processes that reduce and remove risk, is flexible in responding to the changing needs of the organisation, and is focused on monitoring performance through daily routines so that appropriate responses to problems can be initiated when they arise. When such a management system is missing, confusions of responsibility and accountability lead to waste and a lack of responsiveness; with time and energy spent fighting fires and not on building improvement. Gaps in procedure, or excessive regulation, result in unnecessary errors that impact performance without warning. Poor performance monitoring and untimely responses lead to embarrassing repeated failures and a loss of credibility with customers and colleagues alike.

Therefore, in being a healthy organisation that supports effective teamwork, in engaging empowered front-line team members, and in utilising a well-functioning management system; a manufacturing facility can support the intrinsic motivations of its employees, can perform well, and can establish the solid foundations upon which operational excellence is built. Moreover, with proper thought and consideration, I believe that these intrinsic motivations can be deliberately aligned to the goals of the organisation. I've seen that it's possible to bring together the desire to work as part of a team, to work with purpose, to be autonomous, and to be successful and improve; with the need for the organisation to perform, to grow, to improve in its efficiency and capability, and to progress towards excellence.

Inspired by Ohno

Can I prove my conclusions to be correct, or to be comprehensive? Not practically, no. Even if I were to analyse terabytes of data, monitor hundreds of manufacturing operations, and interview thousands of professionals, I couldn't possibly provide a substantive enough argument. The 'three common factors' statement is driven by the sum of my 20+ years of experience, and most importantly was ultimately 'found' when I read 'Toyota Production System' by Taiichi Ohno; the father of the Toyota Production System and the basis for everything Lean that has followed.

In reading Ohno's book, and considering it alongside management theories learned elsewhere, I developed a sense of the environment that Ohno had been operating within when he developed the Toyota Production System. To begin with, I observed that Ohno's narrative inadvertently describes Toyota as having the characteristics of a healthy organisation which enabled effective teamwork. And, when reading between the lines, it seemed to me that Toyota was (and probably still is) a place where workplace politics were minimal, teamwork was the norm, and everyone was aligned behind the goal of 'Catching up with America'.

Also, from what Ohno describes, it seemed to me that Toyota had the basis of a well-functioning management system in place. Ohno is very clear on his understanding of Toyota's performance, the amount of equipment and number of people employed, and the reporting structures in place. It's clear that performance was monitored, organisation structure was defined, and procedures were established; but the freedom to creatively solve problems using 'common-sense ideas' still existed.

And finally, although it was perhaps clear that Toyota wasn't necessarily filled with empowered front-line team members in the 1940's, 50's and 60's; Ohno does frequently describe his respect and appreciation for their role and contribution. Despite the fact that Ohno may not have been particularly great at engaging with them in order to improve (he refers to things such as 'forcing' change, to 'industrial disputes', and to 'shouting at foremen'), it is apparent that he demonstrated a level of patience and respect for their desires and motivations when implementing any change.

In the end, I came to believe that Ohno was operating in an environment that actively enabled him to develop the tools and philosophies that became the Toyota Production System. This was the foundation on which he applied his genius. The health of the organisation, Ohno's respect for people, and the capability of the base management system were what enabled Ohno's intrinsic motivations, and were what underpinned Toyota's transformation. They jumped off the page when I compared them to those environments where I myself had been successful, and more appropriately, when I had not.

So, whilst my answer to 'why' might appear to be simple, I do not wish to gloss over or understate it.

It's therefore worth repeating.

If a manufacturing operation has a healthy working culture that enables teamwork, which is supported by team members who are actively empowered and engaged, and is supported by a well-functioning management system; then that manufacturing operation will be successful in boosting every team member's intrinsic motivators, and will deliver good performance, a positive working environment, and a platform for Lean. That manufacturing facility will perform well, and will achieve a status of being good. And, as a consequence, that facility will have built the foundations that enable the path to operational excellence, and the future achievement of great.

What's the solution?

Answering the question of 'how do I fix all of this?' is something of a challenge. How do you create a healthy organisation? How do you build a well-functioning management system? Is it truly possible to actively engage and empower front-line team members? And finally, how on earth could all of this be integrated together coherently?

For me, it's this last question that is critical. It's the integration of all three factors that is the most difficult, and at the same time the most fundamental. If I were able to lead a manufacturing operation in a way that systematically maintains a healthy organisation, whilst engaging empowered front-line team members, and utilising a well-functioning management system; then that would be extremely powerful. If I could find a way to systemise teamwork and the removal of politics, to integrate a sense of ownership and accountability, and to manage performance daily with structure and procedure; then I could solve the three core problems facing almost every manufacturing facility I have ever experienced. That approach would be truly different from the norm. It could build a facility that is considered good and performs well, and could establish the foundations that would enable that facility to strive to be great and achieve operational excellence. At the same time, it could tap into every person's internal motivations, and align them with the needs and desires of the organisation as a whole. It could even add real and tangible value to the lives of the people that I represent in the process.

After much soul-searching, mistake-making, ongoing learning, honest reflection, and hard work, what I believe I have developed is exactly this. What I have developed, is the *Lean Foundations™* approach.

Lean Foundations™ is a comprehensive approach to the leadership and management of a manufacturing facility. It is comprised of eight inter-related steps that require the coordinated implementation of particular concepts, structures, procedures, tools and methodologies. These are all deliberately designed to specifically address the three common factors; to improve organisational health and teamwork, to facilitate the engagement and empowerment of front-line team members, and to introduce a well-functioning management system. In doing so, they integrate the shared mental models, workplace culture, and management protocols that enable a facility to perform well; and to build the foundations upon which operational excellence through the application of Lean can take root and flourish. What follows next is an introductory description of that 8-Step model.

the8step model

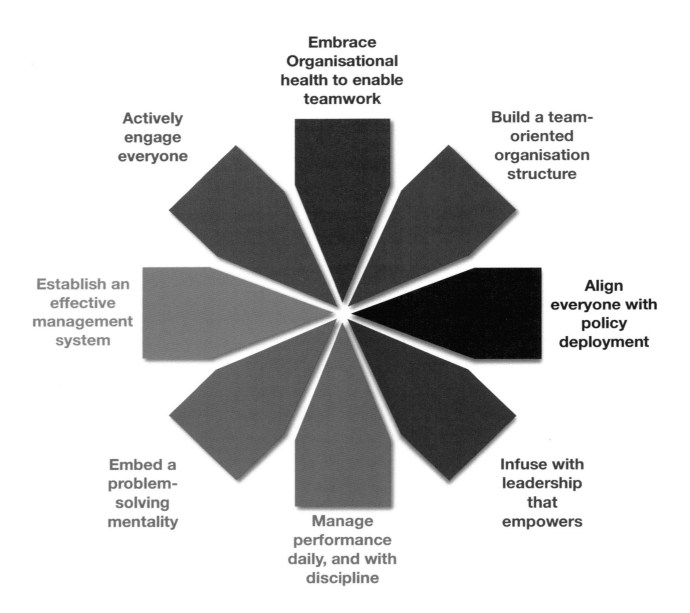

Embrace Organisational health to enable teamwork

Build a team-oriented organisation structure

Actively engage everyone

Align everyone with policy deployment

Establish an effective management system

Embed a problem-solving mentality

Infuse with leadership that empowers

Manage performance daily, and with discipline

Leading any manufacturing facility, regardless of its size or complexity, is a considerable challenge. The management of daily processing and all of its associated problems, alongside the responsibility of the financial, emotional and physical well-being of the people you represent, can be both extremely rewarding and uncomfortably demanding at the same time. I know this to be true because I have been where you are, have sat where you are sitting, and have seen what you now see.

As a result of the time I have spent in numerous factories and plants, I have come to recognise the familiarity of the experiences that many of us face. The three core problems of poor workplace happiness, poor operational performance, and an inability to implement Lean, with their impact on our intrinsic motivators, are an everyday occurrence. And, the three common factors of a lack of organisational health and teamwork, of a lack of engagement of empowered front-line team members, and a lack of a well-functioning management system are, well... common.

Having sought to develop a solution to those common factors, and therefore a way of addressing the core problems; I have found that I've repeatedly encountered the same kind of roadblocks, mindsets, disappointments and challenges in pretty much every facility I've ever entered. I've learned that we all face the same type of obstacles when trying to improve; and all experience the same kind of problems when trying to inspire others to do the same. Like you, I have seen how difficult it is to resolve poor teamwork, have witnessed how a plant can drift without a clear plan of improvement, and have suffered the chaos of a lack of stability and control. It's the constant recurrence of these experiences that have led me to believe that a solution to the three common factors must be achievable, and that these problems had to be something that I could learn to resolve. It's their familiarity and consistency that led me to try and understand what caused them in the first place, and to develop standard responses which eventually would go on to become the 8-Steps of the *Lean Foundations*™ approach. It's this practiced and proven response to these recurring experiences that *Lean Foundations*™ hopes to empower you with.

Below is a short summary of the 8-Steps, each of which addresses at least one of the typical experiences that we all face on a daily basis; and which, when resolved, help to move us forward on our journey towards being a well-performing facility.

STEP 1: Embrace organisational health to enable teamwork

We all know that effective teamwork is important, and that we as leaders are responsible for ensuring that our people can function well in teams. The question is, how do we actually do it? Getting people to function well in teams can be difficult, and knowing how to create the right environment that enables teamwork can be a challenge. In this first Step, we'll explore the concept of Organisational Health, and I'll hopefully persuade you to embrace it as a means of building the truly positive working environment that allows teamwork to flourish. Then, we'll explore the tools and processes that we can utilise to help us introduce organisational health. We'll discuss our purpose and 'Golden Circle', and ideas for creating psychologically safety. By embracing organisational health, we can inject a sense of purpose, we can enable effective teamwork, and can introduce a fundamental building block that can underpin all aspects of our improvement journey.

STEP 2: Build a Team-oriented organisation structure

Enabling teamwork not only requires a healthy environment, but also needs your team to be structured in the right way to encourage and support it. All too often a facility is hindered by a poor organisation structure that lacks key functions and roles, restricts teamwork, and is populated with people who aren't suited to the journey you want to take. Here, we'll discuss how to structure your team so that teamwork is enabled, and we'll review the roles that any factory needs to have in place in order to be successful. We'll also discuss the characteristics that you're looking for in the right people for your facility, and we'll consider how to manage them effectively as a resource. Getting your organisation structure right, and introducing the right people into your team, demonstrates your genuine intent, and starts to fast-track your progress.

STEP 3: Align everyone with policy deployment

Not having a clear plan for improvement is a shortcoming of too many factories. But, fire-fighting can get in the way, and knowing exactly what problems to solve and in what order can be a real challenge. Just keeping your head down and ploughing on sometimes feels like the only option. In this Step, we'll discuss how to create an Improvement Plan that will align your entire team on your journey to workplace happiness and improved operational performance. We'll explore how to use Policy Deployment, and how to introduce A3 thinking and 'X-Matrix' tools to make sure that you're solving the right problems in the right order. And, we can put customer focus, and the respect of our people, at the very heart of our journey. Creating alignment, and prioritising your efforts on your biggest challenges, ensures that everyone pulls in the same direction, and gets your process of improvement really motoring.

STEP 4: Infuse with leadership that empowers

It's easy to make the mistake of telling people what do, and to end up being the only person who makes decisions and solves problems as a result. As a leader of a manufacturing facility, the responsibility can weigh heavy on your shoulders, and the need to be successful can drive you to make the wrong choices on how to lead. The question is, how do you change, and what do you change to being and doing? Here, we'll discuss how empowering leadership can invigorate a sense of ownership and accountability in your team. We'll explore different ideas about leadership that empowers, and we'll consider how to introduce it into your facility. Infusing empowering leadership is like injecting adrenalin into your system, and your improvement journey can become super-charged by the enthusiasm and commitment of your people.

STEP 5: Manage performance daily, and with discipline

A manufacturing facility can face numerous problems every day. Knowing which ones to solve first, and being confident that they're being solved properly, can be a challenge in itself. Add in the desire and pressure to continuously improve, and you could be stretching your team's capabilities beyond breaking point. In this Step, we'll take a look at a daily management system called the 'MDI' process; which you can introduce to help you and your team deal with every problem that comes along, whilst still being able to drive improvement. And, that system can help you maintain a level of discipline and rigor in your management approach, and can help you to drive the right standards in your operational performance. Introducing a daily management process gives vital energy and discipline to your improvement journey, and underpins the mentality of small but continuous steps forward.

STEP 6: Embed a problem-solving mentality

Solving problems effectively is a skill that is all too often missing in most manufacturing facilities. First of all, problems are hidden through a fear of criticism and blame. And then, even when they are identified, they rarely get solved properly the first, second or even third time around. Behind these problems, waste builds up, and people suffer in quiet frustration. Here, we'll explore how you can introduce processes that encourage problems to be identified and shared without finger-pointing and blame. And, we'll discuss how to develop the right kind of problem-solving mentality in your team, with the right tools to support the problem-solving process. Embedding a problem-solving mentality and skillset empowers everyone with the ability to fix what needs to be fixed, and to improve whatever needs to be improved. Your improvement will gather momentum as the path to achieving good is cleared of roadblocks by someone other than just you.

STEP 7: Establish an effective management system

The chaos of poor performance, and the urgency of daily fire-fighting, is the reality of working in manufacturing operations. Developing a thick skin and a resilience to failure is a must. In this Step, we'll discuss how standardisation of processes and procedures can stabilise your performance. And, we'll consider exactly what processes you need, and how you can best introduce them into your facility. We'll also take a look at how your leadership role can change as a result, and how you can oversee and support your team effectively, rather than having to direct and instruct them as the norm. It's establishing a management system of this nature that can give you and your team the capacity and space to breathe, and the opportunity to focus on improvement rather than just survival every single day.

STEP 8: Actively engage everyone

The people who know your processes best, and who experience problems in real time, are those at the very front-line of your activities. Unfortunately, they're also the most likely to be missed out, and the least likely to be involved. It's not unusual for an improvement journey to be delivered through the efforts of a select few, and to therefore fall seriously short of achieving its full potential. The question is, how do ensure that we involve everyone in our pursuit of achieving good, and how can we be certain that we capture every person's valuable perspective and knowledge? Here, we'll discuss the concept of employee engagement, and what kind of factors we need to be conscious of when trying to encourage it. We'll also discuss the activities that you can introduce into your facility that will ensure that everyone in your team is fully engaged. It's through employee engagement that we can find the last piece of the improvement puzzle, and can hopefully deliver genuine workplace happiness with – and within - every member of our team.

Hopefully, you're not surprised by the lack of reference to typical Lean tools such as Flow and Pull, 5S, Kanban, and Value Stream Maps here. Remember, this 8-Step model is designed to provide the environment for those *Lean Basics* to take root; to create the foundations on which they flourish. It's not the place in which their terms are defined or a method for implementation explained. Just as was the case for Taiichi Ohno and Toyota, the application of those *Lean Basics* follows *Lean Foundations*™. In reality, it's the focus on customer centred performance (cost, delivery, quality, profit), and on fully respecting the workforce, that is the true heart of Lean and the Toyota Production System, and not the tools that we've become so obsessed with trying to implement. As a consequence, it's that focus that is integral to the foundations that need to be in place for Lean to truly thrive, and is therefore why *Lean Foundations*™ has committed improved workplace happiness and operational performance to the very heart of its approach.

Does it always work?

Well in my experience to date the answer is yes. Every time I have applied the *Lean Foundations*™ approach it has made a positive difference of some kind, even if the period of implementation has been short, or the process has been constrained by outside influences. Operational performance has improved and stabilised across the board. Employee job satisfaction has increased and people's sense of belonging to something bigger than themselves has developed. As a result, I've been able follow up with the successful introduction of at least the basic elements of Lean in a way that has been sustained beyond my time with an organisation.

However, it hasn't all been plain sailing. There have been a great many bumps in the road, and my understanding of the correct approach has evolved over many years. In each of my experiences, the degree of success in implementation has usually been impacted by the same thing; the length of time given to its application. It's important to note that *Lean Foundations*™ requires patience. Whilst there is always a short-term benefit, results of the kind typically desired by the corporate world are not necessarily instantaneous and take time to materialise. *Lean Foundations*™ is not designed to be a short-term solution, and is not for people looking for a quick fix. It builds capability and structure, it builds understanding and appreciation, it builds something more and for the long-term. It does so in small steps; by establishing simple but effective processes, controls, methodologies and tools that help a leader of any manufacturing facility build the foundations upon which operational excellence, driven by Lean, can eventually take hold.

So, if you're up for the challenge, let's get to Step 1…

STEP

1

Embrace
Organisational
health to enable
teamwork

When I take responsibility for leading a manufacturing facility, the first step on my *Lean Foundations*™ journey is to stop and to take a moment for reflection. Whether as its leader, or as a functional manager within it, I endeavour to recognise that my area of responsibility will come to reflect me and my approach to leadership. It will reflect my beliefs, my management style, my approach to human interaction, my desire for performance and success, and my willingness to listen and engage. Of course, there are outside influences that also have an impact; wider organisational hierarchy, management team peers, company-wide strategies, customer expectations, and the nature of the people in my team. But all of these can be managed and influenced by my leadership approach, and it is my mentality that is the dominant force. That moment of reflection is a humbling experience. It's a reminder that, for the people that I represent, I carry a significant responsibility. My leadership approach will impact their job security, their sense of well-being and happiness, and their willingness to perform and improve.

In spite of this, I also know that I do not function in isolation. I work alongside many others, and I rely upon them to meet their day to day responsibilities in order for the organisation to function. I desire to collaborate with them in order to satisfy my own intrinsic motivations. In reality, it's my ability to work as part of a team, and my ability as a leader to build and nurture effective teams, that ultimately determines whether or not I am successful. All organisations are built on a network of teams, and their ability to function effectively is the engine that drives organisational success. This seems such an obvious point to make, but all too often organisations fall short. When people are able to function together effectively as a cohesive unit they are more able to be successful, and are therefore more likely to drive the success of the organisation as a whole. Manufacturing facilities are no exception here. Whether it's a management team responsible for running a factory, a project team charged with introducing a new product, or a shop-floor team who operate a production cell; their ability to function as a cohesive unit will determine their ability to deliver results.

Having worked in many manufacturing facilities, I've seen all too often the crippling power of poor leadership, and the debilitating impact it can have on the happiness and well-being of the people who are supposedly being led. I've also experienced the impact of poor teamwork and a lack of collaboration, and have seen how a failure to embrace teamwork by people in positions of responsibility can cause it to quickly disintegrate and disappear. And, once it's gone, I've seen how a lack of teamwork can cause repeated and constant failure and distress, and I've experienced the poor performance and low morale which follows.

I've come to realise that my approach to the leadership of my facility is extremely influential, and that my commitment to the creation and encouragement of effective teamwork is especially fundamental to its success. It's for this reason that enabling effective teamwork is at the heart of the *Lean Foundations*™ approach, and is why it's the very first of the leadership responsibilities that must be addressed. It's the primary foundation stone on which everything else is built. Without teamwork, no organisation can perform well; and achieving good on the path to achieving great will be beyond its capability.

In searching for an understanding of what it takes to build and lead effective teams, I have learned that the relationship between teamwork and a concept called 'organisational health' is critical. I believe that the two ideas are intrinsically linked, and that a team is unable to function effectively in an organisation that is not healthy. As a consequence, Step 1 of *Lean Foundations™* aims to encourage you, as a leader in manufacturing, to understand what helps to make teams effective, and to embrace the concept of organisational health as the critical factor.

To begin with, let's explore some different ideas on teamwork and organisational health. In the process, I hope to be able to influence your leadership approach in a way that is positively reflected in your ability to build and lead a healthy team. Following on, I'll outline a variety of practical tools and activities that can be used to develop and sustain organisational health in your manufacturing facility. In utilising these, we can help your organisation as a whole to embrace organisational health and effective teamwork, and can help to create the conditions that increase workplace happiness, improve operational performance, and create a platform for Lean.

WHAT MAKES A TEAM EFFECTIVE?

I would hope that everyone would agree that building effective teams is important. Clearly, organisations function through the transition of material and information from one team or team member to another. Therefore, it stands to reason that ensuring that your teams can function effectively, and can interact with one another successfully, will strongly influence the likelihood of your organisation's ability to be successful too. However, understanding what it takes to make a team effective is a challenge. Complete an internet search on the subject (and I have!) and the 'hits' are too varied and numerous to quantify. The concept of teamwork is widely discussed and analysed on an almost daily basis. In my learning journey, I have found two pieces of work on the subject that I consider to be the most insightful and worthwhile for leaders. They are Patrick Lencioni's definition of the characteristics of an effective team from his seminal book '*The Five Dysfunctions of a Team*', and the findings of Google's '*Project Aristotle*'.

Lencioni's 'Dysfunctions'

In '*The Five Dysfunctions of a Team*', Patrick Lencioni cleverly helps us to understand what makes an effective team by describing what makes a dysfunctional team, and then flipping it. He defines a five-layer model, illustrated in the graphic below, with clear definitions for each layer, and with a logical escalation of cause and effect through those layers, both in the functional and dysfunctional scenarios.

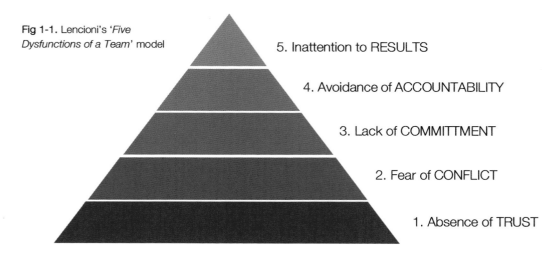

Fig 1-1. Lencioni's *Five Dysfunctions of a Team* model

5. Inattention to RESULTS

4. Avoidance of ACCOUNTABILITY

3. Lack of COMMITMENT

2. Fear of CONFLICT

1. Absence of TRUST

Layer 1 – Absence of TRUST – Refers to the need for team members to be vulnerable with one another, and for them to feel able to be open about their mistakes and weaknesses. This requires them to believe that they will not be criticised, humiliated or taken advantage of as a result. Team members come to trust one another and have faith that they are committed to the group. They're prepared to speak freely and express themselves openly.

Layer 2 – Fear of CONFLICT – Refers to the need for team members to be able to conflict healthily; which means to debate and argue constructively in order to ensure all perspectives are considered and the right decisions are made. Teams that lack trust are unable to conflict healthily; and they resort to underhand comments and whispered politics that damage productivity. Teams that are able to conflict productively show a willingness to disagree in the pursuit of the best solutions.

Layer 3 – Lack of COMMITMENT – Refers to the need for teams to buy-in and commit to decisions and actions that the team need to complete in order to be successful. Without the ability to conflict healthily, buy-in is often lacking, and team members may well stay silent or reluctantly agree to maintain positive outward appearances. Team members who are able to commit fully are focused on delivering success for the team, and are prepared to hold the team accountable.

Layer 4 – Avoidance of ACCOUNTABILITY – Refers to the need for team members to hold themselves and each other accountable in order to deliver their responsibilities. When teams lack commitment and buy-in, team members will be reluctant to challenge themselves and their peers when their actions and behaviours are inappropriate. When teams are able to hold themselves accountable for their results, they are far more likely to deliver a successful outcome.

Layer 5 – Inattention to RESULTS – Refers to the need for team members to put the collective goals and needs of the team ahead of their individual desires. When team members are able to trust, have healthy conflict, commit wholeheartedly, and hold each other accountable, they are far more likely to deliver results.

When team members fail to trust, fear conflict, lack commitment, and avoid accountability, they inevitably fail to deliver the results that the team is responsible for producing. Instead, team members are likely to focus on their own needs and professional ambitions.

Lencioni's view is wonderfully simply yet truly insightful, and I'm sure it rings true for anyone who has ever functioned as part of a team. We've all experienced those feelings of frustration when fellow team members didn't meet their agreed responsibilities because they didn't commit to them in the first place. Or, we haven't spoken up during a debate for fear that the team would react negatively to a contradictory contribution. We've also no doubt been part of a team that has been criticised for failing to 'pull together' to achieve the right result.

The challenge for us as leaders then, is to understand how to create that environment of trust described in Lencioni's Layer 1, and how to encourage the other four layers to develop from it.

Google's 'Project Aristotle'

In November 2017, Julia Rozovsky, a member of Google's People Operations team, published a blog following their analysis of 'What makes a Google team effective'. It was codenamed 'Project Aristotle'. Their findings, based on over 200 interviews with Google employees across 180+ active Google teams, surprised them. They had expected to find that team success was driven by who is part of the team, but what they found was that team success depends on how those team members interact with one another, and how they view their contribution. Like Lencioni, the Google team defined 5 layers, or dynamics, that they believed set successful teams apart from other teams elsewhere.

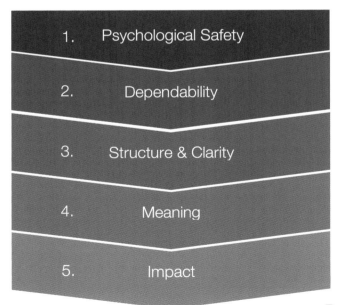

1. Psychological Safety	Team members feel safe to take risks and be vulnerable in front of each other.
2. Dependability	Team members get things done on time and meet Google's high bar for excellence.
3. Structure & Clarity	Team members have clear roles, plans and goals.
4. Meaning	Work is personally important to team members.
5. Impact	Team members think their work matters and creates change.

Fig 1-2. Google's 'Project Aristotle' teamwork model

Interestingly, there are considerable similarities here between the findings of '*Project Aristotle*' and Lencioni's '*Five Dysfunctions*'. Where Lencioni defines the concept of trust, or more precisely vulnerability-based trust, as the first and most critical layer, Rozovsky defines the concept of Psychological Safety, where team members are prepared to be vulnerable with one another, as the first and most critical dynamic. In fact, the Google team found that *"... Psychological safety was far and away the most important of the five dynamics... it's the underpinning of the other four..."*. In addition, the second dynamic of Dependability in '*Project Aristotle*' draws similarities with the ideas of Commitment, Accountability and Results highlighted by Lencioni.

'*Project Aristotle's*' findings in relation to Structure & Clarity, Meaning and Impact also draw similarities to the findings of Dan Pink in his book '*Drive*', and highlight another of our intrinsic motivators. Pink has conducted an array of analyses into what motivates people in the workplace, and has found what he considers to be some surprising results. Whereas we might expect that money is our main motivator, Pink and his team have found that this is only true in a limited number of circumstances, and usually only for a limited period of time even in those circumstances. Instead, Pink has classified our motivations under three main headings; a sense of purpose, a sense of autonomy, and a sense of mastery. The sense of purpose relates to our desire to be part of something important, and to fully understand our individual role and contribution. The sense of autonomy relates to our desire to have control over our contribution and how we deliver it. The sense of mastery relates to our desire to improve and get better at what we do; to be successful and to perform. It's Pink's thoughts on a 'sense of purpose', also supported by Alfie Kohn's description of the importance of 'content' or 'meaningful work' in '*Punished by Rewards*', that align succinctly with the findings of Structure & Clarity, Meaning and Impact by the '*Project Aristotle*' team.

Again, the challenge for us as leaders appears to be to seek an understanding of how to create an environment of trust, or psychological safety, in order to provide the basis for dependability in execution. However, added to this is the need to align psychological safety with the ability to create a clarity of purpose, structure, meaning and contribution. In doing so, we can tap into the intrinsic motivators of both teamwork *and* purpose. It's finding the answer to this challenge that took me on a journey towards understanding the concept of organisational health.

SO, WHAT IS ORGANISATIONAL HEALTH?

My understanding of the concept of organisational health has developed throughout my career. Originally, my awareness was limited to the practice of utilising certain leadership ideals that are well understood in the Lean community. They are often called 'Lean Mental Models'. Good examples of these are provided in Pascal Dennis' book '*Getting the Right Things Done*', where the author describes a number of Lean mental models that need to be utilised to help create an environment where Lean methodologies are embraced. Dennis contrasts conventional leadership with Lean mental models. Ideals such as 'Though-Shalt instructive management' are replaced with 'Leaders as a teacher and coach', or 'Problems are things to be hidden' is replaced with 'Make problems visible'. Similarly, 'Leaders don't go to the shop-floor' is replaced with 'Go see for yourself', and 'Only specialists solve problems' is replaced with 'Everyone solves problems using simple methods'. In drawing these comparisons, Dennis helps to highlight that the mental models we employ as leaders are critical, and that utilising the more positive and proactive approaches can help to build a healthy organisation. In applying these mental models in my own experience, I found that the working environment very quickly became more positive, with teams becoming more effective, and team members feeling more autonomous and able to embrace change and take responsibility. However, at the time, I didn't necessarily understand the full reasons why.

As my career has developed, and as my understanding of what builds effective teamwork has grown, I have come to realise that the approach advocated with these mental models is supported by wider business concepts discussed in some of the management texts that I have read. In particular, I have found that the combination of two concepts gives the most comprehensive understanding. The first of these is 'Psychological Safety', a concept that the findings of '*Project Aristotle*' drew me towards. It's a concept that has been superbly described by Amy Edmondson in her book '*The Fearless Organisation*', and by Dan Radecki and Leonie Hull in their book '*Psychological Safety*'. The second is 'Organisational Health' as defined by Patrick Lencioni in his insightful book '*The Advantage*'. These concepts have helped to broaden my understanding of organisational health as a whole, and have helped me to understand how it's the true answer to building effective teams.

Psychological Safety

The concept of psychological safety has been progressing since Amy Edmondson published her journal article '*Psychological Safety and Learning Behaviour in Work Teams*' in 1999. In the article, Edmondson defines psychological safety as *"... a belief that one will not be punished or humiliated for speaking up with ideas, questions, concerns, or mistakes, and that the team is safe for interpersonal risk taking..."*.

In her latest book, '*The Fearless Organisation*', Edmondson provides a fantastic view of why psychological safety is so critical to the success of an organisation, and how to help create an environment that is psychologically safe. She observes that psychologically safe workplaces are respectful of individual needs and allow freedom of expression, and as a result are more productive, more likely to learn from mistakes, and are more likely to build employee engagement. In their book 'Psychological Safety', Dan Radecki and Leonie Hull provide a fascinating insight into how psychological safety impacts our mental and emotional processes, and define a simple model to help us to understand. They describe the model S.A.F.E.T.Y – Security, Autonomy, Fairness, Esteem, Trust, and You – and outline how different environments can impact each of these senses in different ways depending on our individual sensitivities. They outline different scenarios for each aspect, and demonstrate that productivity levels of the team, and of the individual, are seriously impacted when psychological safety is sacrificed. Radecki and Hull describe with scientific certainty how an attack to a person's psychological safety forces their brain to consume valuable resources, and in the process restricts the parts of the brain that are focused on productive pursuits such as decision making and creativity.

Let's consider the reality of working in a psychologically safe environment. Imagine working in an environment where you feel able to speak up when you believe something is wrong, and feel confident to contribute to a discussion when a valuable point is being missed, because you believe that your ideas will be respected and valued. Imagine working in an environment where you don't feel the need to hide a problem, because your team members are actively encouraged to support rather than criticise. Imagine working in an environment where you feel able to ask for help without fear of being ridiculed or ignored, and where individuals who point the finger and blame are held accountable for their judgement. Imagine working in an environment that considers and respects your personal needs when communicating change or agreeing working conditions. Such an environment is surely going to lead to more effective problem solving, is likely to produce better results first time, and be more productive in the long run.

Most of us would consider that the environment just described is nothing more than a utopian ideal. We've all worked in those environments where keeping your mouth shut and your head down was the safest way to maintain your sanity, and even your job. Expressing concerns over a new initiative that might be slightly off target, or asking a question of someone in a position of authority, can require courage that borders on stupidity. And, doing so simply opens you up to criticisms of negativity and of lacking ambition. Working in such a place can be soul destroying and saps productivity and enthusiasm from even the most committed.

There is, of course, data that supports this point. Gallup's 'State of the American Workplace Report 2017' shows that just 30% of workers believe that 'their opinions count at work', but for those organisations where their result grew to 60%, staff turnover reduced by 27%, safety incidents reduced by 40%, and productivity increased by 12%. (Herway, 2017)

Lencioni's 'Advantage'

In 'The Advantage', Patrick Lencioni describes his view of organisational health as "...The single greatest advantage any company can achieve..." and he passionately defines what it is, why it makes such a difference, and how to introduce it into any organisation effectively.

Lencioni describes a healthy organisation as having clarity in its purpose and structure, with all parts of the business being in harmony and working in unison towards the same aims. As a consequence, a healthy organisation lacks internal politics and confusion, it has high morale and productivity, and has low staff turnover. This sounds over simplistic in its explanation, but take a moment to consider the reality. Imagine a working environment where all functions are working together towards the same objective. Where direction from above is consistent and you receive the same message as the person you are working with from another department, making collaboration and teamwork easy. Imagine working in an environment where politics are actively and publicly dismissed, and individuals who promote their personal goals over those of everyone else are held accountable. Imagine working towards a common objective and being challenged to do so, knowing that it will make a significant contribution to the success of the business and yourself, and being supported by both your peers and manager to achieve it.

Again, most of us would consider Lencioni's description as a utopian ideal. We've all worked in those places where inter-departmental objectives and targets clash, where direction and communication are lacking, and where politics between individuals and functions is the norm. It's a painful and unpleasant experience that we know impacts our ability to be productive and happy at work. We know within ourselves that the healthy alternative is what we crave. Lencioni's description is passionately persuasive and taps into that internal desire. He argues that *"… the seminal difference between successful companies and mediocre or unsuccessful ones… has everything to do with how healthy they are…"*.

And again, there is data that supports the point. A 2017 article in McKinsey Quarterly by Gagnon, John, and Theunissen highlights that the top quartile of publicly traded companies in McKinsey's Organisational Health Index deliver roughly three times the returns to shareholders as those in the bottom quartile. They also demonstrate that businesses that focus on organisational health are more profitable, with an 18% increase in earnings versus as average of 7% for those companies in the S&P500.

Now, in understanding the concept of organisational health defined by Lencioni, we can see that it quite apparently supports the dynamics of structure and clarity, meaning and impact defined by Google's '*Project Aristotle*' and supported by Dan Pink's '*Drive*'. In creating the healthy organisation that Lencioni describes, team members will, by default, be provided with the sense of purpose and importance that they crave, and which will make them more effective as part of their team.

Bringing it together

If we now envisage a working environment in a way that combines the healthy organisation defined by Lencioni, with the psychologically safe environment defined by Edmondson, what we can describe is an ideal that no doubt all of us would strive to work within.

Imagine a workplace where all functions are working towards the same objective, and where that objective has been openly discussed, challenged, and modified where necessary by the team members involved in its execution. Imagine a workplace where direction from above is consistent, and has been communicated in such a way as to consider and respect individual needs. Imagine working towards a challenging objective as part of team, and feeling able to raise your hand and ask for help when you struggle or mis-understand.

Imagine working in an environment that celebrates when you identify a problem, and then rallies a team together to help to get it solved so that you can continue to be productive.

This is the kind of environment that most of us would desire to work within and to be part of. This is the kind of environment that enables effective teamwork.

We can see that establishing alignment through a sense of purpose and meaning, and creating an environment that is psychologically safe, is critical for both individual team members and the organisation as a whole. It's not too difficult to appreciate the impact that such an environment could have on the three core problems of workplace happiness, operational performance, and creating a platform for Lean. An aligned and purposeful environment that allows freedom of expression without fear of retribution is clearly going to help to sustain high levels of workplace happiness. Team members are naturally going to feel more engaged, experience less inappropriate pressure, and achieve a feeling of contribution and value. The knock-on effects on performance are obvious too. Teams that function more effectively solve problems in a more timely and efficient manner, and they achieve their objectives more reliably. The utilisation of Lean is facilitated because individuals and teams feel more able to adapt to change, are more willing to try new and challenging solutions to problems that are slightly different to the norm, and perhaps are actively seeking those novel solutions to problems that they are already trying to solve.

This is why it's this kind of environment that *Lean Foundations*™ seeks to create. This is why it's this approach to organisational health, and its role in supporting effective teamwork, that I hope I have persuaded you to embrace, so that the people that you represent can embrace it with you. It's this approach to organisational health that taps into our intrinsic motivators of teamwork and purpose, and which fuels workplace happiness, operational performance, and provides a platform for Lean.

Just in case you're not quite there, here's one last reference. In her book '*Powerful*', Patty McCord, describes her view of how to build high performing teams based on her experiences over 14 years as former Chief Talent Officer at Netflix. It's no doubt an organisation that has grown dramatically, has pioneered new technologies and services during a journey of constant evolution, and has delivered performance and culture globally recognised as peer leading. Central to her story is a description of the healthy and psychologically safe environment that was actively encouraged, and which underpinned their success.

"… We wanted all of our people to challenge us, and one another, vigorously. We wanted them to speak up about ideas and problems, to freely push back, in front of one another and in front of us…"

Now, the challenge is to understand how we actually do it.

GETTING STARTED

Hopefully the last few pages have been successful in persuading you of the power of organisational health in supporting effective teamwork. As a result, I also hope that you can appreciate why building organisational health and effective teamwork is fundamental to addressing the three core problems.

What we need to do now is to provide you with mechanisms for building organisational health and effective teamwork in your manufacturing facility. To do that, we need to outline how we can establish alignment with a clear purpose that creates meaning for the whole organisation, and describe how we can initiate and sustain psychological safety.

In their books, both Edmondson and Lencioni provide clear and concise methodologies for creating the conditions that they so eloquently describe. But, they serve their individual approaches, and cannot simply be replicated as a result.

It's worth sharing a couple of critical observations at this juncture. For both Lencioni and Edmondson the responsibility for delivering the change lies with the top leader of the organisation. It's not a point that they make explicitly, but it is clearly implied. Also, *Lean Foundations™* is focused on delivering change specifically in a manufacturing facility for two reasons. First, because it's the basis of my experience and is therefore where I feel it's most appropriate for me to contribute. Second, because manufacturing facilities are often led and managed as independent entities. Whether they function as part of a small privately-owned businesses, or as part of a large global group of companies, a manufacturing facility is often able to insulate itself from the influences of the wider organisation, and its leader is able to influence its culture and working practices in line with their own leadership approach. This, by default, can make that leader the top leader of their organisation, and means that they have to accept the responsibility to deliver the required change in the right way. Of course, the ideal would be that the *Lean Foundations™* approach is embraced by a whole organisation, and therefore each of their manufacturing facilities would not have to insulate themselves. But that seems almost too ambitious to hope for.

Bearing this in mind, this part of the *Lean Foundations™* approach seeks to help you, as the top leader of your manufacturing facility, to build a healthy organisation and therefore enable effective teamwork. It does so through the application of 4 sub-steps. They are 'Build the vision', 'Share the vision', 'Lead from the front', and 'Kick-start structure'. Their purpose is to introduce and embed the two features of a healthy organisation: a clarity of purpose and direction, and the creation of a psychologically safe working environment. Let's look at each sub-step in turn.

BUILD THE VISION

As a manufacturing leader, you are likely to be responsible for leading a management team of operational professionals with diverse functional responsibilities. The main aim of this first sub-step is to create a degree of alignment and coherence in that management team. After all, if your management team isn't aligned, how could everyone else be? First, we need to encourage your management team to understand and embrace the power of organisational health and effective teamwork as you have just done yourself. Second, we need to align them with a commitment to a common purpose, and need to encourage them to define and agree the mental models that underpin daily interactions and help to create a psychologically safe environment. At this point we are not looking to develop a detailed plan of action. Instead, we are trying to create a vision of how we will work together, and what we will work together towards, which will help to establish the environment of organisational health that we seek. To help you to do this successfully, I intend to arm you with the knowhow to bring together and utilise three complimentary ideas.

Welcoming change

Change is something that makes people uncomfortable, and can quite easily be rejected and even actively resisted regardless of whether it's a good idea or not. We therefore need to be able to present the desire and need for improvement in a way that will be readily accepted by as many people as possible. We want to create a sense of buy-in and willingness to embrace the *Lean Foundations™* journey that we're about to begin. It's worth recognising that in approaching change in this way, we're already starting to think in a way that is respectful of individual needs, and is therefore helping to create psychological safety.

In searching for a way to introduce change successfully, I was guided towards a wonderful book called '*Switch*' by Chip and Dan Heath. The ideas presented by the Heath brothers are both simple and effective. They describe that we are all guided by two mental processes; our emotional side, and our rational side. Our emotional side is the part of us that guides us towards the things we want to do, or away from the things that we are afraid of. It's this side that draws us toward that chocolate bar we shouldn't really eat, to stay in bed a little longer than we should, or to run away from the miniscule (but obviously vicious and highly poisonous) spider in the bathtub. Our rational side is the part of us that thinks more logically and sensibly, and helps us to make reasoned decisions in the face our emotional responses. It's this side that creates the 'pro's and con's' list when making a big spending decision, which draws up the exercise plan to support that desire for athletic prowess, or which rejects the offer of a second piece of cake.

The Heath brothers help us to understand how these mental processes interact by describing them in the terms of an Elephant and its Rider. The Elephant is our emotional side, and the Rider is our rational side. In theory, the Rider is in control of the Elephant and is determining how it behaves. However, that control is precarious because the Elephant is somewhat larger and more powerful than the Rider. If the Elephant wants to go a different way to the Rider, then it will. We know that our emotional Elephant is the one that has stopped us from quitting smoking, or encouraged us to have extra dessert, or forced us to jump on a chair, even when our rational Rider is calmly letting us know that those aren't the right things to do.

In understanding this interaction, the Heath brothers have related our mental processes to the introduction of change. If change is introduced badly, our emotional Elephant may well react, and may well cause us to respond negatively, even if the rational Rider is desperately trying to maintain control. If change is introduced and it doesn't make sense, our rational Rider may well reject it even if it makes life easier for our emotional Elephant. They have therefore defined a simple process to help to introduce change in a way that makes it easier for us to accept. There are three fairly self-explanatory steps to the process: 'Direct the Rider', 'Motivate the Elephant', and 'Shape the Path'.

In simple terms, 'Direct the Rider' involves providing a clear and logical reasoning behind the need or desire for change so that the Rider is able to understand what is required. 'Motivate the Elephant' involves engaging a person's emotional side when introducing change by appealing to their desires and needs, by inspiring them, or even motivating them through frustration. 'Shape the Path' involves clearing obstacles and providing guidance on how to complete change so that neither the Rider or the Elephant are easily knocked off course.

It's a simple process that has more sophisticated detail to it than I am taking the time to describe here, but it's definitely worth considering as we seek to initiate a significant process of change. When completing the activities for encouraging your management team to embrace organisational health, and for them to define the common purpose and the mental models that will create psychological safety, it's a good idea for us to consider the three-step process defined by the Heath brothers. In doing so we're more likely to be successful in getting their buy-in.

Structuring alignment

Bringing people together and aligning them behind a common objective or cause is not as easy as it sounds. Drawing on the motivations of their Rider and Elephant is certainly an important factor, as is directing the path they take. But providing a logical structure for them to build the shared objective upon has driven me to try a great many different approaches during my career. I'm once again drawn to the work of Patrick Lencioni, and in particular his excellent book '*Silo's, Politics and Turf Wars*' where he describes a four-step model for enabling organisational alignment.

Lencioni's model is shaped by the observation that individuals and teams often respond to a 'rallying cry' or sense of urgency with real alignment and shared focus. If an organisation is on the edge of closure, or a sports team is on the brink of losing a critical match, the team members can find it easier to come together to recover and succeed.

The first step of Lencioni's model requires a leadership team to agree a pre-determined rallying cry (without the need for an emergency) or 'Thematic Goal', which he defines as *"... a single qualitative focus that is shared by the entire leadership team – and ultimately by the entire organisation..."*. His second step is to agree 'Defining Objectives', which he defines as *"... the components or building blocks that serve to clarify what is meant by the thematic goal..."*, and which are again qualitative statements that are shared by all. The third step is to define 'Standard Operating Objectives', which are more tangible and quantitative and define specific targets for success. The fourth step is 'Metrics', which are the specific measurements used to confirm and monitor progress.

In understanding this model, we can see that the first two steps can support the kind of top-level buy-in that we are trying to create at this point in the *Lean Foundations*™ journey. The third and fourth are a little more granular and specific than we need here, but will become relevant later in the process. What we can suggest that we are looking to achieve now therefore, is alignment of the management team to a 'Thematic Goal' and a set of 'Defining Objectives', in order to build that clarity of purpose and sense of meaning required for organisational health. However, if we want to introduce the improvement journey in a way that will enable it to be positively embraced, we should also consider the need to Motivate the Elephant, and to appeal to our emotional side. One way to do that is to try and be a little inspirational.

Combining for inspiration

In his rousingly motivational book '*Start with Why*', Simon Sinek introduces us to an idea that he calls 'The Golden Circle'. It's a fantastically simple but very clever observation about the characteristics that separate those individuals and organisations that are inspirationally successful, from those who are quite simply not. He describes a simple three-layer circular model to explain his thinking.

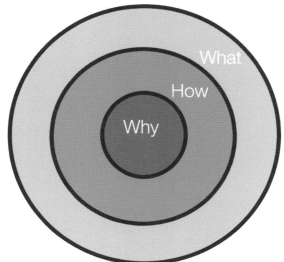

Fig 1-3. Simon Sinek's 'Golden Circle'

Sinek explains that most organisations tend to work from the outside of the circle to the inside when identifying themselves to their employees and their potential customers. Those organisations explain what they do, what service they provide or what product they make, and how they do it differently from the competition (for example, being cheaper). However, the truly inspirational and often more successful organisations work from the inside of the circle to the outside. They describe their 'Why' (their fundamental purpose for existence) and then describe 'How' they meet that purpose and 'What' they do in support of it. One of Sinek's favourite illustrations of this idea is Apple Inc, where he compares the two approaches outlined below…

Outside to Inside looks like… *"We make great computers. They're beautifully designed, simple to use and user-friendly. Wanna buy one?"*

Whereas Inside to Outside looks like… *"Everything we do, we believe in challenging the status quo. We believe in thinking differently. The way we challenge the status quo is by making our products beautifully designed, simple to use and user-friendly. And we happen to make great computers. Wanna buy one?"*

Sinek's argument and illustration are compelling. The second perspective here is dramatically more attractive than the first. We know from experience that because of the way Apple presents itself and its products, there is a desire to purchase them simply to support and belong to their 'Why'. Their products inspire us because of that desire for belonging. It's a compulsion that we may not necessarily be fully conscious of, but it's definitely there.

And it's that same sense of inspiration that we may be able to take advantage of here. In order to really Motivate our Elephant, we want to be able to inspire our management team, and subsequently the whole organisation, on our *Lean Foundations™* journey. To do so, we can bring together Lencioni's ideas with Sinek's; we can realise that Lencioni's 'Thematic Goals' are similar to Sinek's 'Why', that Lencioni's 'Defining Objectives' are similar to Sinek's 'How', and that Lencioni's 'Standard Operating Objectives' and 'Metrics' are similar to Sinek's 'What'. In order to align the organisation, and perhaps even inspire them, we can define our own 'Golden Circle'.

So, how do we go about defining our 'Thematic Goal'/'Why' and our 'Defining Objectives'/'How'?

The Offsite – agreeing a common purpose

Whether you're a manufacturing leader that is new to an organisation, or even one who has been working there for some time, I would propose that we can achieve the alignment we seek by bringing the management team together for a structured but open leadership discussion. The aim in undertaking this discussion would be to lead your management team through a process of reflection and understanding that encourages them to make pre-determined conclusions, and which ultimately results in them defining the standard 'Thematic Goal', or 'Why', and 'Defining Objectives', or 'How', of *Lean Foundations™*. It's possible that the thought of running such an event makes you want to run for the hills (or at least, to throw this book in the bin), but please rest assured that it's not as daunting or as difficult as it may seem. However, if it does appear to be a challenge too far for you to manage, then it's perfectly okay for you to consider employing a professional meeting facilitator to help manage the event. In doing so, it's a good idea to coordinate your requirements clearly in advance, and agree how you will work together to achieve the desired results.

In my experience an event of this nature is best completed off-site, but you could do it on-site as long as it is remote from the day to day operations to avoid being disturbed. It's likely to be an all-day event, and may even take two days. If taking yourself and your whole management team offsite for 1 or 2 days seems laughably impossible, then perhaps run the equivalent half day sessions instead. If you have been working in a facility for some time, you may wish to coincide this event with a milestone; perhaps the start of a new financial or calendar year, or the launch of a major new product. If you're new to a facility, this event is something you can schedule once you've settled into the organisation and have a good idea of how it functions, so perhaps a month or so in.

Running the event effectively is a challenge. It's important that we try and get engagement from the entire team, so creating the conditions for this is something we should consider in advance. By the way, engagement doesn't necessarily mean everyone contributes equally. Some personalities are more comfortable in speaking up and expressing themselves than others, so don't worry too much if some contribute less. We should look to invite the right people, and try and make sure that the invites for the event are raised well in advance, with an agenda clearly described, and a clear message that everyone will have the opportunity to input as much as they feel able. If it's possible to invite managers from functions outside your direct team without causing internal problems then I would suggest that you do so; creating alignment beyond just your own operational responsibility is a real positive.

Consider starting the meeting with an outline of the structure of the event, including breaks and rules around things like mobile phone and laptop use, and reinforce the wish for everyone to feel able to contribute and with freedom of expression. Remember, if this is the first time the team has ever done anything like this, it will take time for them to feel comfortable and to behave appropriately, and you can encourage their involvement by modelling the right kind of behaviour yourself. You can allow people to relax and feel comfortable by reacting positively when a potentially contentious point is raised, by allowing the discussion to flow and not 'telling' people what to think, and by enabling contributions from quieter team members when asking them for their perspective or point of view.

Once the rules of engagement are clear, it's time to try and initiate, encourage and direct the debate. It's not prudent for me to be too prescriptive here as debates of this nature are fluid and individual by their very nature. However, I can suggest that you lead the discussion by asking questions, and that you use these questions to direct the discussion toward the specific conclusions you're hoping to draw. Record the responses using a whiteboard, easel, or post-it notes.

There are two conclusions you are hoping to encourage your team to make…

1. *We suffer from poor operational performance, a lack of workplace happiness, and an inability to utilise Lean.* Questions you can ask your team to draw this conclusion include… Do we need to improve our facility? If yes, what do we need to improve? Where do we lack in performance? Are we being criticised for failing to perform? Are our employees happy and engaged? Do people enjoy coming to work? Are we losing our best employees? Are we able to embed Lean? Do our kaizen events work? Do we see results that last? Do we see facility-wide involvement? The answers that you share will enable you to confirm the three core problems statement – 'we suffer from poor operational performance, a lack of workplace happiness, and an inability to utilise Lean'. This will become the basis of your 'Thematic Goal' – your 'Why'.

2. *We have these problems because we lack organisational health and effective teamwork, we don't utilise an effective management system, and we don't engage empowered employees.* Questions you can ask your team to draw this conclusion include… Do we have a clear direction and sense of purpose? Are we all working towards that common purpose together? Do we think our employees work well in teams? Do they appear to trust one another and express themselves freely? Do you as managers trust one another? Do we conflict with one another healthily? Do our employees feel accountable for their own areas of responsibility? Do we support them effectively to solve their own problems? Do we show empathy and actively listen when they raise a problem? Do we take on responsibility for solving that problem ourselves, rather than support them in solving it? Are our daily processes robust? Do we schedule production effectively? Do we have good inventory control? Do we utilise an Enterprise Resource Planning (ERP) system properly? Do we have good quality controls? It's a good idea for you to provide some understanding of what supports effective teamwork, and what defines organisational health at this point so that you're providing conceptual context to enable their understanding. Maybe you can share our insights from Lencioni's '*The Advantage*' about clarity of purpose and direction, and from Edmondson's '*The Fearless Organisation*' about psychological safety, and the benefits they both bring to teamwork. It may also be useful to share the YouTube vide of Dan Pink's TED talk on '*What motivates us*'. It's a short 10-minute video which really helps to make the point around purpose and meaning. As a result of sharing these points, you're 'Directing their Rider' by providing the rational intelligence that will able them to logically understand. Again, the answers that you share will enable you to confirm the three common factors statement - 'we lack the characteristics of a healthy organisation and effective teamwork, we fail to engage empowered front-line team members, and we lack a well-functioning management system'. This will become the basis of your 'Defining Objectives' – your 'How'.

Now that we've drawn the management team through this process of reflection, we can try to encourage them to align and to agree on how to move forward; but only at a top level, and not with any detail at this point. Here, we can look to agree to define our common purpose, and to find a structure that allows us to do so. We can now introduce Lencioni's model for breaking down silo's and politics, and in particular his 'Thematic Goal' and 'Defining Objectives', and then describe Sinek's 'Golden Circle'. To help with this, I would suggest that you share the YouTube video of Simon Sinek's TED talk on 'The Golden Circle' idea, as it's an engaging way to explain the concept directly.

Once you have introduced the two sets of ideas from Lencioni and Sinek, you will hopefully be able to describe the similarities between them, and as a result to draw your own version of 'The Golden Circle' like the one below...

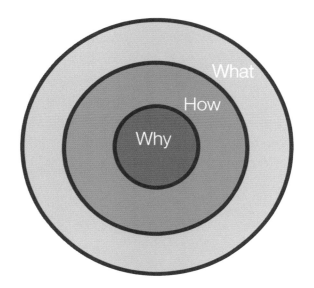

Why: To be a great place to work: to be a happy workplace, with good operational performance, and which is able to utilise Lean.

How: By creating a healthy organisation that enables effective teamwork, by engaging with empowered front-line team members, and by developing a well-functioning management system.

What: To be defined later – by everyone.

Fig 1-4. The *Lean Foundations*™ 'Golden Circle'

You can see here that we've successfully integrated the three core problems of poor workplace happiness, poor operational performance, and an inability to utilise Lean, into our 'Thematic Goal' or 'Why'. We've also integrated the three common factors of lack of organisational health and effective teamwork, lack of engagement with empowered front-line team members, and lack of a well-functioning management system into our 'Defining Objectives' or 'How'. We've created a neat and concise model, and hopefully in the process have established a sense of buy-in with the management team to the process of improvement that we're now initiating. It's also important to note that the buy-in to our 'Why' and 'How' is helping to establish a fundamental feature of Lean culture and practice into our psyche. As I mentioned in the earlier introductions, Toyota has always been focused on adding value for their customer, and on respecting their employees. Our 'Why' and 'How' provides the same focus, only with a slightly different phrasing, and therefore prepares our team to accept that Lean ideal in the future.

There is one further important factor we need to consider at this point. Depending on the nature of your role and the scale of your wider organisation, you may already be working with things like Mission, Vision and Values statements, and these are unlikely to be exactly the same as the 'Why' and 'How' we've just defined. This is not something to be concerned about but is still something that we need to integrate into what we're doing. It's probable that any such statements require performance, improvement and results relevant to your product or industry. Being able to position your 'Golden Circle' as a means of delivering these should be possible. In fact, I've often found that being able to present such a model, and the plan that we'll develop later alongside it, helps to build confidence and a sense of relevance to those Mission, Vision and Values statements, which sometimes seem remote and even meaningless in a local facility context.

Going through this process of realisation with your management team takes time and patience. You could, of course, simply stand up in front of everyone and write the conclusions for them, but that will not result in them accepting or believing them as whole-heartedly as they will if you take them through the process of self-realisation. It's a directed process admittedly; you will be leading them to the conclusions that you want them to make, but this can be very effective, and if led well you can expect everyone to fully buy-in to the conclusions as a result. It's this process that both Motivates their Elephant, and Directs their Rider. By framing the discussion in this way, you can enable them to use logical and rational information to inform their thinking, and can appeal to their emotional desire to solve real problems that affect them and their team members on a daily basis. Engagement with the change process we're initiating here is ultimately created because we're seeking to solve the problems that your management team actually want to solve. At the same time, we're working on problems that will improve the performance of the organisation, which is something that almost every employee will also actively desire. We will be contributing to the overall improvement of the facility in which you work and improving the individual working lives of every person within it. It's a win-win scenario.

Whilst it's difficult to describe here, I have found upon completion of these events, management teams often leave them with a real sense of enthusiasm and hope. This very quickly translates itself to the wider organisation, as managers return to their individual teams to discuss the event. I would suggest that this is something you want to actively encourage. Spreading positive energy throughout a facility is an opportunity that should not to be missed. However, it's important that you all agree on what should and should not be communicated by individual managers. The message needs to be consistent.

What we've achieved at this point is alignment and buy-in of the management team to the common purpose that will provide the meaning and sense of purpose required for organisational health. Now, we need to agree the behaviours that will initiate and nurture psychological safety.

The Offsite – agreeing mental models

Hopefully your offsite meeting is proving successful so far. You may wish to complete the next part in the same event, or to split it into a separate event, either way will work and is entirely up to you.

Our next step is to try and define a number of agreed mental models (or acceptable behaviours – what you call them is up to you) that will support and nurture an environment of psychological safety. These mental models will form the basis of the leadership approach that you will ask the management team to follow, and will be cascaded throughout the organisation so that everyone understands the acceptable methods of interaction. You will have already set the context for this discussion in the previous part of the offsite meeting. You will have sown the seeds of understanding psychological safety and what contributes to it. However, whether you're completing this in a separate event, or as part of the first, it's possibly worth reiterating those ideas at this point to keep them fresh. In particular, there are five specific considerations that it's a good idea to present, these include references to the senses that are impacted by a lack of psychological safety from the Radecki and Hull S.A.F.E.T.Y model discussed earlier…

- *Re-framing failure* – The risk of failure and its potential consequences can have the biggest impact on an individual's sense of psychological safety. If a person believes that failure will lead to criticism and even punishment, regardless of cause, then they may take every necessary step to avoid that failure, including avoiding taking responsibility in the first place, or not taking creative risk to achieve the highest possible levels of success. They may endeavour to protect their sense of self-esteem, and maybe even their sense of security, and may to look to take 'the easy way out'. Instead, psychologically safe environments frame failure in terms of learning, and ensure that making a mistake and learning from it is an extremely valuable process. This of course cannot excuse all forms of failure, and success has to be openly encouraged and embraced as being critically important. A balance has to be sensitively struck. Most importantly, failure of effort and commitment need to be managed critically, whereas failure of performance that is not due to failure of effort and commitment needs to be seen as an opportunity to improve. Where failure results in high risk to an individual or the organisation it needs to be framed as a shared responsibility, and that its identification is seen as a means of protecting everyone.

- *Respect for individual contribution* – The sense that individual contribution is not valued and is ignored, or the sense that an individual is treated differently because of their personal differences, can have a huge impact on an individual's sense of psychological safety. If a person believes that they will be ignored if they raise an idea, point out a problem, or contradict an opinion, then they may simply stop contributing. If a person believes that they are discriminated against because of physical or personality reasons, their sense of trust and fairness may be impacted and they are likely to 'suffer in silence'. They may even express cynicism when others express ideas, undermining them in the process. Instead, psychologically safe environments embrace and respect all individual contributions, with every problem raised at least recorded for resolution in the future, if not immediately addressed, and time taken to understand and appreciate an individual's perspective. Importantly, in a psychologically safe environment, individuals will be held accountable if they inappropriately criticise an alternative perspective. That means comments that are personal or emotive such as 'that's a stupid idea', or 'you don't know what you're talking about' become unacceptable and are openly discredited.

- *Recognition and appreciation* – The sense that an individual's daily contribution is not appreciated or recognised can have a significant impact on their sense of psychological safety. If a person believes that their contribution is simply expected, and that any effort to be successful is just the norm, then they may revert to completing the bare minimum that is required to 'get by'. They may well lose interest in their role, become less likely to volunteer for additional responsibilities, or even resent their workplace and resign. Instead, psychologically safe environments actively recognise and appreciate all contributions, whether they are the normal day to day responsibilities, or additional demands that go above and beyond what's expected. Language such as 'Thank you', 'I really appreciate your effort', 'Thanks for your help', 'That's a great idea', is more are prevalent, but this does not happen by accident and has to be actively encouraged.

- *Enabling freedom of expression* – The sense that an individual is restricted in their role and is only able to add value by following instruction can have a considerable impact on their sense of psychological safety. If a person believes that they have no opportunity to express themselves creatively, to respond to changes in circumstance without asking permission, or to deviate from standard process without risk of criticism, they are likely to become frustrated at a lack of autonomy. They may look to push problems upwards for solution, to lose the ability to think for themselves, and there may be a risk that they will abdicate responsibility entirely. Instead, psychologically safe environments promote ownership and accountability by allowing individuals to modify their working practices in line with changes in demand. They will actively encourage teams to solve problems for themselves, and will embrace individual flexibility in meeting their responsibilities. They will also encourage individual development and personal improvement through the utilisation of training, one-to-one coaching and mentoring, or participation in group improvement activities.

- *What Psychological Safety is not* – Creating an environment that is psychologically safe does not mean that it is 'nice', or that it has low standards. It does not mean that people have to be excessively polite and pleasant with each other, because candid and honest disagreement is, in fact, absolutely critical. It does not mean that responding appropriately to failure means that people become comfortable and underachieve, because performance is absolutely still necessary. Expectation of performance still exists but does so without creating a sense of anxiety. The ability for people to expect high performance and to conflict constructively to achieve it, whilst being able to learn and improve from failure, is the delicate but important balance that you are seeking to achieve.

Again, it's a good idea to present these five points in the context of an open and frank discussion with your management team. Whilst, on this occasion, the outcome of the discussion is not as pre-determined as before, you are looking to lead them toward conclusions of mental models that are along the lines of the ones outlined below...

- *Problems should not be hidden* - Problems are opportunities for improvement, they need to be identified so that they can be fixed.
- *Leaders listen, look, and advise* – Leaders of all levels act as a coach and teacher, they actively listen and support, and only instruct if/when necessary.
- *Failure is a learning opportunity* – Making mistakes is ok, but we have to commit ourselves to our highest levels of effort and to expect to perform. When we fail, we have to take responsibility and ensure that we learn from the mistakes that led us there.
- *Performance is important* – Delivering a quality product, on-time, at an appropriate cost, and safely, is of primary importance, but not at the expense of our health and well-being.
- *Everyone is equal* – No one person's opinion is more important than another, no one person's role is more valuable than another, regardless of their position.
- *Everyone deserves respect* – Inappropriate behaviour and personal comments will not be tolerated.
- *Be dependable* – Your colleagues need and want to be able to rely on you. Deliver your responsibilities, and expect others to deliver theirs.
- *Leaders go, look and see* – When problems are identified, leaders should take the time to understand them so that they can appreciate their impact and be part of the solution.
- *Solve problems together* – When problems are identified, all team members should be involved and consulted on the solution.
- *Say 'Thank you' frequently* – All team members, especially leaders, should actively promote recognition and appreciation with a deliberate and sincere effort.
- *There are no bad ideas* – All contributions and thoughts are valued, and none are dismissed.
- *Celebrate success* – When an individual or team is successful and achieves a positive result, this should be celebrated and recognised.
- *Conflict appropriately* – Conflict is not a bad thing. Disagreement is necessary in order to consider all points of view and to find the right solution. However, conflict must be professional and not personally biased or motivated. It should only come from a desire to seek the truth.
- *Team first* – Everyone should be focused on the performance of the organisation first, then their team, then themselves.
- *Give more than you take* – Add value to the team before you consider your personal needs.

- *Personal Development is important* – Training and learning will be supported by the organisation wherever practical, both individually and for team groups.

You may identify your own versions of these mental models and may adapt them to your specific environment, but thematically these are the kinds of statements that I would encourage you to agree with your management team as part of your discussions. On agreeing them, you are committing to working in line with them yourself, and you are committing to ensuring that everyone in your facility works to them, too. Once agreed, we can make sure they are recorded onto a single document, with appropriate corporate logos added, and with signatures from all the managers involved in the discussion. This point may seem a little excessive, but it will hopefully ensure that every member of the management team has been able to buy-in. It's a final opportunity for them to challenge acceptance, and for them to raise any concerns.

The final item for you to look to agree is how to respond when individuals do not work in line with the mental models. This is what Edmondson calls '*sanctioning clear violations*'. This can be a difficult agreement to reach, partly because individuals within your own management team may well have concerns about their own ability to work in line with the mental models themselves. However, it is important to define simple methods for managing adherence. If not, it's unlikely that the mental models will be maintained and worked towards. If there are no consequences for working away from them, then they will simply become a paper exercise, and the improvement journey you're looking to implement will lose validity and respect. Also, without an understanding of how to manage indiscretions, individuals may well respond inappropriately, and may inadvertently damage the psychological safety of an environment or team as a result. There are different appropriate responses to indiscretions that you could agree, I'm referencing a small number of options here in a simple escalation process. Fundamentally you're looking for your management team to agree the responses that they believe are appropriate.

- *Observation* – Any individual should feel able to raise an observation about an inappropriate comment, response or behaviour directly with the person who has made the indiscretion at any level of the organisation. This should be raised professionally and with non-emotive or personally biased language, and should point out the nature of the indiscretion, and the emotional response it has elicited.
- *Complaint* – Any individual should feel able to raise an informal complaint about an inappropriate comment, response or behaviour directly with the person who has made the indiscretion, and/or with that person's line-manager. A complaint may become necessary if the indiscretion is severe, or if it is being repeated. Again, this should be raised professionally and with non-emotive or personally biased language, and should point out the nature of the indiscretion, and the emotional response it has elicited.
- *Training* – Where necessary, it's worth considering giving some (or even all) individuals some specific training on the nature of psychological safety and the agreed mental models. I would suggest that this type of training is developed in conjunction with colleagues from HR, utilises content from Radecki and

Hull's book '*Psychological Safety*', and in particular helps people to understand their S.A.F.E.T.Y model.

- *Intervention* – Where necessary, individuals may need to be addressed by their line-manager in relation to an indiscretion, particularly if the indiscretion is severe, or if it is frequently repeated. This should be considered as an informal counselling session, but should be documented utilising whatever standard process is in place. Again, this should be raised professionally and with non-emotive or personally biased language, and should point out the nature of the indiscretion, and the emotional response it has elicited. The aim is to educate and coach the individual who made the indiscretion, but please bear in mind that this is not always achievable.

- *Disciplinary* – Where necessary, individuals may need to be taken through an organisation's standard disciplinary process in response to frequent or significant indiscretions. This would become necessary if observations and complaints have been made, if training given, and if interventions completed, but poor behaviour continues. This may seem a step too far, but as we've already discussed, an environment of psychological safety is critical to the success of every individual and the organisation as a whole. It's therefore important to protect that psychological safety, and to demonstrate to everyone that you are wholly committed to it.

Through the course of your discussion with your management team, you can agree an escalation process similar to that described above. These can be added to the document showing the mental models should you wish, or can simply be shared with the wider organisation in the later sub-steps of the process, the choice is yours depending on what you feel is appropriate for your facility.

What we have hopefully achieved by this point is significant and we should take a moment to reflect. We should now have built a degree of coherence and alignment in our management team. Hopefully, the management team has a clear understanding of organisational health and effective teamwork, and has reached an agreement on the common purpose and the mental models that will underpin the daily interactions that help to create a psychologically safe environment. It's important not to over-estimate the level of management team coherence, a small number of offsite events will not reconcile poor management cohesion fully. However, positive steps will have been made, and management team alignment to the common purpose and acceptable behaviours that will underpin organisational health and effective teamwork is an important first milestone in the *Lean Foundations*™ journey. If you believe that you have successfully achieved this, then pat yourself on the back, that's a job well done.

Now we need to get everyone else in your facility on the same page.

SHARE THE VISION

Early in the *Lean Foundations™* journey, it is important to establish with all team members that a change process has started, and that it is a change process that everyone can embrace and be part of. It is not something to be feared or to get frustrated about, because it will be of benefit to all. Now that you and your management team have agreed how you will work together, and what you will work together towards, we can share it with your whole facility so that we can create that awareness. The aim, therefore, of this second sub-step, is to communicate that positive change is coming, to enable everyone in your facility to understand and embrace the power of organisational health and effective teamwork, and to encourage them to buy-in to the common purpose and mental models required to achieve them. To be successful, we again need to consider the ideas of Chip and Dan Heath, and remember that we're looking to engage everyone fully by 'Directing their Rider', 'Motivating their Elephant', and 'Shaping their Path'.

The Town Hall brief

I have found that the simplest way to share the vision is to complete an all-hands briefing session, which is sometimes called a Town Hall Brief. You may wish to do this in one sitting, or in multiple sessions, depending on the number of people in your facility, and the size and configuration of your meeting rooms or assembly areas. To be successful, we're going to need a projector and screen (or white wall), and we may even need a microphone and speakers if the space is large enough. We're also going to need to create a presentation which you can talk alongside. The idea of standing in front of a large group of people may well be filling you with dread by this point and may cause you to give up on the *Lean Foundations™* idea at this early stage, but I would urge you to proceed. After all, you are simply sharing an idea about which you are passionate, with a group of people that you professionally care for. You're in control, here.

The presentation that you display, and your delivery of it, can be constructed in a way that will help to create the buy-in that it's so important to achieve. To help with this, I would suggest that you structure it in a way that reflects the offsite discussion held with your team, so that you take every individual through the same Socratic process that your management team has experienced; only you're unlikely to be seeking individual contributions due to constraints of time. Here's a suggested sequence of messaging that should help you to create your presentation in a way that helps to Direct Riders, Motivate Elephants and Share Paths all at the same time.

- *Change is coming* – You can clarify for everyone that a change process has started, and that a process for improving the facility is underway. You can state that this change process is different, because it will align the needs of the organisation with the needs of every individual within it.
- *The power of teamwork* – You can explain that organisational performance is underpinned by effective teamwork. Briefly communicate what makes teamwork effective, share Lencioni's '*Five Dysfunctions*',

the findings of '*Project Aristotle*', and Dan Pink's theories on intrinsic motivation from '*Drive*'. Perhaps then share the YouTube video of Dan Pink's TED talk on '*What motivates us*' as you did with your management team.

- *The power of organisational health* – You can explain how organisational health impacts the effectiveness of teamwork and share what enables organisational health. Briefly describe Lencioni's concept of organisational health and the need for clarity of purpose. Briefly describe the basis of psychological safety and the impact it has on vulnerability-based trust in supporting effective teamwork.

- *Management team alignment* – You can explain that the management team has agreed on the need for a common purpose, and has agreed on a set of mental models to support psychological safety. Share Lencioni's 4-layer model from '*Silo's, Politics and Turf Wars*', and describe idea of 'Thematic Goal's' and 'Defining Objectives'. Share Sinek's '*Golden Circle*' concept utilising the YouTube video of his TED talk discussed previously. Draw the comparisons between the two concepts.

- *Your Golden Circle* – You can describe the process that the management team went through to develop your own 'Golden Circle', and then share it with your team. Be as empathetic as possible when describing the three common problems and three common factors that make up the 'Why'/'Thematic Goal' and 'How'/'Defining Objectives'. Explain that the 'What'/'Standard Operating Objectives/Metrics' will be defined as part of a whole team planning exercise later.

- *Your Mental Models* – Perhaps share the mental models that have been agreed, and give a clear explanation of each one and endeavour to provide examples of good and bad behaviour as context if you can.

- *Responsibilities* – You could describe the responsibility that everyone has in working to the mental models discussed, and describe the appropriate responses to indiscretions that everyone should follow. Make it clear that supporting psychological safety is of paramount importance.

- *Change is coming* – Back where we started, perhaps re-iterate for everyone that a change process is already happening, and why this is the case. Throw in the reminder that everyone is expected to be involved.

- *There is more to come* – You can clarify that there is more to the change than just what has been outlined so far; that there will be modifications to organisation structure, to daily processes and procedures, to how problems are solved, and to how everyone is actively involved. These further changes will become apparent over time.

Exactly how you deliver these messages is entirely up to you and your personal preferences. You may choose to present simple short messages on each slide or give lots of explanation in each case. You may wish to stand up, or to sit down. You may wish to ask questions and engage team members in discussion, you may not. The exact method of delivery is not important. What you're trying to achieve is a consistent end result; that everyone in your team recognises that a positive change process has begun, that everyone in your facility understands and can embrace the power of organisational health and effective teamwork, and that everyone has the opportunity to buy-in to the common purpose and mental models required to achieve them.

We also need to be honest with ourselves at this point. There is likely to be a mixed response to this briefing session. Some individuals will respond positively and will be excited by the potential opportunity. Some individuals will be neutral in their response and will want to wait and see. Some will be cynical and will 'have heard it all before'. Others, however, may well be outwardly and vocally negative and contradictory, just for the sake of it. Your team members will respond differently based on how effectively you deliver the message, what their personal experiences have been in the past, and what you and/or your predecessors have said and done previously. There is no getting away from this, but it should not discourage us from starting the process. What should encourage the majority of people to believe is a consistency of message and approach over time, with some taking longer to buy-in than others as a natural part of that. However, there will of course be some people who never accept the change. In my experience, some of these people will choose to leave your organisation of their own accord and you will be happy when they do so. Others will eventually need to be removed from your facility, using entirely correct and appropriate processes to ensure legal and psychologically safe compliance. Do not underestimate the fact that all of the other team members you represent are likely to be happy when this happens. They will be aware of the disruptive nature of those individuals and will be looking to you and your management team to address them appropriately. Part of your role as leader of this change process will be to recognise when that removal is required for the benefit of all, and to take the correct and necessary steps to make it happen.

The follow-up

It's of vital importance that the message of the Town Hall brief does not stand in isolation. It's very easy to complete the brief, and then to expect everyone to suddenly change the way they are working. I'm afraid things are rarely that straightforward. There are a number of simple steps that you can take that will help to initiate a little momentum immediately following the Town Hall brief.

- *Reinforce the message* – You can bring all your managers, supervisors, team leaders etc. together for a separate discussion to stress the importance of the message given, and to provide them with a direct opportunity to ask questions. Perhaps give them more guidance on how to follow the mental models provided, or explain the importance of their role in bringing the change process to life. Maybe ask them to seek feedback from their team members.
- *Ask for feedback directly* – You can walk through your facility in the days following the Town Hall brief and specifically ask people for their honest feedback, either as individuals or groups of people. It's a good idea to take the time to listen, and to perhaps even take notes. Perhaps even use the conversations to reiterate points if people have misunderstood or are a little cynical. You can make it

clear that you believe in the change process and are passionate about its success. Your enthusiasm will be infectious.

- *Publicise the messages* – If you have noticeboards or communication boards, then you can print and post copies of the presentation and allow people to read it. Share it on public access computer drives if you can. Maybe email it to everyone if it's practical. Most importantly, you can print out and post the one-page document showing all of the agreed mental models with the signatures of the management team. Look to make this as visible as possible, especially in public areas and meeting rooms.

By following-up in this manner, you should help to demonstrate that you are serious about the change journey that you have initiated, and that this is simply the beginning of the process.

Hopefully, we've now managed to communicate to everyone that positive change is coming, have enabled everyone in your facility to understand and embrace the power of organisational health and effective teamwork, and have encouraged them to buy-in to the common purpose and mental models required to achieve them. Now we need to introduce some specific practices that will properly embed the new working methods that you're trying to encourage, starting with you 'Leading from the Front', and following with developing or modifying certain procedures which will 'Kick-start structure'.

LEADING FROM THE FRONT

Having started the ball rolling on your *Lean Foundations*™ journey, there is an opportunity for you, as the organisational leader of your manufacturing facility, to lead from the front. Your integrity, consistency, and enthusiasm can be the energy that sparks others to join you in the process of change that we have initiated. In completing the offsite session(s), we will have hopefully drawn your management team alongside you. And in completing the Town Hall brief, we will have encouraged team members throughout your facility to start to believe that something different and positive is happening. Now, the opportunity exists to galvanise a real sense of excitement and enthusiasm.

At the same time, there may well be a nervousness and lack of confidence around exactly how to behave appropriately. Naturally, individuals will avoid stepping forward to take the kind of interpersonal risks that we're hoping to encourage. Being the first to be vulnerable takes courage, particularly if that environment has not supported that vulnerability previously. The aim, therefore, of this third sub-step, is to provide you with guidance on how to adapt your leadership approach so that you are the role model for being vulnerable, and for responding correctly to vulnerability. The activities described aim to support you in being the leadership example for how to function in a healthy and psychologically safe organisation.

Admit you don't know

In '*The Fearless Organisation*', Amy Edmondson describes the need for leaders to demonstrate 'Situational Humility' in order to invite and encourage team members to actively participate in the psychologically safe environment. She suggests that leaders adopt a learning mindset, which combines humility and curiosity, and which relates a feeling of transparency and openness in interactions. In his thoughtful book, '*Humble Inquiry*', Edgar Schein describes a similar concept, something that he calls 'Here-and-now Humility'. He explains that this is humility that demonstrates inferior status and vulnerability in interaction, with an acceptance that another party is in a position to know something, or can do something, that you cannot. For a leader to demonstrate such humility, they need to be willing to be vulnerable from a position of authority and status. That takes courage, and when done properly is a means of building genuine trust-based relationships that enable psychological safety.

That idea of 'Situational Humility', or 'Here-and-now Humility', is an important characteristic for us as organisational leader on our *Lean Foundations*™ journey. A simple way for us to achieve it successfully is to accept and communicate our own errors and limitations. To say 'I don't know', or 'I got that wrong' is a way of demonstrating the kind of vulnerability that can build the confidence of your team. This may seem counterintuitive to some. You may expect that your team members want to see 'strong leadership' of the more traditional kind, where leaders tell and instruct. In fact, it's proven that what they wish to experience is leadership that trusts their perspective and contribution as specialists in their given area. For them to be recognised as key contributors and for their organisational leaders to engage with them as equals. Admitting you don't know is a powerful tool in enabling others to step forward, particularly when combined with the simple question 'What do you think?'. It also enables others to say 'I don't know' without feeling self-conscious. You can provide the leadership example that others are able to follow without fear of retribution.

Inquire, and mean it

Both Edmondson and Schein discuss the need for leaders to demonstrate proactive and genuine inquiry, where responses to questions are sought with sincerity and an honest desire for understanding and truth. That kind of inquiry is built on the approach of 'Situational Humility', or 'Here-and-now Humility', and helps to build constructive trust-based relationships. In the Lean community, there are similarities here with the kind of 'Lean Leader' models that feature leaders with big eyes, big ears, and small mouths.

This type of inquiry can be actively pursued in normal day to day interactions. However, in these early stages of the *Lean Foundations*™ journey, it is worth making a deliberate effort to demonstrate this leadership approach. It's a good idea for you to complete a top-level review of the organisation's basic processes, so that you as the operational leader of your manufacturing facility can properly understand how it functions. In the process, you can actively demonstrate your humility and your willingness to learn, and can demonstrate your genuine desire to build open and honest relationships with your team members. To do this well, you'll need to try and speak with every person in your facility on a one-to-one basis to understand their role, and the challenges they face in meeting their responsibilities. It's best to do this by visiting them at their desk or workbench so that they feel comfortable and in control. If you are responsible for a large number of people in your facility and one-to-one sessions are impossible, then you might need to break this down into small groups of responsibility instead, and address groups of team members who work together in process or functional areas. You can ask open questions when completing this activity. Perhaps begin with 'Why', 'What', 'How', 'When', 'Where' and look to make a genuine effort to understand. A good idea is to be seen to take notes, and ask questions that follow on from answers to demonstrate that you are listening. Compare the answers you are receiving to what you would expect. I'm confident that you're going to learn about problems that you didn't know existed or wouldn't have ever expect to find. And, you're likely to see exactly where your team members are 'putting-up' with things that are wrong because they don't feel able to do anything about it. Be prepared to feel disappointed and frustrated but do your best not to express this in a way that makes the person you speak with feel exposed or criticised. You want them to feel able to be honest and open with you. The failure is with the process, and not with the person.

If you are new to a manufacturing facility, this approach is a good way to get to know your organisation and the people in it, and may well be something you do before the Offsite sessions and Town Hall briefs, as alluded to previously. If you have been leading a facility for some time, the approach can be a good way of re-framing your existing relationships in line with the expectations you've now set around organisational health and psychological safety. If your previous leadership approach included more 'telling' than 'asking', then this top-level review presents the opportunity to prove that you have changed, and may even be an opportunity for you to apologise for previous indiscretions if you feel necessary.

The top-level review is important for another reason. You've committed to agreeing the 'What' or 'Standard Operating Objectives' of your 'Golden Circle' with your team. The review provides you with an ideal opportunity to actively seek and gather your team members contributions to this process. It's not the only time that we'll address this, we'll get to it in more detail later in the *Lean Foundations*™ approach, but you can certainly present your purpose for completing the top-level review in this context. This may be more necessary in environments where trust of leadership and management is a significant problem, and your process of inquiry may be mis-construed as potentially malicious or deceitful.

Lead effective meetings

The first thing to say here is that meetings are absolutely fantastic. I know that a great many of you are reading that statement with incredulity and are now certain that I'm crazy, but really, I'm not. Meetings really are great, but only when done properly. In reality, for managers and leaders of organisations, meetings are what we do. We spend our time discussing, agreeing, deciding, sharing, and presenting in a variety of meetings on a daily basis. However, many of us would comfortably say that 'I'd get more done if it wasn't for meetings', or 'My job would be much more enjoyable if it wasn't for meetings'. In '*Death by Meeting*', Patrick Lencioni describes two common problems that cause meetings to illicit these types of responses. Firstly, he draws the point that meetings are boring and lack drama. Secondly, he quotes that meetings lack structure and control. You can, as organisational leader of your facility, take steps to address these two problems with relative ease.

The drama that Lencioni refers to is conflict. Too many meetings lack conflict, and as a consequence do not deliver real and tangible results. We therefore feel disappointment and frustration and believe that the meeting has been a waste of time. In our healthy and psychologically safe organisation, we are actively seeking conflict. Therefore, your leadership approach can encourage that drama or conflict in every meeting setting so that it becomes effective and worthwhile. Lencioni defines three features that encourage that sense of drama. Firstly, create the 'hook', or a sense of drama, by injecting a reason to care and a degree of tension into the meeting from the very beginning; perhaps within the first few minutes. Make the purpose or agenda of the meeting important so that it introduces a sense of drama. Secondly, leaders can encourage everyone to 'mine for conflict', to challenge one another to engage in difficult discussions that are likely to lead to conflict. You can do this by seeking out and uncovering issues about which team members disagree. You can choose not to ignore that elephant in the room, and instead tackle it head on. It's talking about the issues that matter in a constructive but potentially conflicting manner that makes meetings more productive and even enjoyable. Finally, you can give 'real-time permission', or in other words, recognise when conflict happens and appreciate it. When the first signs of conflict appear, you can interrupt and remind the participants that it is good, and be positive and enthusiastic without going overboard. It can be extremely effective in encouraging further conflict.

Lencioni's need for structure relates to what he calls 'meeting stew', where meetings are poorly structured and endeavour to address too many diverse and conflicting points. They fail to provide sufficient time and energy for discussion on each point, or the great number and variety simply can't be addressed sensibly without spending too much time on them. It's this kind of 'meeting stew' that leaves people frustrated because their point hasn't been given proper consideration, or a critical decision wasn't made, or the meeting over ran and impacted everyone's diaries. To address this issue, Lencioni defines a need for specific meetings for specific purposes. Segregating meetings that are tactical from those that are strategic for example. He defines four types of meetings that he would recommend, which we'll get to later in the *Lean Foundations*™ approach.

The point here, for your leadership approach, is to try to make sure that meetings are well structured with a clear purpose and focused agenda. You can aim for any meetings scheduled to have sufficient time available to enable constructive debate and for conflict to take place without fear of over-running. And, perhaps try to make sure that the meeting is seeking to address a limited number of points that are appropriately related to one another in order to avoid some being dropped altogether. This may mean that more meetings are scheduled in order to cover every issue. As long as those meetings are properly structured and managed with the appropriate 'drama', then the more the merrier – yes really! In those kinds of meetings, important discussions will take place, and critical decisions for action will be made.

To help with this approach to meetings, it may be worth sending an email to all employees which describes your expectations of how meetings should be structured and should function. It's likely that as the leader of your facility you won't be in every meeting that takes place; so, setting the expectation with everyone clearly will help you to be present, even if you are not.

Intervene early

As the organisational leader of your manufacturing facility, you're going to be acutely aware of certain individuals that are going to struggle in the healthy and psychologically safe environment that you're looking to create. These are individuals whose behaviour is on the extremes of what is unacceptable, which is popularly known as 'toxic'. Perhaps they are loud and brash and speak their mind without consideration of how they are impacting other people. Potentially they are too direct or even aggressive in their communications, possibly from a position of authority as a supervisor or manager. Perhaps they always make their point from the side-lines and through others, rather than openly, directly, and in public. They may be deliberately negative and may contradict any idea, regardless of how valuable it is. In really extreme cases, they may express prejudice based on race, nationality, sex, disability, gender or sexual orientation.

In all of these cases, not only do you know who these people are, but so does everyone else. Every team member in your organisation will be conscious of the fact that these particular individuals are going to struggle in the new environment that you're seeking to create. You may even find that these people are publicly identified during your Town Hall meeting (it's happened to me – more than once).

Our challenge here is to address these people directly and very early in the process. A good option is to pre-empt the fact that they are going to struggle by holding one-to-one discussions with them. This does not need to be a negative process and you should try and make sure that it is not a discussion where blame is attributed. Instead, this can be a discussion where you are seeking to help them prepare for what they are about to face. These individuals are likely to be aware of their own deficiencies and may be extremely concerned for their ability to survive in the new environment. Their own sense of psychological safety will be threatened; with their senses of security, esteem, fairness, and trust put at risk. You can acknowledge that you recognise that they may be concerned that they are going to struggle, and can discuss ways for them to adapt their approach so that they are more able to be successful. You can also provide them with alternative ways of communicating and engaging with others, and maybe role play scenario's as appropriate.

With some individuals, you will receive a positive response, and you will hopefully note a deliberate attempt to adapt their behaviour positively. This is not a one-step process by the way. You're likely to need to continually coach and nurture their development over time. It's possible that you will need to identify examples of correct and incorrect behaviour with them and constantly encourage their progress. However, some individuals will either be unable to develop, or will not be prepared to change. These are individuals that you are unfortunately going to need to address through the escalation processes defined earlier, to the point that they may either leave of their own accord, or will have to be removed from your organisation. This is not necessarily a pleasant process for you to engage in, but sometimes needs to be done for the good of the whole organisation and the balance that you are trying to create.

By addressing these necessary interventions early, we can demonstrate to every team member that your commitment to organisational health and psychological safety is total. By undertaking the process correctly, you can reinforce psychologically safe behaviours and can provide a perfect example of how to conduct yourself in the most difficult of circumstances.

Be accessible

It's a good idea for you to demonstrate your leadership example as frequently as possible. Modelling appropriate behaviour is a valuable way of demonstrating your commitment to the change journey that you have initiated. A good way to achieve this is through a technique described as '*Management by walking around*', previously termed by Tom Peters and Robert Waterman in their best-selling book '*In Search of Excellence*'. The concept is simple enough. The idea is that as organisational leader of your manufacturing facility, impromptu and unstructured interactions with your team members can offer more opportunities to build relationships and identify problems than more structured equivalents such as meetings. By 'walking around' on a frequent basis and stopping to have informal discussions with your team members, which may be either work related or personal, you can help to establish mutual trust and respect, you can unearth and solve potentially long-standing problems that show that individual needs are important, and you can model psychologically safe behaviours that team members can learn from and apply themselves.

If you can, take the time to walk through your facility daily, but at the very least, try for two or three times a week. In the process, try to interact with as many people as possible. Look to ask questions, demonstrate empathy by being genuine and sincere in understanding their problems, and where possible, get involved to deliver solutions. It's a good idea for you to model psychologically safe behaviour whenever the opportunity arises. You can say 'I don't know' if it's appropriate to do so, express vulnerability and explain how you are feeling, or ask open questions and constructively disagree in order to inject some healthy conflict. If you can, reference your responses in relation to the common purpose and mental models in order to reinforce their importance and relevance.

Some of you reading this will consider what has just been described as normal. It will be a practice that you are comfortable in completing and you may be surprised that it is included here because you're quite simply doing this already. However, there will be some of you reading this who realise that you complete this kind of activity quite rarely, and may feel a little uncomfortable at the prospect. I can only suggest that it is a process that you will find extremely valuable, and that after you complete it on a small number of occasions you will find it increasingly easy to do. You might even enjoy it.

Say 'Thank you'

The subject of 'praise' in the workplace is discussed and considered widely in a variety of literature. And in simple terms, we would all expect that offering praise is a good thing to do. We would believe that saying 'well done' or 'good job' is something that would be considered correct and would encourage improved performance. However, there is actually a substantial amount of evidence to the contrary. There is a growing understanding amongst psychology professionals that offering praise as a reward mechanism is actually counter-productive, particularly in the long-term.

In his book '*Punished by Rewards*', Alfie Kohn argues that praise, and other forms of reward such as financial incentives, have been proven to be reducers of individual and group performance. His view is that rewards are normally issued as a means of maintaining behavioural control from a person in a position of authority, someone such as a manager or even a parent, and that by default that sense of control does not always positively influence an individual's sense of intrinsic motivation. Instead, whilst a person's behaviour may be temporarily influenced as a result of being given praise or some other reward, in the medium to long-term that behaviour may be negatively impacted. Individuals may come to expect their reward, and be unhappy if it is not given. They may feel pressured by the need to maintain performance in order to maintain the delivery of praise, and their performance has the potential to decline as a consequence. Others may consider the reward to be nothing more than a means of establishing control and may reject it, as well as the behaviours that they are supposed to be exhibiting.

Whilst all of this may indeed be true, it seems counterintuitive to reject praise outright. In seeking to create a psychologically safe environment that respects every individual equally, it seems wholly appropriate to give recognition and appreciation. But this desire is subtly different. Recognising and appreciating an individual and/or group contribution or performance with the words 'Thank you' is not necessarily the same as giving praise.

It's this method of recognition and appreciation that *Lean Foundations*™ would advocate for your leadership approach. Taking the time to express gratitude when a task is completed, or when a project is delivered, can add real value to someone's day. And, you can even show appreciation for the normal day to day activities as well as the unusual. Consider expressing your thanks in relation to the effort taken to deliver the result, and if possible, identify specific details that would have required higher levels of effort or ability to complete. Giving feedback such as *"…Thanks for getting that delivery booked in on-time today, that one big pallet must have been particularly difficult… I really appreciate your effort…"* is extremely powerful in demonstrating respect and in building relationships. When giving feedback of this nature, try to be comfortable in doing it publicly, and if you can, encourage others to join in. Peer recognition can often be more effective than that given from a person in authority because it's considered to be more sincere and less controlling. Most importantly, try to be deliberate in giving this recognition and appreciation. Look to make the effort to visit a team or team member at their place of work, amongst their colleagues. By the way, this doesn't mean that you can't say 'well done' or 'good job', they are perfectly acceptable phrases to use, but only in a limited way. Try not to make them the core of your feedback method, they'll lose impact and sincerity quickly if they are thrown around at will.

Learn

Don't just take my word for all of this stuff. Why not go and read the books and materials that I have mentioned for yourself. Get to know the subject matter so that you can fully understand and appreciate it. Consider trying to follow the guidance that they provide. Of course, be prepared to make mistakes in the process and be prepared for your personal learning journey to have ups and downs just as mine has. You're likely to experience happiness and frustration in equal measure, particularly in the early stages, as you develop your own understanding and approach. All of these activities can help you to provide the leadership example that will positively reinforce the *Lean Foundations™* journey that you have initiated. In actively undertaking the suggestions here, you can demonstrate vulnerability, and how to respond to vulnerability, in a psychologically safe environment. You can encourage and model appropriate conflict. And, you can spread understanding, enthusiasm, and passion for the change process. The commitment to organisational health, effective teamwork, and psychological safety, will be growing.

KICK-START STRUCTURE

As the final part of Step 1, we can now complete a number of tangible structural activities which will demonstrate your commitment for the change process that you have initiated. In reality, the details of the remaining seven Steps of *Lean Foundations™* are all designed to embed the concepts of teamwork, psychological safety and organisational health into your facility. However, at this early stage in the journey, there are specific activities that you can undertake which are indicators of real intent and that will help to build concrete mechanisms into the very fabric of your facility. Whether you are new to a facility or have been working as its leader for some time, these are steps that will prove to everyone that you're serious about what you do, and that organisational health and teamwork are important to you.

It's worth mentioning at this point that your ability to introduce some of these measures may be impacted by the exact nature of your role in your manufacturing facility, and perhaps within your wider organisation. Whilst you're likely to be the top leader in your facility for reasons described previously, your ability to influence policies on things like pay may well be affected by exactly how your organisation empowers you in your role. Fortunately, *Lean Foundations™* does not require you to implement every step with religious precision. Take advantage of the parts that work for you - and leave the parts that don't.

Take safety seriously

The role of 'Health and Safety' in our working and personal lives has unfortunately become something of a joke in modern times. We're frequently presented with the idea that 'Health and Safety' is something that should be derided and criticised, brushed off and parodied. We seem to think that it has negatively impacted our freedom and ability to work quickly and easily for fear of 'what might happen but probably won't'. Whilst this may or may not be true, what remains is that every employer has a duty of care to ensure that they provide facilities, equipment and working practices that are healthy and safe for use in the workplace. It's also important to remember that every employee also has a duty of care to work in a safe and healthy manner - a fact sometimes overlooked.

What 'Health and Safety' does provide is an opportunity for you to demonstrate your commitment to the respect and appreciation of your team members as part of creating a psychologically safe environment. In managing 'Health and Safety' appropriately, you can demonstrate that you accept responsibility for ensuring the welfare of your employees, and that you care sufficiently to expend effort, time and even money in meeting that aim. There are a small number of activities you can complete to demonstrate this in these early stages.

First, you can issue instructions that all accidents and incidents have to be reported through to yourself regardless of their severity and frequency. This can be done via email, text message, or phone-call - whatever is convenient depending on the time of day that the issue occurs. You can now follow-up visibly when an accident or incident is reported; you can view the site of the accident, speak with people involved, and commit to take appropriate action to rectify issues and prevent reoccurrence. It's important to do this whether the affected person(s) has suffered a serious injury or not. It's not the result of the accident or incident that is important, it's the fact that it occurred at all. We'll touch on how you ensure that appropriate actions are taken to resolve the issue later in the *Lean Foundations™* approach as part of Step 5.

Second, you can complete routine Housekeeping/Safety Walks through your facility. In the short-term, these can be completed monthly, but as your facility improves you could consider reducing them to quarterly. In typical Lean terms, these walks are sometimes referred to as Gemba Walks, but at this early point in our process we're seeking to keep things relatively simple whilst providing the foundations for greater depth in the future. The idea of the Housekeeping/Safety walks is not complicated. Simply walk through your facility with your management and supervisory team and ask them to identify and photograph/document areas where opportunities for improvement exist, particularly in relation to safety risks and hazards. Perhaps ask your team to compile these photographs into a single document as a means of recording what improvements will be made and by when. A challenge here is to ensure that your team sees the walk as an opportunity for them to ask for support and help to get things fixed, not an opportunity to highlight all that is 'wrong'. That perception will rely on your attitude and approach to the walk. If your demeanour is in any way adversarial, or attributes blame, then the walks will be seen as a punishment. If you are able to be open and supportive, the walks will be seen as an opportunity to learn and to receive help. That help may be given as advice on how to solve a problem, or with authority to spend money to get something repaired.

Third, a good option is to complete an initial top-level health and safety risk assessment of your facility with your management team, particularly with your Health & Safety representative if you have one, and develop a plan to resolve any serious or significant risks. You may believe that there are no such risks under your watch, but I would be very surprised if that were true. Every manufacturing facility that I have ever visited has had unresolved health and safety risks, as it's almost an occupational hazard. The kind of risks you can deal with in this process are likely to be more significant and potentially long-standing, and unfortunately are likely to cost money to fix. We might be talking about air quality issues, excessive noise levels, or lack of accident prevention controls such as light-guards or emergency stops. You might even lack decent fire and evacuation controls such as alarms and extinguishers, or lack sufficient first aid support on site. Whatever the issues, consider this as a way to identify them, to draw up the plan for resolution, and to instigate the release of time and funding where necessary.

Facilitate facilities

Closely linked to the subject of health and safety is the provision of the right facilities and equipment. If your team members are going to meet their responsibilities and perform their role to the best of their ability; they will need access to a huge variety of tools, equipment and machinery which are operational, fit for purpose, and are readily available. By taking the lead in ensuring that everyone has access to the right facilities and equipment, you can once again demonstrate that you respect and appreciate your team members' needs, and will support the creation of a psychologically safe environment in the process. There are two simple activities you can undertake right at the beginning of the *Lean Foundations*™ approach that will support this.

First, consider completing a tooling and equipment audit. You can walk through your facility, once again with your management team, and ask every person in your team if they have good working equipment with which to complete their job. In completing this activity, you can identify two important factors; where equipment is missing, and where it is need of repair or replacement. You can consider all types of equipment in such an audit; not just hand tools for production operatives, but also IT equipment for office-based employees, and also things like lifting equipment for logistics team members. Perhaps make a list and develop a plan to repair, replace and purchase equipment that is needed. Also, consider identifying where you have an excess of equipment in some areas that can be re-distributed or even removed. You might find under-utilised capital equipment that you can use to increase capacity, or to remove to free up floor space. Often on completing these audits I've identified money saving opportunities that have contributed to generating the finances to buy other equipment in turn. You may identify major pieces of capital equipment that have suffered from a lack of investment and care over time. Deciding how to resolve issues with these can be difficult because the costs can be significant. A good option is to undertake a simple cost benefit analysis of different repair and replace options to decide how to proceed. Whatever your choice, it's not a good idea to ignore the problem, as it's only likely to get worse.

Second, consider completing an audit of the buildings and welfare facilities that you provide. Do you believe that the toilet facilities are in good condition, well maintained and of sufficient quantity? Do you provide food and drink facilities and, if so, are they hygienic and clean? Is your building weather proof and comfortable to work in with appropriate levels of temperature control and light (preferably natural light)? Are your offices ergonomically sound? Should you provide relaxation and leisure facilities for use during break periods? Do you have outside areas that you could utilise with appropriate furniture and cover for use in good weather? Are your meeting facilities adequate? Is your facility secure, both during working and non-working hours? Again, it's a good idea to make a list and develop a plan where improvements are required.

Of course, this is all going to cost time and money, and you'll need to make appropriate prioritisation decisions. Thankfully, it's not critical that you resolve every issue immediately, only that you have a plan to resolve them in a sensible order and within sensible timescales. People are generally practical and patient when it comes to spending money, and they will understand that you don't have unlimited funds.

Compensate with care

The question of pay is always a contentious one. If there is anything that can unsettle and unbalance a team, it's money. Our psychological safety is easily sacrificed if we feel that we are being paid unfairly in comparison to someone else, or if we feel that we are being taken advantage of in terms of the value we bring. I've often witnessed leaders be confronted by people questioning their pay, because their sense of fairness and trust has been threatened. Knowing how to deal with this is challenging.

There is a huge amount of discussion amongst psychology professionals around pay and financial rewards, particularly around the influence of pay on our intrinsic motivations. Both Dan Pink in '*Drive*', and Alfie Kohn in '*Punished by Rewards*', argue strongly that financial incentives can be extraordinarily damaging to our intrinsic motivators, and can drive us towards behaviours that are not necessarily in the best interests of ourselves or our team. They cite numerous cases of where financial based incentive plans have actually detrimentally impacted performance. Evidence demonstrates that people come to expect the rewards, and therefore these things become less effective at incentivising performance. Or the rewards drive temporary adjustments in behaviour that fade over time. Worse still, the rewards encourage inappropriate behaviour through a sense of competition that can damage teamwork and collaboration. The simplest example to provide for a manufacturing professional is the role of the bonus for the sales team in winning orders. How often have you felt under inappropriate pressure to deliver a product, regardless of whether it can be produced cost effectively, safely, or at the right quality, simply because the salesperson wanted to receive their bonus? It's certainly something that I have experienced more than once.

Yes, the concept of pay is difficult, but both Kohn and Pink agree on a sensible way to try and manage it, and it's their approach that is advocated in *Lean Foundations™*. They suggest that organisations pay people generously and fairly to try and take the issue of money 'off the table', and then do everything possible to put the issue of money 'out of their minds'. Incidentally, the term 'generously' does not mean paying people too much, because doing so is also proven to be detrimental to performance and teamwork.

Therefore, at this point in the *Lean Foundations™* journey, if your organisation empowers you to do so, it's a good idea for you to consider completing a comprehensive pay review of every member of your team; preferably with the support of your HR team and perhaps with genuine salary comparison data. By doing this you can help to solve any psychological safety problems early in the process, and you may enable your team members to be driven by their intrinsic motivators, rather than by ineffective promises of financial reward.

This does not necessarily mean that you are going to be handing out lots of pay rises. Your organisation may complete standard annual pay reviews at specific times of the year and with clearly allocated budgets and therefore, your freedom to make changes may be restricted. Furthermore, you have the cost base of your manufacturing facility to consider and need to ensure that you're not going to be uncompetitive in the market place. However, you can still use this exercise to identify whether or not you have any serious discrepancies in what your organisation is paying. Are there any gender pay gaps that need to be closed? Is your organisation paying in line with market rates? Are you paying different amounts to people doing the same or similar roles? Are you overpaying anyone? Do you have a bonus scheme in place, and if so, is it working? Do you have different terms and conditions in place for things like sick pay and holidays as a result of legacy business changes? If you do have discrepancies that need to be addressed, then I would suggest that you deal with them at the earliest available opportunity.

Where people are underpaid, I would suggest that you correct their salary, but do so discretely and without unsettling others. If the discrepancy is too large to deal with in one step, perhaps commit yourself to further changes in the future. Where you believe that people are overpaid, you may decide to 'red circle' their salary, putting them outside a normal annual review process for a period of time until the market rate 'catches-up'. If you have an imbalance in terms and conditions, then you can perhaps look to find a way to reconcile these. Be generous here if you can by picking the best options available without damaging your operational capabilities. If you have bonus schemes in place for output, quality, or even attendance, then I would actively encourage you to negotiate and agree their removal. This may be difficult to achieve and may take some time, but the evidence is clear that they don't really work. In fact, the evidence clearly shows that performance improves without them.

If you do not offer terms and conditions that are typically available in the market place then this is the time to consider adding them. I've seen manufacturing facilities that do not offer standard terms for sick pay or compassionate leave, instead having a policy of 'management discretion' in place. I would argue that discretion leads to discrimination, whether conscious or not, and as a consequence, I would always suggest that fair and generous policies are introduced that provide sick pay, paid holidays, and compassionate leave as a standard - and with equal access for all.

An important point to reference here is that many manufacturing facilities and their employees are supported by a trade union of some kind, and in relation to matters around pay and compensation it's appropriate to negotiate with representatives from that union. This can make interaction difficult, potentially even adversarial in nature. I am by no means expert in managing trade union negotiations, and could not declare that I have a one-stop solution for completing them positively. I would simply suggest that you enter those negotiations with the desire to be fair and generous, whilst being responsible for the organisation as a whole for both today and in the future. It is your role as organisational leader of your manufacturing facility to best represent the interests of your employees and the organisation as a whole, and hopefully your application of the *Lean Foundations*™ approach will help to demonstrate these values to any trade union representatives that you interact with.

Enthuse new employees

Having clearly defined the way that you hope to encourage people to work together, it's important not to dilute the message when introducing new employees to your organisation. There is a need to ensure that new team members receive the same message with the same level of passion and enthusiasm so that they also buy-in to the same way of working as their longer serving peers. There are two simple actions that you can take that will support this.

First, consider making sure that your recruitment process clearly communicates the nature of the working environment that you are developing. You can do this by adding appropriate comments into all job adverts, person specifications, and roles & responsibilities documents. Also, if you use external sub-contract recruitment support, perhaps provide them with a full job-brief and clear instructions on how to communicate with candidates on your behalf. We'll talk more about the process of selecting the right type of person later in *Lean Foundations*™, but at this point we're simply taking steps to manage the way your facility is presented to potential new employees. Be prepared for these messages to increase the number of candidates you have for new roles. After all, we are working to create an environment in which people enjoy coming to work, and by communicating this externally in the right way you will encourage people to want to be part of your journey.

Second, you need to induct new employees into your organisation carefully and in a way that establishes their buy-in to organisational health and psychological safety. A good way to do this is for you to be personally involved in the induction process of every new employee. This may be a challenge depending on the size and scale of your facility, but I would actively encourage you to make the effort and investment if you can. Perhaps create a slightly shortened version of your original Town Hall presentation on organisational health and psychological safety and deliver it during the induction of new employees. If you have the time, be the person to complete a plant tour so that you can really embed the message by pointing out live examples of good practice in action. In being involved in the induction process in this way you will be demonstrating to both your existing team, and any new team members, that you are absolutely committed to the importance of organisational health and psychological safety in your facility. It's also a really useful way of reinvigorating the message, because new team members will talk with existing employees about their induction. Their excitement and anticipation in joining their new employer will spread and will re-enthuse your existing team.

STEP 1 SUMMARY

In completing Step 1, I hope that this book has been successful in encouraging you to embrace organisational health as the means of delivering effective teamwork in your workplace. After all, it's teamwork which will be fundamental in underpinning every aspect of your *Lean Foundations*™ journey moving forward. Whilst we've spent a lot of time discussing this idea, I cannot stress enough just how much difference effective teamwork and organisational health can make. They provide the essential corner stone of our well-performing facility, and can start to generate small improvements in operational performance and workplace happiness almost immediately.

I hope that you've harnessed the advice that can help you to properly integrate organisational health concepts successfully into your normal practices and routines. All of the activities that we've discussed can support you in taking some simple early steps, and in making initial structural changes, which can positively reinforce the organisational health and psychological safety of everyone that you're responsible for. And, you can hopefully take the first steps towards enabling your facility to perform well, and subsequently to establish the foundations on which operational excellence is built. The remaining 7 Steps of the *Lean Foundation* approach will enable you to embed these concepts, along with many more, even more fully.

Before we move on to Step 2, it's worth a quick review of what we've discussed so far.

- Teamwork and organisational health are central to the *Lean Foundations*™ leadership approach, they are the key stone on which all of the other Steps are successfully built.

- Effective teams are psychologically safe with team members able to express vulnerability-based trust. They are able to conflict, commit, be accountable and deliver results in a way that shows that they're dependable. And they are supported by a clear structure and clarity of purpose, a sense of meaning, and have an ability to make an impact.

- Working as part of a team, and having a sense of purpose, are two of our intrinsic motivators.

- Bringing together psychological safety with a common purpose is the heart of building organisational health in *Lean Foundations*™ in order to enable our intrinsic motivators and facilitate effective teamwork.

- We can build organisational health and effective teamwork by following 4 sub-steps: 'Build the vision', 'Share the vision', 'Lead from the front', and 'Kick-start structure'.

- 'Build the vision' describes how we can create coherence in a management team around a common purpose. By completing an offsite activity, and by 'Directing the Rider', 'Motivating the Elephant' and 'Sharing the Path' we can develop our own 'Golden Circle' to define our 'Why' or 'Thematic Goal', and 'How' or 'Defining Objectives. We can also agree our mental models for acceptable behaviour and interaction which will help to create psychological safety, and we can define how we will sanction violations to those mental models.

- 'Share the vision' explains how we can create buy-in with our entire team. By completing a Town Hall brief with all our team members, we can introduce them to the concepts of effective teamwork, organisational health, and psychological safety. We can share our common purpose and mental models and can kick-start the *Lean Foundations*™ journey.

- 'Lead from the front' defines a number of activities that we can complete in order to provide the right example of how to behave in a psychologically safe environment, and to enthuse people on the change process that has been initiated. We can learn, say I don't know, inquire and mean it, lead effective meetings, intervene early, be accessible, and say thank you.

- 'Kick-start structure' outlines a number of early actions that we can take in order to integrate organisational health and teamwork in to the fabric of our manufacturing facility. We can take safety seriously, facilitate facilities, compensate with care, and enthuse new employees.

STEP

2

Build a team-
oriented
organisation
structure

Despite instinctively knowing that teamwork is important to organisational success, it always amazes me how often organisations fail to provide a working structure for their employees which facilitates and encourages teamwork to take place. I've often entered a new manufacturing facility and found them to be structured in a way that does not enable people to work together as a team. I usually find that I spend a significant portion of my time, particularly in the early stages of the *Lean Foundations*™ journey, establishing connections between people by changing their roles, reporting lines, and communication channels. Quite often I find that I need to recruit people into new roles that don't exist, but really should. Or I have to remove roles and transfer people to something new, because they really aren't adding any value. I have likened myself to an old-fashioned telephone exchange operator, disconnecting and re-connecting cables so that people can talk to each other as they wish. And this is not my way of forcing people to communicate, it's the opposite. In reality, I'm simply placing them into a context which enables them to voluntarily communicate with the right people at the right time for the right reasons. I'd be surprised if at some point you hadn't shared the same experience.

How many times have you identified a problem, and have been unable to think of the right person to deal with it, because you can't identify the person with the responsibility for it? And how many times do you end up picking that problem up yourself as a result? How many times has someone approached you and asked who they should talk to about an issue that they have, because it's not obvious to them who the responsible person is? How many times have you scheduled meetings, and struggled to select the right people to invite? Or maybe, people haven't turned up to a meeting because they don't think they're responsible for whatever needs to be discussed? Worse, how many times has someone identified an issue, but simply not bothered to do anything about it, regardless of the consequences, because there is no one to help them?

Now that we've embraced the importance of effective teamwork, and have started to encourage its development with practices that are designed to nurture organisational health and psychological safety, it's important for us to provide some solid structural foundations on which it can flourish. The first and most fundamental of the structural changes that we can make is around the organisation structure of our manufacturing facility. We can make sure that we clearly communicate who is responsible for what, that all responsibilities are being covered, that reporting lines and peer groups are clearly understood, and that everyone knows which team(s) they are part of and who their fellow team members are. We can also ensure that we have the right people in our team, and that we only introduce new people who fit with the way that we are trying to work together. Without a clearly defined organisation structure of this nature, which is designed to support teamwork, and is populated with the right people, our aspiration of improved workplace happiness and operational performance is nothing more than a pipe dream. By taking this Step, we can begin to describe our 'What' or 'Standard Operating Objectives' in our 'Golden Circle', and can move forward in earnest on our path towards enabling our facility to perform well, and to building the solid foundations that our aspiration for operational excellence requires.

To help us to achieve all of this, we can work through a series of four sub-steps; 'Modify the matrix', 'Build your matrix', 'Right people on-board', and 'Manage your resources'. In sharing these, I'm hoping to persuade you of a simple but effective approach to structuring your facility in a way that encourages effective teamwork, and which in the process supports later elements of the *Lean Foundations™* approach. A quick reminder here that we're only talking about the organisation structure of our manufacturing facility. I'm not intending to enter into complex debates around the strengths and weaknesses of different types of organisation structure for extensive multi-national companies. Instead, *Lean Foundations™* simply shares the view of what has been seen to work on numerous occasions in various manufacturing environments with different and varied value streams. As with everything, feel free to take what works for you, and to discard what does not.

MODIFY THE MATRIX

If you have the time and opportunity, it's worth completing a quick internet search on 'how to structure an organisation'. Go ahead, take a minute to put the book down, pick up your device, and see what results you get. What you'll probably find is a multitude of different opinions around how many different options there are. I've seen articles, blogs and websites that suggest anywhere between 3 and 8 different types of structure; from functional, to product, to project, to divisional, to matrix, and everything in-between. What's my conclusion from this variety of responses? There isn't a definitive answer. There isn't one way that anyone agrees is the best. And I suppose that's sensible as every organisation is different after all. So, in talking about organisation structure, I have to be careful not to declare something that no-one else does. I can't be so bold as to say that 'this is the right way to do it'. Instead, I can only suggest what I have found to be a successful way to build an organisation structure in a manufacturing facility, and hope that I can persuade you of its merits in the process.

For *Lean Foundations™*, the structural approach advocated is a matrix structure, but it's not a typical matrix structure, it's slightly modified. Let's explore why *Lean Foundations™* advocates this approach first, then we'll look to understand a more typical definition, and can then explore how the version here differs.

Cross functional teams and organisational layers

A manufacturing facility is a complex beast. Regardless of what is being produced, the interactions that take place on a daily basis between various activities and functions require a sophisticated interaction of processes and responsibilities so that goods can be manufactured and shipped. There is a constant 'passing of the baton' that occurs both in the physically real world and in a computerised systematic world. Components have to be ordered by people in purchasing and material planning, inspected by people in quality, and then booked-in and safely moved by people in logistics. Orders have to be received by people in customer service, and then scheduled by production planning. Finished products have to be manufactured by production, perhaps tested and assured by more people in quality, before being shipped by people in dispatch. And this is just within the manufacturing process itself, without thought for all of the many other processes that take place before a part is even produced. It's obviously an over-simplified view, but no doubt you get the point.

To manage this complexity, many organisations will operate with a typical functional organisation structure, which will line up individuals of equivalent authority from different functions in layers alongside one another. A Production Director will sit alongside a Quality Director, a Production Manager alongside a Quality Manager, a Production Supervisor alongside a Quality Engineer, and so on. In that functional structure, teamwork tends to flow vertically, with people in each function focused on supporting their team members within their function. The risk of such a structure is that the desire to improve functional performance overrides the need to manage the performance of the organisation as a whole. This potentially causes unhealthy conflict, and it's possible for some functions to overspeed in relation to others, or to be held back. There are also lots of opportunities for waste and loss of performance to occur in daily operations. There is the potential for individual activities not to take place in a timely manner, for inventory to build up between stages, or for processing to be incorrect if information is not passed on accurately, amongst many others that you have no doubt seen for yourself. The model below provides a crude example...

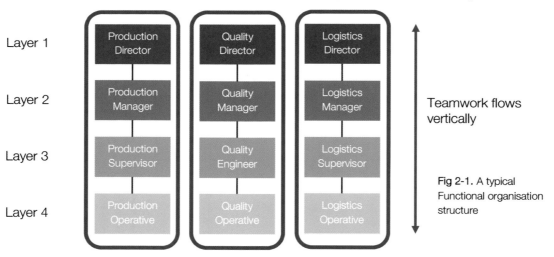

Fig 2-1. A typical Functional organisation structure

Instead, managing the level of complexity so that a facility performs well and reduces waste through the solving of problems that travel across functional lines, requires teams of people to work horizontally across the organisation. In other words, they need to work cross-functionally. It's for this reason that Lean enterprises are often 'value stream' structured. Lean teams are deliberately constructed horizontally to manage and drive the 'passing of the baton', or the 'flow of product and information', across all functions, by bringing people together from different functions and giving them all the shared objective of improving value stream performance. This kind of structure was advocated very early in the Lean community, with

Dan Jones and Jim Womack describing it clearly in their seminal book '*Lean Thinking*' as far back as 1996. They described how *"... the lean enterprise groups the product manager, the parts buyer, the manufacturing engineer, and the production scheduler in the team area..."*. Again, the model below provides a crude example.

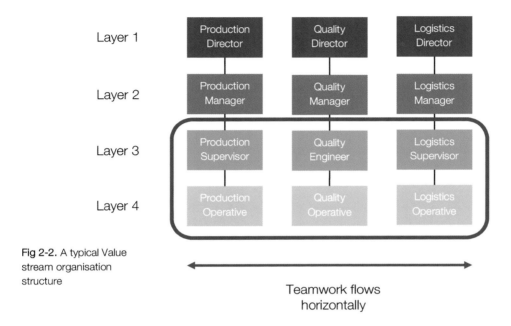

Fig 2-2. A typical Value stream organisation structure

Teamwork flows horizontally

It's for this reason that *Lean Foundations*™ advocates the use of the matrix structure. A matrix structure will take a typical functional organisation, and will superimpose a value stream responsibility across it in order to bring people from different functions together into a team. It forces cross-functionality into the very fabric of the organisation. That cross-functionality can support the kind of teamwork that we have been discussing in *Lean Foundations*™. It can enable, and even require, people from varied functions to come together to express contradictory opinions and conflict healthily. It can also enable more effective problem-solving; because team members from different functions can offer diverse ideas and perspectives, and as a consequence the team delivers results and is dependable. And, it can support the alignment around a common purpose; to improve the operational performance and workplace happiness of the cross-functional team, and by default the organisation as a whole. It can support our 'Why', and in the process can facilitate our 'How'. However, as with most things, there are disadvantages as well advantages.

What is a matrix structure?

A typical matrix organisation structure features both a vertical and horizontal level of departmentalisation, and superimposes reporting relationships in both directions. This means that the people who work within a matrix structure report into two line-managers, both vertically and horizontally, as per the model overleaf.

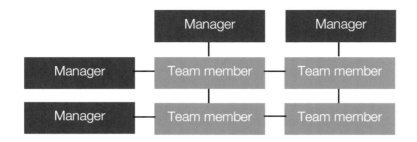

Fig 2-3. A typical Matrix organisation structure

A structure of this nature combines functional management on one side of the matrix, with focused-team management on the other side of the matrix. Managers can share equal authority and responsibility regardless of which side of the matrix they sit, and team members are challenged to work equally with two reporting lines.

Theoretically, the main advantages of a matrix structure are that it allows decentralised decision making, that problem-solving and teamwork within focused-teams are supported, that the flow of product and information through the value stream is managed, and that people can be moved flexibly between these to balance workload and capacity. Matrix structures can also help to restrict the potential for the functional silos described earlier. They reduce the likelihood of functional managers being purely focused on driving the performance of their functional team without consideration for the organisation as a whole. If you've ever been a Production Manager, I'm certain you will have experienced some pretty fundamental disagreements with your Quality Manager colleague in the past, and vice-versa. A matrix structure can, theoretically, help to minimise this kind of unhealthy conflict because functional managers need to support the performance of the focused-team as well as their function.

However, the main disadvantage of a matrix structure is the potential for confusion over authority and responsibility which results from the dual reporting lines. Team members can be asked to complete activities by each manager that can be contradictory if those managers are not aligned. Or a team member's workload and capacity can be misjudged if tasks are being delegated by both managers without effective communication between them. If you've ever worked in a pure matrix structure like this, you'll know that at times it's not fun. Another potential disadvantage is that silos in focused-team direction can occur, with team performance over-riding functional discipline and control. It's possible for process controls that are usually maintained and required by functional representatives to be overridden or to erode because those with functional responsibility are focused on delivering operational performance instead. Matrix structures can also be a little resource heavy, which is never popular in the world of manufacturing where headcount costs are always a point of contention.

The advantages of a matrix structure are all positives for us in *Lean Foundations™*. The decentralised decision making can support the empowerment of front-line team members, and as a result can tap into our intrinsic motivator of autonomy and accountability. And we already know that the support of teamwork is clearly what we're trying to achieve. Not only that, the ability to balance resources in line with workload is a very practical positive, and it helps to provide opportunities for personal development and improvement if team members move between focused-teams. It can therefore support another one of our intrinsic motivators, success and improvement. The disadvantages, however, are a problem. Focused-team silos are just as much of a problem as functional silos. After all, we're looking to enable teamwork that embraces the entire network of teams in our facility so that they can function together effectively for the benefit of the organisation as a whole. And the risk of confusion of responsibility and authority will not help with our desire to provide clarity of purpose and direction.

The *Lean Foundations™* matrix

The *Lean Foundations™* matrix structure seeks to take advantage of the benefits of a typical matrix structure, whilst managing the negatives. It does so by embracing one key feature. Team members are allocated into a value-stream or focused-team, but rather than reporting both functionally and operationally, they are only given one direct line-manager, which helps to manage the risks of confusion and contradiction of priorities. Furthermore, each line-manager is provided with the same direction of prioritisation and purpose from above, regardless of whether they have functional or operational leadership responsibilities. They are all targeted with a focus on delivering value for the customer, and for improving the well-being of our employees. Through the efforts already made with the development of our 'Golden Circle', and with more that we'll address in Step 3, the alignment of all line-managers helps to support integrity and balance of the *Lean Foundations™* matrix structure. Let's explore exactly how the structure works.

First of all, those team members with typical operational responsibilities such as Production, Planning and Logistics, are allocated into focused-teams and report into an Operations Team Manager. The basis on which these teams are segregated is determined by the nature of the manufacturing environment that they occupy. They could be separated by product, by customer, by process, or simply by physical boundaries. Secondly, colleagues from support functions such as Quality, Manufacturing/Process Engineering, and perhaps even Purchasing, are allocated to the focused-teams, whilst maintaining their functional reporting lines. Finally, some 'pure' functional areas sit outside the focused-team structure from areas such Facilities & Maintenance, Trade Compliance, or Health & Safety. In the process, two layers of team are identified, the Core Team, and the Functional Support Team. The Core Team(s) are led by an Ops Team Manager or Supervisor, and the Functional Support Team(s) are led by a Functional Manager or Supervisor. Take a look at the diagram below to get a better understanding…

Fig 2-4. The *Lean Foundations™* matrix

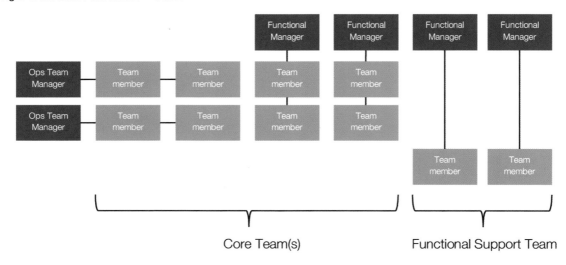

Core Team(s)   Functional Support Team

The Core team acts as a value stream team, or focused-team, and is responsible for the delivery of operational performance of the value-add activity in their value stream. Here, that's the production of components. For other sectors and industries, it could be quite different. The team members who report directly to the Ops Team Manager have responsibility for managing the traditional operational disciplines; Production, Planning, and Logistics. They are the functional specialists in this area and carry responsibility for those functional disciplines. Note that these three functions are combined under the umbrella of Operations. This is deliberate. Their amalgamation breaks down the old-fashioned barriers between the three individual functions. Production Managers chase labour and machine efficiency, Planning Managers chase inventory levels and delivery performance, Logistics Managers chase warehouse and transport efficiencies. They all fight for their own functional performance, sometimes at the expense of each other or even the whole. An Operations Manager is required to balance these three inter-related performance requirements, sometimes on a case by case basis, to deliver the most rounded solution for the benefit of the customer and the organisation.

The inclusion of team members from functions such as Quality, Manufacturing or Process Engineering, and perhaps even Purchasing, within the Core Team(s), gives the Ops Team Manager, and the cross-functional team, additional responsibilities. It requires that team to be fully conscious of process and product quality, of process design and reliability, and of material cost. This responsibility does not have to be seen as a burden however, it can be viewed as an enabler. In holding that responsibility, the cross-functional team has all the functionality necessary to take ownership and accountability of their total performance. They do not have to seek permission to make change, or to utilise people. It is within their remit to decide which problems to fix first for greatest impact, and how to prioritise and balance their own resources.

It's necessary at this point to clarify the importance of the Core Team structure. The primary role of the Core Team is to support the front-line team members in the execution of their day to day responsibilities, and to provide whatever assistance they require to perform. Those front-line team members are ultimately responsible for delivering operational performance; after all, they directly influence what Toyota would call the core indicators of Safety, Quality, Delivery, and Cost, and therefore directly impact customer service and the financial success of the organisation. The role that the Core Team plays in providing support to those front-line team members is therefore critical to the success of your manufacturing facility as a whole, and to the realisation of the last of the core indicators; Engagement.

Functional Managers who have team members as part of the Core Team have two responsibilities. First, they must support the performance of the cross-functional team, and therefore need to be aligned with the Ops Team Managers. Second, they must manage the process control and discipline of their function. In retaining reporting line responsibility to their team members within the cross-functional team, both of these responsibilities are supported. The Functional Managers retain the ability to manage individual activities and people, whilst having to consider the overall performance of the team in the process. The risk that focused-team silos overrule functional discipline is minimised as a consequence.

The role of the Functional Support Teams is to provide functional support and infrastructure, and to manage process discipline and adherence, for the more specialised functions. Areas such as Health & Safety, Trade Compliance, and Facilities & Maintenance, are often functions that provide more generic services to the whole organisation or facility. However, in the *Lean Foundations™* approach, these functions do not work in isolation from the Core Team(s). Instead, these functions define, communicate, train, support, and manage the adherence to policies and procedures that are specific to their functional responsibility so that the Core Team(s) can then work to the policies and procedures that are defined, and are trained and facilitated in doing so. It's worth providing an example here to aid understanding. A Health & Safety Manager can define the format of a Risk Assessment document, can define the procedure for completing it, can define the policy for when it needs to be completed, can train individuals within the Core Team on how to complete it, can support them in completing it when necessary, and can audit and verify that it is completed to the appropriate standard. They should not be the person to complete the Risk Assessment themselves, instead that will be completed by someone from within the Core Team, such as a Team Leader or Production Supervisor. A Facilities & Maintenance Manager would do the same when introducing a TPM (Total Preventative Maintenance) process for example.

This is not necessarily a traditional view of how support functions should operate. Often, I've seen that support functions are expected to complete the activities themselves. Remember, we're trying to tap into our team's intrinsic motivators; teamwork, a sense of ownership and autonomy, a sense of purpose, and a desire to succeed and improve. In structuring the relationship between the Core Team(s) and Functional

Support Team(s) in this way, we are enabling the intrinsic motivators of all team members to come to the fore. The Core Team members will be trained and supported in meeting a more varied and interesting set of responsibilities, they will have more opportunities to improve and succeed, and will achieve a greater sense of autonomy and purpose in the process. At the same time, the Functional Support Team members can achieve a sense of purpose from being able to develop and define the infrastructure of their specialist function, whilst engaging in teamwork with their colleagues in the Core Team(s) in completing day to day tasks. They will also better understand their role in supporting the common purpose of the overall facility.

In seeking to adapt a typical matrix structure in this way, the *Lean Foundations*™ approach hopes to be able to take advantage of the value-stream concept so readily accepted in the Lean community, whilst at the same time managing the risks associated with the more traditional matrix view. I have found there to be considerable advantages from structuring a manufacturing facility in this way, here are just a few...

- By identifying and creating focused-teams, there is automatically a clarity around team structure. Everyone clearly understands what team they are in, and who their peers are in their team.

- The focused-team can be structured so that all key responsibilities are included within the team. There is no excuse for not including a key functionality or team member as the gap becomes transparent and obvious to everyone.

- Leadership responsibility for the team is clearly defined with the Ops Team Manager, so final decision making and escalation of dispute resolution is not confused, and ultimate ownership of performance is clear.

- Decision making authority for day to day activities and processes is decentralised and away from leadership, allowing speedy resolution of problems and supporting a sense of autonomy and empowerment.

- Functional Managers share some responsibility for focused-team performance because their team members are part of the Core Team. The risk of functional silos is removed.

- Functional Managers and their team members retain their responsibility for functional discipline and process adherence, meaning that process control is not overridden and the risk of focused-team silos is reduced. In fact, functional team members tend to become process specialists and are relied upon by the team for their skillset and knowledge. At the same time, process discipline becomes actively sought by the whole team. Specific functional knowledge spreads throughout the team and reliance on specialists is reduced over time.

- The role of support functions is better facilitated and understood, and their relationship with the Core Team(s) enables the intrinsic motivators of purpose, improvement, autonomy and collaboration.

BUILD YOUR MATRIX

You may already have your organisation structure defined in the way I've described here. If not, and your organisation structure is more typically functionally defined, I would suggest you consider modifying it to the *Lean Foundations™* matrix. However, helping you to build your own version of the *Lean Foundations™* matrix structure is a little tricky. I can't possibly define something here that will accommodate all of the individual differences of every single manufacturing facility. Instead, I'm going to try and guide you through some particular decisions that will help you define your matrix structure for yourself. I'll also include some fictitious examples of different structures here to help provide some insight. This isn't an exact science, and you may find that you need to evolve and adjust your structure over time as you come to understand how it's working, and in response to any changes in your facility.

The basis of your cross-functional team

Selecting the basis of how to define your cross-functional team structure is a critical first step. Every manufacturing plant is different, producing different components and parts, utilising different equipment, serving different customers, and structured within different interconnecting processes, so unfortunately, there is no one single answer to the question of how to do this. There are a few points for you to consider when making the decision…

- You are trying to encourage cross-functional teamwork and to manage the 'flow of product and information' along your value stream, or, the process by which your facility adds value to a component or service and supplies it to your customer. Therefore, identifying your value stream or streams is a good starting point. These may be easily differentiated because you have dedicated production lines for different products, or you may only have one value stream which every product will travel through. Each plant will be different.

- You are likely to need to consider the amount of value streams that you can properly resource with cross-functional teams. You may only have one value stream, you may have multiple. You may identify ten value streams, but may not be able to resource ten teams cost effectively, and therefore you may need to consolidate value streams together under the umbrella of a smaller number of Core Teams. You may only have one value stream, but it could be extremely complex, and you may need to break it down into smaller sections to manage it effectively.

- The number of your customer interfaces is an important consideration. You don't really want a customer to have to interface with three or four main contacts from different value focused-teams if you can help it. It has the potential to cause confusion and is a burden your customer won't appreciate.

Your organisational layers

Deciding how many organisational layers you will have, and which layers will be part of the cross-functional teams, is the next step in defining your matrix structure. In simple terms, most manufacturing facilities contain four layers; leadership, management, supervision and front-line. Within each of these layers there may be further differentiation. Let's take a look at each in a little more detail.

- *Leadership* – This is likely to be the level of the organisation that you are operating in. It's responsible for setting the strategic direction and medium/long term goals of the facility, and for oversight of performance and process adherence. It sets the expectations for how a facility is led and managed, and maintains that expectation through daily mentoring and coaching interactions. You may be an Operations Director, Plant Manager, General Manager or similar. You may work in isolation on site with functional peers who are remotely located in central facilities, or you may work alongside functional peers who are located onsite from the likes of Sales, Product Management, Engineering, HR, and Finance. A sensible ratio of leader to manager is 1 to 8. This can be stretched to 12 and reduced to 4 depending on the environment, but with anything outside of this I would recommend some restructuring.

- *Management* – This is the level that drives day to day performance and process adherence through active engagement in problem-solving and leadership of team members. Usually organised functionally, it can also include focused-team leadership if appropriate. Within your manufacturing facility, this can include Operations Managers, Production Managers, Planning & Logistics Managers, Quality Managers, Health & Safety Managers, Manufacturing Engineering Managers, Purchasing Managers, Facilities & Maintenance Managers, Lean/Continuous Improvement Managers, and maybe even Trade Compliance Managers. Typically, these work alongside functional peers from outside normal manufacturing operations roles such as HR, Finance and so on. A sensible ratio of manager to supervisor is again 1 to 8. And again, it could be stretched to 12 and reduced to 4 depending on the environment.

- *Supervision* – For *Lean Foundations*™ this is the most critical part of the organisation structure. It is the people at this level who are instrumental in making the daily performance of your operation actually happen. These are the people who most need to be included in the cross-functional team, and who add the most value in solving problems and leading people. Within your manufacturing facility, this level includes operational supervisors from the likes of Production, Planning, and Logistics; engineers from Quality, Manufacturing Engineering and perhaps Facilities & Maintenance; and buyers from Purchasing. For *Lean Foundations*™, the ideal ratio of operational Supervisor to Front-line worker is 1 to 12 at the most, preferably 1 to 8. However, I've worked in enough manufacturing facilities to know that this is an ideal. I've seen ratio's as high as 1 to 60 in one facility (and they wondered why it didn't perform well?!).

Most organisations would not be prepared to fund the ideal ratio despite the benefits in engagement, performance and control that it produces. If you are really interested in empowering and engaging front-line team members, this ratio has to be embraced, and is critical aspect of ensuring the success of the *Lean Foundations™* approach.

- *Front Line* – This is the level that delivers day to day processing in your facility. The people at this level work on production lines or in production cells, or in logistics roles delivering parts, or perhaps as inspectors, customer service administrators, or material buyers/planners. These are the people who experience problems and waste in real time, and who can add the most insight into how to improve performance and provide solutions. They are also likely to be the most knowledgeable and skilled in the details of the product and the process that they operate. The relationship between these people and their supervisor, and our ability listen to and support them, is a critical success factor.

For your manufacturing facility, depending on its size, I would suggest that you consider a minimum of 4 to a maximum of 6 layers including yourself. These would include an Operational Leader (you), a Management team, a Supervisory level as one or two levels (Group Leader/Production Supervisor and/or Team Leader/Zone Leader), and a Front-line level again as one or two levels (Operative/team member and perhaps Senior Process Operative). The number of supervisory and front-line levels that you need is really something that you'll need to consider based on the size of your team, the number of front-line team members, and the variation of your processes in line with the ratios of team member to line-manager that your organisation is prepared to support.

Deciding which layers are actively included in the cross-functional team structure, and which are part of the Core Team versus the Functional Support Team, also depends on the nature of your facility. In all my experiences, the Supervisory level has been at the heart of the cross-functional team structure because of their importance in leading day to day operations, and for that reason I would recommend that you do the same. I've always included Production Supervisors/Team Leaders, Quality Engineers and Manufacturing Engineers as part of the Core Team. At times I have included people from Purchasing and even Maintenance in the Core Team too, particularly if they have a large role to play because there are lots of parts to buy or a large number of machines to maintain. Sometimes you can divide your front-line team members so that they are also included in the Core Team, sometimes they need to stay functionally separated. If your production process is organised so that you have isolated production cells, then including them as part of a segregated Core Team is easier than if your operation is organised in a way that means every part goes through even process step.

Also, deciding at which level your value stream or focused team leader sits is important. The individual(s) who occupy this role need to have the credibility and authority to manage and lead the performance of their value stream, and to interface with their functional counterparts with gravitas and influence. I would therefore suggest that they occupy a position one level below yours, depending on where you sit. In my career, I have occupied Operations Manager roles, and have had focused-team leaders at a Group Leader Supervisory level who have been supported by Team Leaders, Process Engineers and Quality Engineers in the Core Team. I've also worked as an Operations Director, and have had focused-team leaders at an Operations Manager level who have been supported by Production Supervisors, Planning Supervisors, Manufacturing Engineers and Quality Engineers in the Core Team. Both options worked well because they met the needs of the environment they operated in.

The right functions and roles

The next step in defining your matrix structure is to understand and select exactly what functions and roles you require in your facility, so that you can ensure that you're covering all the major activities comprehensively. At this point I intend to list off the major functions that I would expect to see in any manufacturing facility, with a small description of their main responsibilities. I realise that for some this may seem a little patronising, but please bear in mind that in every facility I've entered I have had to introduce at least one role because it was missing. I would suggest that when you read through this list, you may find at least one role where you think 'I could do with someone who does that in my facility'. Please also bear in mind that this list does not mean that you need one person per role. Roles can be combined in order to manage costs.

- *Production Planning* – Sometimes called Master Scheduling or similar. Responsible for generating an efficient production plan that supports OTIF (On-time in Full), by scheduling production through finite schedule or Heijunka maintenance processes. Can manage capacity and equipment utilisation, as well as order intake in line with capacity. Includes roles such as Production Planner or Master Scheduler. Can be supervised or managed by a Planning Manager, Planning Supervisor, or Operations Manager.

- *Customer Service* – Sometimes part of a Sales or Commercial team, sometimes in Operations as part of the Planning team. Responsible for interfacing with customers, for sales order processing, and communication of delivery expectations and plans. Often a front-line interface with customers and a critical role to listen to. Includes roles such as Customer Service Coordinator or Administrator. Can be managed or supervised by Planning Supervisor, Planning Manager, or Operations Manager.

- *Material Planning* – Sometimes combined with purchasing/buying roles, sometimes separated. Responsible for ordering of raw materials to support the production plan whilst maintaining sensible inventory levels to cope with demand changes and the support of cashflow constraints. Can also monitor supplier delivery performance. Includes roles such as Material Planner or Buyer. Can be supervised or managed by a Planning Manager, Planning Supervisor, Planning Group Leader, Operations Manager, or Purchasing Manager.

- *Purchasing* – Responsible for the identification and selection of best supply solutions for raw materials, along with negotiation of price and supplier relationship management. Often driven purely by material cost, it's sensible to include logistics costs and supplier performance on quality and delivery as part of decision-making criteria. Includes roles such as Buyer, or Purchasing Administrator. Can be supervised or managed by a Senior Buyer or Purchasing Manager.

- *Logistics* – Responsible for the movement and storage of material within your facility, plus the delivery of finished goods to customers and perhaps the collection of raw materials from suppliers. Will manage Goods-In, Warehousing, production line-feed, and Dispatch processes. The focus is inventory accuracy, often through the utilisation of a WMS (Warehouse Management System). Will also lead Perpetual Inventory and Stock-take processes, and will often manage MHE (Manual Handling equipment) and warehouse racking and storage solutions. Includes roles such as Goods-In Coordinator, Dispatch Coordinator, Logistics operative, Warehouse Operative, and Inventory Coordinator. Can be supervised or manager by Logistics Supervisor, or Operations Manager.

- *Quality* – Responsible for management system creation and adherence (where required), and for providing systems and controls for assuring product specification. Will utilise standard quality processes and tools such as Control Plans, PFMEA (Process Failure Mode Effects Analysis), APQP (Advanced Process Quality Planning) to manage quality through process control. Will lead the response to customer quality complaints, with Quality Engineers often expected to be proficient leaders of problem-solving processes. May also manage inspection processes at Goods-In and End of Line with qualified Inspectors. Frequently support with the generation of documentation such as FAIR (First Article Inspection Report) or ISIR (Initial Sample Inspection Report) in Quality Administrator roles. May also manage supplier quality performance and warranty. Management system adherence sometimes requires a Systems Engineer to maintain procedures and complete internal audits. Includes roles such as Quality Engineer, Quality Technician, Systems Engineer, Inspector and Quality Administrator. Can be supervised or managed by a Senior Quality Engineer or Quality Manager.

- *Facilities & Maintenance* – Responsible for ensuring the availability of equipment, machinery and facilities to required standards. Can complete PM's (Planned Maintenance) to reduce likelihood of equipment failure, and can introduce TPM (Total Preventative Maintenance) with the support from front-line team members to reduce further. Often responsible for managing safe contractor working practices, and adherence to legislative requirements related to machinery and equipment. Is likely to be involved in capital expenditure decision-making. Includes roles such as Maintenance Engineer (electrical, mechanical, multi-skilled), Maintenance Technician, and Administrator. Can be supervised or managed by a Maintenance Supervisor or Maintenance Manager.

- *Health & Safety* – Responsible for providing the tools and mechanisms that will support the delivery of a safe working environment. Can develop and implement tools such as Risk Assessments, COSHH controls, Accident/Incident reporting and investigation, Hazard reporting, and Near Miss reporting and investigation. Their focus is to reduce workplace accidents and incidents, particularly lost time and reportable incidents. Often picks-up responsibility for Environmental management also. I have found it useful to combine with Facilities & Maintenance responsibilities because of the overlaps in legal compliance management. Includes roles such as Health & Safety Officer or Health & Safety Manager.

- *Engineering Change Control* - Responsible for coordinating engineering changes with all relevant functions in order to minimise operational cost through inventory utilisation. Will interface with Material Planning, Production Planning, Engineering, and Production to coordinate cutover dates for change, and will manage traceability and documentation. Includes roles such as Engineering Change Coordinator. Can be managed by Planning Manager, Quality Manager or Operations Manager.

- *Production* – Responsible for the manufacture of finished goods through the utilisation of appropriate equipment, people and materials. Should be focused on efficiency, delivery and quality performance, as well as working safely. Includes roles such as Production Operative, Senior Production Operative, and Production Team Leader. Can be supervised or managed by a Production Supervisor, Team Leader, Group Leader, or Operations Manager.

- *Process/Manufacturing Engineering* – Responsible for process design and layout, in order to enable safety and efficiency. Will manage equipment specification and location, and will design with ergonomics and labour utilisation as primary considerations. May also manage tooling, and could be involved in capital equipment decision-making. Usually an excellent support infrastructure for production teams. Includes roles such as Process Engineer or Manufacturing Engineer. Can be supervised or managed by a Senior Engineer, Engineering Manager, or Operations Manager.

- *Continuous Improvement* – Responsible for supporting and encouraging a continuous improvement culture. Primarily a cultural influencer with a strong focus on encouraging the use of the right kind of mental models, will also be involved in training and development of all team members in Lean tools and disciplines through Kaizen events. Can also support with culture audits. Includes roles such as Continuous Improvement Manager, Lean Engineer, and Continuous Improvement Engineer. Can be supervised or managed by Operations Manager or facility leadership role.

As I said, this list is simple and you might consider a little patronising. However, I once entered a facility that had no Production Planning capability, and they wondered why their delivery performance and equipment utilisation was so poor. Another facility had no Process Engineering capability, and they wondered why their labour utilisation was so low. And another had no Quality Engineers, and they wondered why they had a high level of customer quality complaints. Sometimes you can't see something that is as plain as the nose on your face to someone else. I'm a firm believer in having every role covered by someone, whether that someone has to pick up multiple responsibilities, or you have numerous people for each activity. By clearly covering every base you can make it much easier for your team to identify who has responsibility for each discipline, and you can ensure that a particular discipline and functionality is being championed and improved. I often consider my role as being similar to that of the conductor of an orchestra. I am simply in place to guide and direct a team to play in the right way and at the right time. However, if there are key instrumentalists missing, the music will not sound as sweet. You wouldn't create an orchestra without a wind section, or strings. Why do the same in your manufacturing facility?

Core or Support?

The final step in defining your matrix structure is to decide which functions and roles sit within the Core Team, and which functions and roles sit in the Functional Support Team. Again, there are no hard and fast rules here unfortunately. Who you include will depend on a small number of factors…

- The Core Team(s) should always include Production Supervision, Production Quality Engineers, and Manufacturing Engineers. These three roles represent the critical disciplines that are fundamental to the success of the Core Team activities. Where possible, I would also advise the inclusion of Production Planning and Supplier Quality representatives, as again their functionality is extremely valuable to include as part of the Core Team. Unfortunately, this is not always possible due to constraints on resources.

- How many value streams you have versus the amount of people available is a major consideration. If you have multiple value streams, you may need to consolidate them into focused-teams by customer or product type in order to reduce the resource burden, and you may need to minimise the functions you include to do the same. In those environments, you may have to keep some functions centralised in the Functional Support Team, perhaps even the likes of Production/Material Planning for example.

- The nature of the problems you experience most will also have an influence. If you have lots of machinery and equipment that is often breaking down and impacting performance, you may wish to try and include the Maintenance team in the Core Team, even if only for a period of time. If delivery performance or customer quality is your major issue, then including someone from Planning or Quality will add value.

- The volume of the activity that you process is also a consideration. If you make large capital equipment in small volumes with low levels of repetition, then you may not have a large Logistics function with lots of people moving materials and components around your facility. You may therefore decide to keep Logistics as a centralised Functional Support Team function. However, if you are in a high-volume high-mix environment where the timing of the movement of material is critical, then including Logistics as part of your Core Team might make more sense to you.

Some examples

Exactly how you build your version of the *Lean Foundations*™ matrix structure will depend on your thoughts around these points, and the nature of your facility. Here are a couple of fictitious examples of environments to help provide some support for your decision.

Factory A

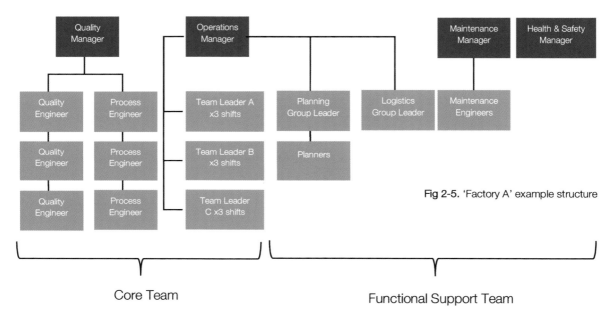

Fig 2-5. 'Factory A' example structure

This facility produces components through 12 self-contained production cells that are operated by anywhere between 3 and 8 team members. Each production cell produces a defined type of part with allocated equipment and for a specific customer. There are commonalities between production cells, with similar types of products being made, but for different customers and utilising different types of equipment. The facility is managed by a Plant Manager, who has a small management team of an Operations Manager, Quality Manager, Health & Safety Manager, and Maintenance Manager, and with a Supervisory level with a number of functional Team Leaders, and functional engineers. To manage it effectively, three cross-functional teams are defined by physical location rather than by customer or process simply because of the variation, and the factory is divided into three to match the team structure. Balancing the number of team members per cross-functional team makes daily management easier. Included in the Core Team are Production Team Leaders, a Quality Engineer, and a Process Engineer, along with front-line team members from Production and line-feed Logistics. In the Functional Support Team is Planning, Health & Safety, Maintenance and central Logistics for functionality like Goods-In and Dispatch.

Factory B

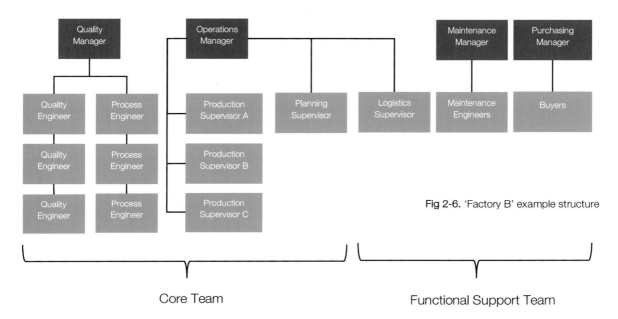

Fig 2-6. 'Factory B' example structure

Core Team

Functional Support Team

This facility produces components through one value stream, which is segregated into three individual process steps. Each process step has completely different characteristics and utilises different numbers of people and types of equipment. Customer orders can be processed through all or just some of the individual process steps depending on the nature of the component required. Orders received come from multiple customers, but each customer sits in one of three typical product types. The facility is managed by an Operations Director, who has a management team including a Production Manager, Logistics & Planning Manager, Purchasing Manager, Quality Manager, and Maintenance Manager, and with a Supervisory Level including Production Supervisors and functional engineers. To manage it effectively, only one cross functional team is defined, but with some segregation for the indirect team members in functions such as Quality, Customer Service and Planning. These are allocated to the three product types and therefore to particular customers in order to manage the number of customer interfaces. The roles of Production Manager and Logistics & Planning Manager are combined into an Operations Manager role. Included in the Core Team are Production Supervisors, Quality Engineers, Process Engineers and Planning. Included in the Functional Support Team is Logistics, Purchasing, and Maintenance.

Factory C

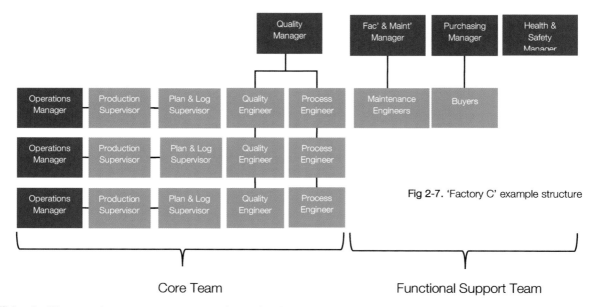

Fig 2-7. 'Factory C' example structure

Core Team   Functional Support Team

This facility produces components through three value streams, each with completely different characteristics and functionality. There are three different products, one for each value stream. The facility is managed by an Operations Director, who has a management team which includes three Operations Managers, a Quality Manager, Health & Safety Manager, Facilities & Maintenance Manager, and a Purchasing Manager. There is a supervisory level which includes a number of Planning & Logistics Supervisors, Production Supervisors and functional engineers. To manage it effectively, three cross-functional teams are created, each with their own Operations Manager, and with dedicated Production Supervisors, Quality Engineers, Planning Supervisors and Process Engineers. Included in the Functional Support Team is Health & Safety, Facilities & Maintenance, and Purchasing.

Hopefully these three examples help you to decide how to create your own version of the *Lean Foundations™* matrix structure. Remember, there isn't one right answer here, and you don't necessarily have to do something once and then set it in stone. Consider setting your structure one way and then evaluate its effectiveness over time. If you feel the need to modify it, then do so but with careful consideration for the potential impacts both positive and negative.

Making the change

Once you've decided exactly how you plan to structure your facility, you're going to need to implement the change in a way that supports the healthy and psychologically safe environment that we're trying to create and maintain. We're potentially looking to make some fairly fundamental changes to some team member's roles, reporting lines, and teammates, so we need to be able to make these changes with sensitivity. To help with this, it's a good idea for us to return to the concepts of 'Motivate the Elephant', 'Direct the Rider', and 'Share the Path'. We need to be able to communicate the planned changes in a way that will enable them to be most readily understood and embraced, and following the advice of the Heath brothers is likely to help us in this regard. I would therefore suggest that you apply the same three-step process that I have utilised on numerous occasions, and which has usually been successful.

First of all, I would suggest that you look to communicate the changes with your team by utilising the following logical argument…

- As we know, we're trying to create a great place to work, by improving workplace happiness, operational performance and creating a platform for Lean – this is our 'Why'

- To achieve this, we're looking to embrace effective teamwork and organisational health, to engage and empower front-line team members, and to build a well-functioning management system – this is our 'How'.

- As our first major structural step on this journey – the first part of our 'What' - we're planning to facilitate effective teamwork by adjusting our organisation structure to a matrix structure which supports cross-functional teams, and in the process enables a focus on value stream performance.

- This matrix structure will draw together team members from different functions who will take ownership and accountability for their value stream performance, and will be provided with all the support they need to achieve it.

- There will be a Core Team or teams (based on your decisions), and a Functional Support Team. Everyone will be tasked with driving value stream performance, with the Core Team(s) primarily focused on this, and the Functional Support Team targeted to assist whilst also driving their own functional discipline and process adherence.

- At this point, it's a good idea to share the whole organisation structure if you can, particularly when presenting to your entire facility. Don't forget, you don't have to include names in the early stages of your discussions in order to preserve points of confidentiality.

- Finally, consider sharing the process that will be followed to introduce the new organisation structure. When will it be complete? Who will take the lead? What type of conversations will take place and with whom? What choices do people have in accepting changes to their roles?

Hopefully you can see that this logical progression of thoughts should help to Motivate Elephants, Direct Riders, and Share Paths all at the same time. Of course, there will still be cynics and doubters, but hopefully more and more people will begin to convert to a more positive outlook.

Secondly, I would suggest that you consider completing your communication on three levels, potentially with support from colleagues in HR…

- *Individual* – Consider taking the time to talk on a one-to-one basis with any person whose role is about to be changed in any way, whether with actual responsibility changes, reporting line changes, or changes to the team they will be working in. I would advise doing this early in the process so that you can gain an understanding of any individual preferences or problems people may have in accepting the changes. You may need to adjust your plans to accommodate them.

- *Team* – Perhaps take the time to bring the cross-functional teams together in order to help them understand clearly who their teammates are and maybe even initiate some early team coherence.

- *Facility* – It's a good idea to share the whole structure with everyone in your team at the same time if you can in order to ensure consistency of messaging. This may mean another mini-Town Hall meeting or meetings depending on your available facilities.

Finally, once your communications are complete, and you have started to implement the necessary changes to the team structure, it's worth making a few subtle but impactful physical changes that will help to reinforce the structural changes you're introducing. Here's a few examples…

- *Co-locate the teams* – Something I would always recommend is to co-locate cross-functional teams in the same office or workspace if you can. By separating people from their functional workspace, and including them in a cross-functional workspace, you really are stressing the desire for them to work together as a team on problems that affect them all, and on the performance of their team as a whole. Even better, locate the team as close to the factory floor as possible, whilst of course providing the best working conditions you can and considering things like noise, natural light and temperature control. You're going to want your teams to frequently visit the shop-floor to understand problems in real time, so why not make it as easy as possible for them to do so.

- *Co-locate management* – Bringing the management team together will also encourage them to work more actively as a team, rather than as functional leaders. I would suggest that it's a good idea for Ops Team Managers to be located with their cross-functional teams, but if you can, it's definitely worth bring your other functional managers into a collective space. In doing so you're also helping to encourage independence in your functional team members. Later in *Lean Foundations*™ journeys I have included Ops Team Managers in the same space as functional managers to really reinforce cross-functional team independence and management team coherence.

- *Segregate the factory* – I would actively encourage you to clearly identify the physical factory space allocated to each cross-functional team. This can be done with line markings on the floor, and signage. If you use line-marking, try to ensure that you don't create any sections of 'no-man's land' between segregated areas. You need to ensure that everywhere has a defined ownership in order to support processes like 3S/5S later in your Lean realisation. This may mean that you need to define areas that sit in cross-functional team ownership, and pure functional ownership.

- *Facility Layout drawings* – I know that it sounds overly simplistic, but I have found that super-imposing de-marked areas on facility drawings to identify ownership really serves to drive home the point. It gives everyone a clear and consistent communication about who is responsible for what. It's a good idea to publish these in public areas in your facility.

There is one final point of consideration here. As part of your restructuring you may well find that you have identified people who are in roles that are no longer required, as well as identifying gaps. It almost goes without saying that if you can reallocate people to a new role it's worth doing, as long as you're happy that they can perform in their new role of course. However, it's also possible that you don't have alternative roles available and need to make roles redundant. This can be unpleasant, particularly if the individual in question is a high performer. It can also be a positive, as it will allow you to deliver some welcome cost reductions, and can potentially deliver a means of taking out a low performer from your team, or to fund new roles that you have identified are needed. Whichever is true, remember that the long-term goal of improving workplace happiness, improving operational performance, and creating a platform for Lean, is what you're striving for.

Key reminders

Now that you have designed and implemented your new organisation structure, there are two simple ideas to remind yourself and your team of on a frequent basis.

First, the horizontal team is more important that the vertical team. Anyone who has worked with me will have heard this phrase a hundred times, and will have seen me move my finger in a horizontal ellipse, then vertical ellipse, to make my point. The cross-functional teamwork that runs horizontally along the value stream and through your focused-teams is more important than the teamwork that runs vertically through functional lines. It's this teamwork that will drive the performance of the value stream through problem solving and waste reduction, and in the process will drive the performance of the organisation as a whole. It's also the horizontal cross-functional team that will nurture and facilitate the kind of teamwork that we're trying to embrace.

That same horizontal teamwork also needs to take place amongst your management team. They need to abandon any previous pre-conceptions around driving functional performance and instead embrace their peers as their primary team. It means that they have to support one another, even at the expense of their functional responsibilities at times. A functional manager should be prepared to sacrifice their own functional requirements for the good of the organisation, sometimes being critical of someone in their own functional team and agreeing with someone in their management team instead. This can be difficult for them, particularly if they have been heavily functionally focused in the past. They will need your constant support and guidance in order to maintain the discipline. I have often found that this kind of horizontal teamwork is more difficult to encourage in your management team than anywhere else. An important point for you to consider here is that the same rule applies to you. Only if you are aligned with your peers, whether they sit in your facility or not, will you be able to ensure that the improvements that you are driving in your facility are aligned with the needs of the organisation as a whole.

Second, having a deliberate focus on horizontal teamwork, and in particular on the importance of the cross-functional team in managing value stream performance, means that we have begun the process of what I would describe as 'flipping the hierarchy'. A typical organisation structure document shows the leadership team at the top, and front-line team members at the bottom, exactly as I have been presenting in the diagrams previously. This has been intentional, I have not wanted to raise any eyebrows at this point. However, as we focus on organisational health and psychological safety in supporting effective teamwork, and as we utilise cross-functional value stream teams to drive operational performance, we start to establish the role of management and leadership as support functions, rather than as figures of hierarchal authority. The role of front-line team members and supervision is where we come to be focused in order to add value, solve problems and remove waste. It's true that the management and leadership layers still carry the responsibility for the overall performance of the organisation, and also maintain the authority to make business critical decisions on things like expenditure and disciplinary processes. But, these decisions are taken to serve and support the cross-functional teams, rather than to dictate to them. It's therefore worth routinely reminding yourself, and your team members, that you and your management team work for them, not the other way around. We'll talk more about this a little later when we address empowering leadership.

RIGHT PEOPLE ONBOARD

In 2001, Jim Collins published his seminal book 'Good to Great'. In it, Collins and his team presented their thorough and comprehensive analysis of a number of companies that had demonstrated a progression from good to great financial performance, and had sustained it over time. The level of detail in the analysis completed, and the importance of their findings, cannot be over-stated, and should not be under-appreciated. They describe eight characteristics that are common to all of the 'great' companies that they identified, the one that we're interested in here is 'First Who… then What'.

Collins argues that a differentiating characteristic of all of the 'great' companies identified, was the fact that they "… got the right people on the bus…". In other words, they recruited and retained the best people to operate their company, and removed the people who were not. Importantly, what he also argues is that getting the right people on the bus came before deciding where the bus was going. His reasoning is simple. It's the right people that will define the right direction. Because they're the right people, telling them where to go and how to get there will not work. Instead, they need to be active participators in the decision-making process around direction and strategy.

For us, that's the equivalent of bringing the right people on board before we define the 'What', or 'Standard Operating Objectives' of our 'Golden Circle'. Our 'Why' and 'How' are pre-defined by our desire to become a great place to work; to be a happy workplace, that operationally performs, and seeks excellence by creating a platform for Lean; and to deliver this through organisational health and effective teamwork, through engagement of empowered front-line team members, and through the utilisation of a well-functioning management system. Our 'What', the detail of the actions that we will take to deliver the 'Why' and 'How' still has to be defined. As Collins suggests, in order to define it well we need to ensure that we have the right people on board first. Having completed a number of these *Lean Foundations*™ journeys myself, I can't stress enough the importance of having the right people in your team. The wrong people will not be intrinsically motivated, will not embrace organisational health, psychological safety and effective teamwork, and will not drive operational performance and workplace happiness. The right people will do all of those things because *they want to*, and not because you tell them to.

The challenge, of course, is identifying who the right people are in the first place. If, like me, you've completed a significant number of job interviews in your time, you'll know it's extremely difficult to discern the right people from the wrong people. At the same time, even when working alongside people already in place in your facility, it can be difficult to decide whether their contribution is positive or not. To help, I want to take you through four complimentary ideas which identify some of the characteristics that you are looking for to ensure that you have the right people for your *Lean Foundations*™ journey.

Type X, versus Type I

Cast your mind back to earlier parts of the book, and hopefully you'll remember that we're trying to tap into the intrinsic motivators of all of our team members. We're trying to create an environment that doesn't suppress our desire to work as part of a team, to work with autonomy and accountability, to be successful and to improve, and to work with a sense of purpose. An obvious question here is, do we all share all of these intrinsic motivators equally? The answer is, of course, no.

In '*Drive*', Dan Pink identifies two types of behaviour that are common to us in the workplace. Type X behaviour is "*… fuelled more by extrinsic motivators than intrinsic ones…*", and is where people are more interested in receiving external rewards from the completion of an activity, rather than experiencing inherent satisfaction. Type I behaviour is the opposite. It is fuelled by intrinsic desires rather than extrinsic, and is where people are less interested in receiving "*… the external rewards to which an activity leads and more with the inherent satisfaction of the activity itself…*". For *Lean Foundations*™, it's clearly the Type I behaviour that we're trying to enable through the development of a healthy, psychologically safe and empowering working environment.

Interestingly, Pink argues that whilst individuals demonstrate these behaviours in different ways and at different times, we all have particular dispositions towards one of these behaviours. We are all inclined to behave more typically as Type X, or Type I. What we are looking for therefore, is to retain and recruit people who have a disposition towards Type I behaviour. It's these people who will best fit into the working environment that we are seeking to create.

Pink offers a couple of important insights into Type I behaviour that it's worth being aware of here. First, whilst we all have dispositions, our behavioural patterns are not fixed. They are traits that are developed through experience and circumstance, and can be learned and un-learned in equal measure. Therefore, someone who is pre-disposed towards Type X can learn Type I behaviour. This means that we can balance our view of some individuals with the knowledge that people can develop the behaviours that we are trying to tap into with our support and guidance. Second, don't assume that Type I's don't care about money and financial reward and can be paid less as a consequence. If a person's pay is not fair and appropriate for their responsibilities and skillset, their senses of trust and fairness will be affected, and their psychological safety impacted. No amount of disposition towards Type I behaviour will correct such mis-management. However, once a Type I is fairly and appropriately rewarded, and money is *"…taken off the table…"*, their intrinsic motivators are able to take the fore.

Givers versus Takers

In his thoughtful book, '*Give and Take*', Adam Grant describes the idea that people can differ in their preferences for reciprocity, or the practice of exchange for mutual benefit during our social and work interactions. Grant outlines the idea of a reciprocity spectrum, with 'Takers' at one end of the scale, and 'Givers' at the other. 'Takers' are defined as people who *"… like to get more than they give…"*, who balance reciprocity in their favour and put their own interests ahead of the needs of others. They believe that their individual success is more important than that of others, and that they should receive credit for their efforts in order to feel worthwhile. Working environments dominated by 'Takers' tend to be paranoid places, with everyone waiting to receive the stab in the back that underpins someone else's success. 'Givers', on the other hand, prefer *"… to give more than they get…"*. They desire to give their time, energy, skills and knowledge generously for the success of others and the whole, and feel success themselves as a consequence. Grant does describe a spectrum, a linear scale between two points, and he argues that our behaviours can shift from one reciprocity style to another depending on our situation and circumstances. However, he suggests that in general we tend to develop a fairly typical reciprocity style which becomes the way we approach most interactions most of the time.

Most interestingly, Grant presents clear information that demonstrates that whilst 'Givers' can be the worst performers in their given profession, in all cases 'Givers' are also the best and most sustained performers, with 'Takers' sitting in between. Because of their generous and compassionate nature, 'Givers' often establish more fulfilling and supportive relationships in return, provide more effective leadership, and are more reliable in delivering performance.

From this simple description, it seems fairly obvious that for *Lean Foundations™*, we're seeking to retain and recruit 'Givers' rather than 'Takers'. It's our desire to build effective teams which function in a healthy and psychologically safe environment, and it therefore seems unlikely that the we will be able to establish or sustain such an environment if it is filled with people whose own self interests are their primary concern. In drawing this conclusion, there are a couple of important points for us to consider.

First, Grant suggests that, in the majority of cases, people will tend to present a style of 'Matcher' when at work. We tend to seek an equality and balance in our interactions; to get the same as we give in order to maintain our sense of fairness and trust. He also identifies that there are some individuals who present as 'Fakers', who pretend to be a 'Giver' in order to receive more in return, but are actually a 'Taker' in disguise. And, he describes those people who are disagreeable 'Givers', who present as people who may be prickly and difficult to deal with, but actually have our best interests at heart. In identifying the right people to be part of our *Lean Foundations™* journey, we need to be aware of all of these behavioural tendencies and be able to spot them in a crowd. Second, Grant is clear that simply recruiting 'Givers' is not enough, because the existence of just one 'Taker' in a small team of 'Givers' can be toxic, and can mean that the 'Givers' simply stop giving in order to preserve their sense of fairness and balance. Worse, they may become 'Matchers' and simply copy the prominent behaviour of the 'Taker'. It's therefore critical that we actively identify and remove the 'Takers' from our team in order to enable the 'Givers' to flourish. In doing so, Grant suggests that we can develop an environment that is characterised by pronoia, the opposite of paranoia. Here, team members operate in the belief that other people are plotting their success, rather than their demise, and that they are working with their best interests at heart. It certainly sounds like the psychologically safe environment we're trying to create.

Growth versus Fixed

In her fantastic book '*Mindset*', Carol Dweck offers a description of two different perspectives that people can have of themselves and their abilities. She outlines that people with a 'Fixed' mindset have a sense that their qualities and capabilities are defined and set in stone; that their intelligence, personality and character are something that they are born with and which determines their ability to succeed in life. The logical conclusion of the 'Fixed' mindset is that being a successful, intelligent, capable and all-round good person is something that is bestowed upon you rather learned or nurtured. Those people, therefore, feel that every situation they face is a test of their personality and character, and can suffer with doubt and fear of failure and rejection. They will respond negatively to failure; they will hide mistakes for fear of criticism, will blame others instead of accepting responsibility, and will avoid taking risks.

People with a 'Growth' mindset have a sense that their qualities and capabilities are things that are learned and can be developed over time. They believe that their intelligence and character is something that can be nurtured, and that success is earned through hard work and determination. 'Growth' mindset people see failure as a learning opportunity, and do not waste time worrying about how great they look when they could be spending time learning to be great instead. They constantly look for opportunities to improve, will take responsibility for their own failure, and are more likely to take risk in order to achieve greater success.

Again, it seems fairly obvious from this simple description that for *Lean Foundations™*, we're looking to retain and recruit people with a 'Growth' mindset rather than 'Fixed'. In seeking to create a healthy and psychologically safe environment, we need to ensure that our team members feel able to identify problems and seek ways to solve them, to hold their hands up when mistakes are made and accept responsibility, and to learn new skills and knowledge in order to become a more rounded and valuable team member. People with a 'Growth' mindset are far more able to support what we're trying to achieve than those with a 'Fixed' mindset. However, it is important to note that both mindsets are learned behaviours based on our life experiences and circumstances. We also move between mindsets at different points in time, and in response to different stimulus. This means that we can balance our view of some of the people in our team in the knowledge that their behaviours can be developed to better fit the environment we're trying to create.

The Ideal Team Player

In his book, '*The Ideal Team Player*', Patrick Lencioni describes what he calls the 'three virtues' that all good team players share. They are 'humility', 'hunger', and 'smart'. The virtue of 'humility' is fairly self-explanatory. He believes that great team players lack ego and concern about status, and are quick to point out the contributions and successes of others rather than themselves. They're team focused and seek group success over individual success. Lencioni defines 'hunger' as a desire to learn, to take on more responsibility, to succeed, and to work hard. He believes that great team players have a real need to do a job well, and will go above and beyond to be dependable and deliver results. The virtue of 'smart' is a little less obvious, and refers to what he calls 'people smarts' rather than intellectual capacity. He believes that great team members are interpersonally aware, are good listeners, and have a good intuition about group dynamics. They're conscious of how their actions and comments impact others.

Most importantly, Lencioni believes that it's the combination of all three characteristics that is critical to defining a great team player. If someone possesses one or two of the characteristics without the others, they are less able to contribute effectively in a team environment. They may be 'hungry' only, and therefore may impose their thoughts and ideas on others. Or they may be 'humble' only, and may contribute little value in terms of effort and inter-personal relationships. They may be 'smart' only, and may be popular and well liked, but offer minimal contribution to the team. If they are 'humble' and 'hungry', but not 'smart', they're likely to make a positive contribution to the team, and are going to share credit and success, but are likely to be mis-understood by the team mates and could have poor relationships with their colleagues. Those who are 'humble' and 'smart', but not 'hungry', are likely to be easy to like because they can interact well and don't seek the limelight, but are likely to offer a limited contribution to the team and are unlikely to be passionate about team goals. If they are 'hungry' and 'smart', but not 'humble', they're likely to be ambitious and potentially manipulative, and will work hard for their own benefit rather than for the team as a whole.

Once again, we can see that the Lencioni's virtues of the ideal team player are exactly what we're looking to retain and recruit on our *Lean Foundations*™ journey. The combined 'hungry', 'humble' and 'smart' team player is going to be interested in supporting and crediting the team, is going to work with energy and passion and a sense of responsibility, and is going to be considerate and thoughtful of their colleagues' feelings whilst still being able to deal with situations of healthy conflict. These are all characteristics that are going to support our desire for effective teamwork, a healthy organisation, and psychological safety.

There are, however, a couple of important points that Lencioni identifies and which we need to bear in mind. First, it's important not to confuse humility with a lack of self-confidence. People who lack confidence may appear to be self-deprecating and therefore humble, but in fact have a reduced sense of self-worth and value. These people can damage team effectiveness because they're not prepared to speak up, to present or defend their thoughts and ideas, or call out others with healthy conflict. Second, those people who are 'hungry' to a point of excess can also be dangerous to team effectiveness. If their hunger drives them to make selfish decisions and to act in a way that serves their own ambitions, they may sacrifice the team in the process.

A combined perspective

So, who are the 'Right People' for us to get and keep onboard? It seems pretty clear that the kind of person we're looking to recruit and retain as part of our *Lean Foundations*™ team is a 'Giver', with a 'Growth Mindset', a 'Type I' disposition, and who demonstrates the virtues of 'humility', 'hunger' and 'smart'. If you could also add a healthy dose of 'bias for action' into the mix; what R. Meredith Belbin might call a 'Completer-Finisher' in his book '*Management Teams*', and which is a trait that ensures that a person delivers their responsibilities with deliberate focus and effort, then you're likely to be onto a winner. That should be easy, right? Well, unfortunately, not necessarily. Despite the fact that there are obvious overlaps in these traits, finding people already in your team, and who can join your team, who meet all of these criteria, can be quite difficult. It's not impossible, but it is difficult. In addition, actually identifying them amongst all of the other people is a real challenge. I'm not going to spend time here describing the best way to interview and assess people against these criteria, I'm no expert in interview techniques and selection processes. However, I can suggest a few simple ideas to help you…

- Now you know what you're looking for, it should be easier to see it. By being aware of these characteristics you should become more able to identify them in others.

- It's a good idea to be very open and clear about the type of person you're looking to include in your team, both in your review and recruitment processes. You may well find that the wrong people deselect themselves in the knowledge that they're not going to fit in your environment moving forward, particularly if you can effectively encourage your team to 'call out' inappropriate behaviour as part of working in a healthy and psychologically safe environment. The wrong type of person will soon become fed up with suppressing their natural urges, or being told that their behaviour is unacceptable.

- Consider involving as many people as possible in an interview or review process, particularly from the team peers and line managers of the roles you're assessing or looking to fill. Allowing people from a team to be part of the selection process for a new team member can be a very empowering and respectful process and well worth consideration.

- You could utilise tools such as Personality Profile Assessments and Myers-Briggs personality profiling, particularly for leadership and management roles where recruiting the right kind of person is absolutely critical to success.

- You could consider compromise in some areas, particularly when they are areas that can be developed with training and exposure to good practice. I often look at a person as a glass which is partially full. I consider how full that glass is when I find it, and how much more I can fill it with my time, energy and guidance, as well as with training and support from others. I also consider how full it needs to be to add value and contribute, and by when. If I believe that I can bring those two levels together in the time available to me, and I have the capacity to do it, then I make the effort. If not, particularly if it's a clear no, then I make the difficult decision instead.

- If in doubt, I would always advise you to make the difficult decision and say no, whether recruiting someone new or assessing someone in your team. If you're weighing up positives and negatives, it's possible that you have too many negatives and you're simply procrastinating.

- When the assessment is an obvious no, whether for a new recruit or an existing team member, I would suggest that you act decisively and with clarity. Anyone who does not fit with the team ethic that we're trying to encourage is likely to have a toxic impact on your speed of progress, and the effectiveness of what we're trying to achieve. They can undermine you and your *Lean Foundations™* journey without even realising it. This is not about being ruthless, it's about being determined in the desire to improve workplace happiness and operational performance. If someone doesn't fit, and isn't going to fit, it's better for everyone involved to make that decision sooner rather than later in my experience.

- If you recruit someone new, and then after a short period of time find that they do not fit in the way that you thought they would, I would advise that you make the difficult decision and release them. This is not an easy decision to make, particularly if you have recruited someone from gainful employment elsewhere. However, I find that it is important for you to see this through. Your team members are looking for you to protect the environment that you are seeking to create from people who cannot function well within it.

There is one last point that I haven't addressed so far, and you may be wondering why. In deciding who the right people are to have on our team, there is always the question of the importance of technical ability versus the value of character and personality. There are a great many sound bites on social media that suggest we should 'recruit for personality, not knowledge' or something similar. My advice here is fairly straightforward. Technical knowledge and skill are always valuable and will be part of any assessment on how much someone fills their glass. In the early stages of a *Lean Foundations™* journey it can often be a much more critical factor, as job knowledge and skills that are particular to the product or equipment within your facility can seem irreplaceable, along with the person who retains them. However, as we progress on our journey, we're going to spread knowledge and skills throughout the team. Therefore, the risk of 'martyrdom', or what I call 'white knight syndrome', where 'indispensable specialists' cause or allow problems to occur so that they can appear to save the day, will be reduced. I believe that the critical factors in making the decision on how valuable technical knowledge and skill are time and energy. Can you spare the time for someone to learn? Can you allow someone the time to develop, to make mistakes and learn from them? Do you have the energy and capacity to support them effectively in that process? If the answer to these questions is yes, then I would always advise that you go for it. I'm often pleasantly surprised at how well someone steps into a new role, or performs following a promotion, when they have the right personality traits and characteristics. If the answer is no, then you're going to need to add technical skill and knowledge into your selection criteria for getting or keeping the right people on board. At the same time, you'll need to accept that you may be missing out on an ideal opportunity to promote from within. Having said that, if you have someone in your team who is particularly toxic, removing them is more important than losing the skills or knowledge they retain. I usually find that the perception of someone's importance is very different from the reality, and there is often another solution waiting in the wings.

MANAGE YOUR RESOURCES

I think that we would all accept that there is a difference between management and leadership. As leader of your manufacturing facility, you're responsible for providing direction and vision, and for motivating and guiding your team to follow it. As the senior manager in your facility, you're also responsible for controlling and coordinating the resources available to you in order to achieve the objective of manufacturing and delivering goods in line with customer expectations. Those resources include your people, and it's easy to forget in the midst of trying to lead them, that you still have to manage them too.

From a management perspective, I have found that it's extremely practical to consider your people in exactly that same way as you would consider your machinery and equipment. This seems crude I know, particularly when considering all of the discussions we've had around things like psychological safety and intrinsic motivators. However, I'm deliberately talking about a pure management perspective only. If we consider our people as a machine-like resource; with a finite capacity, a particular capability, and a level of efficiency, we can learn to manage them in a way that improves their utilisation. We can ensure that they are not overloaded, and are not expected to achieve something that is beyond their capability. In doing so, we can help to maintain their sense of psychological safety, and can enable their ability to be effective as individuals and as part of the team. In the process, we'll support their intrinsic motivator of success and improvement. I'm obviously not advocating this approach in isolation from good leadership; I've provided a significant amount of insight in that area already, and will provide more in later parts of the book. But, managing our people as an effective resource is an important responsibility that will affect our ability to deliver workplace happiness and operational performance. There are a number of tools that I have found useful in this regard which are listed here. Again, I have no desire to be patronising, and if you already utilise some or all of these tools then I apologise for wasting your time. If not, feel free to utilise the ones that work for you.

- *Roles and Responsibilities* – A clearly defined and documented set of roles and responsibilities for every person can be extremely valuable, but are so often not in place. I frequently find that these tools are missing, and believe that they can add significant value in providing clarity of responsibility and ownership that many people in your team will find extremely useful. I would always advise that you take the time to document the roles and responsibilities of every person or role in your facility, and that you do so with a consideration for how those responsibilities meet, overlap and handoff between each other. By doing this you'll be ensuring that there are no gaps that ownership can fall in-between, and you can deliberately build the communication and relationship links that you would encourage your team members to utilise. It's for this reason that I often write all of the roles and responsibility documents myself, but it can be just as effective if you coordinate them between your management team. I sometimes find that part of the reason roles and responsibilities are not documented is because managers and leaders fear that people will stop helping one another if they do so. My experience tells me that the opposite usually happens. Once people properly understand their responsibilities, they can focus on meeting them as a first priority, and then can help others when they have the capacity to do so. And if you manage your resources carefully so that people do have capacity, they will happily help each other in order to be an effective and valued team member. It also means that people know when they are helping, and when they are being helped, and will express and receive appropriate levels of appreciation accordingly.

- *Headcount Report* – Pretty much the very first management report that I create on a *Lean Foundations™* journey is a Headcount Report. This is a simple report showing every person in my facility, identifying their status as either a Direct or Indirect employee, as either a Permanent or Temporary employee; and the role, team or process that they are allocated to. It's a report that I manage on a weekly basis, which is either completed manually or by downloading information from a Time & Attendance system, and which compares a planned headcount allocation with an actual headcount allocation. A report of this nature can help identify where you have imbalances in the allocation of your people between processes, where you have gaps in teams or roles, where you have temporary employees that could be permanent and vice-versa, or where you have incorrect allocations of Indirect and Direct roles.

- *Headcount Projection Report* – The very next report that I create is the Headcount Projection Report, which is a document that is used to forecast the headcount requirements of my facility over time depending on changes in demand and business circumstances. It's obviously closely linked to the Headcount Report, and to demand forecasts. I find that a report of this nature can help to identify when significant changes in headcount requirements are on the horizon, and can help you to justify those changes in requirements to whomever signs off recruitment or restructuring costs, even if that is yourself. It can help you to plan for change effectively, giving you the opportunity to see when it is coming and to take appropriate steps to manage it.

- *Skills Versatility Matrix* – It's normal for a Skills Matrix document to be required as part of a typical management system such as ISO:9001. However, in my experience, it's also normal for that document to be nothing more than wallpaper, despite its usefulness if used properly. I would always recommend that a genuine Skills Versatility Matrix is created and maintained, and is actively utilised as a live tool to inform decision making around things like job allocation, flexibility and availability of critical skills, and training and development requirements. In creating and maintaining a tool of this nature, decision making around who works on what job, regardless of whether that's an office-based or factory-floor based role, becomes much easier and better informed. It also enables that decision making when operations are stable, but more importantly when things go wrong and urgent decisions are required. Having a clear and structured tool in a scenario where someone reports their unexpected absence at the last minute is extremely beneficial, and means that you're not relying on a manager or supervisor's memory or instinct. The inclusion of the word 'Versatility' here is deliberate. A typical skills matrix normally includes a list of names on one side, and critical skills on the other, and cross-references which person has which skills. However, a Skills Versatility Matrix can add more information. It can include the level to which someone is trained and skilled in a role, usually from a scale of 1 to 4, where 1 is an unskilled trainee, 2 is a semi-skilled trainee, 3 is fully-trained, and 4 is able to train others. It can also include a plan for maintaining this level of skill and training, by recording when a person last worked in a role, when their skills level was last assessed, and when they needed to work in the role and be reassessed in order to maintain their skills. How long someone needs to work in a role, and how frequently they need to be re-assessed, is defined by the needs of the individual role. Reaching this level of sophistication may seem a step too far in the early stages of your *Lean Foundations™* journey, but it's certainly something that I would suggest you aspire toward over time.

- *Job Allocation Board* – This is a visual management tool which identifies who is working on each job in your facility on a given day or shift. It's usually used on a factory-floor basis only, but does not have to be. The board shows a representation of your production line(s)/cell(s), and includes spaces for each role which can then be populated with laminated cards that represent each person on your team. The Skills Versatility Matrix is used as a reference tool to decide who is able to work where. When team members enter the facility at the start of their work day, they are required to check the board to see where they are planned to work on that day. Even better, if team members are agreeable, they can enter the facility a few minutes early for their shift, and can be part of the decision-making process for their job allocation. Engagement of this nature can be extremely empowering for those involved. A useful addition to the job allocation process is to include decisions on job rotation and training. Some specific roles can be repetitive and perhaps even boring, or may be more physically demanding, and therefore enabling your team to agree who will rotate and when is a good way to encourage teamwork and a 'giving' rather than 'taking' mentality amongst team members. The same can be achieved by agreeing when someone requires training in a role, or re-training if they have not completed a role for some time.

- *Activity tracking* – Managing the workload and capacity of an office-based person can seem difficult, but can be done. By utilising a whiteboard, or something similar, to list all of the outstanding activities a person needs to complete, with a level of prioritisation and expected time to complete each one, which is then quickly reviewed with them on a daily or weekly basis, you can gain a very clear understanding of exactly how 'loaded' that person is. I would usually only advise this if you find that someone is particularly struggling with their workload, or the decision-making on prioritisation is critical to your operational success.

- *Holiday/Absence Planner* – I know, this really is basic, but you wouldn't believe the amount of times I've entered a facility and found that the simple act of tracking holidays and planned authorised absences is not done. As a consequence, I've seen production cells and machines that have stopped, or office-based processes that are delayed, simply because there are not enough people to operate them, or the people with the right skills and experience are not there. A simple calendar that shows who is planned to absent on a given day, with some practical rules around how many people can be off from the same process or work area at the same time, is usually extremely beneficial and easy to maintain.

- *Absence Management* – I have lost count of the amount of times that I have needed to introduce an absence management policy and process into an organisation. It's only right and proper that an organisation supports its employees when they are unwell or require unavoidable time off work. However, it's also appropriate for an organisation to ensure that its hopefully generous and flexible policies for absence are not abused by the minority, at the expense of the majority. Tracking absence, and defining agreed policies around the number of occurrences and amount of time someone is allowed to be absent from work before appropriate actions are taken is absolutely normal and responsible. It's my experience that nothing frustrates your employees more than when a colleague is seen to be taking advantage of the system, and not being held accountable for it. I would actively encourage you to agree, implement and work rigorously to a set of absence management policies, preferably with the support of your HR team.

- *Activity versus responsibility review* – Another activity I've found useful at times is a review of someone's actual daily activities in comparison to their documented responsibilities. This is an activity that I often complete when someone is struggling to meet the expectations of their role, and there is a need to understand why. I usually create a simple document that divides the working day into 15-minute segments, and then ask the relevant person to populate it with the detail of their activity in each of the 15 minutes. If this is completed over the course of a week, and then reviewed, it's amazing how often you find someone working on things that are not their responsibility and which need to be reallocated to another person in their team. On the odd occasion, I have found that the person is simply 'full', and cannot meet their responsibilities on their own. At other times, I have found that a person's perception of their workload is different than the reality, and it's simply the pressure of normal work that they are struggling to manage. Helping them to cope with this by realising that work is a never-ending process makes the exercise just as worthwhile. The completion of the document and the subsequent review helps to identify and justify the existence of a problem, and then enables informed decision making on how to solve it.

- *Personal Productivity* – I have found on occasions that some individuals struggle to find an appropriate mechanism for managing their, at times, varied responsibilities. It's not unusual for every person to have their own very personal approach to managing their capacity and workload, and for the mechanisms that some people employ to be particularly ineffective. On those occasions, I have found it useful to introduce those individuals to '*Getting things Done*' by David Allen, and have encouraged them to follow his suggestions for managing their workload through the use of specific types of list. It's a thinking and organisation process that I use myself, and have found invaluable in managing my workload very successfully. I wouldn't hesitate to suggest it others.

STEP 2 SUMMARY

Having completed Step 2 of your *Lean Foundations™* journey, I'm hopeful that you've taken a major step forward in building the well-performing facility that we seek. By developing an organisation structure that is clearly defined, that supports teamwork, and that is populated with the right people; you're working to establish the solid footings which will underpin your path to improved workplace happiness and operational performance. Only when you have the right people on-board, and organise them to work effectively together, can you deliver the kind of change that we're seeking to achieve.

I'm confident that we have discussed a number of useful insights that can help you to understand how to organise your facility in a way that supports your desire for effective teamwork and organisational health. The *Lean Foundations™* matrix structure is a practiced and proven solution that can genuinely encourage and support effort teamwork in your facility. And, I believe that we've discussed some valuable ideas around the recruitment and retention of the right kind of person for your team, and how to manage and support them effectively as a resource. You're now one very important step closer to enabling your facility to perform well, and to establishing the foundations upon which operational excellence takes root.

Before we go any further, it's worth taking a small amount of time for a quick review.

- All too often, leaders of manufacturing facilities can fail to introduce an organisation structure which supports effective teamwork. As a result, that facility is likely to struggle to perform well, and may suffer with poor workplace happiness.

- Typically, facilities will utilise a functional organisation structure which will align people of equal authority from different functions, and will encourage vertical teamwork that can restrict organisational performance.

- As an alternative, a matrix structure operates with an added layer of cross-functional working to a functional structure, but this can cause confusion of authority and responsibility.

- *Lean Foundations™* promotes a modified matrix structure, which integrates cross-functional teamwork into the organisation structure, whilst providing structural clarity, enabling effective teamwork, and removing the risk of operational and functional silos.

- The *Lean Foundations™* matrix structure introduces a Core Team to manage the core production activity, alongside Functional Support Teams who provide guidance and support in functional responsibilities.

- The role of the Core Team is fundamental to the success of the *Lean Foundations*™ approach. It's the Core Team(s) that are focused on the core performance indicators of Safety, Quality, Delivery, Cost and Engagement, and which ultimately influence the success of your facility as a whole.

- To build your own modified matrix, you can consider factors such as the basis of your cross-functional team, how many organisational layers you need, what functions and roles you require, who will be part of the Core Team and Functional Support Team, and how you're going to implement the change.

- There are two key ideas to remember and remind others of; the horizontal team is more important than the vertical team, and you are 'flipping the hierarchy'.

- Getting the right people on board is critical to our success. We are looking for people who are a 'Giver', have a 'Growth Mindset', have a 'Type I' disposition, who demonstrate the virtues of 'humility', 'hunger' and 'smart', and have a 'bias for action'.

- At times, we need to manage our people as a resource, and can do so effectively if we consider them as having machine-like capacity, capability and efficiency. In thinking this way, we can effectively support their sense of psychological safety.

Align
everyone
with policy
deployment

3

STEP

It's not difficult to find a manufacturing facility that is simply 'plodding along'. I've witnessed a number of facilities whose primary focus is nothing more than to survive the day; to manufacture and deliver the same product today that was produced yesterday and will be produced tomorrow. Sometimes I find that the leaders of these manufacturing facilities are focused only on meeting their annual budget or monthly sales forecast, and the idea of developing a plan for facility-wide change and improvement is merely wishful thinking. Or, they are over-whelmed by the scale of the challenge in front of them, and have little understanding of how to grasp their numerous and varied problems in order to define and implement a sensible solution. I also meet leaders of facilities who have a desire and perhaps even a plan to improve, but they struggle to realise the expected benefits. On occasions, their plan doesn't address the real problems that are impacting the facility, and causes them to waste time and energy on the wrong things. Often, it fails because their team is not aligned, and they end up working against each other on contradictory activities. At other times, the leaders lack the tools, methodologies or rigor to coordinate the execution of a well-defined plan, and it never quite delivers. Whatever the cause, those facilities lack the impetus and drive that a genuine and effective improvement plan provides, and the employees in those facilities suffer as a consequence. Their workplace is less happy, and their operational performance less capable. Their intrinsic motivator of improvement and success is constrained, and no doubt their sense of fulfilment and satisfaction severely impacted. Worst of all, those employees may have some pretty good ideas about how to improve things themselves, but may not feel that they are in a position to contribute. Their intrinsic motivator of autonomy and accountability takes a hit too.

So far, we have made good progress on our *Lean Foundations*™ journey. We have embraced the importance of effective teamwork, and continue to nurture it with organisational health and psychological safety. We have ensured that our team is on-board with the change process that we have initiated, having achieved their buy-in to our 'Golden Circle', and in particular our 'Why' and 'How'. We have also introduced an organisation structure that actively enables teamwork, and which is populated with the right people to make it work. Now, your facility is primed and ready to drive the kind of change and improvement that we seek. Your people are no longer willing to accept the reality of 'plodding along', they want to solve their problems and improve. They want to come together with purpose, and to add value to the place where they work. They want a plan, and they want to execute it. Fortunately for them, in you, they have a leader who feels the same way.

Having defined our 'Why' and 'How', and having decided on our 'Who', it's now time to identify and agree your 'What'. If we really do want to deliver on our desire for improved operational performance and workplace happiness, it's time to define and implement an Improvement Plan which will drive the achievement of an agreed set of 'Standard Operating Objectives', and will provide the heartbeat of your improvement journey. That Improvement Plan, if focused correctly, can target the problems that impact organisational health and effective teamwork, can drive us towards the empowerment of engaged front-line team members, and can design and build a well-functioning management system. It can be the tool that underpins the transformation of your manufacturing facility, can support and encourage teamwork to take hold, and can be a fundamental aspect of building the foundations that operational excellence desperately needs in order to thrive.

However, the scale of the problems in your facility may well be significant, and your ability to decide which ones are the most important could be challenged. Furthermore, you may wonder how on earth you're going to align your team to deliver the solutions together, and how you can possibly lead and manage the diversity of activities to an effective conclusion. What we need, therefore, is to utilise a process that can define an Improvement Plan which addresses the most significant problems and opportunities in your facility, and then to deploy that plan in a way that aligns and engages everyone with a shared responsibility for its delivery. And that's where Policy Deployment comes in.

Policy Deployment, sometimes referred to as strategy deployment, policy management, or *Hoshin Kanri*; is a planning and execution system which can help an organisation focus its activities and people to address its most significant problems and opportunities. It has three characteristics that add the most value for us in *Lean Foundations™*. First, it's a system which actively engages the people within the organisation in the definition and execution of the plan. Rather than being a purely top down process, it includes elements of bottom-up feedback throughout, and as a consequence ensures that all team members are able to contribute their thoughts and ideas. This means that the problems that are integrated into the plan for solution are relevant and important to the people who operate the facility on a day to day basis, and as a result are much more likely to be the problems that have the most critical impact on operational performance and workplace happiness. Second, it's a system which automatically builds-in alignment across functions and teams. It enables a clear understanding of responsibilities and ownership, and clarifies overlaps and inter-relationships between activities. Third, it's a system which is equally focused on plan creation and plan deployment. That focus on deployment is a real enabler in driving the successful implementation of the plan, and is where other strategic planning processes can fall short. In all cases, Policy Deployment engages and empowers the people involved, it aligns them in their common purpose and direction, gives them autonomy and accountability, provides an opportunity for success and improvement, and encourages them to collaborate and work as a team. For us, it's another 'win-win'.

There are numerous tools that can be used to support a Policy Deployment process. *Hoshin Kanri* is a system that has been actively utilised by Toyota for a number of years, and as a consequence there are a various books and published materials that describe a variety of modified approaches. For *Lean Foundations™*, the approach advocated combines the use of two tools; a version of a 'Strategy A3', along with an 'X-Matrix', with a deliberately simple but well-defined process for their creation and deployment. To support you in understanding this version of the system, we'll work through three sub-steps; 'Tell your story', 'Align with the X-Matrix', and 'Deploy with rigor'. We should remember here that we're not looking to define the business strategy of a global corporation or even a small enterprise, we're looking to agree and manage a simple and effective top-level plan for our manufacturing facility which will drive us towards improvement in operational performance and workplace happiness. Also, I'm not intending to dictate to you the specific content of that plan, I'm simply hoping to describe a process for you to develop that plan for yourself.

TELL YOUR STORY

Our first challenge is to grasp the variety and complexity of the problems that you face on a day to day basis in your facility, and then to define a plan that can help us to resolve them. We know that we have overarching problems of poor workplace happiness and operational performance; and we know that these are impacted by poor organisational health and teamwork, a lack of engagement of empowered front-line team members, and the lack of a well-functioning management system. But these are our broad-brush problems; they are the underlying characteristics of our facility, and result from more ingrained issues that occur daily. Within the detailed fabric of our daily operations, our team members face routine problems that contribute those underlying characteristics. We need to identify what those problems are, prioritise their importance, and then decide how to solve them. We should of course bear in mind that the actions we've taken so far in relation to organisation structure and teamwork are part of that process too.

In addition, we have the opportunity to fully integrate our 'Why' and 'How' into the mindset and daily practice of our team. We can ensure that everyone is fully conscious of the desire to improve workplace happiness and operational performance in their day to day activities. And, we can start to establish a mentality and culture that is focused on meeting that 'Why' and 'How'. In the process, we can continue to embed the Lean ideal of focusing on adding value for the customer, and for respecting our employees.

To meet this first challenge, and to take advantage of this opportunity we need to 'Tell your story'.

Every manufacturing facility has a story to tell, particularly one that is embarking on the kind of improvement journey that we are taking. In telling that story well, we have a fantastic opportunity to sharpen our thinking around our understanding of our problems, and our ideas for their solutions. A3 reports are specifically designed for that purpose. They are formatted so that they can convey the story of an improvement journey or problem-solving activity in a logical and succinct way. Their use enables us to follow and document a scientific thinking process that helps us to understand and communicate our problems, and to clearly define and describe our plan for resolution. They are called A3 reports for an obvious reason, they are printed on a single piece of European A3 paper (equivalent to American tabloid 11" x 17" paper), and there are a multitude of different standard and non-standard versions. Their origin is generally attributed to Toyota, and have been utilised by them as their standard method for communicating problem resolution and strategic analysis for a number of years, if not decades.

For *Lean Foundations™*, the A3 report is a vital tool in supporting the Policy Deployment process. In this first sub-step, we'll work through the completion of the '*Top-Level Improvement A3*', the specific format of which has evolved over a number of years of application and is loosely based on a standard 'Strategy A3'. In doing so, we can achieve a number of important points. First, we can gain a clear understanding of the context in which we're looking to start our improvement journey; why it is important to us, and what may influence us in the process. Second, we can understand the scale and complexity of the operational problems we need to fix, and in the process understand which have the most impact on our 'Why' and 'How'. Finally, we can define and agree our milestone goals or 'Standard Operating Objectives' on the journey, and can detail the projects and activities that will solve our problems and deliver the improvements in organisational health and teamwork, engagement and empowerment, and the capability of our management system.

The A3 can also serve as the tool for oversight of the execution of those projects, with the inclusion of feedback loops for any adjustments in direction that become necessary. It's important to note that this is deliberately scoped as a top-level A3 only. Whilst it will include detailed information on overall facility performance, it's main use is to facilitate and capture our thinking on the main improvement activities of our *Lean Foundations™* journey. The real detail within those improvement activities will be developed later in sub-step 3, 'Deploy with Rigor'. However, before we get started on the A3, we need to talk about the thinking processes that will underpin our approach.

The Scientific method, Theory of Constraints, and the feedback loop

I don't think it would be unreasonable of me to expect that most readers of this book will be aware of W. Edwards Deming's PDCA cycle. The PDCA cycle, or 'Plan', 'Do', 'Check', 'Act', is an expression of the scientific method, and is the foundation of the policy deployment process. In simple terms, it's a mental model similar to those we have discussed previously. However, it's quite possibly the most important of all mental models, because it ensures a systematic and logical approach is taken to the resolution of any situation or problem. Hopefully you can recognise how integral it is to a policy deployment process. If we are to decide what problems need to be fixed, how to fix them, and then to act upon them, it's logical for us to 'Plan', and then 'Do'. And if we desire to perform well, it's also sensible for us to 'Check' on the success of our actions, and to 'Act' in response when appropriate and necessary.

It's also possible that you are aware of Eliyahu Goldratt's *Theory of Constraints*, so eloquently described in his ground-breaking novel '*The Goal*', and later in his book '*What is this thing called Theory of Constraints*'. Goldratt's *Theory of Constraints* concept defines what it calls our 'Thinking processes' for change, and describes a simple six step approach to managing a process of ongoing improvement; 'What to Change',

'What to Change to', 'How to Change', 'Implement the Change', 'Evaluate the Change', and 'Start Again'. Hopefully you can recognise the similarities here with Deming's PDCA cycle, but also note the additional level of detail in the early steps that overlap with Deming's 'Plan'. That additional detail provides useful clarity around how to 'Plan'. It provides simple mental steps that we can follow to properly understand a problem, and to define the means for solving it. It's for this reason that *Lean Foundations*™ combines these two ideas and utilises them together as part of the approach to the completion of the '*Top-Level Improvement A3*', and the policy deployment process. It informs our mental models, and helps us in our desire to ensure that we're working to solve the right problems, in the right way, and at the right time.

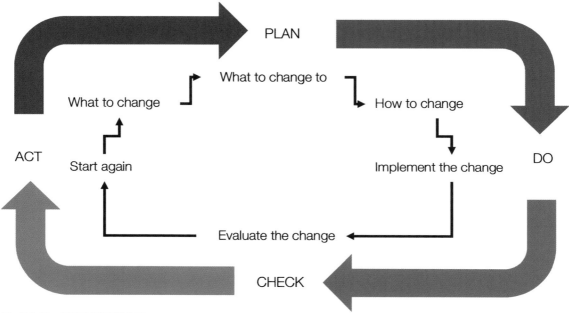

Fig 3-1. The PDCA/TOC Thinking process

It's this thinking process which also forms the basis of our process for bottom-up contribution to the plan. At particular points in our policy deployment process, we're going to actively seek input from our team members, and we're going to ask them to utilise this thinking process to make those contributions. Those layers of feedback loops, sometimes called 'catch-ball cycles', are critical to the success of the development of the plan, and to its execution. They're going to ensure that we're working on the right problems, that we're being successful in resolving them, and that we're adjusting our planned solutions based on what we learn as we progress. They're also important in supporting our team member's intrinsic motivators by giving them a voice, and in ensuring that the planning process contributes to organisational health and psychological safety.

The *Top-Level Improvement A3* – the Annual Offsite

The completion of an A3 of this scale is most successful when it's a collaborative process. Whilst it's possible for you to populate it alone, it's not advisable. We're trying to achieve alignment and buy-in to an improvement plan, to our 'Why', to the 'What' or 'Standard Operating Objectives' of our 'Golden Circle', and to the projects we're going to undertake to achieve them. We therefore need to bring the right people together to complete the A3 as a team, with a dose of healthy conflict included to make sure we agree to work on the right things.

As with our earlier activities, I would propose that an offsite meeting will provide the best opportunity for you to bring together the right people to hold the kind of frank and open discussion you need for this exercise. I find that they usually take a whole day, but again if you need to split it into two half-day sessions for practical reasons then feel free to do so. Also, if completing the session offsite is not feasible for you, I would suggest that you look to isolate the meeting from normal day to day operations as best you can. This offsite meeting will become your strategic planning review, and will be something that you look to complete on an annual cycle each year.

Within the session, you're looking to encourage the type of open and honest debate that we've discussed previously. Psychological safety, and the ability for your team to conflict healthily, is of paramount importance in ensuring that you capture every possible contribution and idea, and cover every base. It's possible that your team is still in the early stages of developing their sense of vulnerability-based trust with one another, so this A3 process provides the ideal opportunity for you to nurture it's progress by modelling and demonstrating good practice.

Who you invite should hopefully be fairly clear. I would suggest that you consider including the key decision makers and process leaders in your team, whether they be part of your management team as functional or focused-team managers in either the Core or Support Teams, or part of the supervisory layer of your organisation. Having completed your organisation structure activities from Step 2 you should find that choice to be a little clearer than perhaps it was for the first offsite, and you should find that you have a greater degree of confidence in the contributions you're likely to receive. The people that you include will become your deployment leaders for the execution phase of the policy deployment process, so please choose carefully. They will need to accept and embrace responsibility for the delivery of the Improvement Plan, as well as being the specialists in their area of expertise. You'll also need to ensure that you cover all functional and value stream responsibilities so that there are no gaps for activities and ownership to fall between.

It's worth noting at this point that it's not necessary for you to wait to complete this planning process until your organisation structure is complete. You'll need to decide when is the best time, and whether or not you can complete the activity if you're still waiting for key roles to be filled, or even if you're planning for less constructive team members to leave. The choice, of course, is yours, and will no doubt be influenced by the organisational pressures and the sense of urgency you have for agreeing the plan.

The *Top-Level Improvement A3* – feedback loop 1

Now that we're clear on who is going to be part of the team responsible for completing the A3, it's time to ask them to prepare for its completion by collating the right data, and by canvasing the right opinions. By completing this activity well, we can improve the likelihood that our A3 will identify and address the problems that have the most significant impact on your facility, and we can support our desire to build a healthy and psychologically safe environment where every person's ideas and contributions are valued and respected. Remember, we're in the process of 'flipping the hierarchy' of our facility, so listening and responding to the needs of our team is a critical step in that process.

In Step 1, I suggested that it could be a good idea for you to complete a top-level review of your facility, and for you to spend time with every member of your team to understand their day to day processes and any problems they face. Hopefully you have completed this activity already, if not, now is definitely a good time to do so in readiness for the completion of the A3. In addition, it's a good idea for you to encourage your management team to complete the same activity, you may even consider completing it together. In the process, you should both try to consider the combined PDCA/TOC thinking model, and should seek to understand every person's activities in terms of 'What to Change', What to Change to', and 'How to change'. Don't be afraid to ask these questions directly, your use of them will encourage the mental model in others. It's a good idea for the questions that you're asking here to be guided towards our ultimate objectives; our 'Why' and our 'How'. We need to understand which problems are most impacting organisational health and teamwork, engagement and empowerment of your team members, and the capability of your management system. Whilst all daily operational problems have an influence on those organisational characteristics, some will have more of an impact than others, and it's those that we will want to focus on resolving first.

This activity functions as the first feedback loop into the A3 process, so I would advise you to make everyone aware that their contributions are going to be integrated into the A3. They are likely to see it as a good opportunity to get the problems that they experience addressed, and it will encourage them to be open and honest with you. It will also make them aware that their contributions are valued and appreciated, and their sense of psychological safety and intrinsic motivators will benefit greatly. Be prepared to identify a long list of opportunities for improvement when completing this exercise, and don't be surprised if you don't get to address them all, particularly in the first instance. Also, don't be afraid to acknowledge when something doesn't need to change. If it isn't broken, don't fix it, but do appreciate it.

The collection of data is important as part of this process. Bringing together information on the core performance indicators of on-time delivery, customer quality, safety, cost (scrap, inventory, labour, efficiency, OEE), sales, and profitability (or your equivalent), is a good first priority. You could also consider collating data on your wider performance indicators, such as supplier quality, inventory accuracy, machine up-time, right first-time, or capacity utilisation, along with potentially many more. When selecting the data to include in your discussions, consider what you already know to be your main performance problems and bring along data that is relevant. However, I would advise you not to over-stretch yourself and your team. Selecting what you do not include is just as important as selecting what you do.

If you can, look to bring data that is presented over time. By stating your performance for a given indicator in weekly or monthly buckets over the period of a year or even more, you can potentially identify trends and change points that may help your understanding of a problem and its cause. What is even better, is if your data is presented so that it is segregated by reason code. If that is possible, you may be able to sort your data into a Pareto chart, with the causes presented in logical order, starting with the one that has the greatest number of occurrences or impact, and ending with the one that has the least number of occurrences or impact. A Pareto graph or chart really helps to identify where you can prioritise your efforts to have the biggest influence in solving a problem. Remember, 80% of your overall issue is likely to be in 20% of your problems, so addressing the 20% first should be your priority.

Whilst data collection is important, I would advise you not to become too embroiled in it. In some organisations, information of the type listed is readily available and easy to present, in others less so. Data is useful because it will help us to tell the story with facts, which tends to be particularly important when having to justify investment decisions for example. However, the opinions and thoughts of your team members are just as valuable, if not more so. In my experience, their intuition and instinct around what is wrong, and what can be done to fix it, is often extremely insightful and rarely far off the mark. Listening to them carefully, and debating their conclusions with logic and diplomacy, can frequently identify the right way to proceed.

The *Top-Level Improvement A3* – the format

The A3 document format below is the one utilised in the *Lean Foundations*™ approach for the policy deployment process. It's used for both the '*Top-Level Improvement A3*', and the '*Project-level Improvement A3*' that we'll discuss a little later in sub-step three, 'Deploy with Rigor'. It features a title panel, and six main content panels; 'Context', 'Current State', 'Goals/Operating Objectives', 'Improvement Projects', 'Action Plan', and 'Review & Follow-up'. Completing each of the panels in sequence, following the directional arrows shown, encourages a logical flow of cause and effect decision-making, and enables the story-telling effect when presenting the information from each panel in turn. Now that we understand the correct thinking processes to use, have decided who will and how we're going to populate the A3, and have gathered the right information about our problems in preparation, we can work through the completion of each panel in turn.

Our aim in completion is two-fold. First, to utilise the thinking processes that the A3 enables in order to develop an effective and comprehensive top-level Improvement Plan which is focused on improvements that support our 'Why' and 'How'. Second, to describe a persuasive story that will interest and engage its reader, and which will encourage the involvement and enthusiasm of its participants. You may well find that you struggle to populate all of the information you discuss into each panel as you go through the process of completion. This is perfectly normal and is nothing to worry about. As you progress, you will be able to consolidate and summarise the most important elements into the one-page document. However, as you complete it, be prepared to utilise a larger space than just the A3 sheet in the first instance.

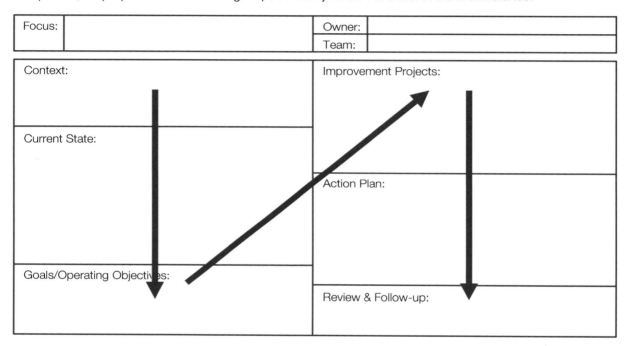

Fig 3-2. The *Lean Foundations*™ A3 format

The *Top-Level Improvement A3* – Focus/Owner/Team

This section of the A3 is fairly self-explanatory, and seems non-descript. However, each element is important in its own way.

First of all, defining the 'Focus' of the '*Top-Level Improvement A3*' will quantify the scope and remit of your improvement journey. It's therefore sensible for you to consider exactly what you're trying to achieve in attempting to utilise the *Lean Foundations*™ approach. This may sound a little silly at this point, as you're obviously seeking to improve workplace happiness and operational performance, and to provide a platform for Lean. And you're obviously planning to complete this by embracing organisational health and effective teamwork, by engaging with empowered front-line team members, and by utilising a well-functioning management system. However, now is a good opportunity to properly reflect on this ambition and to ensure that it really is something that you're looking to achieve for your entire facility. Perhaps, for example, your facility is particularly large and challenging, and it may be sensible to focus your efforts in one area. Or perhaps you have one value stream that is under-performing and needs specialist attention. I would not necessarily advocate a fragmented approach, because concepts such as organisational health and psychological safety need to be applied facility-wide to be most effective. But, your needs versus your available resources may dictate otherwise. The words that you populate into this field can be your own, and should reflect your reality. However, it's sensible that they reference our 'Why'; the desire for improvement in workplace happiness, operational performance, and creating a platform for Lean, and our 'How'; the need to embrace organisational health and effective teamwork, to engage empowered front-line team members, and to utilise a well-functioning management system. In doing so, they provide a useful context for the logical flow of the A3.

Second, it's important to be conscious of the fact that this A3 is owned by you. As the organisational leader of your manufacturing facility, you carry the responsibility for the overall strategic direction and performance of your team, and as a consequence it needs to be your name at the top of the page. In my experience, this sends a powerful message to your team. It demonstrates to them that you understand and accept your responsibilities as leader of your facility, and that you own the improvement journey that you're leading.

Third, identifying all of the people who are part of the A3 team, and therefore who are responsible for its creation, and most importantly it's subsequent deployment, is a critical component of ensuring its success. Defining that ownership from the beginning sets clear expectations for everyone involved. It is up to you who you reference here, but I would suggest that as a minimum you include those people who you have invited to the A3 offsite session(s). Remember, whomever you list will become your deployment leaders and will take the lead in delivering the output of your A3 process, so getting this right is crucial.

The *Top-Level Improvement A3* – Context

The first of the six main content panels can seem a little trivial at first glance. Its purpose is for you to provide the 'Context' on which you are presenting your improvement plan story. It sets the scene for everything that follows, and provides useful information that you may well need to be conscious of during the creation and deployment of your Improvement Plan. This could include information that is relevant to your specific facility, or wider organisational considerations. It might also include macro-economic, political, legislative and societal factors that are impacting your operations, as well as trends in local and regional markets that might need to be considered. As a minimum, it serves as an introduction to the story that you are about to tell, and can include a basic description of the nature of your facility and your team. Consider answering questions like…

- What product do you manufacture? Who are your main customers? What volumes do you produce and what turnover do you achieve? How many people do you employ?

- What changes have occurred in your wider organisation? Has the business structure changed? Do you have a new leadership team? Are there new business strategies? Has anything from above triggered your desire for an improvement plan?

- Have there been economic changes that are impacting you? Is currency exchange a problem? Are you impacted by oil price? Is there new legislation that is affecting you? Are there changes in consumer consciousness that are impacting demand for what you manufacture? Has your political landscape changed and is that affecting your business or ability to recruit?

- Importantly, what has triggered your desire to initiate an improvement plan? Has your local leadership team changed? Is your facility under threat? Why have you recognised that workplace happiness and operational performance is poor?

Completing this part of the A3 allows for a useful period of reflection and understanding within your team. I would advise you not to rush this part in the belief that it lacks merit. I often find that it helps to clarify a sense of meaning and value for the participants of the A3 offsite session, and grounds them in understanding why it's important to complete the exercise.

The *Top-Level Improvement A3* – Current State

The second content panel provides the basis for understanding your problems in detail. By completing this panel well, you will be describing 'What to change', and will be starting to form ideas of 'What to change to'.

In the first instance, it provides the opportunity for you to identify where your facility performs well, and where it does not. Here is where you can utilise the data and opinions gathered during your preparation phase, and present the reality of your facility in all its glory. You can list your main performance indicators, include any tables and graphs that may be relevant, and make pointed statements that communicate the opinions of the people in the A3 session. Now is the ideal time to introduce the opinions and thoughts collated from the top-level review that you and your management team have conducted, and to make use of them to encourage debate and healthy conflict in your A3 team. It's important not to shy away from your reality here, whether that is positive or negative. Your wider team is trusting that your integrity and honesty will support their need for change and improvement. On the flip-side, it's also important not to be unnecessarily or even unfairly critical. A balanced view will gain the most credibility.

Secondly, this is where you can start to understand why you experience the performance that you do. What do you and your team believe to be the causes of the problems? What processes are failing or need improvement and why? Are the processes failing, or is it the people (it's usually the processes by the way, but not always)? Which issues are having the biggest impact on operational performance and workplace happiness and need to be addressed first? You may want to utilise some typical root cause analysis tools here, such as Ishikawa/Fishbone diagrams, Cause and effect diagrams, 5-Why diagrams, a SWOT analysis, or Pareto charts. On the other hand, you may not. I often find that for top-level discussions of this nature, the thoughts and instincts of the team are usually accurate enough. Their ideas and feelings, based on their experience and knowledge, will typically lead you in the right direction, particularly if you have the right people on board in the first place. Don't forget, you're only seeking a top-level understanding, and not granular clarity. For example, believing that you 'have weaknesses in your production planning process' which affects your delivery performance, is sufficient at this stage.

This second panel is also the part of the A3 where I would suggest that you encourage the most debate and healthy conflict. Be prepared to spend the bulk of your time on this panel and ensure that all opinions and perspectives are considered. Really thrash it out, because it will make a huge difference to the clarity and effectiveness of your plan moving forward. Furthermore, the panel is likely to be particularly full of information when complete, and you'll need to work hard as a team to summarise it concisely in a way that tells the story clearly. I have sometimes found it useful to include this consolidation process as part of the debate and discussion, it can help to iron out any final disagreements.

The *Top-Level Improvement A3* – Goals/Operating Objectives

The third content panel is one of the smallest, but is absolutely fundamental in underpinning the direction that your improvement journey will take. Here is where you will need to make a small number of bold and specific goal statements that are the basis of 'What to Change to', and which carry throughout your improvement journey as the 'Standard Operating Objectives' of your 'Golden Circle'. These should be measurable targets which become the headlines of your 'What', and which are goals that drive you towards solving the problems that most impact operational performance, workplace happiness, and your ability to implement Lean. You may well have seen them described previously in a variety of different ways, such as 'True North' statements, or as a 'Value Driven Purpose'.

It's therefore crucial to the success of the *Lean Foundations*™ approach that these goal statements become the heart of your improvement journey, and that you commit yourself and your team to debating them with real intent and purpose. By describing the top-level goals that your team will strive towards in their daily interactions, they add significant value to the remainder of the process, and to your very long-term aims of achieving operational excellence through Lean.

There are a few points to bear in mind when defining these 'Standard Operating Objectives'…

- It is imperative that they are primarily focused on adding value for your employees and customers. Therefore, they should always reference the core indicators of Safety, Quality, Delivery, Cost and

Engagement as a priority. Please understand the importance of this point. These goal statements are integral to the success of your facility, and can serve to embed the right focus on customer and people-centred performance that is central in Lean practice and thought. In later steps of the *Lean Foundations™* journey they will be part of daily operations, so signposting them as part of your 'Standard Operating Objectives' is a crucial step. They also ensure that the focus of your team is on improving workplace happiness and operational performance, which is after all our primary ambition on our *Lean Foundations™* journey. Bear in mind that these indicators are the basis of Toyota's drive for operational excellence. If they are good enough for them, they should be good enough for us.

- You may need to consider targets that are cascaded from above in your wider organisation for things such as Revenue and Profitability, perhaps even for things like Net Working Capital/Cashflow or New Product Introduction. If you do, it's a good idea to try and ensure that your 'Standard Operating Objectives' support these requirements, and do so with goal statements that support the core indicators of Safety, Quality, Delivery, Cost and Engagement at the same time.

- The most motivating targets and goals are those that are achievable, but also stretch our abilities. Be careful to make sure that the 'Standard Operating Objectives' are challenging to yourself and your team, without being ridiculous. Again, this will help with the credibility of what you're trying to achieve. It will also drive a performance mentality. Remember, just because we're promoting a psychologically safe environment, does not mean that we're accepting of sloppy or poor performance. Setting challenging 'Standard Operating Objectives' will help to demonstrate this point, and will support the activities that drive performance excellence later in the *Lean Foundations™* approach.

- Be careful not to try and achieve too much improvement at once. I often find that enthusiasm for the process and a desire to get things right means that everything can be targeted to be fixed at the same time. In fact, on every occasion that I've completed such an activity, the team involved has targeted too much too soon, and fallen short. The second and third cycles usually define more pragmatic and realistic expectations. On the other hand, these can be useful learning experiences, so don't feel that you have to hold back too much.

- The statements need to be S.M.A.R.T. or Specific, Measurable, Achievable, Realistic, and Timebound (there are different versions of this anacronym, but any are valid). Simply saying that you want to improve delivery performance is not enough. You need to be able to say by how much, and by when, and to be defining a target that is able to be delivered in the time available.

Agreeing these goals and targets can be tricky. You are going to be asking your team to commit to something that they will be held accountable for and measured against. If they have experienced a negative reaction to failure against commitments of this nature in the past, they may be reluctant to repeat their mistake. This is a strident test of your commitment to psychological safety, and of your willingness to allow failure in the pursuit of success. I would suggest that you do your best to give a clear and sincere assurance that failure to achieve the targets will not result in blame or inappropriate consequences. Instead, criticism and accountability will only be applied if there is a failure to apply effort and attitude.

There is one final point to make here. These 'Standard Operating Objectives' act as place markers on your journey, if you're making progress towards them, then you're making progress in improving workplace happiness and operational performance, and in creating a platform for Lean. They should be precious to you and your team, and should be protected as a result. At the same time, things change. Business pressures and expectations move, and circumstances may result in you needing to adjust your view. If that becomes the case, be prepared to adapt your operating objectives accordingly, albeit reluctantly and as a last resort, otherwise you're likely to damage organisational health and psychological safety unnecessarily.

The *Top-Level Improvement A3* – Improvement Projects

The fourth content panel is where you will finalise your understanding of 'What to Change to', and begin the process of agreeing 'How to change'. It's here that you can list a series of Improvement Projects that your deployment leaders are going to be responsible for delivering. These should aim to meet the goal statements listed in the 'Standard Operating Objectives' panel, and should look to resolve the problems and opportunities identified in the 'Current State' panel. Be aware, this is the '*Top-level Improvement A3*', and we're only looking to agree the basic steps that we're planning to take on our improvement journey at this point. You're going to be challenging your deployment leaders to create their own '*Project-level Improvement A3*' documents in sub-step 3 of the policy deployment process, and this activity will define these Improvement Projects in much greater detail.

For each Improvement Project, it's sensible to consider the following points…

- Identify the deployment leader responsible, in other words, the member of your management or supervisory team who will take the lead in delivering the project in your facility. That person needs to be functionally capable and responsible, and have sufficient authority and gravitas to lead their given project. Also identify which other team members will support.

- Specify the scope of the project. Which process areas are included? Which products or customers? What is its purpose?

- Define a measurable outcome with progress milestones if appropriate. As with the 'Standard Operating Objectives', these targets need to be challenging in order to sustain a performance mentality. Don't be afraid to make them tough, but do your best to make sure they can be delivered and that the deployment leader accepts responsibility for delivering them.

- Be confident that the projects you identify will positively impact operational performance and workplace happiness. Challenge yourself and your team to justify their inclusion and their scope on that basis.

As an example, you might identify an Improvement Project which will '*Review and upgrade the production planning process*'. The deployment leader could be the Operations Manager, and they could be supported by the Planning Supervisor, and Production Supervisors. You may choose to limit the scope to a particular value stream or production cell, and decide that you want to complete the project in order to improve customer delivery performance. You could set a target of a percentage improvement, or choose an absolute value such as 95% of all orders to be shipped on time, with a 1% improvement per month over 12 months. In improving delivery performance, you will be contributing to the overall operational performance of your facility. Less time and energy will be wasted responding to late deliveries, your team will feel a greater sense of success, and your facility may well win respect and appreciation from your customers and your wider organisation.

Exactly which projects you define, how many, who is responsible for them, how they are scoped, and what you hope to achieve with them, is entirely down to you and your team. They will reflect the nature of the problems that your facility faces, and how you decide to resolve them. There are some projects that are very typical, such as the example given above, and others that will be more specific to you and your facility. One important factor is to ensure that you include improvement projects for every functional and value stream area. These projects will form the basis of individual objectives and development plans for your team members. It's therefore important that they are given improvement objectives that are properly integrated into the activities of the whole team.

It's also a good idea to include projects that support the work already delivered as part of the *Lean Foundations™* journey to date, and for the activities that we will discuss ahead. Having an Improvement Project for developing effective teamwork, and for organisation structure development makes sense, and delivering the content of Steps 4 to 8 will consume valuable resources and time, as well as add value to the 'Why and 'How', so it's a good idea to include those activities in your planning process too. To do this, you'll need to carry on reading, and then to try and relate what you learn to the problems that you're experiencing, and to their solutions. Of course, if I've been successful in making the content of those steps worthwhile, that should be fairly easy to achieve.

These Improvement Projects, alongside the 'Standard Operating Objectives' can now finalise the substance of the 'What' of your 'Golden Circle'. In defining your projects, and combining them with your goal statements from content panel three, you're going to be able to agree a final 'What' statement, and to include it with your 'Why' and 'How'. I would suggest that you take the time to discuss and define this statement with your team as part of this content panel. In doing so you will remind them of the wider context in which the A3 exercise is taking place. Your 'Golden Circle' will now be complete, and can be presented alongside the other documents that we will create throughout the remainder of the policy deployment process. And please, don't forget to recognise the significance of that achievement.

The *Top-Level Improvement A3* – Action Plan, and Review & Follow-up

The fifth content panel, 'Action Plan', is difficult to complete with any level of detail at this point in the process. In reality, you need to complete sub-step 3, 'Deploy with Rigor', before you have sufficient information to scope out a basic plan for each of the projects. To begin with, I would advise you to agree the basic milestones of when the projects will start, and when they are likely to conclude. You may also wish to target a milestone for the creation of the '*Project-level Improvement A3*' for each of the Improvement Projects in order to kick them off with real intent.

How you choose to format these actions plans in this content panel is up to you. I would actively promote the use of a basic Gantt chart which shows the timing of each project's main milestones in weekly or monthly buckets. In sub-step 3, I'm going to be encouraging you to use this action plan panel as the tool for oversight of the alignment and inter-connectivity of all the projects, so a format of this nature helps. However, I would advise you not to strive for too much complexity or detail in this plan, otherwise you'll spend a lot of time administrating it, and not much time using it.

As for the sixth content panel, 'Review & Follow-up', it's not for use at this point. However, I have found it useful to explain its purpose to the team in the A3 creation session. It's in this panel that you and your team will record the outcome of the review sessions that will be completed during the deployment phase of the process, and is where you will identify follow-up actions and changes to the plan that respond to any business changes that may impact it. In effect, it's where we will record the 'Check' and 'Act' phases of our PDCA cycle.

Pause for reflection

It's worth taking a short pause to stop, take a breath, and reflect at this point. We've covered a lot of ground and shared a lot of information on how to complete our '*Top-level Improvement A3*'. In completing this exercise, you and your team have achieved a significant milestone on your *Lean Foundations™* journey.

Your A3 should now provide a clear understanding of the context in which we're looking to implement your improvement journey. It can help you to understand the scale and complexity of the problems we need to fix, has defined and agreed your milestone goals or 'Standard Operating Objectives' on the journey, and details the improvement projects that will hopefully deliver the solutions to your problems and enable the improvement that we seek. Importantly, your A3 will hopefully have targeted your Improvement Plan in those areas that need it most, and where the activities will bring the greatest benefit in supporting improvement in operational performance and workplace happiness. You will also have finalised your 'What' statement, and therefore your 'Golden Circle', and will be able to share it alongside your '*Top-level Improvement A3*', and the other documents we're about to produce. Please don't under-estimate the significance of what you have achieved so far, particularly alongside what you have already delivered with your work on effective teamwork and organisation structure. By now, the enthusiasm and energy in your team is likely to be high, and I'm confident that you're already noticing a change in the way your facility is feeling and functioning.

ALIGN WITH THE 'X-MATRIX'

Our second challenge in the policy deployment process is to ensure that your management team is aligned in the delivery of the Improvement Plan. It's likely that the plan that you have documented within your '*Top-level Improvement A3*' is complex, with a great deal of varied and inter-related parts. Each of your team is likely to be responsible for leading the delivery of at least one project, whilst potentially having a supporting role in others. It's therefore important for us to help them to understand those relationship dynamics, and to help your wider team understand them too. Without this guidance, there is a real risk that certain projects will take priority over others, potentially as a result of the strength of personality of some of your team, or simply as a result of circumstance and opportunity. I have found that the relationships between projects can often be critical, and that progress in one is dependent on progress in another. Raising the capability and performance of your whole facility in all the areas you have identified at roughly the same time is a challenge, but is achievable with the right amount of coordination.

In this sub-step, we'll work through a very simple process for the completion of an 'X-Matrix'; the primary tool in a policy deployment process for visualising the inter-connectivity of individual projects within an overall improvement plan. It's an ideal tool for presenting an improvement plan in a way that highlights the inter-relationships between top-level goals and individual improvement projects, for identifying the connections between projects and the performance improvement we're seeking to achieve, and for visualising the shared responsibilities of a cross-functional team in the delivery of that plan. It's deliberately designed to support our desire for alignment and collaboration across both functional and cross-functional teams. For *Lean Foundations™*, the policy deployment process integrates the output of the '*Top-level Improvement A3*' into the creation of the 'X-Matrix', and in doing so supports the rational and hopefully persuasive story-telling of our improvement journey.

The 'X-Matrix' – the format

First of all, don't worry, an 'X-Matrix' is not a complicated tool, and its integration with the '*Top-level Improvement A3*' makes it even more simple to utilise and populate. In effect, an 'X-Matrix' is a one-page document (usually A3 in size), which presents the logical links between layers of organisational strategy and execution. I have witnessed a variety of formats and methods for completion in my varied experiences, with the version included here having evolved from a number of practical applications.

The diagram below shows what the *Lean Foundations™* blank 'X-Matrix' looks like. As you can see, there are five main areas that need to be populated, 'HOW – Defining Objectives', 'WHAT – Operating

Objectives', 'WHAT – Improvement Projects', 'WHAT – KPI's', and 'WHO - Deployment Leaders'. As with the A3, there is a logical direction of travel, both when it is populated, and when it is read, as denoted by the arrows. The grid sections are also populated as part of the 'X-Matrix' exercise, and are filled with markers to identify the linkages between each of the listed elements.

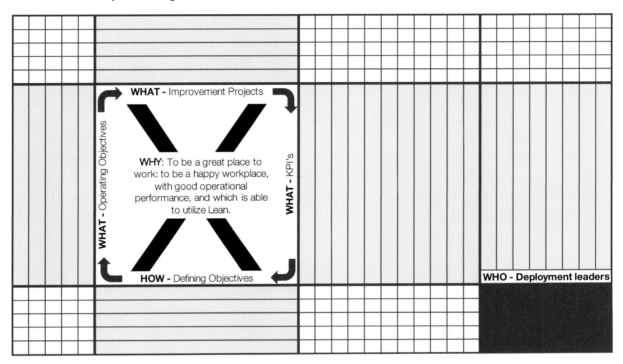

Fig 3-3. The *Lean Foundations*™ 'X-Matrix' - blank

Hopefully you should recognise the common language being used here, and that our 'Why' is clearly presented at the heart of the 'X-Matrix'. Now that we have completed our '*Top-level improvement A3*' we can transfer across the relevant output from each of the A3 content panels in turn.

The 'X-Matrix' – populating from the A3

The process of completing the 'X-Matrix' is one that I usually undertake in the same offsite event as creating the A3. Of course, if you find that time or energy levels are against you, then feel free to adapt your approach as you find appropriate. Four of the five sections of the 'X-Matrix' require a simple read-across from the A3. However, the 'WHAT – KPI's' section will potentially require some further team discussion and debate.

- *'HOW – Defining Objectives'* – This is where you start, and is where you can populate the 'How' statement from our 'Golden Circle' into individual strategic statements such as 'Create a healthy organisation with effective teamwork', or 'Improve engagement with our empowered front-line team members'. Again, I leave the exact wording in this instance to you and your team. The statements need to make sense and add value to you. This is also where you could reference any strategic goals that have been set for you from your wider organisation, such as the requirements for Revenue and Profitability, Net Working Capital/Cashflow or New Product Introduction referred to previously. These are unlikely to just go away, so including them here can make sure everyone in your facility is aware of them, and accepts responsibility for delivering them.

- *'What – Operating Objectives'* – Here is where you can populate the Goal/Operating objectives statements from content panel three of your A3. It's a good idea to keep these statements short and to the point, with the specific measurable performance improvement that you have defined being clearly presented.

- *'What – Improvement Projects'* – Here is where you can list all of the Improvement Projects defined in content panel four of your A3. A small piece of advice here, don't go crazy and define too many projects. Depending on the size and complexity of your facility, and how much of a performance problem it has, I would advise somewhere between ten and twenty projects is manageable, between two and three per deployment leader. If you're going above this level you really do need to have a large enough management team to cope.

- *'What – KPI's'* – Hopefully, when agreeing your Improvement Projects in the A3 session, you will have taken my advice and will have defined a measurable outcome for each project. If so, this is where you can list those measurable outcomes in the form of a Key Performance Indicator. Later in the *Lean Foundations*™ journey, you'll be using these KPI's to support daily management processes. This is therefore a good opportunity to really clarify the details of the KPI's you're going to use. You can name the KPI, define how it is measured, define the target level to achieve, and by when if it is timebound. For example, the KPI could be On-time Delivery performance, measured through the percentage of order lines which you failed to dispatch on the day they were committed, and with a target of 95% to be achieved by the end of the year. You may find that in completing this section of the 'X-Matrix', not all of the KPI's that your wider organisation requires are being included for improvement within your projects. I know this may sound a little strange, but it's quite possible that your priorities on the *Lean Foundations*™ journey are slightly different than those of your wider organisation. In order to make sure you're covering these areas it's a good idea to include these additional KPI's, and to try and correlate them to individual improvement projects as best as you can. It's good practice to try and ensure that your policy deployment exercise is comprehensive in covering all of the activities that you need to complete. If you're working on something that is not on your *'Top-level Improvement A3'* and 'X-Matrix', then either you're working on the wrong thing, or your plans aren't as comprehensive as they could be. A final comment here, as with the definition of the 'Standard Operating Objectives' in content panel three of the A3, and the measurable outcomes of the Improvement Projects from content panel four, it's important that the targets that you define for your KPI's are challenging. I know this is something of a repetition, but if you wish to embed a performance culture that compliments the psychologically safe environment you're creating, this is a really good way to support it.

- *'WHO – Deployment Leaders'* – Here is where you can identify your deployment leaders selected in content panel four of your A3. I would always advise that you also include yourself, even if you do not have a specific project to lead (although if you have taken my advice and defined projects that support Step's 1 and 2, you're likely to be responsible for at least two projects). In doing so, you'll be able to demonstrate your willingness and responsibility to support all of the projects listed when we complete the correlation activities.

On completing all of those steps, you are now half-way to having a complete 'X-Matrix' which displays your *'Top-Level Improvement A3'* in a neat and concise way. It should look something like the example below. I've populated this with some deliberately over-simplified ideas for each part of the 'X-Matrix'. No doubt yours will be much more substantial. All that remains is to identify the links between each of the elements.

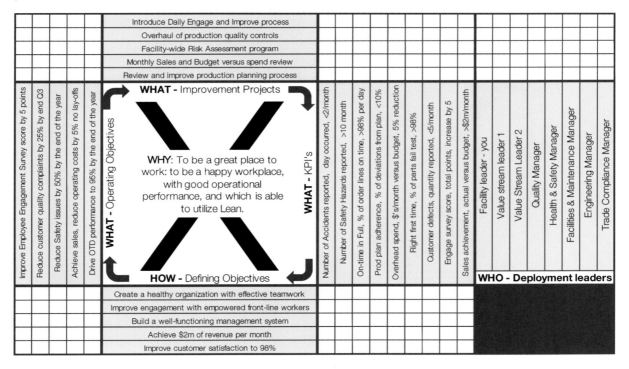

Fig 3-4. The *Lean Foundations™* 'X-Matrix' – partially populated

The 'X-Matrix' - joining the dots

It's in identifying the correlations between each of the elements that the value of the 'X-Matrix' really comes to the fore. Remember, we're trying to support alignment between your varied functional and value stream team members, and we're trying to enable them to complete their overlapping and inter-connected improvement projects collaboratively. We also want to be able to communicate a persuasive story, and to do this we need to be able to highlight the logical links between our top-level goals and Improvement Projects, the Improvement Projects and how we expect them to deliver performance improvements, and the performance improvements and how we expect them to support our top-level goals. It's a circular relationship, and the identification of the correlation between each element is what helps to demonstrate that fact.

In reading the various materials available on the subject of Hoshin Kanri, I've seen a number of different approaches to the process of populating these correlations. Some suggest that only direct correlations between elements are identified, others suggest that two, three or even four layers of correlation are identified. Here, in *Lean Foundations™*, we'll keep things simple and suggest that you identify just two layers of correlation: where there is a direct relationship between elements, and where there is a support relationship.

Top section — WHAT: Improvement Projects

Operating Objectives (left, column order):
1. Improve Employee Engagement Survey score by 5 points
2. Reduce customer quality complaints by 25% by end Q3
3. Reduce Safety issues by 50% by the end of the year
4. Achieve sales, reduce operating costs by 5% no lay-offs
5. Drive OTD performance to 95% by the end of the year

KPI's (column order):
1. Number of Accidents reported, day occurred, <2/month
2. Number of Safety Hazards reported, >10 month
3. On-time in Full, % of order lines on time, >98% per day
4. Prod plan adherence, % of deviations from plan, <10%
5. Overhead spend, $'s/month versus budget, 5% reduction
6. Right first time, % of parts fail test, >98%
7. Customer defects, quantity reported, <5/month
8. Engage survey score, total points, increase by 5
9. Sales achievement, actual versus budget, >$2m/month

WHO – Deployment leaders (column order):
1. Facility leader - you
2. Value Stream Leader 1
3. Value Stream Leader 2
4. Quality Manager
5. Health & Safety Manager
6. Facilities & Maintenance Manager
7. Engineering Manager
8. Trade Compliance Manager

Centre of the 'X-Matrix':

WHAT - Improvement Projects

WHAT - Operating Objectives

WHAT - KPI's

HOW - Defining Objectives

WHY: To be a great place to work: to be a happy workplace, with good operational performance, and which is able to utilize Lean.

Improvement Projects (top rows):

Operating Objectives					Improvement Project	KPI's									WHO – Deployment leaders							
●	▲	▲	▲	▲	Introduce Daily Engage and Improve process								●		▲	●	●	▲	▲	▲	▲	▲
▲	●		▲		Overhaul of production quality controls						●	●			▲	▲	▲	●	▲	▲	▲	▲
▲		●			Facility-wide Risk Assessment program	●	●						▲		▲	▲	▲	▲	●	▲	▲	▲
▲			●		Monthly Sales and Budget versus spend review					●	▲			●	●	▲	▲	▲	▲	▲	▲	▲
▲			▲	●	Review and improve production planning process			●	●	▲					▲	●	●	▲	▲	▲	▲	▲

Defining Objectives (bottom rows):

Operating Objectives					Defining Objective	KPI's								
●	▲	▲	▲	▲	Create a healthy organization with effective teamwork	●	●	●	●	●	●	●	●	●
●					Improve engagement with empowered front-line workers	▲	▲	▲	▲	▲	▲	▲	▲	▲
	●	●	●	●	Build a well-functioning management system	●	●	●	●	●	●	●	●	●
			●	▲	Achieve $2m of revenue per month			●						●
	●		▲	●	Improve customer satisfaction to 98%			●	▲		▲	●		●

Fig 3-5. The *Lean Foundations™* 'X-Matrix' – complete

Now, you can finalise your 'X-Matrix' with an enjoyable and sometimes heated debate with your team to agree the relationships between each of the elements. Starting with the links between 'HOW – Defining Objectives' and 'WHAT – Operating Objectives', and then moving around the 'X-Matrix' in a clockwise direction, you can debate how each of the elements listed under the headings are related, and whether or not their relationship is direct, or support. Take a look at the completed example above to get an idea of what your 'X-Matrix' should start to look like, the circles denote the direct relationship, and the triangles the support.

You can identify each relationship with a different symbol, perhaps a solid circle for a direct relationship, and an open triangle or square for a support relationship. Of course, the format of the symbols is not too important, but the nature of the debate and discussion that the exercise encourages is. You can identify which of your 'WHAT – Operating Objectives' are linked to your 'WHAT – Improvement Projects', and which of your 'WHAT - Improvement Projects' will influence your 'WHAT – KPI's'. You can also use the same symbols to denote the ownership of each of the 'WHAT - Improvement Projects' to their 'WHO - Deployment Leaders', and to identify where deployment leaders will act as a support for others in the completion of their improvement projects. Finally, and importantly, you can identify the relationship between improvements in your 'WHAT – KPI's', and your 'HOW – Defining Objectives'.

Once complete, you will have travelled full circle, and will have drawn your 'X-Matrix' together. It will now visualise how the logical and reasoned output of your '*Top-level Improvement A3*' will meet your desire to build a healthy organisation with effective teamwork, to engage with empowered front-line team members, and to build and utilise a well-functioning management system. The 'X-Matrix' helps to bring the variety and complexity of your top-level Improvement Plan into clarity, and in the process can help your team to understand how their individual responsibilities and activities are related to the whole, and to each other. It enables and encourages alignment across your varied functions and cross-functional teams, and makes your desire for collaboration and effective teamwork abundantly clear. All that remains now is to deploy your plan in such a way that it actually delivers the results you anticipate.

DEPLOY WITH RIGOR

Our third and final challenge in the policy deployment process is to ensure that all of the work undertaken in creating your fantastic '*Top-level Improvement A3*' and 'X-Matrix' does not go to waste. The plan that you and your team have developed is likely to be complex, with a considerable number of inter-related activities that require committed and dedicated application to achieve. It's all too easy for day to day challenges to get in the way of the execution of a plan of this nature. No doubt your available resources are limited and stretched, and in the manufacturing world time is always in short supply. On the flip-side, it's also important that your plan is flexible, and is able to evolve in response to changes in demands and pressures on your resources and time. Organisational expectations and needs do change, and the plan that you have agreed today may well need to look somewhat different in three, six, or nine months' time. Also, it's likely that you and your team will learn of new problems, or develop new perspectives on which problems are the most critical, or on which solutions will offer the most benefit. It was Dwight D. Eisenhower who famously said "*… Plans are worthless. Planning is everything…*", and who are we to argue? We therefore need to be able to utilise a methodology which supports the effective deployment of the Improvement Plan that you and your team have created, and to do so in a way that allows the plan to remain flexible and to respond to change.

In this third and final sub-step, we'll work through a process which will enable the effective deployment of your Improvement Plan, utilising the A3 format described previously, but this time for use by your deployment leaders as a '*Project-level Improvement A3*'. You are now likely to have a clear understanding of the power of the A3 process; and how it's proper application can help us to understand a problem and its causes, to define an effective solution, and to derive a plan for the delivery of that solution. When we utilise this A3 process at the project-level, and combine it with a disciplined and routine review process, we have a powerful mechanism for ensuring that our top-level plan, and the individual project-level plans, are managed and delivered with passion and rigor. At the same time, we can imbue every deployment leader, and their team, with the authority and responsibility for adjusting their plan intelligently in response to changes in circumstance, whilst still delivering on the framework of the overall plan. In doing so, we can realise significant benefits to their intrinsic motivator of autonomy and accountability, whilst ensuring that we maintain the benefits to the motivator of success and improvement.

Cascade the Plan – feedback loop 2

The first activity within this sub-step is the most straightforward, but I would suggest adds disproportionately positive value to your team. I'm sure you remember the Town Hall brief that I proposed that you complete in Step 1 of our journey, and, if you completed it, I hope you recognise the benefits in psychological safety and organisational health that were gained as a consequence. Well, I suggest that it's time to repeat this exercise, this time as a means of cascading both the '*Top-level Improvement A3*' and the 'X-Matrix' to your entire team.

As before, exactly how you choose to complete this is up to you, but I would strongly suggest that you consider sharing these two documents with every one of your team members in this forum. In doing so you can ensure that they are cascaded with consistency, and that they are presented with the enthusiasm and passion that only you can deliver. You have a fantastic opportunity to share the plan that your team has developed, and to demonstrate that it has comprehensively considered as many of your facilities problems and opportunities as possible. It also presents an ideal opportunity to solicit a second round of feedback; to open up the briefing session to a round of healthy debate and perhaps even conflict if appropriate, and to adjust the plan where it's sensible to do so. For this reason, it's sometimes worth cascading your plan through a number of smaller group sessions rather than one large session where people can feel self-conscious and therefore don't speak up. Sharing the PDCA/TOC thinking process as a mental model can help to introduce your desire for feedback, and to give people the confidence to contribute to the discussion. Importantly, you can also communicate how this plan will be delivered, and that each team member will be actively involved through the completion of a *'Project-level Improvement A3'*. Once communicated to your team, you can choose to publish both the A3 and 'X-Matrix', presenting it on noticeboards throughout your facility as appropriate.

In sharing your plan in this manner, the positive impact on your team can be dramatic. All of their intrinsic motivators can benefit greatly; with their sense of improvement and success excited by the opportunities the plan presents, their sense of autonomy and accountability improved because of how they will be involved, their sense of purpose enhanced by the simple fact that a plan exists, and their desire for collaboration improved because they can recognise their role alongside their colleagues and team members. Their psychological safety can also be enriched because they feel involved and engaged in the process. They are likely to feel that their opinions have value, that they are trusted to contribute and participate, and that they can be challenged whilst being supported. In completing an exercise of this nature, I have rarely experienced a negative outcome or perspective. It's quite normal for people to leave excited and enthused by what the plan represents, particularly when following the work on organisational health, teamwork, and organisation structure that has preceded it.

The *'Project-level Improvement A3'* – feedback loop 3

Having completed your *'Top-level Improvement A3'*, you will have identified a number of improvement projects, and in the process will have defined the deployment leaders and measurable outcomes of those Improvement Projects. It's now time for your deployment leaders to rally their own teams, and to complete their own A3 exercises to populate a *'Project-level Improvement A3'*. In cascading responsibility and ownership in this way, you can once again seriously enhance the intrinsic motivators and psychological safety of your team. Exactly as with the cascade of the plan in the Town Hall brief, you're going to encourage senses of trust and accountability, you're presenting the opportunity for success and improvement, you're providing a purpose, and you're encouraging collaboration.

The format and process of completion can be exactly the same as before, although this time I would advise that your role is only to coach and support from afar. For the individual *'Project-level Improvement A3's'*, it's the deployment leaders who are identified as the 'Owner'; it's for them to decide who needs to be part of their 'Team', and their 'Focus' is pre-determined by the title and measurables of the Improvement Project they are tasked with leading. They can lead an exercise for completion of the A3 exactly as you did, following the same guidelines and utilising the same PDCA/TOC thinking processes. As a result, they can identify the nature of their problem, what they believe causes it, what their goals are to solve it, what activities they intend to undertake towards solving it, and can plan how they intend to deliver those activities. The creation of the *'Project-level Improvement A3'* also acts as the third feedback loop in your policy deployment cycle. It cascades clear ownership and accountability to the deployment leaders and their team members, and provides them with an opportunity to shape the direction of the plan as they work to understand and resolve their part of it. In introducing the PDCA/TOC thinking processes through your deployment leaders, you can ensure that your plan is being verified and validated by your team members, and hopefully also encourage the use of those thinking processes in day to day problem resolution.

For you, initially it's a good idea to act as coach and advisor to the deployment leaders in the completion of their individual A3's. You can review it with them once populated and ask simple questions. Is the A3 comprehensive? Does it tell a persuasive story? Do you believe that the problem has been properly defined and understood? Are all the potential causes considered and being addressed? Are the goals achievable and challenging all at the same time? Do the proposed activities properly address the problems? Is the action plan sensibly constructed with clear milestones and responsibilities? Again, I would advise that each 'Project-level Improvement A3' does not need to be an in-depth interrogation and analysis of a problem, as you might find with tools such as an 8D or Practical Problem-Solving sheet. We will explore tools such as these a little later in *Lean Foundations™*, but for now I would suggest that you only need a higher-level analysis of the subject of your improvement projects. Of course, if your team feel the need to utilise more in-depth analysis tools, and have the knowledge and skillset to do so, I would not discourage it. This is their project, and it's a good idea to give them the freedom to deliver in the way they consider to be most effective. However, for Improvement Projects of this nature, I have often found that team members will have a good instinct and intuition for what is wrong, and what needs to be done about it. I've have rarely needed to deep dive into this kind of top-level problem as a result.

It is possible that you may find that the process of completing an A3 document can be a challenge for some, and that people may need a number of attempts before it becomes a truly useful tool for them to use. This, of course, applies to you just as much as it does your deployment leaders. I would encourage you to remain patient as you develop your own skills and those of your team, and persist with the application of the tool. I know from experience how valuable it can be.

Once you're satisfied that each 'Project-level Improvement A3' is populated to the right standard, and that your deployment leaders and their teams have a clear plan that is achievable, you can translate the major milestones to the plan section of your 'Top-level Improvement A3'. In doing so, you facilitate the next activity.

The Monthly review – ongoing feedback

Having communicated the plan to your whole team, and having cascaded the responsibility for delivery of it to your deployment leaders, you might consider the management of the execution and flexibility of your plan to be more difficult. In fact, I usually find it to be much more straightforward. The sense of ownership and accountability that you will have imbued within your team can serve to drive the delivery of the Improvement Plan, almost as if it were driving itself. The passionate enthusiasm of your team, fuelled by the fact that you have the right people on board, can often mean that your role becomes more and more that of a coordinator, coach, or advisor. And, I have found that creating a formal forum for you to function in this role can provide a very effective mechanism for you to have oversight of the effective deployment of your plan, and to enable that plan to adapt to changes as required.

By completing a routine top-level review of the individual '*Project-level Improvement A3's*' with your team of deployment leaders on a monthly basis, you can achieve a number of benefits. First, your deployment leaders will be aware of the monthly review, and will be keen to report progress on their individual plan, thus driving progress on the overall plan. Second, you can understand the challenges that your deployment leaders face in delivering their plans, and can support them in their decision-making processes to recover or adjust their plan accordingly. Third, your deployment leaders can share the status of their plans with each other, and can call on one another for support if necessary, encouraging management level teamwork in the process. Fourth, you can discuss any new priorities or considerations with your deployment leaders in the review, and can adjust the project-level and top-level plans accordingly. Finally, a discussion of this nature is likely to offer significant benefits to the intrinsic motivators and psychological safety of your deployment leaders. In trusting and engaging with them to lead their own projects, and to share the status of those projects with their peers, you can deliberately enhance their senses of purpose, accountability, improvement and collaboration. You might think 'not another meeting', but this can be a meeting with real purpose and which is filled with real drama, and is likely to be a meeting that you and your deployment leaders find extremely valuable. At the same time, your wider team members will experience a ripple of benefit from the fact that the top-level plan is relevant and 'live', and that their inter-connected project-level plans are aligned.

It's the completion of this monthly review that allows you to update content panel five, and populate content panel six on your '*Top-level Improvement A3*'. A really good way to do this is to report the status of your project through the most up to date performance of your goal statements or 'Standard Operating Objectives'. Remember, these goal statements act as markers on your journey, if you're on course to deliver them individually, you should be on course to meet your ambition to improve workplace happiness, operational performance, and your ability to implement Lean. Another option is to present the status of your main KPI's for the same reason. If these are demonstrating an improvement in performance, then you're likely to be on the right track. If not, perhaps you need to consider the activities you've agreed, and whether or not they're the right ones. The 'Check' and 'Act' steps of the PDCA/TOC thinking processes are what keep you moving in the right direction, and ensure you're able to change course when needed. Please don't under-estimate their value.

Embed into Personal Objectives

A final option for the deployment of your plan is to include the detail of the project-level objectives into the personal objectives of your deployment leaders and their team members. Most organisations complete an annual 'Performance Appraisal' process, and as part of that process individuals can be given performance objectives to achieve. I've often witnessed that these objectives can be somewhat under-whelming, and offer little value to the organisation as a whole. They can become nothing more than a box-ticking exercise for managers who have lost faith in the performance review process, or simply cannot be bothered.

However, if those objectives are sensibly aligned to the top-level Improvement Plan, through objectives derived from the project-level Improvement Plans, then they can be somewhat more relevant and topical, and can serve to embed the improvement objectives into the success criteria of every individual. Of course, they need to be relevant to each person. There is no point giving a production operative the objective of improving plant delivery performance for example. But perhaps they could be given the objective of following the production plan at all times, which could contribute to improving delivery performance.

I have found that giving personal objectives in this manner boosts the enthusiasm and passion for the Improvement Plan even further. As we know, one of our intrinsic motivators is success and improvement, and another is working with purpose; if we're given an achievable but challenging objective that contributes to the good of the whole facility, and towards our 'Why' and 'How', then our motivations can be magnified and utilised to even greater effect. One minor note of caution here, it's important to ensure that any changes in your plan are properly reflected in changes to personal objectives. There is no point assessing an individual's delivery of their personal goals if the Improvement Project they were working on is dramatically changed or even moth-balled as a result of business changes that are outside of their control.

STEP 3 SUMMARY

In following Step 3 to create and deploy your Improvement Plan, your facility should no longer be 'plodding-along'. Instead, your facility may well be 'firing on all cylinders', and 'cooking on gas' all at the same time. Hopefully you now have in place a detailed Improvement Plan, which is targeted to solve the problems that most impact workplace happiness, operational performance, and your ability to implement Lean. And, hopefully you also have a process in place for maintaining the alignment and effective execution of that plan. You've taken a major step forward in enabling your facility to perform well, and in building the foundations upon which operational excellence thrives. Before we summarise the main elements of Step 3, there are a couple of final points to make.

First, the *Lean Foundations™* policy deployment system is by no means the most detailed and intensive that you might find if you read some alternative publications. If you take a look at '*Getting the right things done*' by Pascal Dennis, '*Hoshin Kanri for the Lean Enterprise*' by Thomas Jackson, '*Understanding A3*

Thinking' by Durward Sobek & Art Smalley, or '*Managing to Learn*' by John Shook, you're going to find a much more in-depth processes described. However, this is not an accident, it's quite deliberate. Remember, we're only trying to build the foundations for excellence here, and are not trying to apply full blown Lean methodologies. A fully developed policy deployment process is intensive, and in my experience requires a level of capability and experience, as well as an amount of time and energy, that most manufacturing facilities would struggle to provide. The *Lean Foundations™* policy deployment system is therefore defined in a such a way that we experience the benefits whilst not over-stretching our capabilities and resources. At the same time, it can support an evolution towards a more intensive and thorough application in the future by introducing concepts, mental models and tools that are relevant.

Second, what is described here in Step 3 is only one cycle of the policy deployment system. To fulfil the potential of the *Lean Foundations™* approach to policy deployment, it's possible that you will need at least two or three cycles before your performance is stable enough to attempt the implementation of a facility-wide Lean programme. Those cycles are usually annual, and are often aligned with budget-setting processes that are cascaded by your wider organisation. And yes, this does mean that a full implementation of *Lean Foundations™* can take two or three years. This doesn't mean that you have to wait this long to start to utilise more typical *Lean Basics* tools and systems such as JIT flow and pull, Jidoka, or Kanban. It just means that you only introduce those elements as you're ready to do so, and as your Improvement Plan requires it.

To close Step 3, let's take a moment to quickly review the main points.

- An Improvement Plan can add real impetus to a facility and can act as the heartbeat to our *Lean Foundations™* journey. Without it we risk just 'plodding along'.

- Sometimes facilities are unsuccessful with their plan because it doesn't solve the right problems, or the team are not aligned in the execution of the plan, or the complexity of the plan makes it difficult to manage.

- Policy deployment is a system that facilitates the creation and execution of an Improvement Plan. It ensures that the plan is successful by involving everyone in the decision-making process, creating alignment, and focusing on effective deployment.

- By completing a '*Top-level Improvement A3*', we can involve the ideas and opinions of all team members, and can ensure that we are creating a plan which solves the problems most relevant to improving operational performance, workplace happiness, and enabling the implementation of Lean.

- By translating the content of the A3 into an 'X-Matrix', we can visualise the inter-connectivity of the detail within the Improvement Plan, and we can create alignment between everyone involved.

- We can deploy the plan effectively by communicating its substance through a Town Hall brief, by cascading responsibility to deployment leaders through the completion of '*Project-level Improvement A3's*', by reviewing the status of those project-level A3's every month, and by integrating the objectives of the plan into the personal objectives of every team member.

STEP

4

Infuse with
leadership
that
empowers

Early in my management experience, I succumbed to the fairly typical trappings of managers and leaders of organisations of all types, and I told people what to do. I instinctively believed, no doubt through a wide range of sub-conscious influences, that as a manager it was my job to instruct and inform, to make decisions and to get others to act, and to be the driving force that pushed my area of responsibility forward. My intuition for command and control micro-management meant that I found my role far from fulfilling, and I'm certain that it had the same effect for those who reported to me. As I progressed, my responsibilities grew, and my management approach began to fail. I could no longer be in enough places at once to make the right decisions, and wondered why my team were incapable of making decisions for themselves. I couldn't see that my actions drove the indecision in theirs, and that my inability to trust them meant that they no longer trusted themselves.

And then, one day, I saw it, and I decided to change. I realised that I couldn't do everything myself, and that the success of the operational function or facility that I was leading was only achievable through the combined efforts of everyone in my team. Most importantly, I recognised that the people I worked with were unhappy, and came to work every day with genuine reluctance. In some cases, their focus was to do as little work as possible, rather than to achieve as much as they could. My approach constrained them; it restricted their desire for autonomy, and damaged their sense of ownership and accountability. And so, I started to learn, to read the books and articles that I have already referred to, and more that I will refer to later. I tried to adjust my approach, and failed, and then tried again. I sought to find a way to lead a team so that they experienced greater satisfaction from their work, and which enabled my ability to manage my diverse responsibilities at the same time. And that's when I learned about empowerment. I realised that there was a way to lead so that the success of the facility that I was responsible for depended upon my ability to support my team, rather than on their ability to support me. Today, I have evolved my leadership style to something very different, towards a more empowering approach, and I continue to learn and evolve that style, 20+ years later.

A manufacturing facility is a hugely diverse organism, with a great network of inter-connecting components that almost seems to live and breathe independently at times. In such a place, I have learned that the successful delivery of day to day responsibilities, alongside the implementation of an improvement journey like *Lean Foundations™*, cannot be achieved through the efforts of one person alone. And whilst micro-management has its time and place, and can, through sheer force of will, make a difference, it certainly isn't going to deliver the kind of sustained benefits to workplace happiness and operational performance that we're hoping to achieve. That kind of change requires a movement of people; the combined effort of many towards a shared passion for something better. That does not mean that leadership and management are irrelevant. Quite the contrary. They are absolutely critical. But it's the style of leadership and management that is important. The wrong kind of leadership; the kind that micro-manages and commands and controls, can strangle and suppress an organisation and its people. It can reduce our daily interactions and motivations to nothing more than a transactional process where we exchange financial reward for the repetitious completion of a task. On the flip-side, the right kind of leadership; the kind that empowers and engages, can inspire and motivate us to new heights. It can fuel our creativity and enthuse us to achieve more than we ever thought possible, both individually and alongside others as part of a collective movement for change.

We're now three steps down on our *Lean Foundations*™ journey, with five to go. We have embraced the importance of effective teamwork, and continue to nurture it with organisational health and psychological safety. We have ensured that our team is on-board with the change process that we have initiated, having achieved their buy-in to our 'Golden Circle', and in particular to our 'Why' and 'How'. We have introduced an organisation structure that actively enables teamwork, and which is populated with the right people to make it work. We've also developed and deployed a thorough and specifically targeted Improvement Plan which has finalised the 'What' of our 'Golden Circle', and which provides the heartbeat of our improvement journey moving forward. Now, the confidence and enthusiasm of your team may well be high. They are likely to be looking to the future of your facility with great anticipation and excitement, and may be daring to hope that the potential that you have described may actually come true.

At this point, the opportunities before you are precariously balanced, and the way that your team are led, and lead themselves, is crucial. If they are led poorly; if they are told what to do and when, are given no freedom to express their opinions and thoughts, and are restricted in their ability to make decisions and solve problems, then their enthusiasm could be crushed and your *Lean Foundations*™ journey may well falter. Their ability to deliver on their day to day responsibilities, whilst supporting the Improvement Plan, will be constrained. Their psychological safety and senses of fairness, trust and self-esteem could be damaged, and their intrinsic motivator of autonomy may be negatively impacted. However, if you can lead your team well; if you can meet the second part of your 'How' and empower your front-line team members so that they can make their own decisions and choices, can coach and advise them on how to make those choices, and can support them with time, energy and resources in doing so, then their enthusiasm may well flourish and is likely to drive your *Lean Foundations*™ journey onwards. You will have been able to introduce an essential feature of a facility that performs well, and of the foundations upon which operational excellence is built. Your team will be able to find a way to balance their daily responsibilities with their desire to drive improvement, and their senses of trust and self-esteem will grow alongside their intrinsic motivators of autonomy and improvement.

The question therefore, seems simple. How do we ensure that we lead well; in a way that empowers our front-line team members to fulfil their potential, and which at the same time fuels our ambition for improved operational performance, workplace happiness, and the ability to implement Lean? And how do we infuse that leadership into the daily routines of our facility; into our management and supervisory teams and their day to day interactions with their team? Unfortunately, finding the answers to these questions is not as straightforward as it might at first appear. Through my own process of learning, I have achieved a degree of understanding and have developed a leadership approach which, so far, appears to be working (fingers crossed). This understanding of what leadership that empowers looks like, and how to introduce it into a manufacturing facility, therefore forms the basis of what I will share here, and is what we will work through in just two sub-steps: 'Learning to empower', and 'Integrate empowerment'. I do not promise to offer unrivalled insights that will change leadership thinking; I simply intend to share my appreciation of what I consider to be relevant perspectives, and to draw them together in a way that I hope will make sense and add value to you as they have to me. Wish me luck.

LEARNING TO EMPOWER

Our first challenge when seeking to infuse leadership that empowers into our *Lean Foundations™* journey is to try to understand what it looks like, and how to do it. We know that leading our team well, and managing the diversity of our day to day responsibilities alongside our Improvement Plan, requires us to empower our people with the authority to meet their responsibilities themselves. We know that we're going to need to delegate ownership of decision-making and problem solving throughout our organisation, and in the process are seeking to deliver significant benefits to the psychological safety of our team and their intrinsic motivator of autonomy and accountability. But how does this manifest itself, and what behaviours are typical of a leader that empowers?

Understanding this is not as easy as it might seem. The sheer volume of published material on the subject of leadership is vast and hugely varied in the perspectives they present. Add into the mix the idea of empowerment, and the plethora of books and articles is impossible to quantify, never mind summarise. I have by no means read everything that is available, and may well be missing a valuable point of view as a consequence. But, in my learning journey, I have endeavoured to read and practice as widely as is feasible for me. And, as with earlier parts of this book, this first sub-step aims to present a short summary of the material that I consider to be the most valuable and informative on the subject of leadership, and how to use it to empower. It will conclude with the summary of a leadership approach which is centred around the concept of empowerment, and which is advocated by *Lean Foundations™* approach as a result.

Six styles of leadership

In 2000, Daniel Goleman, author of the inspirational book '*Emotional Intelligence*', wrote an article that was published in the Harvard Business Review entitled '*Leadership that Gets Results*'. In this article, Goleman describes six different styles of leadership derived from the extensive research of nearly 4000 senior executives and business leaders: 'Coercive', 'Authoritative', 'Affiliative', 'Democratic', 'Pacesetting', and 'Coaching'. He argues that each of these styles can be characterised by different traits, and that each can have varying impacts on six drivers of organisational climate or culture. These drivers are defined as flexibility (a willingness to make decisions independently), responsibility (taking ownership), standards (expected performance), rewards (workplace happiness), clarity (understanding direction and purpose), and commitment (engagement with the organisation), and are 'scored' by the research for each leadership style in order to provide quantifiable data. Let's take a look at each style in turn.

- *The coercive style* - Is defined as the command and control 'Do as I say' approach, where people are instructed on what to do, when to do it, and how. The research demonstrates that this style is generally an inhibitor of flexibility and responsibility because independent decision-making and ownership are restricted, with it scoring a negative -0.26 for overall impact on organisational climate. It can damage intrinsic motivation by undermining autonomy and accountability, and by restricting a desire for success and improvement.

- *The authoritative style* – Is defined as the 'Come with me approach', where people are guided towards a common goal or purpose, but are also given the freedom to deliver that goal as they see fit. The research suggests that this style particularly encourages flexibility and rewards because the ability of the team to make decisions and act independently is dramatically improved, with it scoring a very positive 0.54 for overall impact on organisational climate. It can provide benefits to intrinsic motivators such as purpose, autonomy, and success.

- *The affiliative style* – Is described as the 'People come first' approach, where the happiness and harmony of employees is the first consideration. This style is a positive contributor to rewards, clarity and commitment because contribution and performance are recognised, with it scoring a positive 0.46 for overall impact on organisational climate. It can positively impact psychological safety through a heightened sense of trust, security, self-esteem and fairness.

- *The democratic style* – Can be summarised as 'An equal voice approach', where all team members are given the opportunity to contribute to discussions and decision-making. This style is a positive contributor to rewards and clarity because individuals are involved and their opinions matter, with it scoring a positive 0.43 for overall impact on organisational climate. It can benefit psychological safety by building trust and a sense of responsibility and ownership.

- *The pacesetting style* – Can be described as the 'Follow the high standard' approach, where a leader sets high performance standards and challenges their employees to keep up. This style is a negative contributor to standards, rewards and clarity as team members may feel overwhelmed and unable to meet the exacting standards, with it scoring a negative -0.25 for overall impact on organisational climate. It can negatively impact psychological safety, with people feeling that their self-esteem and security is threatened, and their intrinsic motivator of success and improvement damaged.

- *The coaching style* – Can be defined as the 'Support each individual' approach, where a leader is focused on developing the capabilities and skills of every person on their team, rather than the specific results of a work-related task. This style is considered to be a positive contributor to standards, rewards and clarity because team members feel supported in their personal development and establish positive relationships, with it scoring a positive 0.42 for overall impact on organisational climate. The independence and autonomy of decision making is improved, because team members feel that any failures will be managed appropriately, and as a consequence their senses of trust and self-esteem benefit, along with their intrinsic motivators of autonomy and collaboration.

Interestingly, the research highlights a clear and positive correlation between the cultural performance of an organisation and its financial performance. It declares that the most effective leaders, with the highest performing organisations, are those who are able to appropriately utilise as many of the six styles as possible, and can adapt their leadership style to the particular needs of any given situation and circumstance. Goleman notes that *"… leaders who have mastered four or more – especially the authoritative, democratic, affiliative, and coaching styles – have the very best climate and business performance…"*.

Hopefully you can recognise that the drivers of organisational climate referred to in the research are strongly related to the intrinsic motivators and senses of psychological safety that we've been referring to throughout our *Lean Foundations™* journey. Whilst terms such as flexibility, rewards, clarity and responsibility are slightly different; their meanings of autonomy, motivation, purpose and ownership are similar. And hopefully, you can also recognise that the behaviours that I have been encouraging in previous Steps are representative of some of the leadership styles that Goleman defines. In our discussions around organisational health and psychological safety, we have effectively been discussing how to present an 'Affiliative' leadership style. We've sought to focus on the happiness of our employees and the harmony with their colleagues and teammates through the promotion of a psychologically safe environment. In our discussions around the creation of the Improvement Plan, we have been presenting a 'Democratic' leadership style. We have sought to involve the opinions and ideas of our team in the various feedback loops of our deployment process. When we have discussed the inclusion of elements of target-setting and the creation of a performance driven mentality, we have demonstrated a 'Pacesetting' leadership style, but have sought to temper the potential negative impacts of this style with our considerations around psychological safety and organisational health. And finally, in defining our 'Golden Circle' and our Improvement Plan, we have provided the basis of the 'Authoritative' style. We've established the basic framework within which we hope to encourage our team to express themselves.

It seems clear that Goleman's perspective is relevant in our search for the right way to lead in order to empower. There are obvious synergies with the 'Coercive' style and my early leadership experiences. It's this practice that I succumbed to, and which was clearly damaging to the organisational culture that I was responsible for, never mind being impractical for managing the complex and varied responsibilities of the manufacturing facility that I was trying to improve. However, in contrast, it seems that in combining the 'Coaching' style of leadership with the 'Authoritative', 'Affiliative' and 'Democratic' styles already established within our working practices, we can access a leadership style which will support our aims. The approach described in each style is based on a need to respect and appreciate the capabilities and feelings of every individual, and as a consequence they align with our already well-established leadership ideals from other elements of *Lean Foundations™*. Furthermore, the 'Authoritative' style in particular is focused on enabling and supporting people to accept and meet their responsibilities within a pre-defined framework, and therefore clearly supports our desire for empowerment. By combining these four styles of leadership, Goleman suggests that we can deliver the most benefit to the six drivers of organisational culture, and can therefore deliver on our ambition to empower our front-line team members in order to improve operational performance, workplace happiness, and our ability to implement Lean.

The 'Servant Leader'

The concept of 'Servant Leadership' was first defined by Robert K. Greenleaf in his essay '*The Servant as Leader*', and has subsequently grown into a significant body of management theory with numerous published articles and books on the subject. It's a philosophy that suggests that the primary goal of a leader of an organisation should be to serve its people, rather than a more traditional view that might suggest the opposite. The idea is simple; the servant leader seeks only to support the needs and wants of the people that they represent, and in seeking to serve them in this way *earns* the recognition and role of leader. A servant leader's priority is to ensure that the people that they serve are supported with whatever is required to enable them to be successful and fulfilled; whether that be tools, equipment, and facilities; or encouragement, motivation and purpose. In shifting the leadership mindset in this way, practitioners of 'Servant leadership' believe that the organisation benefits from both the growing capability of its people, and a growing sense of commitment and engagement from them. Today, the practice of 'Servant Leadership' is growing rapidly, with many large multi-national corporations adopting the leadership style as a means of ensuring a healthy and productive working environment.

Importantly, at its heart, 'Servant Leadership' is underpinned by a genuine sense of humility. In his book '*The Servant Leader*', James A. Autry describes how our typical view of leadership is based on old concepts of power, and that leaders can fall into the trap of demonstrating their level of power by *"... flexing... management muscles..."*. With 'Servant Leadership', that power is inverted and *"...comes from gaining the trust and support of the people..."*. Without humility, how else could a leader demonstrate such a complete commitment to the needs of the people that they represent, whilst at the same time showing no concern for their own?

That humility manifests itself in a variety of ways within the 'Servant Leadership' concept. In much of the literature on the subject, a great number of models are proposed, with a variety of traits characterised. Of course, there are many similarities and overlaps in ideas, with most referencing common traits. For example, James A. Autry defines what he calls the 'five ways of being' as the fundamental attributes of 'Servant Leadership': 'be authentic' by presenting yourself honestly in all your interactions, 'be vulnerable' by being prepared to acknowledge your mistakes and by sharing how you feel, 'be accepting' by being prepared to listen to others and consider their perspectives, 'be present' by being actively engaged in meeting your responsibilities, and 'be useful' by serving others as if you are a resource. Other models include behaviours such as showing empathy by listening and appreciating the feelings and perspectives of others, being altruistic by being selflessly concerned for the welfare of others, showing integrity by being honest and doing the right thing, being empowering by giving others authority to deliver their responsibilities and supporting them in their execution, and being visionary by defining a purpose and persuading others to join.

Once again, it seems clear that 'Servant Leadership' is an important consideration for us in our search for the right way to lead in order to empower. There are obvious synergies with some of the leadership ideas that we've already discussed and will discuss later, particularly in relation to the aspect of humility that we're about to review in 'Level 5 Leadership', but also with the consideration and respect for people that is required for the 'Affiliative' and 'Democratic' styles of leadership described by Goleman. And the manifestation of humble leadership, as defined in the various 'Servant Leadership' models, can be useful in helping us how to demonstrate humility with genuine sincerity, and therefore can support our efforts to empower our front-line team members without fear of being considered disingenuous. I would also hope that elements of 'Servant Leadership' remind you of some of the content already presented in *Lean Foundations™*. We've discussed at length the idea that, as the top organisational leader of a manufacturing facility, we carry a responsibility for the well-being and success of the people that we represent. And the 'Why' of our 'Golden Circle', alongside our desire to 'flip the hierarchy', is a clear declaration of our desire to serve the people in our team, rather than the other way around.

'Level 5 Leadership'

In '*Good to Great*', Jim Collins and his team of analysts, perhaps unsurprisingly, identified a feature of leadership as one of the eight characteristics of the 'great' companies highlighted in their study. Despite actively seeking to downplay the role of the leader in their analysis, the information that they collated on the subject was so strong that they felt it was imperative to include it. They called this characteristic 'Level 5 Leadership'. In itself it seems a fairly vague term, but, as with some of the other published materials we've discussed previously, Collins and his team defined a model with five layers of leadership capability to aid understanding. They suggested that the 'great' companies were led by individuals who demonstrated the traits of all five layers, but were particularly different because they possessed level 5 qualities where others did not. The model below, taken from '*Good to Great*', explains these layers in simple terms.

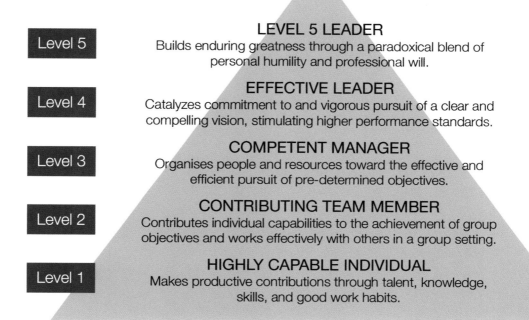

Level 5

LEVEL 5 LEADER
Builds enduring greatness through a paradoxical blend of personal humility and professional will.

Level 4

EFFECTIVE LEADER
Catalyzes commitment to and vigorous pursuit of a clear and compelling vision, stimulating higher performance standards.

Level 3

COMPETENT MANAGER
Organises people and resources toward the effective and efficient pursuit of pre-determined objectives.

Level 2

CONTRIBUTING TEAM MEMBER
Contributes individual capabilities to the achievement of group objectives and works effectively with others in a group setting.

Level 1

HIGHLY CAPABLE INDIVIDUAL
Makes productive contributions through talent, knowledge, skills, and good work habits.

Each of the layers are important in their own right, and hopefully the first four remind you of some of the elements of *Lean Foundations*™ that we've discussed previously. The 'Highly Capable Individual' identified in level one can be considered the equivalent of the 'Right person' that we're trying to get on-board in Step 2, and suggests logically that we are seeking those traits in ourselves as well as the people that we recruit and retain in our team. The 'Contributing Team member' identified in level two draws comparisons with our pursuit of effective teamwork, organisational health, and psychological safety in Step 1. The 'Competent Manager' identified in level three appears to closely align with our discussions on 'Managing our resources' in Step 2. And the 'Effective leader' in level four draws similarities with the leadership approach advocated in Step 3 with the creation of the Improvement Plan and the setting of clear and challenging performance targets.

However, the idea of 'Level 5 Leadership' is a little new to our discussions so far. Collins discusses the traits of humility and professional will with passion. He describes how the 'great' leaders often downplayed their role in the success of their organisation, crediting the contributions of their team, or even blind luck, rather than themselves. These leaders possessed what he called a 'compelling modesty' and refused to discuss their own contributions, whilst at the same time working hard to enable their future successors to be successful themselves. Collins also describes that despite their often reserved and quiet disposition, the 'Level 5 Leaders' possessed an inner determination and desire for success which consistently drove their organisation forward, and which was focused on the performance of the organisation as a whole, rather than on themselves. They demonstrated what Collins calls an 'unwavering resolve' to make the critical decisions which enabled their organisation to deliver results.

In understanding this perspective on leadership, it seems fairly clear that Collin's model has value for us in our search for the right way to lead in order to empower. There is obvious alignment with some of our previous thoughts and activities in each layer of the model, and the level five traits of humility and professional drive are clearly positives that we can adopt. After all, it's humility that can no doubt be the enabler in our desire to empower others, and can allow us to sacrifice any thoughts of personal ambition in order to delegate authority and responsibility for the improvement of our facility to our team. And furthermore, the passionate drive for results can enthuse and energise the team, whilst keeping them on track with delivery of the Improvement Plan, and supporting them with difficult decisions where necessary.

However, it seems that 'Level 5 Leadership' is a rarefied condition that is present in just a few, and as a result you may find that you are asking yourself the same questions that I asked myself on my learning journey. Am I a 'Level 5 Leader'? And if not, can I teach myself to be? In answering these two questions, we should consider that we are all individual, and that some of us are more extrovert and assertive in our nature than others. However, Collins is clear in his belief that 'Level 5 Leadership' can be learned. He hypothesises that there are two categories of people; those who do not have the seed of 'Level 5 Leadership', and those who do. Those who do not are people who are not prepared to put the ambition of creating something enduring above their own personal ambitions. They are driven by what they get in return for their efforts, rather than what they can build for others. If that's you, then guess what, 'Level 5 Leadership' is likely to be beyond you, and I would suggest that *Lean Foundations*™ really isn't going to work for you either. In fact, I would be very surprised if someone of that nature even picked up this book, never mind read this far. Those who do have the seed of 'Level 5 Leadership', and who are prepared to make sacrifices in pursuit of something greater than themselves, can develop their 'Level 5 Leadership' capabilities, and I hope are likely to find *Lean Foundations*™ useful in that aim.

The 'Zapp' of empowerment

In their truly fantastic book '*Zapp: The Lightening of Empowerment*', William Byham and Jeff Cox provide a wonderful insight into the positive impact that empowering leadership can have in the workplace. Their book is presented as a fable, and describes the role of 'Joe Mode', a supervisor in a fictional factory, and his discovery and application of simple techniques for empowering his team in the execution of their day to day responsibilities. The set-up of the story, and the characters within, are all fun; but the message that the book promotes is heart-felt and extremely well delivered.

The idea presented is simple: a team of people who are led in the wrong way, with assertive instruction and micro-management, are likely to be 'Sapped' rather than 'Zapped'. They are likely to be dis-engaged from their responsibilities, will not accept ownership for the problems they experience, and will be unhappy in their role as a consequence. In contrast, a team of people who are led in the right way, with empowerment and respect for their capabilities and opinions, are more likely to be 'Zapped' than 'Sapped'. They are likely to be actively engaged in meeting their responsibilities, will accept ownership for solving problems themselves, and are generally happier and more fulfilled in their role. In the book, 'Joe Mode' learns the value and importance of empowering leadership by observing a colleague, and then by learning to put into practice their actions for himself.

'Zapp' is filled with lots of extremely valuable and worthwhile advice on empowering leadership, and Byham and Cox summarise the main ideas as the story progresses. For example, they define the five main steps that leaders, managers and supervisors should take to 'Zapp' others when discussing performance and solving problems…

- *Maintain or enhance self-esteem* – Make a deliberate effort to protect a person's well-being.

- *Listen and respond with empathy* – Demonstrate that you understand their problem and its impact.

- *Share thoughts, feelings and rationale* – Be open and honest in order to establish trust.

- *Ask for help and encourage involvement* – Seek ideas and suggestions for solutions.

- *The 'Soul of Zapp'* - Provide support without removing responsibility for action.

Added to these five steps, is the understanding of the role of leadership in sharing responsibility, and for maintaining and protecting a culture of empowerment. Byham and Cox describe that *"… sharing responsibility with people does not mean abandoning responsibility…"*, and that leaders still maintain responsibility for setting direction, making top level decisions, ensuring that people stay on course, offering a guiding hand, assessing performance, and importantly being a people smart manager. They are also clear in describing the responsibility of top leaders to protect people from the activities of the wider organisation which might 'Sapp' them; to ensure that managers and supervisors are skilled in the use of the five steps, to be skilled in the use of the five steps themselves, and to recognise and reward performance that results from the use of the five steps.

Each of the five steps of 'Zapp' should hopefully feel familiar to you, thanks in the main to the discussions we've shared on psychological safety, organisational health, and effective teamwork. Terms such as self-esteem, empathy and responsibility for action are hopefully all common place in our now shared vocabulary and understanding. But, the presentation of this logical sequence, concluding with the '*Soul of Zapp*', appears to add real value for us in our search for the right way to lead in order to empower. It seems to provide a very simple but effective methodology for us to cascade through our management and supervisory teams to ensure that they are able to empower their front-line team members. If we can embrace these steps, and in particular the final step of providing support without removing responsibility for action, then we should be able to embed empowering leadership practices into our leadership approach. Furthermore, if we can build in appropriate acceptance of the role that leadership plays in sharing responsibility, and in maintaining and protecting a culture of empowerment, we should be able to embed a very powerful tool into our leadership toolkit.

The art of 'Coaching'

In his engaging book 'ced*The Coaching Habit*', Michael Bungay Stanier presents an excellent insight into the 'Coaching' leadership style defined by Goleman. He describes in very clear and entertaining terms how to utilise 'Seven Essential Questions' that underpin an effective approach towards the 'Coaching' style, and in the process demonstrates a mechanism for empowering others through the use of these questions.

Goleman is clear that the 'Coaching' style is a positive contributor to organisational culture, and Stanier argues that it is also the most under-utilised approach because it is considered too time consuming and difficult to execute. He suggests that modern workplaces, and their leaders, are plagued by the three vicious circles of being overdependent, overwhelmed, and disconnected. He argues that leaders are creating workplaces where their people are overdependent on them for solutions and decision-making, that leaders are becoming overwhelmed by their workload, and that they are becoming disconnected from any sense of fulfilment from their work as a consequence. His proposed solution is to provide a tool that enables leaders to coach others, and to empower their team through this coaching mechanism. He has developed a model of 'Seven Essential Questions' that he suggests support a coaching approach. They are…

- *The Kickstart Question – What's on your mind?* – This a simple way of getting a conversation started and which invites people to share their problems.

- *The AWE Question – And what else?* – This is to ensure that people are given the opportunity to express all of their problems.

- *The Focus Question – What's the real challenge here for you?* – This is to ensure that you are helping people to get to the root cause of their problem, rather than just helping solve the obvious.

- *The Foundation Question –* What do you want? – This gives people permission to ask for what they need to solve their problem.

- *The Lazy Question – How can I help?* – This encourages you not to 'tell' the solution in order to rescue the person from their problem, and instead encourages the person in need to identify what help they want if any.

- *The Strategic Question – If you're saying Yes to this, what are you saying No to?* – This is to ensure that you fully understand the implications of solving the problem presented, and make a logical choice to solve or not depending on sensible prioritisation.

- *The Learning Question – What was most useful for you?* – This is to encourage you and the person you are coaching to reflect on the conversation held, and to appreciate what you have learned.

Clearly, I have over-simplified the substance of Stanier's excellent ideas, and I would certainly advise anyone interested in understanding more to read the book themselves. But, I would also hope that it's obvious that the coaching method described is an important consideration for us in our search for the right way to lead in order to empower. There are discernible overlaps with some of the leadership ideas that we've already discussed, particularly in relation to the 'Coaching' style of leadership described by Goleman, and the '5 steps of Zapp' described by Byham and Cox. And, the nature and progression of the 'Seven Essential Questions' are clearly designed to enable a leader to empower their team members. They encourage team members to identify and discuss their problems, to seek appropriate support, and to be involved in the decision-making process on how to solve their problem in the context of all others. It seems to be a very simple but effective coaching method that can help us to empower our team members to learn and develop whilst solving problems and feeling fulfilled in the process.

The 'Five E's'

So, what is the right way to lead in order to empower our team? What can we learn from the perspectives just presented? Can we combine elements from those leadership styles into an approach that allows you and your management and supervisory team to empower your front-line team members? I believe that the answer to those questions is a simple yes. As a consequence, *Lean Foundations™* suggests an approach to leadership that can be summarised under five headings, all of which begin with the letter 'E'.

These 'Five E's' have developed from a desire to integrate empowerment into every aspect of my leadership approach. I have summarised them below, and whilst I still make mistakes in their execution on a daily basis, I do aspire to achieve the ideals that are described as consistently as I can. I present them here for your consideration in the sincere hope that they offer some value to you as we seek to infuse our *Lean Foundations™* journey with empowerment…

- *Effectiveness* – As with the first three levels of Collins' '5 layers of leadership' model, the first 'E' for consideration in our leadership approach is to be *Effective*: to be a capable individual who is able to make valuable contributions through your own skillset and knowledge, to be an effective team member who is willing to work as part of a team, and to be a competent manager who is able to organise complex and varied resources efficiently to deliver expected results. The suggestion here is simple: if you're ineffective in your role as a manager and leader, then your ability to empower others is likely to be severely restricted. If you're not able to build the basic management framework of organisation structure, teamwork, resource management and process control, your team are unlikely to be successful when you empower them. They are likely to fail because the fabric of the organisation does not support them effectively. Instead, I would suggest that our leadership approach should seek to create a framework of good organisation structure, teamwork and operational process, which provides your team members with the infrastructure that they require to empower themselves. We've already discussed how previous parts of the *Lean Foundations™* approach help us in this aim with the management of resources, with effective teamwork, and through the creation of a team-oriented organisation structure. Later Steps will help further in relation to daily management, problem solving, and process control.

- *Energising* – As with the fourth level of Collins' '5 layers of leadership' model, with the 'Authoritative' style defined by Goleman, and with some of the models within the 'Servant Leadership' community that identify the need to be visionary, the second 'E' for your consideration is to be able to *Energise*: to motivate and enthuse a team of people towards a shared purpose and goal, and to establish their whole-hearted commitment in the delivery of that goal. As with *Effectiveness*, the suggestion here is that the ability to inspire and motivate others towards a common goal provides an element of the framework that people need in order to empower themselves. Without knowing where they are going, or what they are trying to achieve, team members will be unable to make independent choices on what to do, when, and how. Instead, I would suggest that if the aspirations of the organisation are clear, decisions can be made without the need for verification and clarification from a leader or manager, because the direction of travel is already known and understood. Again, with our activities on our 'Golden Circle', and our Improvement Plan, we've already taken considerable steps toward this characteristic.

- *Expecting* – As with 'Level 5 Leadership', and with the 'Pacesetting' style defined by Goleman, the third 'E' for your deliberation is to be *Expecting*: to challenge the organisation to deliver results and a level of performance that is demanding, whilst at the same time being realistic and achievable. Whilst the risks identified by Goleman in the 'Pacesetting' style need to be managed, I would propose that the role of standard bearer is a critical one for any organisational leader. We are all human, and therefore have the potential to relax or take the easy option if given the opportunity. At times therefore, a leader needs to be the person who holds the organisation and the people within it to account in order to deliver the right results. They need to be the voice of consistency, pushing the team towards the pursuit of their goals and performance. Of course, it's important that this is done in a way that is practical and realistic in order to maintain psychological safety and organisational health. We've touched on elements of this characteristic within the definition of our Improvement Plan, and will address it again later in the *Lean Foundations™* approach when we address daily management and process control.

- *Enabling* – As with James A. Autry's definition of 'being useful', and with the 'Democratic', and 'Affiliative' styles defined by Goleman, the fourth 'E' for your consideration is to *Enable*: to provide the organisation and its people with the equipment, facilities, decision-making authority, psychologically safe environment, and guidance that they require to be successful. Hopefully it's obvious that enabling your team members in this way can be an important factor in empowering them. It seems clear that if they do not have the means available to them to meet their responsibilities, then they run the risk of failure, or of having to work much harder to be successful. In the process, their psychological safety is likely to be damaged, and their intrinsic motivators put at risk. Again, we've already discussed some elements of this in previous Steps when addressing organisational health, and will do so again later when we discuss daily management and problem-solving.

- *Empowering* – As with the '5 steps of Zapp' outlined by Byham and Cox, the 'Seven Essential Questions' defined by Stanier, and the 'Coaching' and 'Authoritative' styles defined by Goleman, the fifth 'E' for consideration is to be *Empowering*: to deliberately delegate authority and responsibility for the results of day to day performance and for the delivery of the Improvement Plan to your team members. Whilst the previous 'E's' facilitate and frame empowerment, this final 'E' is intentionally stated in order to reinforce the need to make a specific effort to empower, and to do so by considering the '5 steps of Zapp', and the 'Seven Essential Questions'. If you, and your management and supervisory team, can empower by coaching others carefully through their problem-solving and daily performance management processes, and can do so with empathy and whilst considering self-esteem, then you can be successful in integrating empowerment as a deliberate strategy with deliberate action. It's important to remember the 'Soul of Zapp', and that delegating authority does not mean abandoning responsibility. It's also important to recognise the leadership responsibility for protecting the psychological safety of your team by protecting the empowering world that you are creating, both from external influences, and from the risk of poor execution internally. A final point here is that this does not mean that you should abandon the 'Coercive' style described by Goleman completely. It will still have its uses, particularly at times of emergency and critical business need. It is also a huge part of our more typical thought processes, and will be difficult to give up. Accepting that it exists, whilst making the effort to use it infrequently and only when absolutely necessary, is an important part of learning to empower.

Having summarised the 'Five E's' in this way, I hope that you can see how they effectively bring together aspects of the varied leadership styles presented earlier, and also align succinctly with the leadership approach we've been adopting in earlier Steps of the *Lean Foundations™* approach. As stated previously, my intention here is simply to present an approach to leadership that is clearly centred around empowerment, and which can, if you choose, be integrated into the approach that you and your management and supervisory team embrace. However, it's important to note that the 'Five E's' are underpinned by a fundamental way of being that I believe all of us can endeavour to adopt, and which needs a little further discussion here.

The role of humility

Humility is a trait that we've discussed in detail within 'Level 5 Leadership' and 'Servant Leadership', and is no doubt a trait that can add value to our leadership approach. However, we may feel that being humble is a challenge that we cannot meet. For some that may well be the case. As we discussed with 'Level 5 Leadership', there are individuals who are driven by their own professional desires and ambitions, and are not prepared to sacrifice them for the benefit of others. Humility is therefore likely to be beyond them. But, like Jim Collins, I believe that these people are generally in the minority. For the rest of us, there is hope, and that hope comes in understanding how humility truly manifests itself.

Humility does not necessarily mean that you need to be quiet and reserved in the way that a typical introvert may be. Nor does it mean that you have to lack charm or personality. Humility is still something that you can express even if you are the life and soul of the party. This is a challenge that I have faced myself early in my career, having at times been accused of being a strong personality that others struggled to cope with. I have found that taking on board the advice of professionals such as James A. Autry, and in applying the following seven points in my daily interactions with others, my approach has benefited greatly.

- Be authentic – Present your true self consistently, be honest with others about who you are.

- Be vulnerable – Acknowledge your mistakes, and share your thoughts and feelings with others.

- Be accepting – Appreciate others for who they are, listen to them and consider their perspectives.

- Be inclusive – Realise that you cannot do everything yourself, and be prepared to seek and accept help.

- Be equal - Accept that you are not always the expert, and that others are likely to know better than you in their area of expertise.

- Be 'power-less' – Realise that any authority you have is earned, and then given to you.

- Be altruistic – Desire to help others ahead of helping yourself, and care for and respect every person.

Hopefully you can appreciate that these are aspects of humility that all of us can choose to adopt, regardless of our strength of personality, and whether or not we are more introvert or extrovert in our nature. They can underpin our leadership style and approach, and as a consequence can enable us to demonstrate humility as a way of being that is completely normal and within our capabilities. I know that they have helped me, and will continue to as I challenge myself to develop my humility further. I hope that they can also help you too.

INTEGRATE EMPOWERMENT

Having combined the 'Five E's' leadership style with a genuine approach to humility, hopefully we have defined an approach to empowering leadership that we can infuse throughout our facility. The 'Five E's' are very much centred around the desire to empower others; to provide them with the framework upon which they can accept responsibility, drive independent improvement, and willingly accept and implement change for the benefit of the whole. If delivered properly, we should be able to meet our aspiration for improvement through the deliberate empowerment of our team, rather than through forceful command and control micro-management. In the process, we can support the second aspect of the 'How' of our 'Golden Circle', and can bring together the combined strength of our entire team in delivering on our ambition for improved workplace happiness, operational performance, and the ability to implement Lean.

Our next challenge, therefore, in meeting our desire to infuse empowering leadership into our *Lean Foundations*™ journey, is to understand how we can integrate the leadership approach we have defined into our daily operations. We need to ensure that empowering leadership is fully embedded into the way that we work, so that it becomes normal and part of our routine daily management systems. And we need to be confident that the actions and behaviours of both yourself and your management and supervisory teams reinforce empowerment, rather than restrict it. Here, in this second sub-step, we'll discuss a number of quick and simple activities and methodologies that are deliberately designed to support empowering leadership in the right way, and which you can introduce early in your *Lean Foundations*™ journey. These integrate fully with the more in-depth actions that we will take in Steps 5 and 6, which are designed to deeply embed empowerment into daily operations. I hope that you find these first activities to be of use.

Train, train, and train some more

The first activity in this sub-step is probably the most obvious, but I would suggest can also add the most value. I'm sure that you can appreciate that elements of the leadership style that is advocated will be new to both yourself and your management and supervisory teams, and therefore training them in the content and application of that leadership style is vital in ensuring its successful implementation. In delivering the right training in the right way, you can ensure that your entire team is equally aware of the nature of empowerment, is conscious of your expectation that people will lead in a way that is empowering, and will accept the responsibility that is given to them when they are empowered.

Exactly how you choose to train them is up to you. It may be worth completing the training with external training providers as support, or you may feel able to undertake it yourself by compiling the training material from the content described in this book. The approach that you take will of course depend on how comfortable you feel with the material yourself, whether or not you can afford external support, and which type of approach you believe would be the most effective with your team. In my experience, this is training that I have always asked my Continuous Improvement Manager to deliver, with my support. I happen to have been fortunate enough to have worked with an excellent C.I. Manager over the last 10 years, who is also an extremely effective training provider (thanks Mark). But, even if you're not as lucky as I have been, I would suggest that Continuous Improvement professionals are usually experienced in delivering training events, and therefore may well be a good option for you in your circumstances too.

In delivering the training, I would suggest that it's worth considering two essential points. First of all, it's important to be very deliberate when choosing the content of the material that you're training. At this point in the *Lean Foundations*™ journey, the training that I often ensure is delivered is what we call 'Lean Awareness' training, and covers a wide range of important subjects. Obviously, leadership style and empowerment are a significant portion, but also included is training around teamwork, psychological safety and the right way to conflict healthily, problem-solving (which we'll get to in Step 6 in more detail), and even *Lean Basics* such as 'The Seven Wastes'. There are a significant number of overlaps and interdependencies in these subject areas, as we've already seen ourselves in our discussions so far, and if you're taking the opportunity to train your team, it may be worth bringing these ideas together in order to demonstrate how closely related they are.

Secondly, it's important to make sure that you are selective about who you put through the training, and who you train those people alongside. Training of this nature provides an ideal opportunity to build teamwork and relationships within teams. It can therefore be a good idea to put people through the training in team units. For example, you could schedule one session for your entire management team, a session for each of your cross-functional Core Teams, and even a combined session for all of your functional support team members. You can also schedule sessions for each of your production teams, depending on how your production area is organised. Perhaps you have production cells, or lines that are split into specific work areas, or perhaps machining centres with dedicated operatives. Whichever way they are segregated, bringing them together as a team unit on this kind of training helps to identify them as that team unit, as well as ensuring that they learn something new. You may also think that it's not worth training people such as Quality Engineers, Buyers, or Production Operatives in empowering leadership. However, empowerment is a leadership trait that you would do best to embed into every area of your organisation. As a consequence, it's a good idea for everyone to understand what empowerment looks like and how it works, whether they are the person who is leading through empowerment, or being led. In doing so, anyone who is being led inappropriately can challenge the person leading them if necessary.

One final point to remember here, please do not assume that one training session will be enough. It's a really good idea to schedule at least two if not three sessions, perhaps each with slightly different content or delivery methods in order to keep it fresh. You could deliver the ideas and theory in one session, and then conduct role-play exercises and teamwork games in another. Remember, you're trying to wash the brains of the people you represent, in the process cleaning away any bad habits, and it's unlikely that you will be completely successful in engaging and educating every person in just one attempt. It's therefore worth planning for that eventuality from the very beginning.

Lead by example, one situation at a time

Perhaps unsurprisingly, an extremely important factor in establishing empowerment as the primary leadership approach in your facility is for you to provide a strong leadership example in your day to day interactions. If you communicate your desire for people to be empowered through extensive training, but then consistently use a 'Coercive' style of leadership instead, you're likely to lose credibility very quickly, and are likely to damage the trust that people have in you and your *Lean Foundations™* journey.

In many ways, it's appropriate for you to be exaggerated in your use of empowering leadership; to ensure that you make a deliberate effort to allow people to make their own decisions, but to coach them by using the 'Seven Essential Questions' when needed. To ensure that you're 'Democratic' in decision-making by asking for input on decisions, to be 'Affiliative' by being deliberately considerate of the well-being of the people you're interacting with, and by being 'Authoritative' by using the '5 steps of Zapp' when supporting problem-solving. In the simplest terms possible: stay out of your people's way, but be available to help when needed, and help in a way that guides rather than instructs. In almost over-emphasising the point, you can demonstrate your commitment to the leadership approach, and will enable others to feel comfortable in doing the same. At the same time, the benefits to the psychological safety of your team can be significant, as you're likely to identify opportunities to coach and manage failure through to a positive conclusion.

Of course, the main challenge here, is in understanding when to step back and empower, and when to step forward and support. As a leader, it's important to empower others, and to pass on responsibility. It's also important to support where necessary, and not completely abdicate responsibility. There is a delicate balance to strike, and a seemingly mystical art to learn. However, there is advice available to us that can help. In his fantastic book '*Leadership and the One Minute Manager*', Ken Blanchard describes an approach to leadership that he calls 'Situational Leadership®', and which provides guidance on how to align your leadership approach with the level of competence and commitment of each individual that you're responsible for managing. He describes a clear and detailed model that presents the practical relationship between the level of direction and emotional support someone requires, with their level of competence and confidence. And, Blanchard argues that good leaders adapt their style and approach to each individual, and to each circumstance and requirement placed upon that individual, in order to ensure that they are led and managed successfully and responsibly.

The model aligns four levels of individual development, with four leadership styles. The 'enthusiastic beginner' is someone who is of low competence and high commitment, and who can require a high level of direction and a low level of support. Here, a directive or 'Coercive' style may be the most practical style to adopt. This person needs to develop their understanding and competence, and requires direction in order to manage the effective completion of a task. The 'disillusioned learner' is someone who is of low to some competence, and low commitment; with their low-level of understanding causing them frustration. They can require a high level of direction and a high level of support, and as consequence a style that coaches with a combined 'Coercive' and 'Affiliative' approach may be the most practical. This person still needs some level of instruction, but also needs emotional support to alleviate their frustration. The 'capable but cautious' person is someone who is of moderate to high competence, and variable commitment; as their development progresses through the learning cycle. They can require less direction, but still need emotional support, and as a consequence a style supports through a combination of 'Democratic' and 'Coaching' approaches is likely to work best. Finally, the 'self-reliant achiever' is someone who is of high competence and high commitment, and therefore requires little direction or support. This person simply needs intermittent support and alignment with colleagues, and therefore an 'Authoritative' approach is probably the most sensible.

Blanchard's book is certainly informative and perceptive, and I would highly recommend that you read it if you can. In understanding the concept of 'Situational Leadership®', and in learning to apply its clear logic, we can offer an excellent leadership example to our management and supervisory team, which they can then cascade themselves throughout their team. The idea that one single leadership style can be used in multiple different scenarios is clearly flawed, and by adapting ourselves to each situation as is presents itself, we can ensure that empower responsibly whilst supporting and instructing where necessary.

As a final point here, it's also important for you to strike the right balance with your team when being 'Expecting'. There will be occasions when poor performance is unacceptable, or a response to a situation is not sufficient, and as a consequence you may feel the need to intervene. My advice here is to try and avoid slipping into the 'Coercive' style at these moments, particularly as this is when you will be at most risk of doing so. You may feel frustrated or disappointed in the failure, and may be under pressure to get the problem resolved. As a consequence, it's easy to resort to the tried and tested method of instructing your team rather than supporting them. Here is where your commitment to empowerment will be most tested, and where you can demonstrate your resolve by following the 'Seven Essential Questions' proposed by Stanier. In coaching others through your challenging situation, you can also coach yourself through a more empowering process of leadership, particularly if you can consider Byham and Cox's '5 steps of Zapp' at the same time, and can be empathetic and encourage involvement in the problem-solving activity.

However, on occasions, the use of the 'Coercive' style will be both appropriate and desired. In situations of high importance, or even emergency, your team may well be looking to you for a decisive and determined response. The challenge for you, and your management team, is to recognise when these occasions occur and to respond accordingly.

'Start of Day' meetings

It is possible to integrate empowering leadership into your operations to such an extent that it becomes the norm, but without it feeling like a burden. One of the easiest ways to do this is to introduce the 'Start of Day' meeting into every front-line team unit. These short 10 minute 'Start of Day' meetings can be deliberately designed with empowerment at their heart, by ensuring that their purpose is to identify, report and resolve problems that people have experienced in the day to day execution of their responsibilities.

The format is simple; a manager or supervisor will bring their team of front-line team members together for a discussion at the start of working every day, and will review the previous day's performance. Where under-performance is identified, the team is challenged to understand why, and if necessary to task themselves to prevent its reoccurrence. Where the team is unable to solve the problem themselves, they are able to task their supervisor or manager to seek appropriate support from outside their team. Meetings of this nature are fairly typical in production areas, and are sometimes called 'Start of shift meetings' or 'Team meetings', but there is absolutely no reason why they cannot be completed across a facility in office-based areas too. By completing a meeting of this nature, all front-line team members can be actively involved in problem-solving processes, and can be encouraged to accept responsibility for performance when it is both good and bad. The meetings can also be used to delegate issues upwards in the organisation structure, enabling the 'flipping of the hierarchy' concept we've discussed previously and ensuring that managers and supervisors are positioned to serve the team rather than the other way around. Such meetings can also provide an ideal opportunity to recognise and reinforce good performance, and in the process can be used to show appreciation in a way that can improve psychological safety and a person's intrinsic motivator of success. As a minimum, they help to simply communicate status, and ensure that everyone within a team is fully aware of how a team is performing in relation to its responsibilities. However, it's important to note that robust action has to be an outcome of such meetings. Identifying problems and under-performance, without a real attempt to improve, will only damage psychological safety and intrinsic motivators rather than improve them. To help with this, you may consider joining these meetings yourself on a routine basis, perhaps once or twice a month. In doing so, you can help to identify problems that are lacking the right support for resolution, and can intervene where you think necessary. Such an intervention adds real value in demonstrating your commitment to supporting your team, and can boost commitment and enthusiasm considerably.

These 'Start of Day' meetings are an important feature of the *Lean Foundations*™ approach, and will integrate into the Daily Management process that we'll discuss in Step 5. I would actively encourage you to adopt them as a result. Again, their format is entirely up to you and will reflect how your facility is structured. If you have production cells with individual team leaders or supervisors in place, then they can be easier to identify and organise. If your facility is a little less straightforward, then you're likely to face a little more of a challenge. Hopefully, the work you've done in re-organising your team structure in Step 2 will help. Certainly, the clear identification of the Core Team(s) and Support Team(s) should give a strong indication of how to differentiate who can and should be involved. It's important to note that these meetings are different to the meetings we'll discuss in Step 5. The teams that we're talking about here are not the Core Teams necessarily, but are smaller teams of front-line team members within the Core and Functional Support Teams, such as a Production Supervisor and their Production Operatives in a production cell or line, a Purchasing Manager and their Buyers, or a Logistics Supervisor and their Logistics Operatives.

The meetings tend to be completed in the area where the team is based, assuming working conditions permit it, and are usually supported by a 'Team Board'. This can be a small whiteboard where the information you're discussing can be recorded, along with any actions. I would suggest that you include a summary of your main Safety, Quality, Delivery, and Cost performance indicators in the discussion, but only in very quick and basic terms. Were there any safety incidents? How many parts were produced versus target? Were there any quality issues? Did you have any cost issues such as scrap? Were all orders produced on-time? Having reviewed the team's basic performance, it's a good idea to quickly identify any issues which caused problems or impacted performance, and to discuss them so that they are understood, and ideas for solutions can be offered. As a final point, it's important to take notes on actions, with a clear description of what the action is, who is responsible for it, and when it needs to be completed. That action may include escalation to the daily meetings we'll discuss in Step 5. These are actions that can then be reviewed each day to ensure progress is maintained and communicated throughout the team, and issues that are not being resolved can be escalated. You may remember that in Step 2 we discussed the potential for the use of tools such as a Skills Versatility Matrix, a Job Allocation Board, and a Holiday/Absence Tracker. These are all tools that at different points in time I have integrated into these 'Start of Day' meetings with great success, and I would encourage you to consider doing the same.

What I have just described above is typical of a 'Start of Day' meeting in a production area, but as I've already stated, there is absolutely no reason why these can't take place in office-based areas. In fact, I would actively encourage you to include them in some of your more critical functional areas, particularly in Planning and Quality. Here, the performance and problems you're discussing are going to be much more functionally focused, and as a consequence can be focused on driving functional improvement in support of your Core team activities. Whether you do include them will depend on exactly how your facility functions and how it is organised following your efforts in completing Step 2.

Importantly, whomever is leading these meetings will need to be trained in the 'Five E's' leadership approach. These people are likely to be your front-line supervisors interacting with your front-line team members, and their ability to lead in the way that you are endeavouring to promote is going to be critical to the success of your *Lean Foundations™* journey. Their interactions with your front-line team members are far more frequent than yours, and therefore if you're going to be successful in empowering your team, those front-line supervisors need to lead as you would want them to.

There is one final point for consideration. You may well be reading this suggestion and thinking that 10 minutes spent discussing is 10 minutes spent not producing or working, and that it is therefore a waste. I can only offer you the benefit of my experience, and the assurance that you will more than recover that 10 minutes through the improvements that you're likely to achieve. The simple act of empowering your people so that they can solve their own problems can ignite a passionate involvement in problem-solving and performance improvement. It can help to solve problems that may appear trivial, but are usually extremely valuable, because they have been identified by the people who live with them every day.

The 'Daily Audit'

The use of a 'Daily Audit' process can also integrate empowering leadership into your facility in such a way that it becomes routine, but only if this audit process is a little different than the norm.

Typically, an audit is completed by a manager, and assesses whether or not a process area or cell is performing in line with a standard condition. Where it's not, team members within the process area are tasked with taking remedial action to recover. However, the 'Daily Audit' proposed here flips this process on its head. Instead, the audit is completed by a team member or supervisor from the Core Team, and is completed in order to assess whether or not the team unit is being appropriately supported and empowered by the Management or Functional Support Teams. Where it's not, the Management or Functional Support Teams can be tasked to give further support.

A 'Daily Audit' of this nature needs to be carefully designed and integrated into your Daily management system, some elements of which we'll be discussing in greater detail in Step 5. First of all, the audit questions need to be specifically selected. Secondly, the reporting method needs to be established robustly so that it enables intervention activities to be initiated when necessary, and overseen by yourself if needed. The audit can be fully integrated into the 'Start of Day' meeting, with the audit document being completed as part of the meeting process.

In determining the audit questions, you obviously need to consider the specifics of your manufacturing facility and the way that it operates. At the same time, I can suggest some questions here that help to give an idea of how such an audit process can work…

- Have there been any health and safety incidents in the last 24 hours?

- If yes, are appropriate containment actions in place?

- Are all safety controls in place – e.g. Fire Extinguishers correctly located? Fire exits clear? First Aid kits available? Trained First Aid and Fire Marshals on shift? Lifting equipment controls in place? Emergency stops functional?

- If no to any of these points – is support from the Management or Functional Support Team required for resolution – and if so has it been provided?

- Have all performance issues been raised and adequately discussed?

- If yes, are appropriate actions agreed for resolution?

- Is support from the Management or Functional Support Team required for resolution – and if so has it been provided?

- Is your equipment and machinery operational and functioning correctly?

- If no - is support from the Management or Functional Support Team required for resolution – and if so has it been provided?

Hopefully you can see that these example questions are written in such a way that they confirm whether or not the team that is completing the audit is working with empowerment. Either, a question confirms whether or not the team has acted where they can, and therefore they have chosen to utilise the freedom to resolve their own problems. Or, a question confirms whether or not the team requires support from elsewhere, and whether or not that support has been provided.

In developing an audit such as this, and in completing it on a daily basis in each team or production area, a score can be derived, with a positive answer scoring 1, and a negative answer scoring 0. Wherever a score is less than the maximum, management intervention can be required to understand why, and to decide how to follow-up for resolution. Normally, I would encourage these scores to be published on the 'Team Boards' described for the 'Start of Day' meeting, and potentially even on the whiteboards that we'll discuss as part of the Daily Management process in Step 5. I have even had the scores reported as part of a weekly KPI process so as the facility leader I can provide oversight and can coach intervention where necessary.

Whilst you may consider that such an audit process is a little intense, I've seen on numerous occasions that it helps to embed an empowering leadership approach into the fabric of daily operations. The audit becomes a tool that team members and their supervisors can use to ask for help when perhaps other mechanisms have failed. It gives them a strength of voice, particularly when overseen and supported with intervention from yourself, that perhaps they would lack in normal circumstances. On the flip-side, it can be used to ensure that team members are taking responsibility when it's appropriate to do so. Your intervention could be to coach them on a solution that they can develop for themselves, rather than to simply expect it to be delivered to them. I've also found the use of the process to be extremely beneficial in helping my understanding of day to day performance problems, and of the capability of my team to resolve them independently.

The 'Help Provider'

A feature of a psychologically safe environment, and an empowered one, is that people are prepared to ask for help. Being empowered means that team members have the authority to solve their own problems, but does not necessarily mean that they have the ability to do so, and therefore need to ask for help. At the same time, asking for help requires courage, and the knowledge that such a request will be responded to positively and with respect. Experience tells me that requests for help are only forthcoming if they receive an appropriate response more often than not. If you find that in asking for help you receive nothing, then it won't take long for you to stop asking and to simply put up with whatever problem you're experiencing. On the other hand, if you ask for help and receive it willingly, you're likely to be prepared to ask again.

For this reason, I have often ensured that for each team a role of 'Help Provider' is nominated and clearly identified. This person is usually the Manufacturing Engineering representative within the Core Team, mainly because they are the most diversely skilled and are best placed to support team members with their request for help. I have ensured that being a 'Help Provider' is documented as part of their roles and responsibilities, and that everyone in the team is fully aware that those responsibilities have been defined. By identifying the role in this manner, I have found that any stigma attached with asking for help simply disappears. Where people were previously reluctant to express an apparent weakness, the 'Help Provider' role removes any sensitivities and encourages people to step forward with their request without fear of retribution or criticism. It also ensures that when help is required, it is reliably delivered, and as a consequence people feel confident to ask for help in the future. I find that such a simple step provides considerable benefit to the process of identifying and solving small but cumulatively significant problems.

At the same time, as we saw in Step 2, the primary role of all of the Core Team members, regardless of their function, is to provide support and help to the front-line team members in the day to day execution of their responsibilities. It's therefore important when defining the 'Help Provider' role not to remove the responsibility for helping from other members of the Core Team. You need to be able to strike a sensible balance.

Performance-manage like a parent

When seeking to provide leadership and management that empowers, we have the opportunity to consider an approach which does more than just empower people in the execution of their day to day responsibilities. If considered carefully, we also have the opportunity to empower every person to take responsibility for their own personal development, as well as the development and performance of the operation as a whole.

A typical tool for managing individual performance over time is the 'Performance Appraisal', which has been adopted in various formats by many organisations worldwide. However, in a great many cases, the appraisal process can be completed in such a way that it misses the opportunity to encourage individual empowerment, and instead disengages people from taking ownership for their development. They can often be a soul-destroying experience for many people in the workplace, and can seriously damage their psychological safety and intrinsic motivators. If done at all, 'Performance Appraisals' are likely to be an annual experience only, may well be completed by a line-manager who 'scores' certain criteria based purely on their personal view, and who potentially discusses negative points never previously mentioned. Routine and constructive feedback and discussion throughout the year can be non-existent, except perhaps from the odd emotional outburst or celebratory pat on the back.

In his book 'Punished by Rewards', Alfie Kohn discusses the nature of 'Performance Appraisals' in the modern workplace. He considers that they have the potential to be both damaging to our intrinsic motivators, and also a benefit, depending on how they are conducted, and how they are integrated into wider business decision-making around things like pay and incentives. Kohn suggests that organisations tend to complete a performance review process for one of four reasons: to determine pay and bonuses, to make employees perform from a desire to receive a good review or out of fear of receiving a bad one, to sort employees on the basis of performance so that promotion decisions are easier, and to provide feedback in order to help the employee do a better job. He argues that only the last of those four reasons is truly beneficial, because it offers the possibility for managers and leaders to work with their people, rather than making decisions that *do* something to them. Where performance reviews are utilised to decide things like pay or promotion, a judgment is required, and an outcome that impacts the individual is imposed. Such judgments can be considered unfair and personally biased, and run the risk of damaging psychological safety and intrinsic motivators even if handled with the greatest sensitivity. However, where a performance review is utilised to discuss opportunities for personal improvement through a shared evaluation and assessment, individuals can be empowered to own their personal development, and can be given appropriate support to achieve it. In doing so, their psychological safety and intrinsic motivators are likely to be greatly enhanced.

It's this fourth reasoning to individual performance management that *Lean Foundations*™ advocates. In seeking to support our team members with appropriate feedback and open discussion around their performance, we can support them to achieve the personal development that will benefit them, and the organisation as a whole. If we can interact with them as a parent would with their child, and can advise and support as part of a process of continuous learning and development, whilst appreciating their strengths and achievements, then we can potentially empower them to take ownership of their individual development journey themselves. In the process, we're likely to significantly enhance their psychological safety and intrinsic motivators. There are a number of points for us to consider here…

- Whilst an annual 'Performance Appraisal' is an important event, it should not stand in isolation. I have found that holding one primary formal discussion which is deliberately open-ended and time-flexible is extremely valuable, but it functions best when supported by further formal and informal interactions. You could consider including three additional formal quarterly discussions as the year progresses in order to 'touch-base' with progress and maintain focus. Also, if you can, consider integrating monthly informal discussions, where you 'create' more casual opportunities to discuss how someone is performing in relation to their agreed objectives. Take advantage of opportunities for a discussion at the end of a meeting, or when passing in a corridor in order to keep things relaxed. These kinds of conversations can help to demonstrate that you are available to support, whilst still reinforcing a small amount of expectation of progress where needed.

- The 'Performance Appraisal' discussion, whether formal or informal, needs to be a two-way conversation where ideas and thoughts can be exchanged in pursuit of supporting the personal development of the individual in question. It should not be a series of judgments about one person that are declared by another. As the manager or leader, your role is to offer insight and perspective that adds value for the individual, and to encourage them to accept responsibility for their performance and any improvement that may be required in it. In many cases, organisations provide a standard structure to utilise, with categorisation around things such as 'Bias for Action', or 'Customer Focus'. These can help to guide the nature of your conversation and provide a framework around what good performance looks like, versus the performance of the individual that you're discussing. I would advise you to be careful not to pass judgment during these discussions, and perhaps instead look to encourage self-reflection and self-awareness.

- The 'Performance Appraisal' can endeavour to encourage personal reflection of the positives that each person contributes and experiences in their daily activities. A focus on their strengths rather than weaknesses, and successes rather than failures, can build confidence and encourage engagement. And, fostering a sense of gratitude for the elements of their role that they enjoy and appreciate can enhance their sense of workplace happiness.

- It's a good idea to train your managers and supervisors in how to complete an effective 'Performance Appraisal' process before asking them to undertake them with their team. I would also advise that you cascade the appraisal process; that you complete them with your management team before they complete with their supervisors and so on. In doing so, you can provide a leadership example from which a standard approach can be understood and applied downstream.

- Where possible, do not link the outcome of the performance review discussion to pay or other rewards. Where your organisation's approach requires this, I would advise you to try and neutralise the links between the two as much as possible, and to consider pay and incentives in line with our thoughts and discussions in Step 1.

- It's always a good idea to create an Individual Development Plan as an outcome of the annual discussion, and to use it to monitor progress during your follow-up conversations. This Individual Development Plan should be agreed between both parties, and can be focused on personal development goals as well as on tangible targets and objectives that are linked to the overall Improvement Plan for your facility. We'll discuss this in more detail in Step 8.

- Often 'Performance Appraisal' processes do not include front-line team members who work in Production areas, which always seems strange to me. They are, after all, often the bulk of your workforce and make the most significant contribution to the daily performance of your facility. I would therefore advise that you always include all layers of your organisation in the 'Performance Appraisal' process, and simply adjust your expectations of what each individual can and will offer according to the responsibilities they carry.

- I would advise you, as top leader of your manufacturing facility, to openly discuss your thoughts and feelings around each of your wider team members with your management team before they conduct their 'Performance Appraisals'. It's important that as a management team you are consistent in your understanding and approach to every individual throughout the year. In doing so, you can ensure that team members receive feedback from yourself that is aligned with feedback from their individual manager. I have often completed these discussions as a whole management team because of the overlaps in management relationships that exist in the matrix structure that you're likely to be working with. Together you can also use this forum to identify the people that you would consider not to be the 'Right People' on board, and can agree a shared plan to address those individuals with consistency.

STEP 4 SUMMARY

In completing Step 4 of your *Lean Foundations*™ journey, you have hopefully taken significant steps towards empowering your team members, and in the process will be taking full advantage of the capabilities and potential of everyone in your team. By embracing empowerment as your primary leadership approach, and by infusing empowering leadership throughout your team and your facility, you're likely to be experiencing a genuine sense of positivity and change for good. The ability of your team to manage the great diversity of daily challenges, alongside their implementation of the Improvement Plan, is no doubt far in excess of what you could have achieved if you were driving it alone. At the same time, the well-being of your team will be improved, despite a potentially greater workload and activity level. Their senses of self-esteem and trust will no doubt be greatly enhanced; and their intrinsic motivators of autonomy, improvement, and collaboration are likely to be enriched. Workplace happiness is surely improving, and operational performance will gradually be benefiting as problems are progressively solved. You're definitely heading in the right direction, and are making real progress in enabling your facility to perform well, and to build the foundations upon which operational excellence can take root.

Having now introduced empowering leadership into your facility, Steps 5 and 6 provide the details of an in-depth daily management and problem-solving process that really take empowering leadership to new heights. Before we get to these, it's worth considering one last point.

We've already established that you're likely to be the top organisational leader of your manufacturing facility, and that as a consequence you have a degree of independence in the execution of your leadership responsibilities from your wider organisation. However, this does not mean that you're necessarily completely empowered to make the right decisions for your facility. I know from experience that you may have some autonomy in day to day issues, but are likely to be constrained when it comes to decisions around things like recruitment, capital expenditure, and budget setting. I also know how frustrating this can be.

If, as the person reading this book, you are actually a business leader or owner such as CEO, Vice President, Managing Director or similar, rather than the operational leader of a manufacturing facility, then I'd like to give you some advice on behalf of all of the operational leaders that work for you. Please empower your operational leaders. How?

First of all, accept that they know their facility and all of its problems better than you do. Be prepared to listen to them, and to support them in solving their problems. This will be difficult for you I'm sure. In your position, expressing humility and accepting your lack of knowledge in comparison to a factory leader will be a struggle. But it's a good place to start. On more than one occasion I've been told by a CEO or CFO what was wrong with my facility, despite the fact that they only visited it for a few hours on a single day in a given year. On very few occasions have I been asked what is wrong and what help did I need to fix it.

Second, realise, as Toyota have, that '*Operations is where it's at*'. Toyota's success is built on a deliberate focus to strive for operational excellence as their core strategic differentiator. They know that, if you can deliver operational excellence; you deliver customer service, profitability, and employee well-being. Focusing your whole business on driving operational excellence will empower your facility leaders to be at the heart of improving your business, which is exactly where they want to be. Assuming you have the right ones of course.

To close Step 4, let's take a moment to quickly review the main points…

- Leading a manufacturing facility with a command and control leadership style is likely to be ineffective. It's likely that you will struggle to control your wide and varied responsibilities, and you'll almost certainly damage workplace happiness and operational performance

- A leadership approach that seeks to empower all team members, and which encourages decision making and problem solving throughout, is likely to be much more effective in dealing with the diverse challenges of our *Lean Foundations™* journey, and can also improve workplace happiness in the process.

- In seeking an understanding of how to lead with empowerment, we can consider the 'Six leadership styles' described by Goleman, 'Level 5 Leadership' defined by Collins, the various approaches to Servant Leadership originally described by Greenleaf, Byham and Cox's 'Zapp' of empowerment, and Stanier's 'Seven Essential Questions' for coaching.

- The 'Five E's' of 'Effectiveness', 'Energising', 'Expecting', 'Enabling' and 'Empowering' seek to describe a leadership approach that has empowerment at its heart. These can be combined with an achievable approach to demonstrating humility, which together can be utilised as our leadership approach in *Lean Foundations™*.

- It's important for us to fully integrate empowering leadership and the 'Five E's' leadership approach into our daily routines and systems so that command and control leadership is discouraged.

- To do this we can train all of our people in empowerment, can provide an exaggerated leadership example ourselves, can practice 'Situational Leadership®', can introduce 'Start of Day' meetings and 'Daily Audits', can define the role of 'Help Provider', and can complete 'Performance Appraisals' in a way that empowers.

STEP

5

Manage performance daily, and with discipline.

Have you ever noticed just how much things can change in a manufacturing facility? Everyday you're confronted with new challenges, new orders to deliver, new problems to solve, new issues with customers or your team members. Your production equipment can break down, your suppliers can deliver late, your team members may not turn up for work, or your customers can change their mind. Often it can feel like the issues are simply queueing up behind one another, waiting for you to fix the one in front before the next one raises its head. At other times, they all seem to come at once, and you end up feeling punch drunk from the constant barrage. Knowing which one to solve first can be a challenge in itself.

And yet, on the other hand, sometimes things do not seem to change very much at all. Your production processes are likely to look and operate in the same way today that they did a year ago, and a year before that. Your team members are following the same processes that that they have done for some time. And the problems that you're experiencing every day can have a repetitious pattern that isn't necessarily transparent to everyone, but is most certainly there. It's quite possible that you've been completing Kaizen improvement events on a routine basis, and therefore some parts of your facility do look and work differently than before, at least on the surface. But, that concept of continuous improvement; that elusive ideal that suggests at a world where things change for the better every day, almost autonomously, can seem nothing more than fantasy.

Have you also noticed how things can drift in a manufacturing facility? How problems don't always get solved as quickly as they could, or opportunities are not taken advantage of when they present themselves. You might well have the right people in place, with good teamwork, and maybe even a great plan that everyone supports, but you and your team still struggle to make things happen. At times it seems that you all need a good hard push to get things done, which makes empowering leadership really difficult, and means that your 'Coercive' side is desperate to break free. It's almost as if the constant change that you and your team confront every day, is stopping you from working on the continuous improvement that you're so eager to embrace.

In 'Good to Great', Jim Collins and his team identified a 'Culture of Discipline' as one of the eight characteristics that differentiates great companies from the rest. This does not mean that the great companies they identified were overly harsh in the management of their people. It instead means that these companies were filled with leaders, managers and team members who applied a fanatically disciplined mentality and approach to the execution of their strategies and plans. Because they were filled with the right people, and because the right people had defined the right plan, they were passionate and deliberate in fulfilling that plan to its utmost potential. And interestingly, Collins is clear that this focused discipline was not delivered through bureaucracy and red-tape, but instead through a balanced approach to working within the framework of the plan created, whilst also being given the autonomy and accountability to be flexible within that framework.

Hopefully you can recognise the steps that we have been taking on our *Lean Foundations™* journey towards that *'Culture of Discipline'*. We are actively embracing organisational health and psychological safety as a means of delivering effective teamwork, and in encouraging a sense of autonomy and responsibility in our team. We have built a team-oriented organisation structure which is filled with the right people to drive your facility forward. We have developed a detailed and thorough plan which supports our strategy of becoming a great place to work by improving workplace happiness and operational performance, and by creating a platform for Lean. We have also ensured that our objectives and targets within that plan are challenging and will stretch the capabilities of your team. Finally, we are embracing a leadership approach that actively empowers our team members, and gives them the freedom to deliver their daily responsibilities alongside the need for improvement. Everything, therefore, is primed for that *'Culture of Discipline'*.

However, it still feels like we're missing something. We've provided the basis for the *'Culture of Discipline'* that Collins describes, but how do we cope with the constant change that is restricting our ability to continuously improve? How do we ensure that we are not so busy surviving today, that we forget or run out of time to improve for tomorrow? How do we prioritise the things that we need to work on, from the things that we do not? And how do we systemise that approach into our daily routines and processes?

Over time, and almost by accident, I have found that the answer to these questions is relatively straightforward. I've learned that the solution lies in the way that we manage ourselves on a daily basis, and requires us to build management routines that systemise standard thinking processes and behaviours into our daily operations. By doing so, we can ensure that we respond to problems, and manage our performance, in a consistent and structured manner, regardless of whether we are trying to continuously improve, or manage constant change.

In his wonderfully perceptive book *'Toyota Kata'*, Mike Rother describes how Toyota has incorporated improvement focused thinking processes and behaviour routines into their management system. These help them to identify exactly what *needs* to be worked on to drive improvement, whilst at the same time supporting their ability to adapt to their ever-changing environment. The *'Improvement Kata'* that Rother describes follows an extremely similar logic to the PDCA/TOC cycle we defined previously in Step 3, and seeks to identify the current condition, the target condition, the plan for change, and the obstacles to be resolved in the pursuit of delivering change, whilst considering the basis of their long-term vision and plan as a guide. Whilst the terminology is slightly different, the similarities with 'What to Change', 'What to Change to', 'How to change', and 'Implement the change' are hopefully clear for all. Rother has identified that Toyota has embedded this thinking process into everything that they do, and at every level of their organisation, and in doing so helps us to understand what makes Toyota's management system so different to the norm.

It's this intensity of approach that Step 5 of *Lean Foundations*™ seeks to support you to establish in your facility. The consistent drive for improvement, alongside the ability to adapt to constant change, and the disciplined pursuit of the long-term vision, is absolutely necessary if we're going to meet our desire for improved operational performance, workplace happiness, and the ability to implement Lean. By now we have created a healthy organisation that embraces effective teamwork, have built a team-oriented organisation structure, have completed our 'Golden Circle' and properly defined our 'How' and 'What' alongside the 'Why', and have embraced a leadership style that seeks to empower our team. Next, we need to begin the process of building the management practices that systemise standard thinking processes into our daily routines. We need to start to build the well-functioning management system that can drive us forward. In doing so, we can introduce yet another of the essential features of a facility that performs well, and of the foundations upon which operational excellence is built.

For *Lean Foundations*™, the first of the three steps required to build that well-functioning management system, is to develop and implement a robust daily performance management process. What is advocated here in Step 5 is the implementation of what *Lean Foundations*™ calls the 'MDI' process, or 'Managing for Daily Improvement'. I have learned, after numerous applications, that this process can provide a forum for the '*Culture of Discipline*' that Collins described. And, alongside the utilisation of the PDCA/TOC thinking processes, can provide a process upon which we can implement standard behaviours into our daily routines, similar to the '*Improvement Kata*' utilised by Toyota. It can provide a structured forum that encourages a disciplined pursuit of good performance, and enables our ability to adapt to constant change whilst pursuing our Improvement Plan. We'll work through just one sub-step to describe how to implement this 'MDI' process; 'Introducing MDI'. Hopefully I can persuade you of the merits of the 'MDI' process, and encourage you to introduce your own version of it in your facility. Following on from this, in Step 6 we'll discuss the right approach to problem-solving, and how to introduce a methodology that ensures that problems are solved effectively. In Step 7, I'll endeavour to present a more detailed discussion around the wider aspects of a well-functioning management system.

INTRODUCING 'MDI'

The 'Managing for Daily Improvement' process advocated here has evolved over the last 15 years of my leadership experience. I first started to use a daily meeting process when I inherited responsibility for leading a facility that was identified for closure. I found it to be extremely beneficial in bringing people together to drive improvement, whilst coping with the challenge of daily change, despite the adverse conditions we were operating under. The simple act of bringing the team together on a daily basis, and applying a routine and systemised approach to the management of our performance, to the pursuit of improvement, and to the resolution of daily problems, was extremely powerful and led to significant improvement in our performance in a short period of time. Unfortunately, despite our (albeit belated) best efforts, and even considering the significant improvements we made, we could not reverse the original decision. The facility I was responsible for closed with the loss of almost two hundred jobs. It's not an experience I would choose to repeat, but the daily management process we established is something that I learned a great deal from, and have chosen to apply over and over again. I came to realise the value of that daily management process in driving performance, and in facilitating improvement whilst coping with constant change, and have sought to take advantage of it ever since. Later versions have evolved from that early manifestation, following input from knowledgeable colleagues and skilled lean practitioners, and today it takes the fairly sophisticated form that has come to be called 'MDI'.

To encourage you to embrace the 'MDI' process in your facility, we'll begin by discussing the basic premise of the 'MDI', how it can add value to our desire to drive operational performance with discipline, and can support our desire to manage constant change whilst striving for continuous improvement. Following this, we'll then discuss the basic principles upon which it is based, and how it works in daily practice in conjunction with a set of standardised whiteboard tools. I'll then offer some support to you on how to introduce your own 'MDI' process into your facility.

Why the 'MDI'?

In simple terms, the 'MDI' process functions by combining three elements…

- A daily meeting routine which is established in all team areas. Building on the activities in Step 2, a daily meeting with defined protocols is scheduled in each Core Team area. The primary purpose of that meeting routine is to provide a forum where teams are empowered to manage operational performance, and to solve problems in the pursuit of improving operational performance over time. This 'MDI' meeting takes place in addition to the 'Start of Day' meeting advocated in Step 4.

- The daily meetings are underpinned by a set of basic principles which are understood and applied by every team member taking part. The purpose of these basic principles is to shape how the 'MDI' meetings function, and to guide the behaviours and thoughts of the team members involved.

- The meetings are supported by standard whiteboard tools that are specifically designed to enable the individual team to manage their own operational performance, to solve their own performance related problems, and to manage the execution of individual actions from their Improvement Plan.

As you can see, the 'MDI' process is, in effect, nothing more than a simple but well-defined daily meeting process which utilises standard meeting protocols, standard whiteboard tools, and a set of basic principles that guide the way it functions. However, the key strength of the 'MDI' process is that it supports the disciplined pursuit of good operational performance, and enables any manufacturing facility to strike the balance between managing constant and unpredictable change whilst striving for continuous improvement. And it does so because of two key points.

First of all, as I've outlined, the primary purpose of the 'MDI' process is to drive operational performance. The daily meetings that take place are deliberately designed to discuss and address problems relating to the core performance indicators of Safety, Quality, Delivery, Cost and Engagement. This focus is at the very heart of their existence, and as a result the disciplined pursuit of performance improvement becomes central to every Core Team member's daily working life. At the same time, whilst that responsibility primarily sits with the Core Team, the meeting process is actively supported by Functional Managers who have team members within the Core Team, and also by the Functional Support Teams. As a consequence, they also become focused on driving operational performance by default. Therefore, by implementing the 'MDI' process, and by requiring your teams to utilise it, everyone in your facility becomes focused on driving operational performance.

Secondly, it does so by providing a standard forum and methodology for both the management of normal daily change, and the management and execution of the Improvement Plan we've already defined. It utilises exactly the same tools, behaviours and thinking processes for either scenario, and encourages teams and team members to independently prioritise what *needs* to be worked on first. They can choose to manage the challenge or challenges that have arisen today, or to work on the actions agreed within their Improvement Plan, depending on the level of prioritisation that they define. Once a team has agreed their priorities for a given day, they can utilise the same thinking processes and whiteboard tools to properly analyse, define, agree and manage the actions required for resolution. And, even when choosing to prioritise daily change, they can do so with clear consideration for the needs of their overall Improvement Plan at the same time.

At its heart, therefore, the 'MDI' process is based upon a relatively simple idea. But as a consequence, when properly applied it is extremely effective. This may seem like an exaggeration, but please do not under estimate the value of this structured daily meeting. It's a meeting which empowers team members to manage their performance and solve their problems, but does so by requiring them to follow a set of guiding principles, and by utilising a set of complementary tools, which encourages them to prioritise and solve problems in the most logical and sensible way to support the improvement we have targeted. Just as with Toyota's '*Improvement Kata*' identified by Rother, and with the '*Culture of Discipline*' identified by Collins, the 'MDI' process provides the framework on which the continuous improvement we seek on our *Lean Foundations*™ journey can be delivered, whilst coping with the constant change that we'll experience on the way.

As a final point of consideration, it's also important to appreciate just how much the 'MDI' process compliments so many of the other aspects of our *Lean Foundations*™ journey. As we already know, we're striving to improve workplace happiness, operational performance, and to create a platform for Lean. In reality, we're seeking to create the foundations that will enable us to achieve operational excellence through the implementation of Lean. We also know that the operational performance of our facility is ultimately determined by our ability to deliver on the core performance indicators of Safety, Quality, Delivery, Cost, and Engagement. As a community we're learning, perhaps the hard way, that it's the right kind of focus on these points that is at the true heart of Lean. And finally, we know that to deliver on these core performance indicators, we need to properly support our front-line team members. We need to empower and engage them, to enable them with a well-functioning management system, and to enthuse them with a healthy organisation that embraces effective teamwork.

Now, considering that persuasive logic, it's hopefully clear to see how the 'MDI' process can actively support aspects such as effective teamwork, can provide a forum for healthy debate and conflict, can support the empowerment of front-line team members, and can be an effective component of a well-functioning management system. It brings people together and encourages them to take responsibility for their performance, and the performance of their team. It provides them with a forum for making decisions, for seeking support, for healthy debate and conflict, and for escalating concerns. And, as part of a wider management system, it provides a clear methodology for responding to and resolving issues as they arise in real time. In simple terms, it's a win-win.

How does it work – the basic principles

First of all, there are a number of basic principles that underpin the 'MDI' process which shape both how it works, and how the people using it think and behave. I have come to realise that some of these basic principles are closely linked to ideas presented by Mike Rother in '*Toyota Kata*'. Having read his book a number of years ago, and compared it with the 'MDI' process, it's obvious to me that by sheer luck and coincidence much of what Rother identifies in Toyota's approach is also shared in the 'MDI'. Hopefully that's a good sign.

- *The 'MDI' process happens every day in every area of the facility* - Change happens daily, and the ability to improve only happens as a consequence of consistent small steps towards a long-term objective. Therefore, the process which manages that change and delivers that improvement has to happen on a daily basis.

- *The 'MDI' process is focused on driving the performance of the core KPI's of Safety, Quality, Delivery, Cost and Engagement* – Operational excellence is only delivered through a rigorous and disciplined focus on performance, and particularly in the KPI's that reflect a commitment to the respect of our employees, the respect of our customers, and the respect of our financial security.

- *The 'MDI' process is aligned with the Improvement Plan* – The overall Improvement Plan is always a factor for consideration when assessing performance and deciding priorities. It provides guidance of direction and helps to enable empowered independent decision-making.

- *The 'MDI' process is committed to solving problems* – Improvement is only delivered as a consequence of solving problems; of fixing things that are not correct. Managing constant daily change also requires the ability and willingness to solve problems that occur in real time.

- *The 'MDI' process utilises the PDCA/TOC thinking process* – Regardless of whether the problem at hand originates from the desire to work towards the Improvement Plan, or from dealing with daily change, the approach taken in solving it is consistent. Following the logical thinking process of 'What to Change', 'What to Change to', 'How to Change', 'Implement the Change', 'Evaluate the Change', and 'Start Again', provides a simple mechanism that all team members can learn to apply consistently regardless of the nature and origination of the problem.

- *The 'MDI' process works at the process level* – The Improvement Plan and Policy Deployment process is focused on driving improvement at the organisational level, by considering top-level facility-wide issues. However, the 'MDI' process is focused on solving problems at the detailed process level, where tangible improvement is really delivered.

- *The 'MDI' process utilises facts and information rather than opinion* – Whilst the top-level Improvement Plan was happy to consider intuition and instinct in deciding on direction and priorities, the 'MDI' process solves problems at a process level and therefore needs to utilise facts and information to ensure that proposed solutions are effective and comprehensive.

- *The 'MDI' process is a team-based activity* – Cross-functional teamwork is required to deliver continuous improvement whilst dealing with constant daily change. Therefore, all members of the Core Team and Support Team are required to be involved. At the same time, the 'MDI' process is not reliant on the individual leader of the facility, and can continue regardless of who is in charge at the time.

If you choose to introduce the 'MDI' process in your facility (and I would strongly advise you to do so), it's important that you and your team appreciate and understand these eight simple principles. They provide clear guidance of how the 'MDI' process should function, and how each team member should endeavour to think and behave when operating within it. By following the basic principles provided, everyone can apply a disciplined approach to the pursuit of operational performance, and can be consistent in their approach to the delivery of the Improvement Plan, and the management of constant daily change.

When implementing the 'MDI' process, I would suggest that it's a good idea for you to share these eight principles with all of your team members, and to ensure that they understand and appreciate them fully with appropriate training if necessary. I would also suggest that you consider documenting and presenting them on the whiteboard tools that I'll describe in the next section so that they can be constantly reinforced throughout every daily meeting.

How does it work – the meetings and boards

As I've already stated, the 'MDI' process is built around a structured and well-defined daily meeting process, which utilises a set of standard whiteboard tools. It's a process that has evolved over a number of different applications into its current form, and is now fairly well established. However, as with anything, it's open to improvement and is often tweaked to each environment in which it is applied.

The meeting process is actually a sequence of two meetings, the first being the 'Performance & Plan' meeting, and the second being the 'Report Out' meeting. Each meeting utilises the same three whiteboard formats, the 'Information Board', the 'Team Performance Board', and the 'Issue Resolution Board'.

The 'Performance & Plan' meeting is undertaken by the Core Team, and can last anywhere between 20 and 30 minutes. It has three primary objectives. First, the meeting requires the Core Team to review the operational performance of their area of responsibility over the previous 24 hours, and to determine what actions if any are required to address any performance issues. Second, the meeting requires the Core Team to 'plan for today', and therefore tasks them to discuss and agree things like production schedules, capacity constraints, delivery plans, and customer specific requests. Third, the meeting serves as a daily touch-base with the status of their Improvement Plan or Projects, and again requires the Core Team to update the status of any open actions, and to decide on any further actions that are required to maintain the progress of their plan.

To meet the first objective of reviewing the previous day's performance, the Core Team focuses on using the 'Team Performance Board'. The format of this board is designed to support two primary activities. First, it needs to be able to identify current performance of each of the core performance indicators of Safety, Quality, Delivery, Cost, and Engagement. Importantly, it also needs to be able to compare this current performance with recent performance, so that trends can be identified and responded to when necessary. Second, it needs to provide a means for recording actions taken by the Core Team in response to performance issues, in the process identifying who is responsible for their completion, and by when.

Figure 5.1 presents an example format.

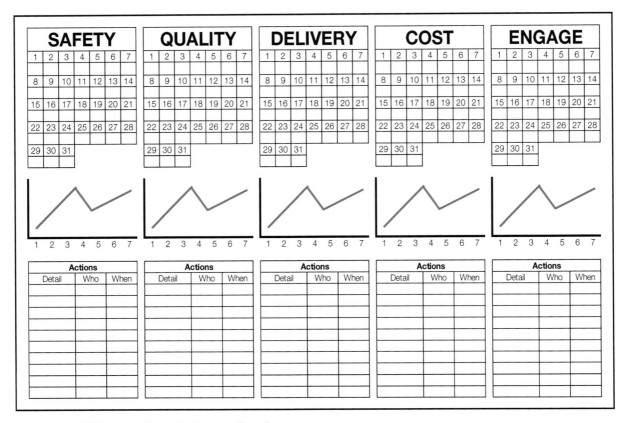

Fig 5-1. The 'MDI' process 'Team Performance Board'

Of course, your format does not need to look exactly as this does, but this is a format that I have used successfully on a number of occasions. The Core Team is required to populate the daily performance as part of the discussion, and to determine and record what actions are required, who within the Core Team is responsible for completing them, and when they need to be completed by. You're likely to find that as you're dealing with daily issues, the actions are mainly of the 'short and sweet' variety, and are things that are hopefully relatively straightforward to resolve in a short space of time. In addressing their performance in this manner, it's important that the Core Team are encouraged to be aware of and to utilise the basic principles of the 'MDI', and in particular the PDCA/TOC thinking processes. It's also important that they're encouraged to prioritise, and where possible to only address issues that are real problems so that they maintain the capacity to consider the needs of their Improvement Plan too. They can of course, use the part of the board that contains the graphical data of the performance over time to help inform their decision-making process. Where trends are negative, action may be more likely to be required versus one-offs. It's here where information from the 'Start of Day' meetings proposed in Step 4 can also be included. It's likely that members of the Core Team have led or been part of 'Start of Day' meetings with their teams in production, quality, or planning and logistics. As a consequence, they're already aware of the previous

168

day's performance, and may be well informed of the causes of any issues from the team members who were part of their 'Start of Day' meeting. Including any issues from those meetings helps to reinforce their validity and value, with the 'MDI' meeting effectively acting as an escalation route for issues from the 'Start of Day' meetings.

In identifying and discussing problems, it may become obvious that a particular problem is a high priority and requires considerable focus. For example, I have always ensured that any accident that occurs in my facility is treated as a high priority issue, along with any customer quality complaint. In addition, it may also become apparent that the Core Team is unable to resolve a problem independently, and may require assistance from the Functional Support Teams, both from within Operations, and from external functions such as Engineering, Commercial, or Product Management. In both of these circumstances, the Core Team is then encouraged to utilise the 'Issue Resolution Board', and is required to populate the details of that problem onto it.

This 'Issue Resolution Board' has a much more prescribed format, and is something that I would advise that you utilise as shown below. The format is deliberately aligned to the basic steps of a typical problem-solving approach, which we'll explore further in Step 6. Its purpose is to enable a slightly more detailed problem-solving mentality and approach to be applied to more complex and challenging problems, and to facilitate the solving of those problems by the appropriate team members from both the Core Team, and the Functional Support Teams, including those from outside of Operations.

Date	Priority	Issue	Containment			Root Cause & Countermeasures	Action	Who	When
			Action	Start	Days				

Fig 5-2. The 'MDI' process 'Issue Resolution Board'

In the 'Performance & Plan' meeting, it's the responsibility of the Core Team to populate the first half of this board. They should define the problem, the day it occurred, and the level of prioritisation it occupies. They should also endeavour to identify a containment action if possible, and to record when it became effective, and how many days it's been effective for. Following on from this, the issue can then be discussed as part of the 'Report Out' meeting, which I'll go through later in this section.

Be aware, in the early stages of introducing an 'MDI' process, you're likely to identify a lot of problems. Issues that you weren't even aware existed often come to the surface as team members take advantage of having their voice heard, or as investigations into problems identify more and more issues. Here is where the ability to prioritise really comes to the fore, and the ability of yourself and the Ops Team Manager to coach the Core Team through the challenge becomes critical. At the same time, it's a great opportunity to reinforce empowerment, and in the process organisational health and psychological safety.

To meet the second objective of the 'Performance & Plan' meeting, and to 'plan the day', the Core Team is required to utilise the 'Information Board'. This board is the most flexible in terms of content and format, because in reality every manufacturing facility is different, and works in different ways. Most importantly, the board needs to include a form of 'production plan' that is appropriate to the individual facility. It might be a finite production schedule for each cell or line in the Core Team area, or it might be a top-level capacity analysis. If you're leading a JIT facility, it might simply be a Buffer/Stock and expected hourly demand tracker. It's this 'production plan' that the team should review and agree as part of the 'Performance & Plan' meeting. Remember, the Core Team is likely to include Production Supervisors, Quality Engineers, Manufacturing Engineers, and perhaps even a Planning Supervisor or a Logistics Supervisor. A daily discussion around a production plan between these team members can add significant value in ensuring that delivery performance is a priority, that it's achieved, and that any cross-functional problems restricting it are highlighted in advance and resolved. For example, perhaps a quality hold is in place on a particular component, and as a consequence a scheduled customer order is at risk of being delivered late. The 'Performance & Plan' part of the 'MDI' process can highlight the risk, and can task the appropriate team members with resolving the quality issue so that the delivery can be achieved. In my experience, delivery performance is often a repetitive problem in a manufacturing facility, and this simple daily discussion can add significant value in improving it.

In addition, the 'Information Board' should also include any other relevant data and information that the team will need to use. I have always included a copy of the overall Improvement Plan, and any local Improvement Plans that have been developed by the individual team. I would also include a copy of the top-level 'X-Matrix'. The inclusion of these plans allows for team members to remind themselves of their medium and long-term objectives as a team, and provides a point of reference for them when determining prioritisations of activity in relation to daily challenges when meeting the third objective. You might also choose to reference your Quality Standards, or your Health and Safety and Environmental policies. You may share an organigram for the particular team area, or a Holiday/Vacation and planned absence chart. You may publish the reports associated with any customer quality complaints, or for any health and safety related incidents that have occurred within the team area. This is also where I would suggest that you present the 'MDI' process 'Basic principles' list, so that it's always available as a reminder. The options are pretty endless, and are basically open to the requirements of the individual team and your individual facility. I would suggest that you agree the content of this board with each team in your facility, and in the process ensure that it covers all eventualities. Of course, it can evolve and change over time as each team becomes more adept at utilising the 'MDI' process.

To meet the third objective of the 'Performance & Plan' meeting, and to touch-base with the status of their Improvement Plan(s), the Core Team is likely to utilise all three board formats. Firstly, they will use the 'Information Board' in order to access a copy of the top-level Improvement Plan, and any team-based Improvement Plans. They can be expected to quickly understand the status of their plan, and to determine whether any particular activities are outstanding or need to be discussed. Secondly, they can utilise the 'Team Performance Board', where any open actions can be reviewed, or new actions can be raised based on the level of capacity of the team. Finally, the 'Issue Resolution Board' can be used, where any critical, difficult to solve, or shared issues can be raised in order to enable a more detailed analysis and resolution, or to seek support from Functional Support Teams in the 'Report Out' meetings. Again, at this stage it's important to encourage the Core Team to be aware of and to utilise the basic principles of the 'MDI', and in particular the PDCA/TOC thinking processes.

It should be noted here that even with the effectiveness of the 'MDI' process in balancing the challenges of daily change with the desire to continuously improve, there will be times where daily change is overwhelming. If you've worked in a manufacturing environment for long enough, you'll know this to be true. My advice here is to be prepared to go with the flow. When the daily challenges overpower the Improvement Plan, there will be a need to reschedule the Improvement Plan. Remember, as Dwight D. Eisenhower said "*… Plans are worthless. Planning is everything…*", and egotistically hanging onto a plan that going to fail is not worthwhile, particularly when managing important daily challenges is what has got in the way. You're going to damage the psychological safety and intrinsic motivators of the team, and you're going to appear 'Coercive' in your management style when you're trying to empower. Please be prepared to adapt, and be appreciative of the fact that you know exactly why you've had to do so, and have made the right choices in the process.

The 'Report Out' meeting is led by a representative of the Core Team (although all Core Team members can be present if they wish), and involves representatives of the Functional Support Teams, and managers of functions that have team members who are part of the Core Team. So, for example, it would include the

Ops Team Manager, and a representative from perhaps Purchasing, Health & Safety, and Facilities & Maintenance. It could also include the Quality Manager, and representatives from other functions such as Engineering, Commercial, or Product Management. Importantly, it's also the forum that you can join as leader of your facility. It's sensible for it to last around 20 to 25 minutes. The 'Report Out' meeting has two primary objectives. First, the meeting requires the Core Team to report their performance for the previous day, and their plan for the current day, to the rest of the team. In doing so they are able to demonstrate that they have control, and are managing their responsibilities alongside the needs of their Improvement Plan or Plans. Second, the meeting provides a forum for the Core Team to ask for help, and to utilise a slightly more in-depth problem-solving methodology when receiving that help through the use of the 'Issue Resolution Board'.

To meet the first objective, the Core Team utilises the 'Team Performance Board', and the 'Information Board'. Using the 'Team Performance Board', they are required to report out a brief summary of their performance for the previous day, and any actions that they have agreed to resolve performance issues. They should also communicate where they have chosen to work on actions relating to their Improvement Plan. Using the 'Information Board', they are required to share the details of their production plan for the day, communicating any challenges that they may have in achieving customer deliveries, and any actions they're planning to take to mitigate the risk.

As hopefully you can see, the 'Performance and Plan' meeting is an empowering experience for the Core Team members. They're required to take responsibility for the performance of their area, and are supported with management tools to enable them to meet that responsibility. Therefore, it's important in this first part of the 'Report Out' meeting to carefully manage the responses of the Management team and Functional Support Team representatives. It can be very easy for individuals to respond 'Coercively' if they feel that the Core Team is not managing a problem effectively, or has not selected the right problem to manage in the first place. If this happens, the empowering benefits of the 'MDI' process can disappear very quickly, and the psychological safety and intrinsic motivators of the team can be severely damaged. Instead, this part of the meeting provides an ideal opportunity to coach Core Team members if necessary, or to demonstrate appreciation and recognition for a job well done when appropriate. It's an opportunity for you as leader of your facility to model the right behaviour, and to encourage it as a consequence. It's also an ideal opportunity for you to challenge and correct the wrong behaviour if necessary. If it's managed properly, the benefits to empowerment, and to psychological safety and intrinsic motivators, are significant. You should look to ensure that this part of the 'MDI' process is very carefully managed as a consequence.

To meet the second objective, the Core Team utilises the 'Issue Resolution Board'. With support from all of the other attendees, the team can review the status of any problems and relevant actions for each of the issues listed. Where new issues are raised, a mini problem-solving discussion can be held with all team members. This discussion should endeavour to agree how to contain the problem if not already done, should seek to define the root cause, and should consider what countermeasures can be introduced and the actions that are required to implement them. These actions can then be recorded on the 'Issue Resolution Board', with clear responsibilities and expected completion dates identified. It is possible that a problem that arises is too complex to resolve in a brief morning meeting, and therefore may need to be taken offline. We'll discuss methodologies for supporting this in Step 6, but it's important at this point to note the offline investigation as an action on the board. Where issues have been raised previously, the team can discuss the status of any open actions, and can update progress accordingly. Here is where the Core Team is able to hold members of the Functional Support Team to account with support from members of the Management team, and even yourself. If actions are not being completed in a timely manner by Functional Support Team members, or perhaps other priorities are getting in the way, this part of the 'MDI' process helps to identify the issue, and provides the opportunity for resolution. In this circumstance, it's sensible to expect your Management team members to be able to agree to re-prioritise activities in order to support the Core Team. In addition, it may be necessary for you to escalate issues to your peers if actions from functions outside of Operations are not being completed. It's also perfectly acceptable to encourage your peers to join the 'MDI' process every now and again so that they can offer their direct support, and can demonstrate their commitment to the process.

Everything that I have just described may seem extremely intense. You may wonder how on earth it can all be contained in two 20 to 30-minute meetings. However, experience tells me that it can; sometimes easily, and sometimes not so easily. When you first get started, it's unlikely that you'll cover everything as people get used to the process. Even after a while of operating with it, some days just blow you out of the water. But, after just a few days of using the 'MDI' process, I usually see the early signs of the positive outcomes that I would expect. And, within a month, it becomes the norm, and the people that use it never want to go back to what they had before. The 'MDI' process empowers the Core Team, because it expects them to take responsibility for their performance, and provides them support in achieving that expectation. It also provides a forum where empowering leadership can be demonstrated; where managers and leaders can coach, advise, support, and engage. The 'MDI' process provides control of the day. It learns from and solves problems from yesterday, and seeks to highlight risks and mitigate them today. The 'MDI' process enhances organisational health and psychological safety. It demonstrates that people are trusted, it aligns their activities to the long-term purpose of the facility, it enables them to collaborate with one another, it drives them to improve, and it gives them autonomy and responsibility. The 'MDI' process provides a forum for the disciplined pursuit of operational performance. It puts operational performance at the heart of every team member's daily priorities and thought processes. The 'MDI' process also provides a forum for balancing daily change with continuous improvement. It enables teams to identify their priorities, and gives them the opportunity to select what *needs* to be worked on first to make the most significant impact. If there is one thing in *Lean Foundations™* above all else that makes a real difference, it's the 'MDI' process.

Setting up your 'MDI'

Getting your own 'MDI' process started may seem a little daunting, but it's actually quite simple. It only requires you to consider a number of easy to resolve practicalities. Take a look at the main ones that I've listed below…

- *Train your people* – I would advise you not to throw people into the deep end with this. Using the information presented previously, train your people on how the process works, and in particular on the 8 basic principles of the 'MDI'. It will make the introduction of the process far easier.

- *Sourcing the whiteboards* - I have found that it's best to ensure that these whiteboards are magnetic, that they are individually mobile and on wheels, are positioned so that you have access to both sides, and are large enough to contain everything they need to (around 1800mm x 1200mm). They're usually fairly easy to procure from your stationery and equipment provider, and are relatively inexpensive. Of course, depending on the number of Core Teams you've established, you may need quite a few.

- *Creating the whiteboards* - You'll need to decide exactly how you're going to create and administrate the boards, in particular the 'Team Performance Board'. In the past, I've used lining tape or permanent marker to define the lines, and have wiped it clean at the start of each month, leaving only the open actions and the over-time performance data in the graphical area. On other occasions, the Core Teams have printed a blank formatted sheet from a large printer and have transferred the actions and performance trend information from the previous month onto it, before swapping it with the sheet from the previous month. The choice, of course, is yours, depending on what equipment you have access to, and how much time you can spend administrating it.

- *Board location* - I have usually defined a specific location on the factory floor or within an office for the boards to occupy in each of the team areas, and have even painted the floor a different colour to clearly identify that location. It's also here that your daily meetings will take place, so you need to identify a location where the environment and noise conditions can support the right kind of healthy and sometimes conflicting discussions. At the same time, it's good to keep the boards in the actual production area, so that all team members can see the meetings taking place, and can review the boards when the opportunity presents itself. It can give them the confidence that issues that affect them are being addressed.

- *Team Performance KPI's* - You will need to select exactly which KPI's you wish to use to reflect the core performance indicators of Safety, Quality, Delivery, Cost and Engagement. Will you use Accidents, Reportable Accidents, or Hazards reported? Will you use Customer Returns, Right First Time, or Supplier Rejects? Will you use On-time in Full to Commitment, or to Customer Request, or if you're a

JIT facility perhaps Line Stops, Delivery Gaps or Buffer size? Will you use Scrap, or Labour Efficiency, Cost of Poor Quality, or Overtime? Will you use Attendance, number of Issues Raised (perhaps in the Start of Day meetings), or Improvement Ideas? The choice here is yours, depending on the nature of your manufacturing facility, and where your priorities lie. Whichever you choose, it's important to ensure that they are already part of your top-level Improvement Plan and your 'X-Matrix' in the 'What – KPI's' panel.

- *Team Performance daily recording* - Hopefully you've recognised that the numbered squares under each of the core performance indicators represent days of the month. You'll need to decide whether to populate these squares with actual numerical values, or with colour-coded indicators such as a green circle for on target, an orange circle for just below target, and a red circle for well below target. Again, the choice is yours. I've used both options in the past and have found that both have their strengths and weaknesses. The numerical values offer more detailed information, and help when trying to correlate with the graphical information. The colour-coded indicators help to draw the eye and highlight trends and anomalies.

- *Team Performance graphical recording* - The graphical area is designed so that you can show performance trends over time. You'll need to decide exactly how long you wish to present data for, relevant to your circumstances and administrative processes. You'll also need to decide how you're going to populate this area. Will it be with a printed graph that you attach perhaps once a week, or will it be something that is drawn on the board and is manually filled in with whiteboard pens.

- *Team Performance actions* - The action area can get somewhat busy. You'll need to define rules around how many actions can be raised, what demonstrates that an action is complete, and who is authorised to remove/close an action.

- *Meeting schedule* – You'll need to decide who is required to attend each of the meetings, both the 'Performance & Plan', and the 'Report Out', and will need to schedule the meetings into everyone's diaries. Today, that's usually somewhat easier with the use of email and diary management software tools. I would advise that you schedule the meetings in at set times, early in the day, and that they very rarely if ever change. All other meetings should be rescheduled around them in order to emphasise their importance, and only major events should ever cause them to be cancelled. Where you have more than one Core Team, I would advise that you schedule the 'Performance & Plan' meetings to take place at the same time, and for the 'Report Out' meetings to take place at staggered times following this so that Functional Support Team members can travel from one 'Report Out' meeting to the next. To give you an example here, I once ran a facility with three Core Teams. Their 'Performance & Plan' meetings all took place from 08:30 to 08:55. The 'Report Out' meetings took place at 09:00 to 09:20, 09:20 to 09:40, and 09:40 to 10:00. This may seem like a lot of time in meetings. However, the Core Teams were only in meetings for a total of 45 minutes, and the Functional Support Teams were only in meetings for a total of 60 minutes. And, in some cases, different representatives from the Functional Support Teams attended different 'Report Out' meetings, reducing the time even further. Even without this, spending up to an hour in a series of meetings each day, and in the process gaining a full understanding of the status of the facility, should hopefully be considered as extremely beneficial, and by no means a waste of time.

- *Engaging non-Ops support* - When seeking to invite team members from outside your operational responsibilities from functions such as Engineering, Commercial, or Product Management, it's of course important to maintain positive relationships and to seek agreement and approval from your peers in those functions. By engaging those functions, you will be influencing their workload and priorities, and this can cause friction if not managed carefully. At the same time, it's important to involve them as the 'MDI' process can help to extend the *'Operations is where it's at'* mentality, and can influence these non-operational functions to take operational performance seriously.

- *Information Board format* – You'll need to decide exactly how to present your production plan or schedule information, and you'll need to decide what other information you think it's relevant to include.

- *Issue Resolution prioritisation* – You'll need to decide how you will communicate prioritisation on the 'Issue Resolution Board'. Will you use numerical values, or alphabetical? And will you have one, two, three or more layers of prioritisation?

- *Delegate* – The best piece of advice I can give you is to delegate responsibility for setting this up to your teams. Once you've trained them, task them to implement it. They'll love it – trust me.

STEP 5 SUMMARY

In completing Step 5 of your *Lean Foundations*™ journey, I hope I have successfully persuaded you to introduce the 'MDI' process into your facility, and I hope I have provided you with sufficient information to enable you to do so successfully. If so, you will have introduced a massively significant process into your facility. All of the steps taken up to this point have added value to our desire to improve workplace happiness, operational performance, and our ability to utilise Lean. However, now that you've introduced the 'MDI' process, you will have provided a tool and forum for everyone in your facility to put all the other Steps into practice on a daily basis. And, you'll have introduced a level of discipline, married with a sensible ability to balance priorities, that will really drive your facility forward. It's also important to remind ourselves of just how much we should benefit from placing daily operational performance at the heart of every team member's daily routines. Even those functions who are not operationally responsible will be drawn into the process, assuming of course that you can encourage them to be drawn in. This is where your persuasion skills will be most tested. I would actively encourage you to develop positive and constructive relationships with your peers (as I suggested at the end of Step 1), and to seek their support in agreeing this working philosophy with their functions for the benefit of the facility as a whole. It can be difficult, and personalities can get in the way, but I can testify that it is achievable, and that there is opportunity for mutual gain for both parties. (*By the way, this is exactly why I asked CEO's, Managing Directors, and VP's to realise that 'Operations is where it's at' at the end of Step 4 – if you're one of these people, you can help here by setting the expectation that all support functions prioritise their activities to support operational performance – just as Toyota have*).

In drawing Step 5 to a close, let's take a moment to quickly review the main points…

- It's not unusual for manufacturing facilities to face constant daily change, whilst not necessarily seeming to change very much at all. It can appear as if constant daily change restricts the ability to continuously improve.

- The most successful organisations are able to demonstrate a '*Culture of Discipline*' in the pursuit and execution of their performance and plans.

- In *Lean Foundations™*, the 'MDI' process is advocated as a means of introducing a '*Culture of Discipline*', and as a means of introducing a Toyota like '*Improvement Kata*', which can embed improvement focused thinking processes and behaviour routines into our management system.

- The 'MDI' process is a well-defined daily meeting process which utilises standard meeting protocols, standard whiteboard tools, and a set of basic principles that guide the way it functions. Its purpose is to provide a forum that enables a team to drive operational performance with discipline, and to facilitate the prioritisation of the management of daily change alongside the pursuit of an Improvement Plan.

- The 'MDI' process has eight basic principles which shape both how it works, and how the people using it think and behave. It's critical that all team members involved in the 'MDI' process understand and appreciate these 8 basic principles, and engage with them when part of the meeting process.

- The 'MDI' process functions with two inter-connected meetings, the 'Performance & Plan' meeting held by the Core Team(s), and the 'Report Out' meeting involving both the Core Team(s), and the Functional Support Team(s).

- The 'MDI' process utilises three standard format whiteboards, the 'Information Board', the 'Team Performance Board', and the 'Issue Resolution Board', in a structured and well-defined process.

- The 'MDI' process may appear a little daunting to introduce, but is actually fairly straightforward and simply requires the completion of a number of practical activities.

- The introduction of the 'MDI' process on the *Lean Foundations™* journey is a truly significant milestone. It brings together all of the elements we've addressed so far, and enables psychological safety, empowerment, and our intrinsic motivators.

6

STEP

Embed a problem-solving mentality

All too often, when I'm working hard to make progress on a *Lean Foundations*™ journey, I find that I'm confronted by the same challenge. On numerous occasions, I have seen that the ability of my team to forge ahead is restricted by their ability to accept a very simple idea. *Identifying problems is good*.

It seems that, whilst we all know that fixing problems is a good thing to do, none of us want to be the one to actually identify the problem in the first place. Either we're afraid that we are the cause of the problem, and don't want to be blamed for it. Or, we don't want to risk damaging professional relationships by pointing out a problem that someone else is responsible for. It's all too easy to seem like you're making an accusation, when in fact you're just trying to get something resolved. It's even possible that we don't want to raise an issue that's going to create more work, just when we're all busy enough. As a consequence, problems can remain hidden and don't get solved. And, even when they do raise their head, people instinctively react defensively. Unhealthy conflict can arise, and genuine efforts to solve a problem can be lost in the midst of a heated debate. Worst of all, people can become apathetic, and stop bothering to raise problems in the first place. They find workarounds that are inefficient, and which carry with them an inherent level of frustration and disappointment. Or they 'sandbag' their processes; building excess inventory, or over-inflating the time required, in order to compensate for the problems that they face.

Even after the implementation of the previous Steps of *Lean Foundations*™, I often witness this kind of reluctance. Despite all of the focus on improving psychological safety, organisational health, and teamwork, the mindset of hiding problems can sometimes endure. It seems to be ingrained into our psyche, and therefore takes considerable effort to change. And this is only part of the challenge. Alongside our reluctance to identify problems, is a lack of understanding on how to solve them properly. It's not unusual for someone to suggest that a problem has been solved, only for it to reoccur again in the very near future. Or, for a solution to be put in place that causes greater problems elsewhere. Even when good solutions are identified, they can often fall by the wayside when people habitually return to their old ways of working, or when the new working methods are not passed on properly to new employees. Taking the quick and easy option can often be the norm, with assumptions about the cause of a problem leading us to jump to poorly defined conclusions about the right solution. It can be rare for us to take the time to properly understand, diagnose, and then solve a problem once and for all.

In his hugely influential book '*The Toyota Way*', Jeffrey Liker seeks to improve our understanding of Lean, by providing a comprehensive insight into Toyota's culture and management systems. He summarises 14 management principles that Toyota have integrated into their daily routines and processes, and he gives some insight into how those principles have influenced Toyota's success. In defining these 14 principles, Liker sub-divides them into four categories, and highlights 'Problem-Solving', and the development of a problem-solving mentality, as the critical fourth category. He describes how Toyota have embedded problem-solving into their DNA. How they encourage their employees to stop production when a problem occurs in order to destigmatise problem identification and to encourage continuous improvement. How they have integrated the Japanese practice of *hansei*, or deep and thoughtful reflection, into the evaluation of their individual and team performance so that feelings of blame are replaced with a willingness to learn. And how they have developed and institutionalised a problem-solving approach that rigorously facilitates root cause analysis and countermeasures.

In developing the *Lean Foundations™* approach, and having learned from Liker's '*The Toyota Way*', I have endeavoured to find ways to replicate Toyota's culture and methodologies in relation to problem identification and problem-solving. I have sought to find a way to encourage my team members to view problems as opportunities for learning and improvement, rather than as sticks to be beaten with. And, I have looked to develop a problem-solving approach that is easy to understand and apply, without being too time consuming and cumbersome. In some ways, this part of *Lean Foundations™* is often the most challenging aspect of the journey, as the mentality of defensiveness and 'quick and easy' can be so deeply ingrained. In my experience, there is a cultural battle to be won in changing the way people think and behave, and it requires constant and consistent leadership over a protracted period of time to truly embed it. However, I believe that it is possible. And, I believe that it's a vital component of building a facility that performs well, and for establishing the foundations upon which operational excellence can grow. Without the ability to identify and solve problems, any process of improvement will be fundamentally flawed, even with all of the previous Steps of *Lean Foundations™* in place. Our efforts to introduce Policy Deployment, empowering leadership, and the 'MDI' process, will fall short of meeting their full potential if we cannot encourage our team members to abandon their intuition to hide and defend their problems, and to embrace a more deliberate and capable problem-solving methodology.

So far, we've made considerable progress on our *Lean Foundations™* journey. We are actively embracing organisational health and psychological safety as a means of delivering effective teamwork, and in encouraging a sense of autonomy and responsibility in our team. We have built a team-oriented organisation structure which is filled with the right people to drive your facility forward. We have developed a detailed and thorough plan which supports our strategy of becoming a great place to work by improving workplace happiness and operational performance, and by creating a platform for Lean. We have also ensured that our objectives and targets within that plan are challenging and will stretch the capabilities of your team. We are embracing a leadership approach that actively empowers our team members, and gives them the freedom to deliver their daily responsibilities alongside the need for improvement. And finally, we have begun the process of building the management practices that systemise standard thinking processes into our daily routines, by introducing the vital and transformative 'MDI' process.

Our next challenge, therefore, is to ensure that we do not waste all of our previous efforts, and that we find a way to help our team members to unlearn the deeply ingrained mindsets around problem identification and problem-solving. We need to be able to introduce working practices and methodologies which actively encourage them to identify problems with enthusiasm, rather than with fear. And, we need to introduce a problem-solving process that enables effective and practical root cause analysis and countermeasure, rather than slapdash solutions that stem from a 'quick and easy' mindset. Following the example set by Toyota, and resulting from my own process of *hansei*, the *Lean Foundations™* approach has developed a number of tools and methodologies to support the challenge that confronts us. We'll work through just two sub-steps to help you to introduce these ideas into your facility: 'Be positive about problems', and 'Problem-solving practically'. I hope that, in presenting these sub-steps, I'm successful in supporting you in transforming the mental models of your team members, so that they can fully embrace the power of problem-solving as the route to improvement.

BE POSITIVE ABOUT PROBLEMS

Changing mindsets is difficult and takes time, particularly when they are based on deeply held cultural stereotypes. It's important at this point not to underestimate the challenge before us, and to be prepared to commit the time, thought and energy to the endeavour. However, the fact that this mindset exists within some or even all of our team members is just a problem in itself. Having identified its existence in the first place is a positive. It's not our fault that it exists, nor is it the fault of the people who hold it. It may even be a trait that we share ourselves. But now that we have identified it, we can understand its damaging effects, and we can take advantage of the opportunity to do something about it. I have found, through a simple process of reflection and basic problem-solving, that there are things that can be done to improve the mindsets of our team members around problem identification and problem-solving. What's described here are a series of simple activities and processes that you can introduce into your facility, and which I believe can make a difference to how your team think. In the process, you can remove a restricting barrier, and introduce a potent catalyst for improvement, which can energise your *Lean Foundations™* journey, and which can support your desire to build the foundations on which operational excellence is built. Let's get to it.

Train your people – the 'Water and the Rocks'

As you may have expected, the first activity in this sub-step is to train your people. I have found that the best way to adjust how people think about problem identification and problem-solving is to make them fully aware of their unconscious mindsets and mental biases. However, simply pointing them out is not necessarily enough. And so, I've come to utilise a very well-established Lean idea to help the training process.

First of all, as with all the other times that I have suggested that you train your team members, exactly how you chose to do it is entirely up to you. As I have stated previously, you may decide to complete the training with external training providers as support, or you may complete it yourself by compiling the training material from the content described in this book. In this particular scenario, I would suggest that it is something that you could do yourself, or it could be done by your Continuous Improvement Manager (if you have one in your team of course). It may even be something that you chose to integrate with some of the other training sessions I've mentioned previously. For example, I have often included it as part of the 'Lean Awareness' training that I discussed earlier in Step 4.

When delivering the training, I find that it's a good idea for it to cover both aspects of our problem. First, how we as individuals can instinctively shy away from raising problems. Second, how poor problem-solving processes can impact our operational performance, and what good problem-solving looks like. What I have found to be most important, is that the training should be very direct in pointing out the mindsets of hiding problems and 'quick and easy' solution chasing. I believe it's important to confront the problem of these mindsets head-on, and to be able describe their potential to hold back the improvement journey that you're on. And that's where the well-known Lean metaphor of the 'Water and the Rocks', illustrated in the graphic below, can help.

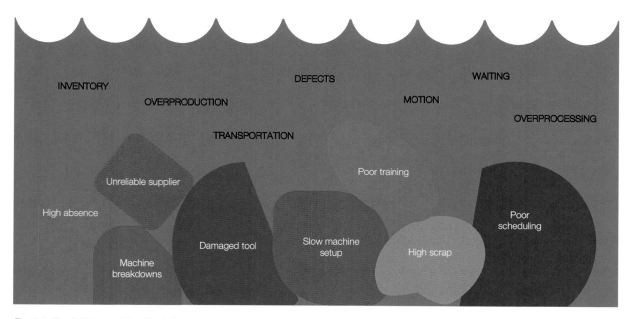

Fig 6-1. The 'Water and the Rocks'

The idea is quite simple. In the metaphor, the water on which a ship is sailing represents waste, and the rocks that sit below the water level are problems. Because of the mindsets of hiding problems, of taking the 'quick and easy' option, or of following the path of least resistance, when finding a problem, we often raise the water level in order to avoid it. In effect, we add waste into our processes, such as inventory, or additional time, and as a consequence we make ourselves less efficient, less effective, and add burden to our already busy working lives. It's also likely that as a consequence, we'll be disappointed and frustrated with the fact that we have to manage such inefficiencies, and therefore impact our workplace happiness.

Hopefully you can recognise how this uncomplicated metaphor can help your team members understand the importance of both identifying problems, and then properly fixing them. By describing how our unconscious biases influence our behaviour, it's much easier to help people to appreciate the impacts they have, and the need to change them. Often, I'm able to support the training with real life examples from the particular facility that I'm working within. I've been able to point to high levels of inventory of raw materials that are being held to compensate for a supplier whose delivery performance is unreliable. Or I've been able to identify additional overtime costs resulting from the need to replace lost production time as a consequence of equipment breakdowns. To be brutally honest, it's never difficult to find the examples in the early stages of a *Lean Foundations™* journey. It's even worth asking your team members to provide some of their own examples, I'm confident you'll find that they have plenty. You may even consider using these particular examples when demonstrating a good problem-solving process in practice, using the approach that's described in the second sub-step.

What I've also found to be an important part of the training activity is to ensure that I demonstrate empathy with everyone involved. It's critical that I do not blame them for behaving as they do. And it's vital that I am able to appreciate the impact that workarounds and poor problem-solving practices are having on their sense of fulfilment and workplace happiness. The training provides an ideal opportunity for me to support the psychological safety of my team, and to enthuse their intrinsic motivators by offering them the opportunity to raise problems and to solve them. Their sense of purpose, and their desire for personal and group improvement is usually boosted. And, in the empowering environment that we've already established, their senses of autonomy and teamwork are stimulated when I challenge them to make the appropriate changes to their thought processes, and their working practices.

One final point here. In some scenario's, when I've delivered this training, a small number of people have expressed disinterest in raising or solving problems. They consider waste and inefficiency to be someone else's problem, and are happy to just turn up for work on a daily basis regardless of what is going on around them. I make this point because you may consider that some of your people may react in the same way. My advice here is straightforward. The wastes that you will identify impact everyone. They do so because they damage the operational performance of your facility, which in turn puts its long-term security at risk. If your people cannot appreciate this obvious fact, then guess what? You still have some of the wrong people on board, and you still have a task to complete to change this. It's important that you complete training with every person in your facility. No one person should be excluded, including your front-line team members on your production shop floor. And the same applies to the process of removing the wrong people. It just as important to remove them from the front-line as it is to remove them from support and management roles.

A gentle reminder

Having delivered training that deliberately addresses the mindsets that hold back problem identification and good problem-solving, I think it's worth reminding your team, and perhaps even yourself, of just how much *Lean Foundations™* is focused on supporting a problem-solving mentality. As a consequence, you and your team members can recognise how much the identification of problems, and the subsequent development of their solutions, has become the norm for you, potentially without you even realising it.

First of all, at its very heart, *Lean Foundations™* has embraced the idea of *hansei*. The practice of deep and meaningful reflection is what has resulted in the identification of the three common factors of poor organisational health and teamwork, a lack of a well-functioning management system, and a lack of engagement of empowered front-line team members. Without the ability to honestly reflect with unreserved self-criticism, I may never have recognised the problems of poor workplace happiness, poor operational performance, and an inability to implement Lean. And I may never have identified the three common factors as the reasons why they exist.

Second, you may have noticed that each of the 8-Steps of *Lean Foundations™* begins with the identification and acceptance of the existence of a problem. For example, in Step 3, we talked about the problem of not having a plan for improvement. And in Step 5, we talked about the problem of not being able to manage constant change alongside continuous improvement. In each case, we've identified that a problem exists and have not tried to hide from it or compensate for it. Instead, we've sought to put in place solutions that have been carefully designed and tested through the application of a practical problem-solving approach. That may seem like a coincidence, but it's not. I've deliberately written the book in this way to try and desensitise any ingrained mindsets that you may have yourself around problem identification. In the process, I hope that you will also have transmitted the same mentality to your team when delivering the *Lean Foundations™* approach.

Third, the *Lean Foundations™* focus on the creation of a psychologically safe environment is a critical factor in enabling every team member to feel comfortable in identifying and raising problems. Whilst some people will still feel reluctant to identify problems even in this environment, those people can be encouraged to have faith that they will not be criticised, or be seen as being unnecessarily critical. However, without a focus on psychological safety, it's extremely unlikely that people will feel secure enough to raise their hands when needed. In fact, in my experience, the only people that do raise problems in those environments are either the highly self-interested (whom you really don't want on your team), or the extremely courageous.

Fourth, when defining the characteristics of the 'Right People' to recruit and retain on our *Lean Foundations™* journey, we discussed a number of ideas that mean that the people we have in our team are more likely to be comfortable in identifying problems, and seeking to solve them properly. In his entertainingly simple but effective book *'Problem Solving 101'*, Ken Watanabe (not the famous actor), describes the characteristics of effective problem-solvers, and also describes those characteristics that restrict a person's ability to want to solve problems. Written for children, his book describes these characteristics through caricatures of typical personalities, based on cartoon characters of children such as 'Mr. Go-Getter', 'Miss Dreamer', and 'Mr. Critic'. His definition of a problem-solving kid includes characteristics such as a willingness to accept and overcome challenges, a desire to identify root causes and to act, and an enjoyment of learning from their mistakes and successes. These traits ring bells of similarity with the 'Growth Mindset', the 'Giver', the 'Type I' disposition, and the 'bias for action' traits that we talked about in Step 2. If you've been successful in recruiting and retaining these kinds of people into your team, as well as removing those people with the wrong traits, you're likely to be in a much healthier position when it comes to your team identifying and solving problems with rigor.

Finally, in the Steps we've introduced so far, and in what will follow, we have introduced a number of very user-friendly tools that support the identification and practical solving of problems. The Policy Deployment process described in Step 3 is a vital part of the journey we're on, and is heavily focused on identifying both top-level and process level problems, and for defining practical solutions for them. The description and utilisation of the PDCA/TOC thinking processes described as part of the Policy Deployment process, and utilised in the 'MDI' process, is clearly a defined methodology for identifying and solving problems. The 'Start of Day' meetings and 'Daily Audit' processes described in Step 4, are specifically designed to support empowerment through the identification and solving of problems. And the 'MDI' process is all about problem identification and solving in order to drive operational performance. In fact, you may well be a little punch-drunk from all that problem-solving practice.

Systemising problem identification

If we're genuinely going to embed honest and unbiased problem identification and problem-solving into our working practices, we need to find a way to systemise them into our daily routines. It needs to become habit; to become so comfortable we consider it normal. Fortunately, we've already taken significant steps towards this aim. The 'MDI' process, 'Start of Day' meetings, and 'Daily Audits' all help to destigmatise problem identification, whilst at the same time introducing structured but simple processes for the ongoing management and resolution of any problems that are raised. However, there are even more opportunities for us to introduce problem identification and resolution processes which both add value and help to overcome any unconscious bias or ingrained mindsets. These processes can also help to support our desire to empower our team members, to improve our operational performance, to tap into our intrinsic motivators, and to encourage psychological safety and organisational health. They're yet another win-win.

- *Production Stop process* – Perhaps the most obvious and impactful way of demonstrating that the identification of problems is important, is for a problem to be so important that it stops production. In *'The Toyota Way'*, Jeffrey Liker defines 'Build a Culture of Stopping to Fix Problems' as the fifth of the fourteen principles of the 'Toyota Way', and describes how Toyota value this fundamental act as a key part of their management system. However, in my experience, most manufacturing facilities have not learned from Toyota's example, and actually operate to the contrary. Production stoppages are considered abhorrent, and all and any steps are taken to ensure that they do not happen, including the side-lining or ineffective containment of critical problems. Even those related to health and safety or quality can be poorly responded to or even ignored. Therefore, introducing a process that allows for controlled production stoppages can have a dramatic impact on the confidence and commitment of your team to the new mindset that you're trying to encourage them to embrace. I would stress that it's important to introduce such a process with control. As I've said on numerous occasions, all manufacturing facilities are different, and therefore have different opportunities and risks associated with stopping production. For example, a Tier one JIT facility that is supplying into the automotive industry is likely to be operating on small inventory buffers and with minimal excess capacity for catch-back of under production. They're unlikely to be able to stop production frequently or for long, without disrupting their customer. Whereas an industrial products manufacturer with 16-week lead times may have slightly more of a chance. Whatever the scenario, I would advise that you define a process which provides clear guidance around the kind of problems that should trigger a production stop, what response is required, by when, and by whom. Also, it's important that each production stop is highlighted and escalated to the appropriate level of management for your business, depending on their frequency and severity. I would also suggest that you think carefully about who is allowed to stop production. It's an extremely empowering decision, and therefore offering it to your front-line team members shows great trust and helps to support that empowering leadership style that you're hoping to embed. And, as a final consideration, it's also a good idea to define exactly who decides whether or not production is ready to re-start. You might want to include the person who originally stopped production to ensure they are now happy to continue. Or, if it's a health and safety or quality issue, you may want to include the relevant functional manager or supervisor in the agreement. There isn't a one size fits all answer here. It's about whatever you and your team agree works for your facility.
- *Hazard Reporting process* – A fantastic mechanism for encouraging problem identification, whilst at the same improving the health and safety of your facility, is to introduce a 'Hazard Reporting' process. Hazards can manifest themselves in a huge variety of ways, and I've often found that the best way to identify and remove them is to ask the people at the front-line of your operations to identify them. They

will be able to tell you where the ergonomics of their workstation is affecting them, where trip hazards exist, where access to a fire door or extinguisher is restricted, or where a production process puts them at risk. Whatever the scenario, I've found that the act of populating a simple A5 document with their name, work area/team, date of occurrence, and a description of the hazard, is both extremely useful and empowering all at the same time. Your team members feel that their concerns are understood and listened to, and that their well-being is important and respected. And, the identification and the resolution of a problem often leads to small but cumulatively significant benefits to operational performance. If nothing else, the reduction of hazards reduces accidents, and the reduction of accidents reduces the level of absence of your skilled employees. I usually locate these A5 documents throughout my facility, and in particular at the 'MDI' board area which can act as a focal point for your team. I've also found that it's important to define who is responsible for receiving and closing out any issues that are raised. And, as they are health and safety risks, it's usually a good idea to ensure that containment actions are taken immediately. You could also consider that the 'Information Board' in your 'MDI' area can be a good place to record any hazards raised and the status of their resolution.

- *Facilities Issue Reporting* – As we discussed in Step 1, managing the effectiveness and availability of the facilities and equipment that your team require to meet their responsibilities is a really powerful way of supporting the organisational health of your facility, and the psychological safety of your team. At the same time, introducing a process that enables your team to report when the facilities and equipment that you provide are not working properly, also encourages the problem identification and solving mentality. Again, as with the 'Hazard Reporting' process, the solution here does not need to be too complicated. A simple A5 document that asks for key information around who reported the issue, which equipment or facility is affected, what is wrong with it, and where it's located, can be enough. And again, it's a good idea to define who is responsible for receiving and resolving any issues reported, and perhaps for recording the issues on the 'MDI' boards. As an extension of the process, depending on the nature of your facility and how critical your machinery and equipment availability is, you may consider expanding the process. I've previously worked in facilities where machine availability significantly impacted operational performance and customer satisfaction. As a consequence, I utilised this process to record the time the issue was reported, and then resolved, and therefore the total time the equipment was unavailable. This data then supported my Productivity and Overall Equipment Effectiveness (OEE) calculations, which subsequently supported my ability to analyse and then improve my performance over time. I've also utilised this process to record the consumption of spare parts for the repaired machines, or even office facilities, thus enabling effective stock control in my Facilities & Maintenance team. Whichever level you take your process to, remember that your primary aim is to encourage problem identification and resolution, and therefore it's important not to allow a negative stigma to be attached to the number of issues raised or the speed at which they are resolved. It's not unusual for a Facilities & Maintenance team to develop a poor reputation in a manufacturing facility, and it's important to try and prevent this from disrupting the new mindset that you're trying to establish. If there are too many issues raised for your team to cope with, or they are not being closed off quickly enough; this is simply another problem that you and your team have identified, and which you can analyse as you would any other problem in order to define a resolution.

- *Improvement Ideas scheme* – Many organisations choose to introduce an 'Improvement Ideas' scheme as a means of encouraging engagement and involvement of their employees. I always like to introduce such a scheme in order to encourage the problem identification and solving mindset. After all, an improvement idea is effectively offering to identify and solve a problem. When introducing a scheme like this, once again it doesn't need to be too complicated. A simple A5 document that asks your team members to record their name, the problem that they've identified, their proposed solution, and the expected benefit if it is implemented is all it really needs. In some cases, I've seen organisations offer incentives for raising improvement ideas. They may offer payments for 'Idea of the Month' or something similar. If you remember all of the discussions we've already had around such incentives, you'll probably guess that I'm not a fan. Personally, I want my team members to offer improvement ideas because they are driven by their intrinsic rather than extrinsic motivators. I want them to raise the ideas because it will help them to improve, will support their team mates, or will contribute to the overall purpose of improving the facility; not because they might receive a bonus in their pay. In order to support this, I've found that it's really important to make sure that any improvement ideas raised are reviewed and responded to appropriately. If the idea is not accepted, there needs to be a good reason why, and it needs to be fed back to the person who raised it. If the idea accepted, it needs to be tasked to an appropriate person for completion, and again feedback needs to be given to the person who raised it. The act of implementing the improvement, and thus solving the problem identified, is likely to give huge satisfaction to the person who raised it, and should encourage others to raise their own ideas in turn.

Hopefully you can see that each of the processes described above can help you to systemise problem identification and resolution into your daily routines, and in the process can influence the mindset of your team so that they feel far more comfortable when doing so. In introducing processes such as these, I have found that it's really important to be aware of a couple of key points.

Firstly, when a problem is raised in whichever forum, it's a good idea to make sure that you address it properly. It's all too easy to damage the psychological safety of your team, and in particular of the person who raised the issue, if you don't respond to it in the right way. This does not necessarily mean that you have to fix it there and then. It means that you take the time to discuss the problem, agree that it exists, agree the appropriate course of action to resolve it, and prioritise its resolution alongside all of the other problems you are working on. As a result, you need to be able to record, prioritise and monitor the progress of problem resolution for each of the processes that you establish. For example, in the case of the 'Hazard

Reporting' process, I have always asked that all hazards raised be reported through the supervisor of the area where the hazard exists. That person is then responsible for containing it, recording it on the 'Information Board', and also reporting it to the Health & Safety Manager. The Health & Safety Manager is then given the responsibility for recording the issue on a register document, for monitoring its resolution, perhaps supporting that resolution with technical expertise if required, and for reporting the number of hazards received as a KPI. I have also worked in exactly the same way with the 'Improvement Ideas' scheme, this time with my CI Manager taking the lead. They will record each idea raised, monitor the status of its implementation, and will report the number of ideas raised as a KPI. In managing the process in this way, I ensure that each issue is captured and driven to a resolution if appropriate, and ensure that confidence in the process is maintained at the same time. It's a positive feedback loop that can easily go the other way if not managed carefully.

Second, it's important to report and communicate to your team the number of times your production line is stopped; or an improvement idea, hazard, and facility issue is raised. The really difficult part of this is being able to be positive about the frequency at which these things happen. Surely, lots of hazards, machine breakdowns, or production stoppages are a bad thing after all? And, of course that's true. But at the same time, having none of these is worse because it means that problems are being hidden or worked around, and are impacting your ability to perform. I've found that a way to help this conflicting perspective is to target an expected level of performance. You may believe that you should receive ten improvement ideas per month, or five production stops; depending on the nature of your facility and the number of people you employ. And therefore, when your performance is outside of these expected areas, you can either appreciate the result, or ask that your team identify and raise more problems. In reporting the performance of your problem raising processes in this manner, you're really reinforcing your desire for your team members to embrace problem identification as a positive.

Finally, experience tells me that you're going to identify and raise lots of problems when you introduce these processes. You may find that you're flooded with them. It's therefore sensible to stagger their introduction, and to ensure that your team can cope with the volume of problems that are being generated. It's also a good idea to have a prioritisation methodology which enables you and your team to make the right choices about which problems to solve first. This can help you to explain why a problem has not yet been resolved if a period of time has passed, and when it will be.

Lead by example… again

As with most things, the leadership example that you provide will set the tone for how your facility functions on a daily basis. Therefore, when it comes to identifying and solving problems, it's crucial that you practice what you preach, and model the right behaviour. This can manifest itself in a number of different ways.

First of all, you can raise problems yourself, perhaps even in areas that you are personally responsible for managing. In doing so, it's a good idea for you to demonstrate a humble and critical reflection of your problem. Alternatively, when identifying problems elsewhere, you can endeavour not to appear critical, can demonstrate empathy with the fact that the problem exists, and can offer support to resolve it.

Second, when someone raises a new problem with you, do your best to try and react in the right way. You can choose to listen attentively, to not take the problem personally, to not react emotionally with anger or disappointment, and to ask questions that help you to understand the problem better. Staying calm, and presenting a logical rather than emotional response can encourage your team members to do the same when they are confronted with a problem themselves.

Third, when a problem becomes apparent, it's a good idea to 'go to gemba', or, 'the actual place' that the problem is occurring. This is likely to mean a visit to the production floor, and is where you can ask inquiring questions and demonstrate 'Situational Humility' as we discussed all the way back in Step 1. By doing so, you can demonstrate that problem identification and resolution is so important you're prepared to commit your valuable time and energy to it.

Fourth, you can deliberately seek out problems which result in the need to stop production. I've often completed an end of line inspection of finished components in order to identify a quality problem that requires rectification, and forces production to stop in order to complete a sweep of everything else in process. This helps to demonstrate my commitment to quality, and helps to demonstrate that the identification of problems that stop production is both acceptable and encouraged.

Finally, when completing the routine walks through your facility that we discussed as part of 'Management by walking around' back in Step 1, you have the opportunity to hear about problems during your conversations with your team members. When holding these conversations, you have the option to ask if your team members are experiencing any problems, and can encourage them to report them in the most appropriate way available. It could be through their 'Start of Day' meeting, or through a 'Hazard Report'. You could even choose to raise the problem on their behalf, having again demonstrated 'Situational Humility' when seeking to understand the problem properly, before raising the appropriate form, or passing it to the relevant member of your team.

PROBLEM-SOLVING PRACTICALLY

Hopefully you've taken on board some or all of the suggestions above, and you're now well on the way to influencing your team's mindset around the identification of problems. Their willingness to raise problems without fear of blame, and without fear of appearing to blame others, is a critical part of the *Lean Foundations™* approach. Problem-solving is a vital skill in delivering improvement, and our path to the foundations that support excellence will not be achieved without it. But please, don't relax your efforts in this area. Your leadership example needs to be consistent in order to ensure that your team do not slip into their old habits.

However, encouraging your team to be comfortable when raising problems is, of course, only one side of the coin. On the flip-side, we need to have the confidence that once problems are identified, we have a capable and effective mental approach and toolkit for solving them. In fact, without that mindset, and without those tools, it's highly likely that your team members will continue to feel apathetic towards raising problems in the first place. After all, what would be the point in raising problems if they don't get resolved properly? And so, we now need to explore what a good problem-solving mindset looks like, and then consider what tools we can introduce with your team in order to support it.

Thinking like a problem-solver

There are a small number of well-known and well-defined standard problem-solving processes that are often utilised in the manufacturing world. You may have heard of Toyota's Practical Problem Solving (PPS) process, Ford's 8D methodology, or Motorola's Six Sigma approach. If not, and you're interested to find out more, you might want to take a look at 'The Toyota Way' by Jeffrey Liker to understand Toyota's PPS, at 'Introduction to 8D Problem Solving' by Donald Benbow and Ali Zarghami for Ford's 8D methodology, and believe me when I say that there are seemingly thousands of options for Six Sigma books. Each of these approaches to problem-solving are slightly different, but at their heart they have a number of similarities.

First, they are all multi-step processes that utilise the principles of the scientific method of 'Plan', 'Do', 'Check', and 'Act' to guide the sequence of those steps, and the mental approach that a problem-solver should apply. Second, they are all tools for analysing problems at the process level. Third, they are all driven by data and facts, rather than opinions and feelings. Fourth, they all seek to establish the root cause of a problem in order to ensure that corrective actions are effective. And fifth, they all endeavour to balance thought and action in equal measure so that there is a genuine result from the problem-solving process.

For Lean Foundations™, I have developed, over numerous different experiences and iterations, a problem-solving methodology that is in effect a hybrid of the PPS and 8D concepts. Like them, it follows a multi-step process, seeks to identify the root cause of a process level problem with data, and includes clear action plans for implementation of effective containments and countermeasures. However, I have developed this more simplified methodology as a first step in enabling my team to think with a problem-solving mentality. Some of the elements of 8D, PPS and Six Sigma can be a little complicated to learn, and to become expert in applying. I've therefore found a need for a less complex approach that helps to bridge the learning gap. Also, I have found that individually, the 8D and PPS approaches have small gaps in the practicality of their application, hence the combination of the two here. And, I've found that the Six Sigma approach is best suited for use with problems that can be analysed through statistical methods and with

192

large data sets, rather than with more typical day to day problems. I believe therefore, that the methodology advocated here is a little simpler to understand, slightly quicker and easier to train and apply, and yet still effective. If you've ever tried to introduce one of the more typical problem-solving methodologies previously, you may have found it difficult to sustain because of the challenges involved in getting people to think in the right way. Hopefully, you may find this approach a little easier. And please remember, at this point we're only seeking to build the foundations upon which excellence takes root, we are not seeking to build excellence itself. Therefore, we need to introduce ideas and tools progressively, so that our team members can develop their skills and thinking processes as we develop our organisation.

The *Lean Foundations™* practical problem-solving approach (PPSA) follows a simple seven step methodology, as illustrated in the graphic below.

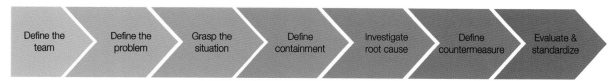

Fig 6-2. The *Lean Foundations™* practical problem-solving approach

Each of the steps of the PPSA are straightforward to complete, and follow a logical path to help any user understand and intervene with any kind of problem, regardless of its severity or scale. Hopefully you'll also notice the alignment here with the PDCA/TOC thinking process that we discussed back in Step 3. We should consider that whilst a little later we'll discuss some tools to support the use of this problem-solving approach, what we're hoping to do in the first instance is to enable our team members to utilise this approach as a mindset. We want them to be able to learn and apply this way of thinking whenever they confront a problem, even if they don't necessarily have a standard tool to hand that enables them to document or record their thoughts. If they understand the process well enough, a blank piece of paper, or an empty whiteboard, can end up being that tool. Let's take a look at each of the 7 steps in turn…

- *Define the team* – This may seem fairly innocuous at first, but I've found it to be vitally important. Some problems can be solved by one person, but not often. Normally, it requires a team. Identifying exactly who needs to be part of the team is therefore very important. If you don't involve all of the right people, you may well miss out on valuable expertise and ideas. I normally endeavour to be as cross-functional as possible, and to include as many different technical and experiential contributors as is practical. When someone in your team is confronted by a problem for the first time, they need to consider exactly whose help they need if any in order to understand and solve the problem correctly. For small day to day problems, that may just be a Maintenance Engineer, or a fellow Core Team member. For more complex problems it may require a cross-functional team that also includes Functional Support Team members.

- *Define the problem* – This step requires a simple description of the actual problem at hand, but often gets contaminated with a description of an assumed root cause. It's important not to jump to conclusions, and therefore you should work hard to ensure that all that is defined here is a quantifiable description of the problem. Ask the simple questions of who was involved or identified the problem, where it occurred, when it occurred or was identified, why it was identified, and what is the impact in terms of the number of parts affected or amount of inefficiency caused. For example, let's assume a member of your team has identified a puddle of water on the floor in their work area. The problem description could be something like…
    o Who identified it: Jane Smith.
    o What is the problem: A puddle of water in the work area.
    o When: This morning at start of shift.
    o Where: In Stamping production cell, next to the control panel on the Stamping machine.
    o Why: I nearly slipped in it.
    o What is the impact: It is a potential slip hazard.

    Note this example problem description does not include any supposition on what may have caused the puddle of water in the first place. It's very easy when describing a problem to state a cause such as *"… a leaking water pipe has created a puddle of water next to my machine…"*. But when describing the problem in this way it's all too easy to influence the direction of the problem-solving activity, potentially leading you to address the wrong cause, or solve the wrong problem. It's therefore important to try and avoid this basic but frequently occurring error as much as possible.

- *Grasp the situation* – This step can take a little practice to get the hang of, and requires a more detailed description of the problem. It's also this step that can really help to point you in the direction of the root cause of a problem if completed well. Can you identify the exact point of failure? Can you collate information that helps you to understand when it first occurred? Do you need to go to '*gemba*' to understand it in full (the answer is nearly always yes by the way)? Can you replicate the failure in some way? Can you suggest some potential reasons for the failure? It's important to address this step with an open mind, and to compare the situation you find with the standard that you would expect in order to help to properly describe the nature of the problem at hand. Do this well, and you make the rest of the process much easier. In the case of our basic example above, by visiting the work area with the puddle of water, can you identify any obvious sources of a leak? Are there any water pipes nearby? Does the roof leak in this area? Has a team member's drink been spilled? Is the water contaminated with any other liquids such as oil that might give a clue as to its origin? If you turn on the nearest production machine does the water leak re-start and the puddle get larger? By asking simple questions, by going to '*gemba*', and by keeping an open-mind, you can start to narrow down the possible causes of the problem and describe it in much greater detail.

- *Define the containment* – This step requires you to define a containment action that will prevent the problem from impacting your customer, your performance, or your employees. For example, you might need to introduce additional inspection if it's a quality problem, increase capacity if your production machine is breaking down, or ask someone to wear additional personal protective equipment if it's health and safety related. Once you have a containment in place, you need to monitor its effectiveness and ensure that it's not leaking failures. If you find that you're still experiencing failures downstream from your containment, you need to re-assess that containment. In the case of our 'puddle of water' example, you'll perhaps mop the floor, put up a wet floor sign, and ask your team members to monitor the situation. You might even need to introduce the ultimate in puddle control, the faithful bucket, for catching any drips and to prevent the puddle from returning.

- *Investigate the root cause* – This step is sometimes the most challenging, and has the aim of identifying and then investigating the impact of *all* of the potential root causes of the problem. Here, you're looking to hypothesise and list ideas for every and any potential root cause, and then to investigate each hypothesis. To help this process along, and in the early stages of developing the skillset of my team, I usually advocate the use of simple brainstorm diagrams in order to explore the logical paths of cause and effect that then identify potential failure modes. An 8D or PPS would advocate the use of slightly more complicated tools such as Ishikawa diagrams, or Cause and Effect trees. These take a little more expertise and practice before they become second nature, but of course, you can utilise them if you feel your team are capable. For a little help in understanding these better, take a look at '*The Problem-Solving Memory Jogger*' by Michael Brassard. The first challenge here is getting the investigating individual or team to list *every* potential cause, rather than just the one or ones that they are instinctively drawn to. It's important to encourage the problem-solving team to keep coming up with options, even when they think they've exhausted all of them. By doing so, you can reinforce the mentality that their first instinct isn't necessarily the only one they should follow. The next challenge is to ensure that each potential cause is investigated with an open mind, is thorough, is supported with data as much as possible, and most importantly penetrates to the true root cause of the problem rather than stopping at the first layer. It may also be necessary to identify both the root cause of the failure, and the root cause of non-detection. If the problem has escaped your facility and impacted your customer, has damaged your operational performance, or has perhaps caused someone to be injured, then it's often worth understanding not only what caused it to occur, but also why it wasn't spotted in advance. For our basic 'puddle of water' example, your hypotheses are easy enough to imagine, and are likely to include a leaking pipe, a leaking roof, or a spillage of some kind (it's a basic example after all). Testing these is likely to be fairly straightforward. When it rains does the roof leak? Can you identify any drips on local water pipes? Or are there any buckets of water used in the locality that may have been accidentally spilled? However, this is only the first level of the problem cause. If the roof does leak, then why? Is there a hole in the roof, or is water gathering and seeping through because its weakened over time? If there is a hole, what caused it? If your pipes are leaking, is it because they're rusty and worn? Or, is it because they were recently maintained and not tightened properly? The key here to successfully solving the problem is to penetrate below the first layer of the problem, and to keep probing until you find the ultimate root cause. To help this, Toyota encourage the use of a 5-Why mentality, where team members are expected to ask 'Why' as many as five times (or more if necessary), when they find the cause of a problem. The approach forces the problem-solver to keep penetrating the problem until the true root cause is identified. Without this mentality, you're likely to only solve the first layer of the problem, and therefore risk the problem returning. You might patch the roof, but the hole may reappear because the issue that caused the hole to appear in the first place was not resolved. This mentality takes a little time and consistent application to learn and develop fully, but it's a skill that you really need to encourage and support in your team.

- *Define countermeasures* – Having investigated all of the potential root causes, and having identified those that you consider responsible for the problem, you can now brainstorm, define and implement appropriate countermeasures for resolution. When completing this step, it's important to ensure that your countermeasures address all levels of the problem properly. In our 'puddle of water' example, you could just tighten the pipe. Or, if the pipe is rusted and worn, you could replace the pipe, and ensure that its tight. By fixing the true root cause of the problem, you'll prevent it from reoccurring.

- *Evaluate and Standardise* – Once your countermeasures are in place, it's necessary to evaluate their effectiveness. Is the problem solved, and can you demonstrate it with data over time? A really good way to confirm that your countermeasures are effective is to try and turn the problem on and off. If you remove your countermeasure, does the problem return, and vice-versa? If your solution isn't working, then you potentially need to re-evaluate your solution, your root cause identification, or even start the problem-solving process again. If you can demonstrate that the problem is resolved, then it's a good idea to modify your management systems, procedures and process controls with whatever new methodology you have introduced. By doing so you can ensure that your changes become standardised, and old working methods do not return. For our 'puddle of water example', you can ask your team members to monitor the situation for a period of time. If the puddle doesn't return then you've been successful. If it does, then you're going to need to take another look. Bearing in mind of course that a second puddle may well have been caused by a completely different problem this time around. If the puddle is resolved, you might consider updating your planned maintenance systems so that the pipe is checked more frequently. And if you really want to take things to the next level, you could inspect all of the other water pipes in your facility to identify the potential for them to leak too. Taking the lessons learned, and applying them in order to prevent future problems from occurring elsewhere, demonstrates a really high level of problem-solving practice.

Hopefully you can recognise that nothing that is presented here is too complex or difficult to learn. Each of the seven steps are straightforward to understand and follow, and can easily become habit if practiced sufficiently. There are important elements to focus upon within each step, but they are certainly not beyond the capability of the strong team that you're building. Of course, if you would prefer to follow an 8D, PPS or even Six Sigma approach, the choice is yours. Whichever choice you make, in introducing a problem-solving approach like this to your team, you can hopefully encourage them to apply its logic each and every time they confront a problem in their day to day work, regardless of its complexity or scale. To embed it fully takes effort and training, and benefits greatly from being consistently supported with coaching from a capable problem-solving practitioner. I'd therefore strongly advise you to train your team extensively in this area, and to become that capable problem-solving practitioner yourself if you can't identify someone in your team. I believe that, if you commit the time and energy to this cause, you can arm your team with an invaluable tool for improving their problem-solving skills. And, in the process, you will have significantly influenced your ability to improve the operational performance of your facility, the happiness of your team, and their ability to implement Lean.

Some problem-solving tools

Our final step on the path to improving our problem-solving capabilities, is to take a look at some of the tools that we can introduce to support the problem-solving mentality we're trying to establish. There are a variety that are available to us, but the three that are referenced here are the ones that I've found to be the easiest to use and introduce with my team at this stage of a *Lean Foundations*™ journey. They are also very much aligned with the *Lean Foundations*™ practical problem-solving approach that we've just discussed. In each case, it's important to ensure that you train your team in their use. Therefore, I would suggest that the training that I referenced in the previous sub-step should look to present these tools and their completion as part of that session. Doing so will also support the training of the practical problem-solving approach at the same time.

The first, and hopefully most obvious tool, is the 'Issue Resolution Board' included in the 'MDI' process. If you turn back to Step 5 and take a look at the format of this board, you'll see that it's been deliberately designed to follow the steps of the *Lean Foundations*™ practical problem-solving approach. The steps are obviously a little condensed so that they fit onto the board, and so that each problem can be addressed quickly and easily as part of the short 'Report Out' meetings that are scheduled every day. But, the intent to reinforce the right problem-solving mentality is clear, and its inclusion in the cross-functional 'Report Out' forum is very much a calculated decision. The 'MDI' process is likely to be the first level of escalation for a problem that cannot be solved by a Core Team member when its raised with them. Therefore, the inclusion of this first level of problem analysis and investigation, whilst uncomplicated, is a valuable tool that is more than sufficient to address the majority of problems that arise. The fact that team members from a variety of

Functional Support Teams are included within the 'Report Out' meeting, makes that initial level of problem-solving more effective and easier to complete. The support that your Core Team needs to solve its problems is already in the right place at the right time.

The second tool is one that many Quality professionals will be familiar with. Typically, particularly in the automotive and aerospace industries, when a customer experiences a quality issue with a supplied product, they will ask their supplier to complete an 8D or PPS document. Sometimes these customers have standard formats themselves, and other times they expect their suppliers to utilise their own formats. And usually, it's representatives of the Quality function that are responsible for completing them. They're often A3 in size, and present the logical flow of the problem-solving process very much like the A3 documents that we discussed in Step 3. Below is a format that I have developed to support the seven-step process of the *Lean Foundations*™ practical problem-solving approach, and which has become known as a PPSA document. This is a document that I encourage my team members to utilise when they're confronted with a particularly challenging problem that may take time to properly understand and resolve. Certainly, it's something that I would always advocate for analysing customer quality issues, but it can also be used for internal problems that require a little more time and energy than the 'Issue Resolution Board' in the 'MDI' process can offer.

Fig 6-3. The *Lean Foundations*™ PPSA document

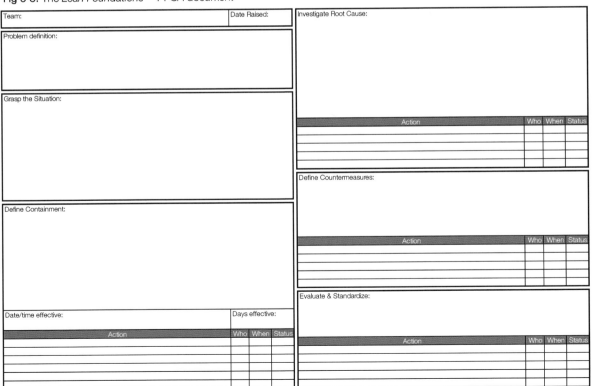

Often, a problem is recorded on the 'Issue Resolution Board', and has a PPSA document raised too. The headlines of the problem, and the steps that the team are taking to resolve it, are populated onto the 'Issue Resolution Board', and the latest version of PPSA document is presented on the 'Information Board'. You'll see that each of the seven steps of the process are clearly identified, and are supported by empty boxes ready for completion. It would be more typical for an 8D or PPS form to be populated with pre-defined tools like a blank Ishikawa diagram or 5-Why table. However, on the PPSA document, the empty boxes allow the user a choice about what tools to utilise when completing their problem-solving activity. They also provide space for photographs to be included when 'grasping the situation', or data and charts to be included when 'evaluating' the effectiveness of the countermeasures. You'll also see that there are action log sections for each of the last 4 steps, where activities have to be agreed and implemented. These action logs help to manage the status of what has been agreed, who is responsible for delivering it, and by when. Like the A3's we discussed in Step 3, these PPSA documents allow the user to 'tell the story' of their problem-solving journey with the information that they present. To begin with, they can take a little practice to learn to complete, primarily because the user is likely to want to present more information than they have space for. But, with practice, they become easier to use and can be invaluable tools in both supporting the mental problem-solving process, and communicating its effectiveness.

In my experience, it's not unusual to find that these types of document are only utilised when a customer requires it, and by members of the quality function. However, I would actively encourage you to utilise them far more widely. This means training your entire team in how to use them, and potentially may require you to specifically ask for them to be used when the right opportunity arises. It's also a good idea for them not to be completed by one individual in isolation; different perspectives help to ensure that the right problem-solving approach is correctly applied. And finally, I would also recommend that you review each of the PPSA documents yourself on completion, particularly those that are addressing customer quality or health and safety issues. You can then use the review activity to coach your team members in their completion where appropriate. In a worst-case scenario, you might even challenge the quality of the solution and suggest that the process needs to be re-started.

The third tool advocated here provides a final level of escalation of problem-solving activity. If the 'Issue Resolution Board' is not sufficient, and the use of the PPSA document is too isolated, then I would propose that you set up a PPSA meeting room, which includes a large whiteboard that is formatted in exactly the same way as the PPSA document above. Where a problem is technically complex and requires input from a large number of varied team members to understand, or is likely to need a large amount of investigation into multiple potential failure modes, these meeting areas can be extremely valuable. By calling a cross-functional team together, and by using the 'PPSA Board' to guide an open-minded and free-flowing team discussion, I've experienced much higher levels of success at solving the problem at hand. It does take a more skilled practitioner to lead the discussion, and so I would advise that you are selective about whom you ask to utilise this tool. But with practice, I've found it to be extremely effective. I also believe that it provides significant additional benefits. It can positively impact teamwork, contributes to a sense of purpose, and improves the well-being of your team members by sharing the burden of a complex problem rather than imposing it on a particular individual. The board is populated as part of the team discussion exactly as the PPSA document would be, with supporting information and documentation attached as appropriate. It's also a good idea to nominate someone to translate the contents of the board onto a PPSA document for record purposes. The availability of camera's on smart phones has made this somewhat easier in the last few years! What I would add is that these meetings rarely operate as stand-alone activities. Problems that are complex enough to require this approach normally require several meetings over a number of days or even weeks, so it's useful if you're able to leave the whiteboard populated for follow-up discussions. If you find that you have lots of these types of problem, you might consider using large pre-printed documents rather than a whiteboard, so that you can manage multiple problems from the same room.

STEP 6 SUMMARY

In completing Step 6 of your *Lean Foundations™* journey, I hope you've been successful in influencing the mindset and skills of your team when it comes to problem-solving. There is no magic switch that suddenly changes the way people think, but I trust that you're seeing the signs that your people are happier and more comfortable to embrace problems, and to solve them with rigor and enthusiasm. In introducing the 'Water and the Rocks' concept, and in launching processes like 'Hazard Reporting' and the 'Improvement Ideas' scheme; I'm convinced that you will have elevated the confidence of your team to identify and raise problems. And, by introducing an effective problem-solving mentality like 8D or the *Lean Foundations™* practical problem-solving approach, alongside their supporting tools, you will have provided them with the capability to solve those problems both independently and conclusively. As a consequence, your improvement journey will be super-charged with the power of effective problem solving; and your path to improved operational performance, workplace happiness, and the ability to implement Lean, will be significantly easier to navigate.

As a final point, at varying stages in the implementation of Step 6, you may find that your team become a little over-whelmed by the number and scale of problems that are identified. The utilisation of the 'MDI' process, and its ability to support prioritisation is key here. As is the ability to reflect and maintain your perspective. Your facility is manufacturing components of some kind. But, except in truly exceptional circumstances, what is being produced is unlikely to be so critical that it's going to change the world. The problems that you're identifying and solving are taking you and your team towards improving your own working lives, and not those of every and anyone else. Is it really necessary to solve that problem now? Or can it wait an extra few hours or even days? I've often described a facility in the early stages of a *Lean*

Foundations™ journey as an 'Injured person', with a great number of minor cuts that are slowly bleeding. These cuts don't cause the person to lose their life, but they do cause them discomfort and unnecessary pain. Each cut represents a problem, and every time a problem is identified and solved, the discomfort is alleviated. Even if the problem is only temporarily contained, and a band-aid is applied, the effect is the same as long as the containment is effective, and the band-aid sticks. And therefore, in the early stages, you may need to apply lots of band-aids to alleviate your pain and discomfort, and to enable your team to have the time and energy to solve problems fully at a later stage. Don't be afraid of just applying band-aids if you really need to. The journey is a long one, and you will want to make sure it's as painless as possible for everyone on the way.

In drawing Step 6 to a close, let's take a moment to reflect on the main points…

- It's not unusual for people to hide or ignore problems from a fear of being blamed for them, or from a desire not to appear to blame others. As a result, these ingrained mindsets can severely restrict the process of improvement that we're so keen to encourage.
- It's also not unusual for attempts to solve problems to be unsuccessful because root causes are not properly identified and corrected, or solutions that are implemented fall by the wayside over time.
- There are steps that we can take to encourage our team members to identify and raise problems, and to educate them on how to solve problems effectively.
- To encourage them to identify problems, we can train them on the 'Water and the Rocks' concept; we can remind them of the problem-solving processes already built into the *Lean Foundations™* journey so far; we can introduce processes such as 'Hazard Reporting' which systemises the identification of problems to the point of routine; and we can provide a positive leadership example when identifying problems ourselves.
- To improve our team's problem-solving capabilities, we can train and continuously coach them in the use of standard problem-solving methodologies such as 8D, PPS, or the *Lean Foundations™* practical problem-solving approach.
- To support our team's problem-solving mentality, we can encourage them to use tools such as the 'Issue Resolution Board' in the 'MDI' process, a PPSA document, and a 'PPSA Board' in a PPSA meeting.

STEP

7

Establish an effective management system

It's not too difficult to find a manufacturing facility that is seemingly out of control. In such a place, whilst everyone has a pretty good idea of exactly how things should work, it seems rare that things ever actually do work in the way they might expect. The fact that an order is received, manufactured, and then delivered can appear to happen through some mystical accident, rather than as a result of a deliberate process of control and execution. The problem with this approach, of course, is that all too often things go wrong. Lead times are inaccurate and deliveries are late, quality control is insufficient and customers complain, material is ordered from an unapproved supplier and rework is required, or corners are cut and accidents happen. The act of fire-fighting becomes an art, and supposedly 'indispensable specialists' become the 'white knights' that ride in to the save the day. Whenever I'm confronted with this kind of environment, I'm told that *"… we work this way so that we can be flexible…"*, or *"… this is how we are able to be responsive to our customers…"*, and *"… standard procedures will just restrict us…"*. Of course, I'm usually told this by the one or two 'indispensable specialists', whilst everyone else is anxiously hoping for some semblance of control and order to be introduced. They desperately want to put the fires out once and for all. They want their facility to perform well, and to meet or even exceed their customer's expectations. And they want to find the time to work with their colleagues on the fantastic ideas that they have for improving how they work, or for developing that new product. Instead, their time is consumed with responding to the problems that the lack of control and order creates.

Every now and again, it's also possible to find a manufacturing facility that is the complete opposite. It has procedures and processes that determine every action, and systems that dictate clear methods for the execution of daily tasks. However, even in this environment things still go wrong. Whilst lead times might be accurate, deliveries can still be late when a simple documentation error holds them back. Quality controls may be in place, but they may slow down the process and add time and cost. Material might well be ordered from the nominated supplier, but perhaps their lead-times are too long and their quality is below specification. And corners may not be cut, but at the same time opportunities may well be lost. Whenever I'm confronted by this kind of environment, I'm told that *"… this is just the way we do things…"*, or *"… this is how we've always done it…"*, and *"… following procedures is how we make sure people follow the rules…"*. Here, things only change when the Systems Engineer or Industrial Engineer can find the time to audit a process; and even then, the changes can be minimal because of interactions with other processes that would also need to change. People are still confronted with the daily fire-fight, and the 'indispensable specialists' still exist. But people find that their ability to respond to the fires is restricted, and they yearn for the freedom to act independently and without need for approval. They want that order to be delivered on time, that quality issue resolved, or that cost avoided. Instead, they have little choice but to pass problems up the management structure for resolution.

When working through a *Lean Foundations*™ journey, I'm often confronted by one or the other of these scenarios. Usually it's the former; and the time and energy of myself and my team is almost completely consumed with dealing with problems that have arisen as a result of a lack of procedure and control. Every now and again, it's the latter; and my time and energy are spent both fighting fires, and trying to break down the barriers that are restricting independent choice and the freedom to take ownership. My ability to build a psychologically safe environment, to introduce a team-oriented organisation structure, to develop an Improvement Plan, to integrate empowering leadership, to introduce an 'MDI' process, or to embed a problem-solving mentality; is severely impacted by constant emergencies, caused by either the lack of procedural control, or the constraints that restrict my team's ability to independently change their procedures for the better.

Whilst reading this book, you may well have wondered just how you could possibly find the time to make the changes that I've talked about. You may be thinking about the poor performance of your facility, and the constant fire-fighting in the core performance indicators of Safety, Quality, Delivery and Cost which consumes your day. Or, you may be well on the way to making the changes we've already discussed, and now find that your performance is not progressing as you might have hoped because of a lack of control, or because your procedures restrict flexibility and choice. So, what's the answer?

In 'The Toyota Way', Jeffrey Liker identifies principle six of the fourteen principles that underpin Toyota's success as: 'Standardised Tasks Are the Foundation for Continuous Improvement and Employee Engagement'. He describes how Toyota have managed to avoid both the chaos and constant failures of an uncontrolled process, and the equally dysfunctional and disempowering effects of an excessively controlled process. A key feature of Toyota's management system is the standardisation of all tasks; from those on the production floor to those in support functions. It's this standardisation which underpins the repeatability of their processes, and the excellence of their performance. And yet, despite this focus on standardisation and control, they've been successful in marrying flexibility and choice into the management of their procedures. They have been able to introduce standardisation as an enabler of innovation and improvement, whilst at the same time ensuring that their daily performance is reliably sound. They have been able to build a well-functioning management system that enables them to perform with repeatability and control, and still allows them to adapt and improve.

It's this kind of well-functioning management system that I have strived to find a way to integrate into the Lean Foundations™ approach. The ability to define and work to standard procedures that control the execution of daily tasks in order to reduce and remove failures, is a vital component of delivering good performance, and of creating the capacity required for such widespread and all-encompassing improvement. At the same time, creating the environment that actively enables my team to adapt those standard procedures, is essential for enabling choice, and for supporting innovation. Without procedures that establish control, my facility will underperform, and will be too busy to improve. Without the freedom to make change, my facility will lack the flexibility and enthusiasm required for improvement.

We're now six steps down on our *Lean Foundations™* journey, with just two to go. We've embraced organisational health and psychological safety, we've built a team-oriented organisation structure which is filled with the right people, we have developed a detailed and thorough plan, we have embraced a leadership approach that actively empowers our team members, we have introduced the fundamental 'MDI' process, and we've started to embed a genuine problem-solving mentality within our team. The progress we've made so far is truly fantastic, but there is still a little way for us to travel.

Our next step on our *Lean Foundations™* journey is to build the well-functioning management system that helps us to establish control and deliver good performance, whilst at the same time preserving our ability to respond to change and to improve. We need to standardise our operating and production processes in order to establish control, and to reduce or even remove the pressure to fight fires in our core performance indicators of Safety, Quality, Delivery, and Cost. We need to introduce management oversight protocols that help us to maintain that control, and which enable us to provide support where it is needed most. And, we need to introduce mechanisms that facilitate flexibility and choice, in order to empower our team to improve and innovate. In the process, we can create the capacity that allows our team to drive the improvements that they are so eager to introduce; and we can continue to support their intrinsic motivators, can enhance their sense of psychological safety, and can empower them to make choices and take the lead. A well-functioning management system of this nature is a fundamental feature of a facility that performs well, and is an essential characteristic of the foundations that enable operational excellence. Without it, our *Lean Foundations™* journey towards achieving good will fail, and our aspiration for a future that is great will never materialise.

We'll work through three sub-steps to help you to introduce this well-functioning management system into your facility; 'Standardise to stabilise', 'Oversee, and offer support', and 'Liberate with choice'. I hope that in sharing these sub-steps, I'm able to support you with the introduction of a management system that genuinely enables the controlled execution of daily tasks, alongside the ability to adapt and improve. Let's get to it.

STANDARDISE TO STABILISE

It's quite normal for the primary production activity of any manufacturing facility to be enabled by the combined efforts of multiple operational support functions. They manage customer orders, administer paperwork, move parts, and raise invoices, amongst a great many other activities. Not unusually, those support functions can often operate through the consistent application of well-established working practices, rather than by following anything more structured and controlled. People may tend to follow habitual routines and ways of working that have been in place for some time, and which have become the established norm. Whilst these may generally work, it's still possible for a lack of concentration or a misunderstanding to result in failure, despite or even because of the often-repetitious nature of the tasks.

In your own experience, you may also have seen that the primary production activity of a manufacturing facility can often be completed through the application of the same kind of well-established working practices and habitual routines. Someone who has not worked in the manufacturing world might expect the production of components to be more effectively controlled; but it's not unusual to find that 'job-knowledge', and the learned practices of experienced skilled team members, is relied upon to excess. I've certainly seen examples where the transfer of production activities from one facility to another results in the loss of 'hidden factory' knowledge, and causes major disruption and pain.

In both scenarios, when standardising these working habits and routines, we have the opportunity to establish structure and control that reduces or even removes the risk of failure. That standardisation enables us to build repeatability and control into the way that we work, so that we can stabilise our operational performance, and give ourselves the opportunity to breathe and think. By reducing the number of safety incidents, by improving delivery performance, by reducing quality complaints, and by preventing excess costs, we can take away the constant noise that occupies our minds and consumes our energy. At the same time, we can improve our operational performance, and can gain credibility with our customers and our wider organisation. Most importantly, we can feed the intrinsic motivators of our team, and can strengthen the organisational health and psychological safety of our facility.

Commonly, standardisation takes the form of defined procedures and processes, often documented and maintained as part of business or quality management system. A process is a series of inter-related tasks that turn inputs into outputs, whereas a procedure is a prescribed way of undertaking a process. By choosing to definitively describe our processes, and the procedures that we follow to complete them, rather than simply functioning through habit and routine, we can provide ourselves with a set of tools that can help us to standardise the way we work. This is certainly the approach that *Lean Foundations™* is keen to promote and follow. But, it's by no means a new idea or rocket science in its application. And, whilst some manufacturing facilities will operate, albeit poorly, without such processes and procedures; a great many operate with them, and still do so unsuccessfully.

Nevertheless, for *Lean Foundations™*, standardisation through the creation of defined procedures and processes is the cornerstone of the well-functioning management system that we're seeking to introduce. Where *Lean Foundations™* is a little different, however, is that it seeks to learn from Toyota's example, and addresses four key considerations to ensure that this approach to standardisation is effective. First, processes and procedures need to be defined for all of the key supporting operational activities, with all of the critical features and characteristics that make them effective included. All too often I have seen operational performance suffer because certain key processes are missing altogether, or are completely dysfunctional. Second, those operating processes need to be introduced in a way that encourages people to use and follow them, rather than as something to be ignored in favour of a quick and easy alternative.

Third, the primary production activity needs to be standardised in order to reduce and remove the risk of variation, and to enable repeatability and control over time and through change. And finally, all of the processes need to be managed in way that promotes their constant and consistent application, whilst being flexible enough to respond to change and empower innovation. We'll take a look at the first three of these considerations in this sub-step, and will address the fourth in the second and third sub-steps.

As a small warning, I would like to add that in much of what I share here, I may be in danger of over-simplifying, or perhaps even being considered a little patronising with the content. For example, when attempting to describe the kinds of processes that a well-functioning management system should include, I can only do so in basic terms because of the individual nature of all manufacturing facilities. If you do find this to be too obvious, or perhaps a little demeaning, then please accept my apologies in advance, but my hands are a little tied. I'm endeavouring to be everything to everyone from a manufacturing perspective, and therefore hope to offer as much insight as is practical, whether it applies in every scenario or not. I hope that, despite this, what I share here proves to be useful.

The right operating processes

Our first challenge on the road to standardisation, and the stability and control of our performance that it supports, is to have an idea of what kind of operating processes we should have in place, and what features they should include.

To help, I've explored the typical operating processes that you might expect to find in any manufacturing facility, and which if are missing, or are inadequately defined, will contribute to a lack of control and poor performance. I have endeavoured to list as many of these as is practical for each function of your team, and have tried to include some description of the kind of good practice features they should include. But, please bear in mind that they are only the processes that I would expect to be in place in order to deliver a facility that performs well, and not necessarily a facility that is targeting excellence in the short-term. As a result, the list is by no means exhaustive for every function; but I would certainly hope is sufficient to help us to establish the right foundations on our journey towards improved operational performance, workplace happiness, and the ability to implement Lean. Oh, and by the way, there's a lot of information here. Feel free to pick out the parts that are relevant to you and your facility…

Health & Safety - the Health & Safety function is responsible for providing the tools and mechanisms that will support the delivery of a safe working environment. Typical processes include…

- *Accident and Incident Reporting and Investigation* – Unfortunately, accidents and incidents, including near misses, will occur. It's vitally important to ensure that any that do occur are properly reported, and are comprehensively investigated with a view of putting in place controls that prevent them from reoccurring. Key features should include…

- o A reporting and escalation discipline that ensures that all issues are reported, and that you as facility leader are properly informed when an accident occurs. This can emphasise the importance of health and safety with your team.

- o An investigation procedure and document which follows a practical problem-solving methodology. The document can be a slightly modified PPSA document, with the 'Grasp the Situation' section including data collection that is specifically related to accident occurrences, including a reference to the nature of any injuries and their severity. The process should define expected timescales for completion of the investigation, and the introduction of containment activities and countermeasures. It should also define who should complete the investigation. Normally, I would ask the manager or supervisor of the injured person to undertake the exercise, supported by the Health & Safety representative of my facility for technical guidance.

- *Emergency Response* – Part of the reality of leading a manufacturing facility is the knowledge that at some point you may well experience an emergency of some kind which needs to be managed. This may range in scale from a small accident that requires minor first aid, to a major incident that requires the involvement of the emergency services. These are often some of the first procedures I will review and update as part of any *Lean Foundations*™ journey for my own peace of mind, and I would recommend that you do the same. Good points to consider are...

  - o The number of trained First Aid representatives, Fire Marshals and perhaps even Spill Teams you employ across your entire facility, and for all shift patterns. You'll need to consider how you will maintain the right quantity to meet legal requirements when your circumstances change. You'll also need to ensure that training is constantly refreshed and up to date.

  - o How your fire and evacuation procedures are defined, with clearly identified protocols for assembly, emergency service contact, alarm control, and building re-entry.

  - o What the correct processes are for response to an emergency that occurs outside of normal working hours, with clear escalation and communication policies.

  - o Critical responses for Disaster Recovery in the event of major impacts on your business.

- *Risk Assessment management* – Your facility is filled with risks and hazards, and each of your major processes will need to be routinely assessed for those risks in order to identify and introduce controls which will minimise their impact. In many countries there is a legal requirement to complete such Risk Assessments. Important considerations include...

  - o The Risk Assessment document format; with numerous standard templates available on the internet, often provided by national health & safety bodies.

  - o The method for Risk Assessment completion; which should include the need to identify all risks within a process, the prioritisation and scoring of each risk, and the identification of any controls that are in place to manage the risks. It should also define who is responsible for completing the Risk Assessments, and for implementing the required controls. Rather than being completed by your Health & Safety representative, I would recommend that they are completed by the supervisor responsible for the process area, with technical support and guidance from your Health & Safety Representative. You could also consider involving any front-line team members that work within the process area.

- o The method for communicating Risk Assessments: with consideration given to how they are presented in the work area that they are applicable to.
- o The method for updating the Risk Assessments; with controls required for reassessment when a process changes, and for annual reassessment to maintain relevance. I would recommend that you create a risk register, which lists all of the processes that require a Risk Assessment, and the date of completion and required reassessment.

- *PPE Management* – No doubt your facility requires the use of Personal Protective Equipment, such as safety shoes, or hearing protection. You'll therefore need processes that…
  - o Identify where PPE is required, how that requirement is defined (usually as a result of a Risk Assessment), and how business changes that influence the requirement are managed.
  - o Define how PPE is issued, which can ensure everyone is provided with the equipment they require and can help to manage costs.
  - o Outline how the requirement for PPE is communicated, including the positioning and type of signage used across your facility, and its inclusion in things like Standard Work documentation.

- *COSHH management* – Many facilities utilise substances that are hazardous, and therefore a process is required for the Control of Substances that are Hazardous to Health. Key points to remember are…
  - o You'll need a register of all hazardous substances used in your facility including a material data sheet for the substance, a definition of the storage methods needed which might include segregated and clearly labelled containerisation, the risks associated with their use, and the controls required when they are used.
  - o You'll need to manage and authorise the introduction of new substances into your facility, which requires interaction with functions such as Engineering when developing and introducing new products. Again, involvement of supervisors and managers from associated work areas where hazardous substances are used can be a good idea.

- *Legal Compliance* – Your facility will no doubt have a number of legal compliance requirements that are both general to industry, and specific to your production requirements. Your process here should look to include…
  - o A Legal Compliance Register which lists all of the controls that are required, and which is then used to track when those requirements have been assessed and need to be reassessed.

Consider requirements such as LEV testing, air quality, noise levels, display screen equipment use, racking assessments, and lifting equipment audits as some of the more typical examples.

- *Waste control and disposal* – Often, your Health & Safety representative will also pick up environmental management responsibilities, and as a result may take the lead in managing the control and environmentally sound disposal of waste from your facility. Be aware, if you manage this process effectively, you're likely to reduce your costs, and perhaps even generate some revenue from recycling. You'll need processes that…
    - o Manage the segregation of waste into categories such as wood, paper, plastic, and metal.
    - o Control and segregate hazardous wastes including lubricants, paints, and chemicals, depending on the nature of your manufacturing process.
    - o Record and retain all documentation in order to monitor and report waste levels to relevant regulatory bodies.

Quality – the Quality function is responsible for the documentation and administration of your management system, and for managing controls that assure your product specification. Typical processes include…

- *Customer quality issue response* – Unless you're in a very fortunate position, it's likely that you're going to experience customer quality issues of some kind. It's therefore a good idea to ensure that whenever a customer makes a quality complaint, you initiate a very thorough and customer focused response. Remember, delivering value for the customer is a key aspect of our journey towards excellence. Good practice processes include features such as…
    - o Clear escalation of the issue when it is first communicated by your customer, with all key team members made fully aware, and responsibility for investigation and resolution clearly defined. I've seen examples where a bell was rung, or an alert email was sent to the Core Team.
    - o The use of a well-defined Practical Problem-Solving Approach and document for investigation of the issue, and communication with your customer. Here I would recommend that you use the PPSA document described in Step 6, or something similar. Your process could include the need to define of a cross-functional team, or the option to use a PPSA meeting room.
    - o The definition of expected timescales for completion of the investigation, and the introduction of containment activities and countermeasures. Typically, we might talk about 24 hours for containment, and one week to one month for countermeasures depending on your industry standards and the technical nature of the problem.
    - o The definition of when and how you should communicate with your customer. It's really easy to be so focused on investigating and fixing a problem that you forget to let your customer know what you're doing about it.

- *Alert process* – It can be useful to develop a 'Quality Alert' process which cascades all customer quality issues throughout the facility. This can help to raise awareness and can create lessons learned opportunities in other parts of your plant. Things to consider here include…

  o The format of your 'Quality Alert' documentation. You'll need to decide what details you'll want to include, and whether or not you'll cascade containment actions in this forum.

  o Where and how the 'Quality Alerts' are cascaded. You could utilise the 'Start of Day' meetings discussed in Step 4 as a forum for sharing the details of the quality issue with all team members, and could publish the alert on the individual whiteboards in each team area.

  o How you can evidence the communication has been received. You could ask team members to sign the alert forms, meaning that they also serve as training records. I've also used similar processes for the communication of accidents, or major health and safety related incidents, and have found similar benefits.

- *Definition of production quality controls* – Any production process contains risk linked to product quality. Issues such as the level of technicality, repetition, labour skill, and raw material variation along with a great many others will impact the reliability and repeatability of your process. Therefore, your Quality team are usually responsible for defining appropriate controls within your process which help to minimise and manage any risk. You'll need processes that…

  o Use tools such as a Control Plan, combined with a PFMEA (Process Failure Mode Effects Analysis), to assess and define the quality controls you need. Together, these work very much like a Risk Assessment but for quality, and are typically created for each individual production process. I would normally ask the Quality representative in the Core Team to own them, but for the whole Core Team to be party to their completion and management. The Control Plan and PFMEA will identify each and every risk, will score it for severity and frequency, and will outline the controls required to manage any risks. Importantly, the control plan should also identify the response required when controls lapse or fail.

  o Define appropriate process controls such as inspection points, poke-yoke devices, checking fixtures, data recording and monitoring (Statistical Process Control – SPC), or buddy-checking.

  o Specify traceability and documentation controls, depending on your environment and industry.

- *Incoming inspection management* – Like you, your suppliers will be manufacturing organisations. And, they're likely to be experiencing the same problems that you are. Therefore, inspecting the components that you receive from your suppliers is a necessary evil. Your processes should include…

  o Clarity around the specific equipment required for completion of any inspection, depending on the technical nature of the product you're manufacturing.

  o Definition of the type of inspection required, and the inspection method.

- Clear controls around selection of suppliers and parts that require inspection, including the definition of when inspection is required. You might decide that inspection is required when a part is delivered for the first time, when components contain critical features, and for a period of time after a previous quality issue has been identified.
- Strong controls around the recording and documenting of all inspections completed, organised by supplier and by product type so that you can complete appropriate analyses of where your biggest supply chain quality problems exist.
- Protocols for how to respond when a component fails inspection.

- *Supplier quality management* – Management of supplier quality involves much more than just incoming inspection. If your facility is accredited with a quality management standard such as ISO:9001 or IATF:16949, you will be required to routinely audit your supplier capabilities, and in particular to manage changes originating from new product introduction or engineering change. Key features include…
  - The use of tools such as First Article Inspection Reports (FAIR), Production Part Approval Process (PPAP), or Initial Sample Inspection Reports (ISIR).
  - The creation and management of a Supplier Quality Assurance Manual (SQAM), which can be rolled out with every supplier, and which defines the quality responsibilities of both parties.
  - A method for recording and monitoring supplier quality issues, and for asking suppliers to respond to any issues with PPSA documents or something similar. Your Supplier Quality Engineers can support the completion of these documents if needed, and can audit the effectiveness of the countermeasures taken by your supplier.
  - A stock sweep process for the inspection of potential risk parts when a supplier reject is identified. This could involve third party support and be a rechargeable activity.
  - A supplier audit process, both for initial supplier selection, and for ongoing management.

- *Calibration controls* – You're likely to be using equipment that requires calibration in your facility, even if that's just a tape measure. You'll therefore need a process that…
  - Maintains a calibration register, defines when calibration is required, and describes which suppliers are used to complete that calibration. It will also need to define how to respond when significant process changes occur.

- *Scrap monitoring* – Responsibility for scrap monitoring can sometimes sit with your Quality team, and other times may sit more with Production. Regardless of who manages it, you're likely to need to define a process for reporting scrap, and for analysing it. It is possible that for you scrap is insignificant, and not something worth managing. But for everyone else, a good process considers…
  - Clear segregation and identification of scrap material, including information such as the reason, the quantity, and whether it is a supplier issue or an internal issue.

- Well-defined mechanisms for assessment and analysis. Where scrap was a significant problem, I found it useful to include the topic as part of the 'MDI' process, and even required the scrapped items to be brought to the 'MDI' boards for review and discussion by the team.
- Clear protocols for recording of scrap so you have a full understanding of the scale of the problem, and can manage the financial implications. If you're utilising an Enterprise Resource Planning (ERP) system, this can be straightforward. If not, you could be defining something quite manual and paper driven.

- *Engineering change control* – Again, you could easily put engineering change management as the responsibility of another function, perhaps Planning or Engineering for example. But, I find the Quality team to be good at policing the introduction of engineering change because they are then controlling the specification of the product. Your processes should…
  - Be able to manage both running changes and immediate changes.
  - Be able to manage the interface of all relevant functions to manage a change effectively, such as Product Engineering, Production, Planning, Quality, Logistics and Manufacturing Engineering. They are all likely to be involved in agreeing and implementing the effective change date, and for communicating with your customer.
  - Have the capacity to cope with the volume of changes appropriate to your facility. It may be prudent for you to recruit an Engineering Change Coordinator, and to create an Engineering Change Committee which involves all of the relevant functions.
  - Be able to manage excess and obsolete inventory costs associated with any changes.

- *Management system administration* – As I've mentioned previously, your facility may well be accredited with a quality management standard, and as a consequence you will have a need to maintain a management system that supports the standard. It is not unusual for a management system such as this to be applied only as a box ticking exercise in order to receive accreditation and a certificate. It's also typical for it to be thrust at a Quality Manager and for them to be expected to simply deliver it. I would strongly advise you to embrace whatever standard you are working to, and to ensure that it is widely integrated into your facility. Good practice suggests…
  - That you recruit a Systems Engineer to maintain it if you can afford to.
  - That you have standard process and procedure document formats that clearly identify responsibilities and ownership for each process step.
  - That the system has clear protocols for document control, and for managing change.
  - That annual review activities are completed.
  - That Internal process audits are scheduled, completed, and acted upon appropriately.
  - That processes and procedures are owned by individual managers and supervisors, and not by the Quality team in isolation.

- *Warranty management* – This is not necessarily relevant to every manufacturing facility, but certainly some. If your organisation offers a warranty on the product that you manufacture, then it's likely that you have warranty claims against your product. I would suggest that you consider…
  - Integrating warranty management into your Quality team.
  - Creating processes that record all warranty claims by type, product and cost. You can then pareto failures, and can respond to those with the highest frequency of occurrence or cost.
  - Establishing a process for reviewing warranty claims, with a focus on identifying repetitious issues that can be fed back into the production process to reduce warranty issues in the field.

Planning – the Planning function is responsible for generating production plans that support customer requirements, and for generating material schedules that support the production plan, whilst managing inventory levels. Typical processes would include…

- *Production scheduling and control* – All manufacturing facilities require some form of production control activity. That activity seeks to balance process capacity, order scheduling, sales forecasting, schedule execution, material availability, inventory levels, and sales order processing. They're focused on achieving good on-time delivery performance and lead-times. A good process will consider…
  - Whether daily finite scheduling, Heijunka mechanisms, or JIT sequencing is used as the primary control method. Finite scheduling processes tend to be chosen where product variation is high, and flexibility is a must. Heijunka led processes tend to be chosen where product variation is minimal, and product is shipped from stock. JIT sequencing is usually determined by the nature of the product, and the expectations of the customer.
  - How daily finite scheduling processes (if relevant) sequence orders for production based on customer due date, and the particular constraints of the relevant process. Included here is the need for specific controls that manage order intake in line with capacity, forecasting to support material availability, process constraints, line balancing, and schedule communication.
  - How JIT sequencing processes (if relevant) function, including electronic communication, information exchange, buffer size, material kitting, labelling and many more. Included here is the need for controls that manage capacity utilisation, buffer control, and product mix in line with pre-agreed guidelines in order to manage material availability and process burden.
  - How Heijunka scheduling mechanisms (if relevant) function, including the design of the build triggers, the management of capacity and product variation, the definition of stock levels, and the management of order intake in line with minimum and maximum stock guidelines.
  - How Sales and Operational Planning (S&OP) processes work, and how they interface with daily scheduling processes.
  - How product variation will influence inventory levels and space requirements, both lineside and in warehouse locations.

- *Sales Order Processing* – Sales Order Processing is the activity that receives and processes customer orders into your facility. Your process will need to include…
    - A strong link to the production scheduling process in order to ensure that aspects such as stock availability, capacity, and material availability are considered when accepting and committing delivery. Some organisations consider Sales Order Processing as a Customer Service activity, and integrate it into Sales. Or, there is a current trend to disconnect Sales Order Processing from the manufacturing facility completely, with centralised 'Customer Service Centres' springing up in low cost countries to save money. For me, this is a mistake, and I would strongly suggest that the activity remains within the Operations team in order to retain the links to the scheduling process. Remember, good customer service is delivered as a result of effective operational capability and is owned by Operations, not by Sales.
    - The definition of procedures which ensure product specification is clear and manufacturable, and which may well involve interfaces with Product Management or Engineering.
    - The method for communicating with customers, including order confirmation, due date commitment, on-time delivery expectations, and shipping confirmation.
    - The management and retention of paperwork, and the communication of terms of supply.
    - The effective control of the Sales Order book, including ERP system data maintenance.
- *Material scheduling* – Part of the responsibility of the planning team is to order and forecast the delivery of materials required for the production process, whilst also ensuring that inventory levels are managed in order to minimise impacts to cashflow. You'll need processes that…
    - Order materials in line with production requirements and stock holding plans. This may be through the utilisation and management of an MRP functionality within an ERP system, or through manual processes that can be more labour intensive.
    - Are flexible and can cope with peaks and troughs in demand.
    - Monitor the delivery and receipt of material from suppliers, alongside internal inventory levels, in order to maintain material availability for production.
    - Manage the replacement of material that is rejected back to suppliers for quality reasons.
    - Manage the impacts of engineering change and minimise the risk of obsolescence.
    - Manage excess and obsolete stock levels and disposal.
    - Maintain a clean orderbook and manage overdue orders from suppliers.
    - Manage system parameters such as minimum order quantities, lead-times, and pack sizes.
    - Highlight potential stock-out risks.

Purchasing – the Purchasing team are responsible for the identification and selection of best supply solutions for raw materials, along with negotiation of price and supplier relationship management, and for the definition of purchasing terms and conditions. Typical processes would include…

- *Supplier selection* – The identification and selection of suppliers is an obvious requirement for the Purchasing team. Here, you'll need processes that…
  - Clarify the selection criteria for new suppliers; with guidance on the quality, safety, financial, environmental, and perhaps even moral and legal standards that they need to meet. There may also be geographic or political constraints defined by your organisation. It's a good idea for supplier selection to look beyond just material price. Instead they need to include considerations such as total logistics costs, tooling costs, and supplier performance and capability. I've seen numerous examples of parts being resourced to new suppliers because of price, only for savings to be wiped out by additional costs caused by poor quality and delivery, or additional logistics costs that were ignored or missed in error.
  - Define the requirements for advance assessment of suppliers, supported by the Quality team.
- *Pricing and supply agreement* – Once suppliers are selected, it's necessary to agree the supply requirements and pricing for the required components or materials. Often, these can be agreed as one-off purchases, or as long-term agreements. Good processes include…
  - Definition of payment and credit terms, delivery terms, price breaks, packaging methodologies, and how forecasting and delivery methods are completed. I would always advise that a Purchasing team involves their colleagues from Logistics and Planning in defining any agreements with suppliers in order to ensure a comprehensive solution is defined.
- *Supplier relationship and performance management* – Whilst day to day performance discussions tend to take place with Supplier Quality Engineers and Material Planners, it's a good idea for the supplier performance relationship to be overseen by the Purchasing team. As a result, the Purchasing team will have a clear picture about the performance of the supplier when it comes to awarding new agreements, and selection for new components. It also means that your Core Team members have a route to escalate supply problems if necessary. Good processes include…
  - Mechanisms for reporting and sharing performance. You might want to consider sending monthly or quarterly performance reports to each of your suppliers, or only to those that are underperforming if your resources are limited.
  - The management of contact details so that escalation is an easy option.
- *Purchase order management* – There are legal considerations when placing purchase orders, and there is often a need to control expenditure in line with budget. It's quite typical for a Purchasing team to manage these requirements. You'll need processes that…
  - Define purchasing terms that are referenced with every purchase order, and which are approved by your organisation as appropriate.
  - Define the levels of allowed expenditure for each person, and where authorisation is required. Many organisations utilise standard processes for the approval of expenditure by members of

the management team. Some do not. Whilst there is a clear logic to their existence, there is also a delicate balance to find. We are trying to empower our team members and to establish relationships based on trust in order to strength psychological safety. Restricting the ability of our team members to spend money where it is necessary can negatively impact this endeavour. I would propose that a balance is struck, and that processes are developed that allow team members to authorise their own expenditure where they have budgets in place, and up to a sensible value. It may be necessary to determine budget owners, and for expenditure to be approved by those budget owners when requested. I would only advocate escalating sign-off approval for expenditure outside of budget, or of significant one-off value.

Logistics – your Logistics team is responsible for the movement and storage of material within your facility, plus the delivery of finished goods to customers and perhaps the collection of raw materials from suppliers. Typical processes would include…

- *Inventory control* – Having a clear understanding of exactly what inventory you have, where it is, and what condition it is in, is absolutely critical to the success of your process. I'm sure every single person reading this book has experienced the impact of a stock loss on their production process. It's therefore extremely important to have robust inventory control processes in place. If there is one area that I would suggest you really focus on in order to reduce any pain you're feeling in your facility, then inventory control is it. Good processes…
  - o Manage the accuracy and integrity of activities such as material receiving, stock transfers, finished goods booking, material back-flushing or component issue and works order booking, dispatch processing and invoicing, scrap booking, quarantine processing, and supplier returns. As part of this, you'll need to consider paperwork management and even archiving requirements. I would suggest that when you define these processes, you try and envisage every potential scenario that your team members may confront in order to provide them with instructions on how to proceed.
  - o Control your warehouse and location management structures, both systematically and physically. If you are utilising an ERP system, these processes and warehouse structures are going to need to be built around how that system works. If you're not, then once again it's going to be somewhat more manual and labour intensive. Either way, you should consider that the systematic world and physical world need to match, so that every movement in the physical world can be replicated in the system world. You may choose to implement an integrated Warehouse Management System (WMS) with barcode scanning controls if you have a significant material and logistics activity to manage. These can be challenging to set up and properly maintain, but do add value in the long-term.

- Manage the stock-taking and cycle counting/perpetual inventory activities. If you can, I would always advise replacing a stock-take process with a really capable cycle count/perpetual inventory process. No matter how good your stock-take process is, it's likely to add just as many errors as it takes out. And, if you introduce a cycle count process, please remember that its main purpose is to find a stock error and to investigate and correct the original cause of that error. If the stock is incorrect because someone forgot to book something in, then get it booked in. Otherwise your invoice matching processes in your Accounts Payable/Receivable team will fail. It's too easy just to cycle count the stock to make it correct, but this should only be done as a last resort. If you need to, you could add sign-off processes and authorisation limits for stock adjustments to drive the discipline.
  - Control traceability and shelf-life depending on your industry and the nature of your products.
- *Delivery transactions* – Depending on your circumstances, your facility may well be responsible for arranging the collection, transportation and delivery of goods to your customer; or your customer may collect. You'll therefore need processes that…
  - Manage the arrangement of transportation, and the completion of the appropriate documentation, particularly where export and trade compliance controls are relevant. This can be tricky to navigate with legal and financial regulation implications. So, if you're required to manage this, I would definitely advocate that you recruit knowledgeable professionals onto your team such as a Trade Compliance Officer, or train your current team well.
- *Line-feed* – Your Logistics team are also likely to be responsible for 'feeding' your production line with parts. If this is not the case in your facility, and your Production team collect their own parts, I would strongly advise you to introduce some line-feeding capability into your Logistics team. Your Production team are skilled operatives that need to be focused on value-add activities, not on collecting parts. You can make them far more efficient by establishing line-feed processes that are centralised into Logistics. Your process will need to consider…
  - The equipment required for the movement and storage of your material.
  - The amount of space required both in your warehouse and lineside for all your material variants.
  - The ergonomics of moving the parts, along with the frequency with which they need to be replenished. Here, you could consider utilising Kanban or supermarket processes to trigger the replenishment activity.
- *Equipment management* – Your Logistics team will also be responsible for managing a variety of equipment, such as Manual Handling Equipment (MHE) like fork-lift trucks or cranes, and warehouse equipment such as racking and ladders. You'll therefore need processes that…
  - Define the quantity and type of equipment needed to support your production requirements.
  - Require start of shift checks to ensure that equipment is safe to use.

o   Manage routine maintenance and servicing in order to maintain availability and compliance.

Facilities & Maintenance – your Facilities & Maintenance team are responsible for ensuring the availability of equipment, machinery and facilities to required standards. Typical processes would include…

- *Breakdown response* – The most obvious activity for your Facilities & Maintenance team to manage is the breakdown of equipment and machinery. This, of course, includes shop-floor equipment, as well as your offices and wider facilities. Key points to consider are…
    - o   Try and make reporting a problem quick and easy, and accessible by any team member in order to support empowerment.
    - o   Look to define a level of priority, record data around the time taken to respond, and monitor trends in failures. We should remember we referenced this kind of process back in Step 6.
- *Planned Maintenance* – In order to minimise lost time from equipment breakdowns, it's a good idea to introduce a planned maintenance and service programme, particularly with your most critical machinery and equipment. Good processes include…
    - o   Controls that define when planned maintenance is required, who it should be completed by, and whether or not external support is required. You may utilise third party software to manage this process, or you may just use a spreadsheet. It really just depends on how much equipment you have to manage, and how critical it is to your ability to produce. This process can also be closely linked to the Legal Compliance Register we discussed as part of the Health & Safety section, with equipment testing and maintenance appearing on both documents. You'll also need to be able to manage changes to your equipment listing.
- *Sub-contractor management* – An integral part of the maintenance of any manufacturing facility will be the utilisation of sub-contractors. Service engineers, and specialist technicians, will always be required. You'll therefore need processes that…
    - o   Manage the health and safety aspects of the practices that these sub-contractors follow, both for their safety and the safety of your team members. These often include the submission of Risk Assessments and Methods Statements (RAMS), and perhaps evidence of Insurance.
    - o   Manage approved contractor listings, which could define training or induction for contractors to work on your site.
- *Critical Spares* – As part of ensuring equipment availability, and for supporting planned maintenance, it can be a good idea to maintain a level of inventory of critical spares for your machinery and equipment. If that's the case for you, I would recommend that you define processes that…
    - o   Control which critical spares are required, for what equipment, and how those spares are routinely replenished if utilised.
    - o   Manage the shelf-life of your spares if appropriate.

    o   Consider the introduction of new equipment into your facility, and how you will define which spare parts would be classified as critical.

Manufacturing Engineering – your Manufacturing Engineering team is responsible for process design and layout, and equipment and tooling specification, sourcing, and management. Their primary focus is in supporting the efficiency and capability of the production activity. Typical processes would include…

- *Production Line design* – For some, the idea of 'designing' your production processes will be a little unusual. For others, it will be the norm. Your Manufacturing Engineering team would usually take the lead in designing your production processes so that product and material flows, and so that the production process is as efficient and safe as possible. You'll need processes that…
  - o   Provide standard guidance around typical process design for your production activity, with reference to aspects such as layout, material flow, ergonomics, environmental conditions (lighting, heating), tooling requirements, material replenishment requirements, activity balance, and quality control needs. It's not unusual for your Manufacturing Engineering team to utilise tools such as PFMEA, Control Plans, and Risk Assessments to support this process.
  - o   Provide guidance on how to source and specify new equipment and machinery, particularly where you already have established supplier relationships and service agreements in place.
- *Standard Work management* – Standard Work is the term often used to describe the working processes utilised by Production team members when actually producing components. These are tools we'll refer to a little later, but are often generated by the Manufacturing Engineering team in conjunction with the Production and Quality teams. You should look to develop processes that…
  - o   Outline the format of these tools, the frequency at which they are to be reviewed, how they are presented, and how they should be updated when production processes change.
  - o   Define how Standard Work should be introduced to the Production team, and how frequently Standard Work adherence needs to be assessed.
- *Tooling management* – In many facilities, the use of tooling for specific processes such as CNC machining is the norm. You'll therefore need processes that…
  - o   Control how that tooling is stored and maintained, how it is routinely checked, and how damage is reported. It's all too easy to fail to deliver an order because a tool was damaged and not reported. You might even consider extending this process to include tooling that you own, but which is utilised and retained by a supplier.

To ERP or not to ERP – many manufacturing facilities will utilise a fully or partially integrated ERP system, many will not. Often, there is a question as to whether to introduce such a system, and whether it can add value. In my experience, the answer to this question is a resounding yes. In introducing and utilising an ERP system, there can be benefits of increased processing speed and reduced resources, in the sharing and retention of information, and the control of specifications and key data. As a consequence, if you have the option, then I would always encourage you to try and implement such a system, and to build your processes and procedures around its correct application. However, their implementation and ongoing management can take considerable effort and require a clear appreciation of their functionality. I've been involved in many ERP system implementation projects, and have seen all of the typical errors of judgment; from underestimating the time required (expect 12-18 months as a minimum), to the insufficient commitment of resource (try and build a cross-functional team with dedicated resource if you can), to ownership with the wrong function (giving an implementation project to Finance or IT to lead is a common mistake), and to the complete lack of understanding from senior leadership about the implications (it's just running MRP isn't it?). An ERP system is fundamentally a tool to enable your operating processes to function, with outputs into Finance, and supported by IT infrastructure. I'd therefore always recommend that Operations take the lead in its implementation and management.

People Management – there are certain processes that are likely to be defined by your HR function, and which may not report directly into yourself in Operations. However, I believe it's important to reference a small number of the most critical of those processes here because of the impact they can have on the day to day management of your facility. If you're missing any of these, or the ones you have are inadequate, you'll need to work with your HR team to get them changed.

- *Absence Management* – You might be surprised to know that a great many manufacturing facilities fail to establish clear and structured processes for the management of absence from work. As a result, absence can become a real problem, and I've seen it to be as high as 10% of a team or more. Therefore, it's really important to define some clear processes that help to manage absence to practical levels, whilst still supporting those team members that really need it. You'll need processes that...
    - Properly record and report absences, and follow up with appropriate action where required.
    - Provide clear guidelines around what levels of absence are acceptable, and what actions are triggered at different levels of absenteeism. There are standard scoring mechanisms you could use such as the Bradford Factor for example. It's usual to consider both length of time off, and frequency, when determining the outcomes of absence.
    - Communicate expectations on payment during periods of absence. Personally, I would always advocate generous policies for payment during absence. I've often seen absence payments restricted for all team members out of the fear that one or two might abuse the benefit. If your processes are robust enough, you will minimise the risk. And, if you recruit and retain the right people, you'll reduce it further.
    - Allow for authorised absences, for compassionate leave, and for planned absences like maternity and paternity leave, medical appointments, and even sabbaticals.

- o Require Return to Work Interviews (RTWI) to be completed, preferably before someone is allowed to return to their workstation following absence.
- o Provide guidance on how to manage people on long-term absence, particularly in relation to helping them return to work, or in relation to accepting that they never will. There is a delicate balance here, and I would again suggest that you are as generous and compassionate as possible, and respect the needs of each individual in every circumstance.

- *Performance Management* – Unfortunately, there are always likely to be scenario's where someone in your team is not performing to the required standard. It's likely that you'll face this situation more than once, particularly in the early part of a *Lean Foundations™* journey when you still have some of the wrong people onboard. It's therefore a good idea to define a structured process for managing sub-standard performance. This helps to enable your supervisory and management team, reduces the risk that the process will be handled poorly, increases the likelihood that poor performance can be corrected, and helps to maintain the psychological safety of the rest of your team who are performing well. Good processes include…
  - o The definition of an escalating series of management interventions based on the response of the individual who requires performance management. For example, the process could begin with a manager or supervisor initially identifying a performance issue in an informal conversation, then could follow with a more formal coaching conversation, then could follow with a formal performance management conversation, and then finally with a very clear and structured performance management review that could have similar outcomes to a disciplinary process. The number of steps that are defined, and your mechanism for recording them, can depend on your personal preferences and the circumstances of your facility.

- *Disciplinary & Grievance* – You might consider the need for disciplinary and grievance processes as a little unsavoury, but I'm afraid they are always a necessity. If you don't have them, I would suggest that you address this with some urgency with support from your HR team. You'll need to include…
  - o A Disciplinary process with an escalating outcome depending on the severity and repetition of issues, along with clarity on how long a disciplinary outcome will remain on record. You'll also need to define guidance on who should complete each stage of the process, including initial investigation activities, the disciplinary meetings, and an appeal process. Typically, it's good practice to have different people completing each stage in order to maintain impartiality. Of course, there are some situations that could be considered as Gross Misconduct, and could result in immediate dismissal, so it's important to reference these. My experience here is based on UK Employment law, which is potentially slightly different to other parts of the world. I would suggest you take appropriate guidance from legal bodies relevant to you.

- A Grievance Process that can help to provide your team members with the opportunity to raise concerns and protect themselves from poor management practice, without fear of retribution. This process will need to be fair and transparent, and is something that I would advise you protect vigorously. Remember, part of your responsibility as the top leader of your facility is to protect your team, even if that means you have to protect it from someone within it.

- *Toolbox Talk process* – a big part of your improvement journey is the training of your team. Sometimes, those training exercises are formally structured and are delivered in a specific training environment. At other times, they could be a little more informal, and perhaps take place at a workstation or even on a production line. This is where a 'Toolbox Talk' process can be extremely useful in training out important minor changes to working practices. You'll need to introduce a process that…
  - Defines the 'Toolbox Talk' form. This is usually a simple document that outlines the material that needs to be trained, such as a minor process modification, or the introduction of a temporary quality control following a customer quality issue, and then records the details of the individuals who have received the training outlined. It might include photographs and diagrams to illustrate the changes or controls that are being introduced.
  - Describes how the form is utilised, and how it is retained for training record purposes.

Please note that the functions and processes described here are primarily those that you as an operational leader would be heavily involved in defining or utilising on a daily basis. There are, of course, a great many other processes that tend to be owned by other functions outside of Operations, but which are equally as important. Consider, for example, annual budget processes, new product introduction, product specification and design, and accounts payable and receivable activities, to name just a few. If you have challenges in these areas which are impacting your operational capabilities, I would advise you to work with your colleagues and peers in the relevant functions to gain improvements that make your operational environment function more effectively. This can be a challenge depending on the nature of the relationships you hold, which is why I would always encourage you to keep them as positive as possible. Often, I have found that failings in these processes have a greater impact on operational performance than flaws in my own operating procedures. However, I usually work hard to get my operating processes and procedures to the right standard before I start knocking on the doors of my peers. By doing so, I find that the problems with those processes are much more apparent, and my peers are much more receptive to the need for change. Particularly if I'm offering the support of my team when deciding how to change. Again, the message to the potential readers who are CEO's, Managing Directors, and Vice Presidents is to remember: *'Operations is where it's at'*. Any support you can offer that integrates this vital concept into your organisation will make a big difference.

Defining *your* operating processes, and making them stick

Now that we have an idea of the kind of operating processes and procedures that we might find in a typical well-performing manufacturing facility, our next challenge is to introduce the same level of standardisation into your particular facility. Your individual requirements and needs will be different from any others, and we therefore need to find the right way for you to define and introduce operating processes and procedures that work for you. We also need to ensure that we introduce them in a way that is sustainable, and which encourages their practical application today and into the future. Whilst this might seem a difficult task to achieve, my experience tells me that it's actually relatively straightforward, although potentially time consuming. *Lean Foundations™* recommends the following of three practical steps which will help you to get to where you need to go.

Prioritise your efforts – First of all, it's a good idea to decide just how big a problem your lack of control and stability is for you. If your operational performance is poor and unstable, as is the case for so many, then it's likely that you have problems in your core operating processes and procedures, and need to work on them to improve. You may therefore decide that you wish to build the improvement of these processes into your top-level Improvement Plan and your 'X-Matrix'. Of course, in doing so, you'll need to prioritise which processes need to be improved, and where they sit amongst the other Improvement Projects that you have defined. You may remember that back in Step 3, I had suggested that you would need to incorporate some of the learning from later Steps of the *Lean Foundations™* approach into your top-level Improvement Plan. Well, here we are.

Process Mapping for improvement – Second, having decided how important the task of stabilising your processes is, and which of your operating processes you feel most need to be improved, it's time to get on with the activity of actually improving them. I've found that the most successful method for defining or improving processes and procedures is to complete process mapping exercises. These are usually led by the manager or supervisor of the function that owns the relevant process, and are sometimes facilitated by a Continuous Improvement Manager as the process mapping specialist. The exercise needs to involve all of the relevant process contributors, which usually requires participation from multiple functions, and follows a simple methodology.

- The process mapping activity begins by defining the 'current state', and carefully describes each and every step taken to complete the process. This can usually take some time, and often requires a large amount of back and forth discussion as people suddenly remember a step they had previously forgotten. When mapping the 'current state', it's important to map how you actually work, rather than how existing process documentation may say you work. This means that the approach is effective whether you already have documented procedures or not. I also find it useful if you can be as granular as possible when describing each of the steps. The more detail, the better the result. Personally, I usually encourage the use of swim lane diagrams when defining processes in order to help to clarify the transfer of responsibility between functions, and to show the passing of time. I also find that they make process mapping exercises of this nature much easier to facilitate.

- Once the 'current state' is defined, the process mapping team are then tasked to identify the weaknesses of the process they have described. Multi-coloured sticky notes can be useful here.

- Next, the process mapping team are tasked to define a 'future state' process map which addresses the weaknesses of the original process. When defining this 'future state', it's important to develop a solution that is appropriate and relevant to your facility's current level of development. For example, there is no point trying to introduce a fully functioning JIT system to solve your delivery performance issues if you don't have the basics of flow in place. And, there's no point trying to introduce full blown 5S processes, if you don't have the right organisation structure and management systems in place. Remember, you will have retained and recruited the right people onto your team, and will be encouraging them to express themselves. As a result, you're likely to enable the introduction of varied and extremely capable solutions based on previous experiences, rather than there being a reliance on the inputs of a particular few specialist (who aren't necessarily very special). You've also introduced a problem-solving mentality, which means that your team are much more able to identify and analyse the problems with your processes, and to suggest practical solutions for resolving them. If anything, you'll be flooded with options, and will need to manage the selection of the right ones carefully. As part of this, it's important to bear in mind that whilst the definition of the 'future state' is an extremely empowering experience, it can also be daunting, as people realise that their contributions will really count. In these situations, I usually endeavour to ensure that the psychological safety of the team is protected so that they feel able to express themselves fully. I've found it to be a good idea to present process mapping exercises of this nature as a learning opportunity, and as something that will respond to change without blame or criticism of failure.

- Once the 'future state' is defined, the team are then tasked to define an implementation plan which needs to consider the most appropriate way of introducing the new process. It could just be that a switch is flicked, and people work to the new process from the start of a new week. More likely, there are more significant steps such as IT functionality changes, training of people, modifications to documentation, and perhaps even communication with customers and other stakeholders.

- Finally, once the implementation plan is defined, it's important to monitor progress of implementation, and the success of the new process. If it's not working as expected, then the team will need to evaluate why, and will need to adjust accordingly. This may result in secondary process mapping exercises.

If you and your management team have chosen to integrate the improvement of certain processes into your top-level Improvement Plan and 'X-Matrix', then these process mapping activities can easily be defined as Improvement Projects, and can be delegated to the relevant functional manager or supervisor as

'Project-level Improvement A3's'. As a consequence, whilst the specific methodology of the process mapping exercise is a little different to a normal A3 problem-solving process, the approach to improvement, and the use of the PDCA/TOC thinking process, is very much the same.

Institutionalise – Finally, after defining your priorities, and creating your new operating processes, you'll need to introduce them into your operation in such a way as you make sure they stick. Having completed the process mapping exercise as you have, you're already in a much better place than if the processes had been created in a different way. It's not unusual for processes and procedures to be independently defined by a Quality Manager or a System Engineer in order to complete a box ticking exercise for business management system accreditation. Instead, by drawing a team together in a process mapping exercise, I usually find that the new processes are more successful, and that they are more widely and readily embraced by the team who developed them. To help this along the way, there are a couple of other actions that I can recommend…

- *Document* – It's important to document your procedures and processes, preferably in a standard format that is easy for everyone to understand and follow. If you have documented procedures already in place, then take a look and see if you could actually use them to complete the processes they are related to. If not, it's worth reviewing the format, even if you're happy that your operating processes actually work. Often, Quality professionals are encouraged to keep documented processes as simple as possible in order to make auditing them easy and at low risk of failure. This means that a process or procedure can be seen to be followed in different ways during an external audit, but an auditor would be unable to report a non-conformance. Personally, I would encourage a more balanced approach, where procedures and processes are more accurate in their detail. For me, this makes following them easier, and therefore ensures that they are more likely to be followed. It also reduces the opportunity for interpretation, which reduces the potential for variation and loss of control. Remember, processes and procedures are different, and for each activity in your facility you may well document both a process, and the procedures that are used to complete them. There are also practicalities to consider when documenting your processes and procedures, such as system maintenance and revision control. This tends to be where your Systems Engineer comes in.
- *Define responsibility* – Ensuring the clear definition of the ownership of each process, and of each activity within a process, is a vital part of making a process stick. The use of swim-lane format process maps will help with this, but you may also consider utilising tools such as a RACI matrix that define the people and functions who are 'Responsible', 'Accountable', 'Consulted' and 'Involved' in any process or activity. Whichever mechanism you use, it's important that ownership is clear, and is readily accepted.
- *Maintain accessibility* – Once your procedures and processes are documented, it's a good idea to make them as accessible to everyone as possible. This may mean paper folders, or more typically

today, means access is available via a shared network folder. You might want to ensure that files are Read-Only protected with controlled access to make change. To help with maintaining accessibility, you might want to ensure that shortcuts to the relevant folder are added to every person's computer.

- *Train people* – And yes, once again, there is a need to train people in the new way of working. It may seem like I keep saying the same thing, but really, training is critical. If people do not understand their role in a new process, or exactly how they are supposed to function, then the likelihood of it being introduced successfully is very low. You could complete this training with formal and structured sessions, or via the use of the 'Toolbox Talk' process described a little earlier.

- *Induct carefully* – Training your current team members is only half the job. As with all organisations, you will always have a turnover of employees, and as a result you'll need to introduce your processes and procedures with new employees in a way that ensures they are embraced and applied correctly. I have found that the introduction of new team members, with their own ideas and historical working methods, can be the biggest risk to the stability of your established controls. To help to manage this risk, I have learned that the development of robust induction and new employee training programmes can be extremely helpful. By introducing new employees in a controlled manner, with detailed training on the defined working methods of your facility, you can minimise the likelihood that your processes become diluted. This potentially requires the creation of training documentation for each activity, or could just mean that you ask colleagues to train new employees in line with the established procedures, and then sign them off when the training is considered complete. You might even consider an informal buddy-check by a supervisor or manager, or perhaps yourself.

- *Leadership walk through* – As part of the completion of a process mapping '*Project-level improvement A3*', you may wish to consider completing a leadership walk through of the newly functioning process. By asking the process mapping team to systematically walk you through a series of real time examples of the process that has been improved, you can personally evaluate its effectiveness, and can recognise and appreciate the efforts of the team. Most importantly, you can gain a personal understanding of how the process works, and can encourage its correct application and use by others.

As I said a little earlier, you may look at the steps I've just described for defining and introducing the right kind of operating processes and procedures into your facility as a little over-simplified. But, all too often I've seen that these straightforward steps have not been followed, and as a consequence, facilities suffer with poor or non-existent processes that impact their daily operational performance. These activities may seem unsophisticated, but I would suggest that they are also very effective.

The right production processes, the right way

The final challenge on our path to stability, is the standardisation of our core production activities. Here is where the potential for disruption is at its greatest, and where the impacts on your operational performance are most evident. If a production activity is completed incorrectly, then waste is created immediately, and the ripples through your process are substantial. The poor execution of an assembly or machining activity can result in scrap, lost time, rework, additional inspection, a late delivery, and then a customer quality complaint. All of which adds considerable burden to your management resources, detrimentally impacts your operational performance, and damages the reputation of your product and your facility. Worst of all, I'm confident that in the majority of cases, you won't even know that these things are happening. Your front-line team members, supervisors, and managers could be dealing with them so habitually that they may not even bother to identify them as problems, and may not consider them as rocks upon which they're constantly pouring water. Standardisation of your production activities removes the reliance on 'job knowledge', and is a vital step to establishing control whilst providing the foundation for deliberate and focused improvement.

However, whilst it's crucially important that we achieve standardisation in your core production activities, it's also important to do so in a way that is appropriate to your current level of organisational development and capability. Just as with defining the 'future state' of your operating processes, there is no point trying to introduce fully functioning Standard Work controls, disciplined 5S methodologies, and sophisticated poke-yoke devices, if your team are not yet practiced in more basic controls, or are too busy fighting fires to find the time to learn. We therefore need to introduce tools and methodologies that will help us to establish a level of control that is sufficient for our facility to perform well, so that in the future we can enhance those controls in order to perform with excellence. Hopefully you remember the 'Injured Person' analogy from the end of Step 6? Well, the same idea applies here.

Bearing all of this in mind, *Lean Foundations™* recommends a number of simple but effective initial steps that will help to establish an effective level of control of your core production activities, without over-stretching your resources…

- *Basic Standard Work* – Standard Work processes are systems for communicating and managing the correct method of completion of a production activity. Fully functioning Standard Work processes would normally develop Standard Work documents for each production activity, which include features such as a sequential description of each step of the production activity, the time it should take to complete them, the key quality and safety features to consider when completing them, what tooling and machinery is needed and when, and what PPE should be used, along with potentially many more. That process would also utilise those documents to train front-line team members, and to routinely assess the ability of those team members to recall and repeat the correct working method. Here, *Lean Foundations™* proposes that you develop your own format for Standard Work, of which there are a great many available on the internet, but that you only include the elements that you consider necessary in these early stages. They take time and resource to create and to maintain, and therefore you need to decide their content carefully. I would advise that you generate Standard Work for every production activity in your facility if you can. Normally, Standard Work documents are created and maintained by your Manufacturing or Process Engineering function, which believe it or not, I often find does not exist in some manufacturing facilities. I would also advise that the generation of the Standard Work documentation closely involves the individual front-line team members who complete the production activity every day. It's important to capture their customs and practices, and to document their 'knack' or working method. Bear in mind that if you work across different shifts, you need to consider the working methods of all of the front-line team members on every shift. You may encounter differences, and then you're faced with the challenge of deciding which one is best, and of convincing the others to change. Once you have created your Standard Work documents, you can now ensure that all your front-line team members are correctly trained, and in the process have a valuable tool to support the management of the Skills Versatility Matrix that we discussed back in Step 2. You also have a means of training new team members when they first enter your production process, and thus reduce the risk of disruption often unintentionally caused by new-starters. I usually ensure that Standard Work is available for review at the workstation for which it is written, with it sometimes being openly displayed in a location where it is easy to refer to. However, this is not necessarily a critical factor, because the Standard Work activity can become ingrained in mental processing and muscle memory, rather than being followed through the reading of visual aids. As a final point, some manufacturing processes take second or minutes to complete and have very few steps, others can take hours and have hundreds of steps. For the latter, the creation of Standard Work documentation is more difficult, but it is still achievable. I know, I've done it. Even in this scenario I would strongly advise you to proceed. It may also be a good idea for you to consider including the creation of Standard Work as one of your Improvement Projects on your top-level Improvement Plan. This can help to prioritise its importance, and manage the impact on your resources.

- *Introduce 3S* – Most of you will have undoubtedly heard of 5S, the workplace organisation method whose name is derived from the fact that it functions as a five-step process, with each of the steps beginning with the letter 'S'. The application of these steps of 'Sort', 'Set in Order', 'Shine', 'Standardise', and 'Sustain', helps to organise a workstation in order to increase the safety and efficiency of its operation. 5S is a fantastic methodology which can really help to make a difference to the stability of a production activity. It ensures that tools are located properly and are readily available, that materials are placed close at hand, and that safety hazards are removed or contained. However, it can be difficult to properly maintain without the correct organisation structure and management disciplines in place. All too often a 5S programme will fall short of being properly sustained beyond a short period of time. To begin with, I would always recommend that you complete 3S activities, which in simple terms set out to fulfil the first three steps of the 5S methodology. By 'Sorting' a workstation and removing unnecessary equipment, material and tooling; by 'Setting in Order' a workstation and defining a place for everything; and by 'Shining' a workstation and cleaning it thoroughly; you can make a significant difference, without burdening yourself with the creation of management controls which support the last two steps. Don't get me wrong, if you feel able to go the whole way, then please do so. For me, I tend not to try to complete full 5S until my team and facility is ready, but it is usually one of the first steps that I would employ when implementing *Lean Basics*. You may wish to integrate a 3S programme into your top-level Improvement Plan, as with some of these other activities, particularly if you're considering rolling it out across your entire facility. I would advise that you break the activities down into bitesize chunks, and that each activity takes place in clearly identifiable team areas. 3S events are generally led by a Continuous Improvement Manager, with complete attendance from all members of the relevant team, including supervisors and potentially other Core Team members from Quality and Manufacturing Engineering. It's typical for a 3S event to generate significant actions for other functions, including Facilities & Maintenance, and for an action plan to take a little time to fully complete. By introducing 3S, you'll gain significant improvements in process reliability and stability, and should at the same time see increased motivation of your front-line team members. I've often seen that a 3S or 5S activity leads to increased levels of pride and satisfaction from all of my team members, and that they can serve as fantastic team-building exercises.

- *Labour Allocation management* – In my experience, a critical factor which affects the stability of the production activity is the allocation of the correctly skilled personnel. I have seen, on numerous occasions, that supervisors and managers can make poor choices when allocating front-line team members to their workstation. They can fail to properly consider whether they have the appropriate training, skills or experience for the role. Worst of all, they can then abandon individuals to 'figure it out', sometimes with the help of a team member on the next workstation. As you might imagine, the risk of disruption in this scenario is significant. I would therefore advise that you maintain clear protocols for the correct allocation of team members to the correct roles. To support this, the Job Allocation board discussed in Step 2 is a really useful tool, particularly when used alongside the Skills Versatility Matrix. I have also overseen the planned allocation of labour in weekly planning meetings, which we'll discuss a little later in the next sub-step. To help your supervisors and managers, it's important to include additional headcount as 'Absence cover' above and beyond the minimal amount you require to meet your operational demand. This is often difficult to justify with the powers that be, because it appears to be purely additional cost and headcount for the sake of it. However, absence is inevitable. Your employees will be entitled to paid annual leave, and even if you manage unauthorised absence well, you'll still experience a level of around 2 to 3% in most industry sectors. Therefore, to maintain your operational efficiency, and to reduce the risk of disruption, you need skilled and routinely trained Production team members to backfill absenteeism. Of course, you can minimise the number that you need by managing absenteeism well, as we discussed a little earlier, and by defining rules which limit the number of people who can take paid annual leave at the same time from the same process area.

- *Temporary Labour management* – Alongside the management of labour allocation, it's also important to properly manage the introduction of temporary labour. Many facilities will utilise temporary employees in order to flex their capacity when demand changes. This is a positive tool and can help to avoid the negative impacts on your core permanent employees of potential headcount reductions when demand reduces. However, I have seen occasions when the ratio of permanent to temporary employees is unhealthy. If this ratio creeps above 10-15% of your total direct headcount, then disruption to your production processes can be considerable. Temporary workers are, by their very nature, transitory, and can leave your facility at very short notice. You may expend considerable time training someone, only to lose them again shortly after, and then need to start the training process again with someone new. That approach adds significant burden to your supervisory and management teams, and can build an unacceptable level of risk into your process control, damaging your operational performance in the process. To help, I would advise that you keep the ratio of temporary to permanent employees healthy, and that you compensate your temporary employees equally with your permanent employees in order to encourage their retention. This could include equal terms for paid holiday, sickness and so on. I would also encourage you to recruit permanent employees from your pool of temporary workers for the same reason.

- *Process design and control mechanisms* – Earlier in this sub-step I referenced production line design as an important process for your Manufacturing Engineering team, and referenced production quality controls as an important process for your Quality team. Bringing these two processes together; to design your production processes effectively, and to build in quality and safety controls, can significantly contribute to the standardisation of your production processes. The design of your production processes can improve the access of the correct tools and equipment, can enable accessibility and accuracy through improved ergonomics and lighting, and identify control risks through the completion of a PFMEA. The use of a Control Plan, and the introduction of specific process controls that manage those risks, can reduce variation and minimise the potential for issues to leave your facility, or even occur in the first place. Please do not under-estimate the value of these activities.

- *End of line Inspection and Rework* – I make this recommendation a little reluctantly, in the knowledge that it really shouldn't be needed. However, as a last resort, it may be necessary for you to consider introducing end of line inspection and rework activities into your production processes. If you find that you're constantly bleeding quality issues to your customer, and you need to protect them from the lack of control in your production process, this may be the best way to reduce or even remove the issue. When introducing an inspection process, sometimes called a 'firewall' or 'special measures', you should remember that 100% inspection is not 100% effective, and you may therefore need to introduce multiple layers to be certain. If you choose this path, then I would advise you to create very clear inspection methods and documents, to record each and every completed inspection carefully, and to ensure that each failure identified by the inspection team is correctly responded to. In reality, an inspection process of this nature should be temporary, but all too often it can become almost normal, and can add burden to your facility. It therefore needs to be introduced carefully, to be viewed as an activity that is independent and a reflection of your customer, and should be removed as soon as it has done its job. If it is applied properly, and is used to identify your biggest issues, and then to implement effective in-line process controls which prevent repeat failures, it can become an effective tool for supporting problem-solving. It can also be used as a means of improving your Standard Work, and for re-training your front-line team members. Furthermore, by including a rework activity that is offline, you can minimise short-term disruption to production flow.

- *Supplier Quality Management* – An often significant factor in the level of disruption experienced on your production line is the quality of the material that you're receiving from your suppliers. If you know this to be a major problem for your facility, then it's probably a good idea to make Supplier Quality Management a priority for your Improvement Plan. You may need to increase incoming inspection activities, and perhaps recharge your suppliers for the cost, or you may ask your suppliers to increase their own inspection activities at their cost. If you have the capability and resource, you could consider completing joint problem-solving processes, particularly as your team are hopefully becoming more skilled problem-solving practitioners. This can help to build constructive relationships with your supply-base, as well as helping to stabilise your facility.

- *Product rationalisation* – As a final thought, you could consider working with your Engineering and Product Management colleagues to try and reduce the product variation that travels through your production process. The greater the variation you have to manage, the greater the risk to process stability, and the greater the implications on your process design and supporting activities. More variations mean more inventory, more lineside storage and space requirements, more warehousing, more material order processing, more supplier management and so on. If possible, and I've seen that it rarely is, it may be worth exploring the opportunities for product rationalisation or the de-listing of certain product types. This, of course, is very dependent on the nature of the product you manufacture in your facility. But if this is something that does affect you, then it may be worth a try. Your colleagues in Sales can often be reluctant to support such an activity, but if you can conduct the right analysis of your historical sales which demonstrates a small number of sales are achieved from a large number of variants, you may be able to get them onboard.

OVERSEE, AND OFFER SUPPORT

As you can probably imagine, standardising the way that you work can take some considerable time and effort. The activities outlined above are not quick fixes that happen easily. But, the benefits in stability that they bring are substantial. Imagine working in an environment where your daily performance is repeatable and reliable, where you deliver your customer orders on-time most of the time, where your customers rarely experience quality issues, where your employees seldom injure themselves, and where your operating costs are predictable. That environment is achievable if you standardise your activities with the right processes and procedures. It sounds too good to be true I know, but please believe me when I say it is possible.

That's not to say that you will achieve perfection through standardisation of course. Problems will still occur, and performance issues will still arise. But the frequency of the occurrence will decline dramatically, and the ability of yourself and your team to concentrate on improving your facility will grow as your level of standardisation grows. And, because of the skills you've given your team in problem-solving, and the tools and forums you've provided to support their ability to manage and respond to change, the resilience of your facility will have improved dramatically. Your team's ability to adapt and modify their standard behaviour in line with any changes to their working conditions will be enhanced, and everyone will feel more in control even when problems occur. Most importantly, as your operational performance improves, and the effort required in delivering it reduces, the levels of happiness in your facility will increase. Your team will feel that they are achieving positive results, and their intrinsic motivator of success will be enhanced. And, their sense that the improvement of the organisation is being fulfilled through their combined efforts, will enhance their intrinsic motivators of collaboration and purpose.

For some operational leaders, this moment in the *Lean Foundations*™ approach may come with a degree of insecurity and confusion. If you have achieved stability, have empowered your team, have provided them with clear direction, have encouraged teamwork, have introduced the right organisation structure, have driven performance with the 'MDI' process, and have taught your team how to solve problems, what is your role now? In the past, you may well have been the person at the heart of every activity. You quite possibly spent your time forcing performance, solving every problem, and making every decision. Now, all of that is in the very capable hands of your team, and happens without needing your involvement.

This does not mean, of course, that you're no longer required. It simply means that your approach to the delivery of your responsibilities has changed. You now really are functioning as the operational leader of your facility, rather than as an operational 'doer'. And instead of being one of the 'indispensable specialists' that saves the day, you're becoming a leadership specialist who is building an exciting and capable future for your team. It's at this point in the *Lean Foundations*™ journey where your own activities can become less tangible and distinct, and you may get a real sense that your job involves 'knitting fog', rather than doing anything concrete or quantifiable. But, this is just a feeling, and is not an accurate one. Your role now is more critical than ever, and your value to your facility and your team, whilst less obvious, has perhaps never been greater.

In order to enable your new approach to your responsibilities, it's time for you to develop the leadership and management protocols that support your ability to maintain what you have spent so much time and effort building. You need to be able to oversee daily operations to ensure that the procedures and processes your team have developed are effective and continue to be applied, whilst enabling you to intervene only when absolutely necessary. And, you need to be able to see when your team members need guidance and support from either yourself or someone else in your team, but perhaps are unaware and are struggling along the best they can. This is where you can develop the tools that will help you to skim across the surface of your facility; asking questions and monitoring progress, then diving in to support or intervene when needed. This is where we can help you to introduce the mechanisms that will support your desire to manage with 'Situational Leadership®', as we discussed back in Step 4, and where you will be able to identify what style of leadership to use, and when. In this second sub-step, we'll explore a couple of key ideas that will help you to achieve this aim, and which can also help to ensure that the standardisation activities that you have instigated remain intact.

Management meetings for leadership

You may remember that moment of amazement, or perhaps anguish, back in Step 1, when I suggested that meetings are fantastic. Your eyes may have bulged in disbelief, or you may have held your head in your hands in exasperation, but I still believe it to be true. And, once you've finished reading this part of the book, I sincerely hope that you do too. Because, meetings are now the place where you are most likely to do all of your work, and spend all of your time. It's in meetings where you are most able to fulfil your role as operational leader, and where your responsibilities for overseeing performance and process stability, and of providing the right kind of leadership and guidance, are most effectively met. Specifically, it's in establishing and leading key management oversight meetings that you can most add value and fulfil the core responsibilities of your evolved role. It's these kinds of meetings that I strongly recommend you introduce if they do not already exist.

The right management oversight meetings serve to report the status and performance of your facility in key functional and operational areas; and as a consequence, enable you and your management team to assess, debate, and encourage the right response from your team when that performance deviates from standard. The key here, is ensuring that you hold the right management oversight meetings at the right time, and that you discuss the right things in the right way. We've already discussed, back in Step 1, that effective meetings require drama through conflict, and control through structure, in order to make them interesting and valuable. However, I have learned that effective management oversight meetings also require three other things…

- *The right reports* – We've already seen throughout our discussions on problem-solving that effective analysis of a process-level issue is only possible through the interrogation of sound data and information. Therefore, for a management oversight meeting to function properly, appropriate information and data that is relevant to the specific subject matter of the meeting is critical. This may well be in the form of a KPI report, an expenditure by cost centre versus budget report, a sales report, or something similar. Whatever it is, it needs to be accurate, and developed so that it adds value to the meeting that it supports. We should remember that KPI's and information influence our behaviour and our decision-making processes. Ensuring that data is accurate and presented in the correct context therefore is essential.

- *An action log* – All too often meetings take place, and discussions are held, but firm agreements on how to proceed are lacking, and issues can drift over time. You may have heard the story of the four people called Everybody, Somebody, Anybody and Nobody. Between them, they had an important job to do. Everybody was sure that Somebody would do it. Anybody could have done it, but Nobody did. Somebody got angry about that because it was Everybody's job. Everybody thought Anybody would do it, but Nobody realised that Everybody wouldn't do it. It ended up that Everybody blamed Somebody when Nobody did what Anybody could have done. Whilst this is a slightly quirky and amusing tale, I'm sure you can understand its sentiment, and can relate to its meaning. I believe that an important aspect of my role as operational leader is to ensure that meetings do not conclude in this manner, and that clear and defined decisions are made on how to proceed in relation to any issue. The use of an action log in each and every management oversight meeting forum can help to encourage this behaviour, and I would definitely recommend that you use them too. At the same time, an action log can help to keep track of the achievement of any actions, and can ensure that people within your team are held accountable for meeting their responsibilities. The action log I create is not complicated. It simply records the action, the date raised, the person responsible for completing it, the amount of time agreed for its completion, and therefore the date that it's due. I always ensure that responsibility for actions are accepted, that the nature of the action is properly understood, and that the timeline defined is initiated by the person accepting the action with limited negotiation from myself unless absolutely necessary. I also endeavour not to over pressurise the completion of actions unnecessarily. If other issues get in the way, or priorities change, then I'm always willing to adjust my expectations on when actions are due for completion. This helps to manage the psychological safety of my team, and ensures that I imbue a sense of trust and empowerment.

- *The right approach* – The right approach to these management oversight meetings will have a strong influence on the approach of your management team in the execution of their daily responsibilities. That approach will also influence the way the individual meetings function, and their outcomes. We know that we are actively seeking to empower our team members, and to enthuse their intrinsic motivators.

Therefore, utilising these meetings to instruct and dictate actions is going to damage our ability to achieve our aims. Instead, these oversight meetings can seek to identify variances to standard, and to request that the responsible teams or team members communicate their plans for resolution, with any requests for support as they feel appropriate. The role of the meeting then changes from instruction, to the evaluation of the suggested course of action, and may propose or request modifications. It can also provide advice, and offer support from either management team members, or even other operational functions that may be able to add value. Leading these meetings so that they function in this manner is a pivotal role for you as operational leader of your facility. In leading in this way, you can directly influence the empowerment of your entire facility, and can ensure that your leadership example is infused into the way that people think and feel. The benefits to psychological safety and workplace happiness are immeasurable.

So, now we understand what to include as part of our management oversight meetings in order to make them effective, what meetings should we hold, and when? In 'Death by Meeting', Patrick Lencioni recommends that an organisation should endeavour to function with four layers of meetings; 'The Daily Check-in', The 'Weekly Tactical', 'The Monthly Strategic', and 'The Quarterly Offsite'. In Lean Foundations™, I propose a slightly modified version of this structure for the effective leadership and oversight of your manufacturing facility, with five layers rather than four, some of which we've already touched on in earlier Steps…

Daily performance review and problem-solving – Hopefully it's pretty obvious to you that this meeting layer is delivered through the 'MDI' process, and even the 'Start of Day' meeting discussed in Step 4. From an oversight and leadership perspective, this meeting process provides you with the ideal opportunity to touch base with the management of daily performance. You can attend as an observer, and can offer advice and support as and when you feel it necessary. You might even choose to intervene if you feel a planned course of action is incorrect, but I would advise you to do so rarely, and carefully. Your influence on the psychological safety of your team is considerable as a consequence of your position. Therefore, you need to be sensitive to the needs of your team, and to intervene only with coaching and encouragement wherever possible.

Weekly Tactical – The purpose of the weekly tactical meeting is to provide a timely forum for you and your management team to review recent performance in your core indicators of Safety, Quality, Delivery and Cost, and to assess short-term plans for future resource and capacity utilisation. I would propose that you hold two separate meetings to support this aim. First, a weekly management meeting. And second, a weekly planning meeting.

- *The weekly management meeting* – The primary purpose of this weekly management meeting is to review the operational performance of your facility for the previous week, and to evaluate whether appropriate actions have been defined and implemented for recovery as necessary by your team. This enables you to oversee both the operational performance of your facility, and the effectiveness of your team in utilising the systems and working methods that you have introduced to support them. I would usually plan to hold these meetings every single week, and would aim to do so as early in the working week as possible whilst allowing enough time for the right information and reports to be collated. Normally, I would invite my entire management team, including Ops Team Managers and Functional Team Managers. This can help to build the teamwork mentality across your management team, and reinforces the idea that horizontal teamwork is more important than vertical teamwork. For the meeting agenda, I usually include the same key items. First, a quick general news update which can share information from the wider organisation, and may inform your team of more specific issues within Operations. Second, a review of your key performance indicators. Of course, these need to include the core indicators of Safety, Quality, Delivery and Cost; but exactly which specific KPI's you use, and how you choose to present them, is up to you. I would recommend that you generate a standard KPI report document which can be retained for analysis purposes, and which can be shared throughout your facility on your various whiteboards. I would also suggest that your KPI discussion assesses the previous week's performance, understands where performance has deviated from target, and evaluates the proposed responses to those variations from the responsible teams or team members. You may need to suggest alternative actions, to request further investigation, or to suggest that your managers intervene with coaching and support for a better solution. A review of this nature allows you to intervene where exceptions require it, and enables you to encourage the right behaviours and responses to problems and poor performance. If you're lucky, you may simply be able to recognise and appreciate the performance you have, or the completeness of the proposed response. Third, depending on the nature of your facility and your responsibilities, I would suggest that you complete a review of your orderbook status. Are you delivering your budgeted or forecasted sales? Are you receiving sufficient orders to support that forecast or budget? Are any actions required to support achieving the numbers that your organisation is going to hold you accountable for? After all, whilst building a happy, healthy and efficient facility is important to us; we still need to protect the financial security of your facility and ensure that the sales and profitability are delivered. Fourth and finally, it's a good idea to complete an open action review. No doubt as you're progressing through the three previous agenda items you will debate and agree actions with your management team, which can be recorded in the relevant action log. This final part of the meeting can review the status of any actions from previous meetings, and can ensure that your management team are held accountable for their completion.

- *The weekly planning meeting* – The primary purpose of the weekly planning meeting is to review the planned utilisation of your key capacity and resources for the week and month ahead. This helps to ensure that your operational load is supported by your operational capability. Whilst this may seem to be a little obvious to some, I have seen numerous manufacturing facilities that do not complete this simple exercise, and then suffer greatly as a consequence. Again, I would usually plan to hold these meetings every week, this time towards the end of the working week, but with enough time to adjust the plan if necessary. Normally, I would invite my entire management team, as there are potential capacity constraints within every function that it's a good idea to consider. The meeting agenda is relatively straightforward. I usually review in detail the orderbook versus planned capacity in detail for the following week, and then assess into the future in slightly less detail. Your facility will have unique requirements, with lead times and planning needs that are specific to you. It's possible that you may need to look into the future with more detail if your lead times are longer, or your operational capacity less able to be flexible to change. Reviewing your capacity means considering the availability of your people, your equipment, and your materials for your production process. It also means assessing the capability of your support functions in areas such as Logistics for line-feeding and Quality for inspection. It's in this meeting that you can properly plan for known absence and holidays, and can even plan for the correct allocation of your people to the roles they are most skilled for. You may even consider discussion of the specific sequencing of your production schedule, or the expected product mix on your JIT sequence, in order to prepare properly. A potential outcome of these meetings is the agreement to increase capacity through the recruitment of either temporary or permanent team members, or through the use of overtime. Or, you may need to reduce your capacity, and may consider balancing your available labour in your facility, or perhaps introduce flexible working. Here is also where you can see long-term changes to your orderbook coming, and can take appropriate actions to plan and respond. This might include forecasting higher material requirements, and preparing your supply chain. Experience tells me that this one weekly planning meeting can add significant value to your ability to manage your facility. It can have a huge impact on improving on-time delivery performance, as well as helping to build stability through the planned management of future change.

Monthly Tactical - The purpose of the monthly tactical meeting is to provide a forum for you and your management team to review your operational performance in specific functional areas. It may not necessarily be practical to review these areas on a weekly basis, or they may require additional focus and value attributing to them. I would propose that you hold a minimum of three separate meetings to support this aim. First, a monthly Expenditure versus Budget review. Second, a Health & Safety review. And third, a Quality review.

• *The monthly Expenditure versus Budget review* – In meeting your day to day responsibilities, you're going to need to spend money. Therefore, it makes sense to ensure that you're planning to spend the right amount to maintain the financial security of your facility, and that you're not spending outside of that plan without good reason. I would propose that you bring your management team together on a monthly basis to review your expenditure versus budget to support this aim. To complete the meeting effectively, it's likely that you're going to need support and attendance from your Finance team with reports and data. I usually request a report that breaks down budget and expenditure by cost centre, with each cost centre allocated to an individual manager for control and approval of spend versus budget. I would normally review expenditure of things like direct and indirect labour costs, overtime and temporary labour costs, overhead costs, material purchases, and facilities and maintenance costs. These are often broken down into much greater layers of detail to aid understanding and analysis. You may wish to see the absolute values also represented as percentages of sales values in order to highlight where changes in sales levels impact your ability to flex your costs. Of course, where expenditure is away from budget, you need to be able to understand why, and to review the decision making of your team when expenditure choices are made. This can be a real test of your ability to empower your team. If they are given responsibility for managing a budget, you will need to allow them to make and learn from mistakes when doing so. This can be expensive, and therefore can test your patience. As with all other situations of empowerment, your ability to coach and guide your team through this process will add significant value in promoting your preferred leadership style in your facility. I would also utilise this meeting to manage activities that are targeted to reduce costs. It's sensible to include cost saving initiatives in your annual improvement plans, and no doubt in your early improvement cycles there will be plenty of opportunity to save money. Here is where you can confirm that those targeted savings are being delivered. As a final point, I would also suggest that you include Capital Expenditure as part of this monthly meeting. CapEx can sometimes take several months to execute because the specification and ordering of major pieces of capital equipment can take time. Therefore, you CapEx review could look to ensure that projects are on target for completion so that annual capital budgets, and the opportunities for improvement that they represent, are not lost.

- *The Health & Safety review* – As we've discussed previously, maintaining the health and safety of your employees is quite possibly the most critical of all of your KPI's. Therefore, I would always recommend that you meet routinely with your management team to discuss the health and safety performance of your facility. This meeting is likely to review the number of accidents and incidents that have been reported, and to review the status of the investigations and the relevant corrective actions. As a consequence, you may well be repeating some of the content of your weekly management meetings. However, I would still propose that you complete these sessions in order to emphasise the importance of health and safety, and in order for you and your team to be able to invest more time in understanding the actions that have or are planned to take place. Again, you need to provide oversight, and to coach and advise alternative action if you feel it necessary. You may also choose to use this forum to review the status of the Hazard Reporting process we discussed back in Step 6, and perhaps even the status of your Risk Assessments, COSHH Assessments, and Legal Compliance Register that we discussed earlier in the previous sub-step.

- *The Quality review* – Second on our list of priority KPI's is quality. Nothing is going to annoy a customer more than poor quality, and nothing can provide more disruption in your facility than your own quality problems and those of your suppliers. Therefore, I would always recommend that you complete a monthly Quality review with your management team to oversee the total quality performance of your facility. This meeting can cover all aspects of quality; from customer complaints, to warranty, to supplier issues, to production scrap, to inspection performance, and to internal process audit results. In reviewing your performance in these areas, it's again important to ask your team to provide the right information and data, and for them to be prepared to share any PPSA documents in order to communicate the status of both customer and supplier complaints. Here you're looking for trends and patterns in performance, are hoping to encourage your team to problem-solve effectively, and to introduce control measures that prevent reoccurrence over time. I have found that a monthly review of this nature, combined with the problem-solving approach described in Step 6, can really help to slowly but surely improve quality performance across the board.

These are the three primary monthly tactical meetings that I would advise for all manufacturing facilities. However, you may feel a need for there to be more. I have seen examples of meetings such as monthly inventory reviews, where inventory reduction was an imposed target from the wider organisation. I've also seen the same for purchase price variance (PPV) reduction targets, or Value Analysis Value Engineering (VAVE) initiatives. You may also have major new production introduction projects running, and need to review those routinely too. Whatever your particular circumstances, I would encourage you to be comfortable in scheduling the right meetings at the right frequency in order to ensure that your team is pulled together to have the right debates, and possibly conflicts, at the right time.

Monthly Strategic – We discussed this monthly strategic meeting in detail in Step 3, when I presented the monthly review of your '*Top-level Improvement A3*' alongside the '*Project-level Improvement A3's*'. From an oversight and leadership perspective, this forum provides you with the ideal opportunity to guide your management team through the execution of their projects. You can offer advice and support, can encourage team members to work together and to support each other, and can endeavour to present the right leadership example to your team when plans fall behind or need to be changed. It also offers you the opportunity to expect your team to perform, but to do so in the right way.

Annual Strategic – The annual strategic meeting is also one that we've discussed previously back in Step 3. The offsite session that you will have used to generate your top-level Improvement Plan, is one that you should look to complete every single year. It provides the opportunity as a team to oversee the performance of your entire year, and to re-set your plans accordingly. It also allows you to adapt to other changes in your wider organisation and in society as a whole if necessary. I find that these sessions can trigger new levels of enthusiasm and motivation in my team, and can remind them that whilst they're confronting problems every single day, they will have made significant progress in resolving them, and will be delivering major improvements to the capability of your facility as a consequence.

Audit like you mean it

Whilst the humble meeting is a much-maligned management tool, perhaps disliked even more is the dreaded audit process. All too often, auditing is seen as an administrative burden that is required to ensure compliance with a relevant management system accreditation, rather than as useful mechanism for management oversight and intervention. I've seen numerous examples of internal audit schedules failing to be followed, of process audits being rushed through in the days running up to an external audit, and of external audits being 'managed' through to completion by a highly stressed Quality Manager with limited and reluctant support from their peers.

Instead, for *Lean Foundations™*, the audit process is a powerful and fully embraced tool, which can inform and enable your understanding of the capability and stability of your standardised processes. With capable audits that are responded to with professional integrity, it's possible to maintain oversight of the management system infrastructure which underpins your operational performance. Think of them as a structural inspection of your building foundations. If those inspections show that your foundations are sound, the rest of your building is more likely to be sound too.

Here, I'm going to touch on three types of audit that I believe are a good idea to introduce into your facility, and which if responded to properly can really add value to managing the stability of your standardised processes.

- *The functional audit* – As we discussed earlier in Step 2, part of the role of your Functional Support Teams is to provide your Core Team(s) with the functional support and infrastructure for the completion of activities related to the more specialised functions. For example, a Health & Safety Manager may define the format and process for the completion of a Risk Assessment, and will train and support the Core Team members in the completion of their own Risk Assessments. As part of this responsibility, I also find it useful to ask the managers of these Functional Support Teams to develop and complete routine audits of Core Team activities in relation to functional disciplines. This may mean that a Health & Safety Manager audits Core Team compliance in the following of Health & Safety good practice; such as maintaining access to fire and evacuation equipment, to maintaining a safe environment, and to the correct segregation of COSHH materials. And, the same can apply for a Quality Manager and the following of Quality controls, such as the correct use of error proofing devices, or of the right measuring equipment during inspection activities. When introducing audit processes such as these, I tend to ask my functional managers to complete the audits on a monthly or quarterly basis, to design them so that a performance score is reported as a percentage, and to complete the audits in all team areas. I then often integrate the output of these audits into the monthly tactical meetings relating to the relevant function, and ensure that performance is discussed and reviewed. In doing so, I can support the importance of the audit activity and performance, and gain valuable insight into the capability of my team in following the relevant practices. You could also consider using these audits to follow-up on the effectiveness of new controls that have been introduced in response to any safety or customer quality issues that have occurred in the previous month.

- *The internal systems audit* – Whether you have an accreditation with a relevant quality or business management system or not, I would always advocate that once your processes are standardised, you task trained members of your team with the completion of comprehensive process and procedure audits. These are slightly different to the functional audits, in that they are seeking to understand where processes and procedures are being followed, rather than where controls are correctly used. Such process audits tend to take place annually by process, and are usually completed by a Systems Engineer or another member of the Quality team. However, you can train anyone in your organisation to complete process audits, and I would strongly recommend that you diversify the responsibility if you can. It's a good idea to ask people from different teams or functions to audit parts of your facility that they do not normally work in. This helps to give a fresh perspective during an audit process. Importantly, process audits will assess whether or not processes and procedures are being followed, and whether or not they correctly represent the working practices for completion of a task. Again, I would normally ask that the results of these audits be reported in the monthly Quality review discussed previously, and as part of this discussion I would be working to ensure that all processes were audited in line with the planned schedule, that appropriate actions were agreed and defined between all parties, and that those actions were being properly addressed. Typically, actions of process audits tend to be poorly defined, or tend to drift into obscurity. Working the audit and associated corrective actions activity well can enable you to keep your processes and procedures fresh, and to maintain the sense that they are an important part of your management system.

- *The external audit* – You may, like me, have made the mistake in the past of treating an external audit like a personal examination with a pass and fail result. Over time, I've come to appreciate them as a valuable learning opportunity, and as a tool for identifying where improvement in process stability can be achieved. I would actively encourage you to consider them in the same way, and to enthuse your team to embrace them also. Rather than asking your Quality Manager to manage an external audit independently and with limited supported from their peers, I would suggest that you involve everyone in your team in supporting an external audit process. Why not task individual managers with preparing their own functions for the audit activity? And, why not ask them to lead the audit activity with the external auditor when it is completed in their area of responsibility? Again, as with the process audits, it's important that any non-conformances identified are owned by the responsible person, and that they take the lead in determining and implementing the right actions for resolution of issues in their area of responsibility. For you, reviewing the results of an external audit can provide a useful third-party view of the capability of your management system, and gives a useful additional oversight perspective. In reviewing the plans for resolution of non-conformance, you also have the opportunity to coach and guide your team to the right solutions if required.

LIBERATE WITH CHOICE

Building oversight mechanisms into your daily operations such as the ones listed above can take a little thought, and in some ways may require you to think differently about the way you perform your role. Now that you're developing your facility through the *Lean Foundations*™ journey, you're going to need to think of yourself as the person who is conducting your orchestra, rather than as a multi-talented musician within it. As a result, you need to be able to stand in the right place, to be positioned where you can oversee what everyone is doing, and can intervene appropriately when needed. The meeting and audit processes we've described can put you in that right place, and can enable you to see the right things. It's now down to you to respond to them in the right way.

However, now that you've encouraged your team to standardise their activities, and have built effective oversight mechanisms to ensure that they remain stable, it's important to enable them to change. This may seem a little crazy after you've spent so much time and effort in getting your processes in place. But, as we know, change happens, and the flexibility and willingness to adapt is important to our ability to respond to our ever-changing needs. We need to be able to integrate that flexibility into our team so that they are able to respond to the needs of your customers with confidence and a clarity of purpose. And, we need to be able to adapt our processes so that they remain relevant and actively support our desire to tap into the intrinsic motivators of our team, to drive operational performance, and to improve workplace happiness.

I know that I've experienced poor customer service when buying products or paying for services. I also know that poor customer service is often caused by a poorly defined process, and by the inability of the employee using that process to change it in order to correct whatever problem they face. I've also experienced good customer service, and know that it usually results from a well-defined process, or is perhaps at its best when a process fails, but the person I'm interacting with is able to adapt and do the right thing. When this happens, I'm impressed with the commitment and responsiveness of the individual, and I'm impressed that the organisation they work for empowers them to make the right choices. It encourages me to use them again.

If I choose to walk in the shoes of the employees in both of these scenarios; I know that in the case of the former, I'm frustrated and disappointed to have let my customer down. I feel disempowered by my organisation, and definitely don't feel trusted to make the right choices. In the case of the latter, it's the opposite. I feel successful because I've resolved a customer issue and made them happy. I also feel trusted and empowered by my organisation to do whatever it takes to support our customers. I know which of those environments I'd rather work in and would enjoy more, and therefore it's that environment that I always try to recreate for the people I represent.

As you know, we've already taken significant steps towards building that place. In focusing on psychological safety and organisational health, and in working with an empowering leadership style, we've taken major steps forward. In addition, there are a couple of specific ideas that I can suggest here that help to incorporate this mindset and approach into the standardisation activities we've already completed.

- *The right process owners* – I know it sounds simple, but just by defining the right process owners for each of the processes and procedures that you've already defined and documented, you can help to cascade a sense of ownership and accountability into your team. To help this further, I would suggest that you don't necessarily take the easy option and define functional managers as the process owners. Instead, cascade them at least one level lower in your organisation structure, and pass ownership into your supervisors and engineers. By defining them as the owners, you can also give them the power to make change, and to build flexibility and the ability to adapt to various typical scenarios into their processes. You can also carry this process ownership throughout your entire management oversight protocols, and can ensure that when process audits are complete it's these owners that are part of the audit process, and who are responsible for resolving any non-conformances. Also, by identifying process owners by role, rather than by person, you can ensure that any changes in personnel are managed with clarity.
- *A process for change* – Another really simple mechanism for enabling flexibility is to define a specific process for implementing changes to process and procedures. If your process owners are provided with clear instructions on how to make a change, and are empowered to do so without having to seek approval from elsewhere in your team, then they will feel much more able and willing to make changes as and when they need to. This process for change does not need to be complicated, and simply needs to define the requirements in terms of a newly documented process, who it needs to be submitted to for document control purposes, and how it should be cascaded through your organisation so that it is widely understood and accepted. This might be through the use of something simple like a 'Toolbox Training' form, or through more structured training if the change is more significant.
- *Deviation and Concession process* – An easy way to encourage flexibility in your processes is to establish a mechanism that allows people to work away from process, but ensures that effective controls are still in place and records the alternative way of working. Deviation and Concession processes encourage people to recognise when they are restricted by a process or specification, and allows them to formally request to work away from standard, but in a controlled way. If these processes

are established with appropriate approval requirements, they can be useful methods for empowering your team to adapt to their circumstances.

- *Encourage standards, enable choice* – The most important activity you can complete is to ensure that your team understand that they are empowered and can choose not to work to a standard process or procedure if necessary. It's a delicate balance to strike, but you need to be able to encourage your team to follow standard processes, whilst at the same empowering them not to if they feel it's necessary. This requires you to deliver the right message from the very beginning, and to continually reinforce this message through all of your daily interactions. The ideal forums for this are in your oversight meetings. Whether it's as an observer in the 'MDI' meetings, or in your weekly or monthly tactical meetings; when assessing your operational performance and discussing problems, you can set the right example. You can ask if standard processes were followed, and if not, can understand why and what was done instead. If the reason for working away from standard is because of a failure, then it needs to be addressed as such and corrected. However, if the reason for working away from standard is deliberate choice in order to respond to a problem, then it can be appreciated, and the person recognised for making the right choice in the wrong circumstances. Of course, actions may still be required to modify the process in order to prevent the need to work away from standard in the future. However, what is important is how you choose to react to the choices made by your team, and to be positive in order to reinforce their psychological safety and willingness to adapt in the future. I know this sounds simple, but it can be difficult to remain conscious of this need at all times.

STEP 7 SUMMARY

In completing Step 7 of your *Lean Foundations™* journey, I hope you've been successful in standardising your operating and production processes, and as a result have stabilised your daily operational performance. If you have, you're hopefully finding that the number of fires you're fighting has reduced, and that the time and mental capacity of your team to focus on improving rather than surviving has increased dramatically. You will have taken a major step forward in building a well-performing facility, and in establishing the good foundations that will enable the path to excellence in the future. At the same time, if you can be successful in building the right options for choice and flexibility into your systems, your people can be appropriately empowered and responsible for implementing change when needed.

Much of what we've discussed in this Step may appear overly simple and almost too easy. And yet, so often I've seen that it's not done, and that a factory simply functions through custom and practice rather than structure and control. It seems strange to think that many facilities operate without standard processes and procedures, and therefore lurch from one problem to another every day. However, despite this lack of stability, they find a way to stumble through and get to where they need to as a result of the determination and resilience of their team. Often, it can seem that the wider organisation accepts this as the way things are done, and is either unable to understand or does not care about the pressures that this places on the people that work within such an environment. Or, they see Lean as the solution, and require Lean improvement activities to take place without understanding that the problems can only be resolved by building the right foundations in the first place, and not necessarily by introducing a Kanban system, or completing a Value Stream Map. Perhaps the issue here is that this process of standardisation takes time, and can't be completed overnight. It can take several months and even years to work through your entire management system step by step. And as we know, short-termism is an infectious disease that permeates many organisations today.

But, please don't let this discourage you. I cannot stress enough the value of completing the activity of building your management system, and stabilising your processes through standardisation. In the process, you'll elevate your role, and will change the value you add to your team. And, if you build in the ability to be flexible and responsive to change, your team's sense of empowerment will grow. Their psychological safety and sense of trust and autonomy will flourish, and their commitment to the purpose of improving your operational performance, workplace happiness, and the ability to implement Lean, will thrive.

One last point here, you may find it absolutely necessary to complete this standardisation activity in one or two of your more critical processes right at the beginning of your *Lean Foundations™* journey. Returning to the 'Injured Person' analogy from Step 6, you may find that there are burning issues that are causing your facility to bleed so heavily, you need to address them before you do anything else. Don't be afraid of dealing with these issues early on in the change journey, whilst you're working on activities in the earlier Steps at the same time.

In drawing Step 7 to a close, let's take a moment to reflect on the main points…

- It's not unusual to find manufacturing facilities which are operating without defined processes and procedures in place, and which suffer from lots of daily operational problems as a consequence.
- It's also possible to find facilities that have excessive regulation of their processes and procedures, which restricts creativity and the ability to adapt to change.
- In order to help both scenarios, it's possible to introduce standardised processes that stabilise performance, whilst also introducing management oversight protocols and building in flexibility which allows for choice.
- To standardise operating process, supporting functions can define the right basic processes with the right features to ensure that they are successful.
- The basic processes and procedures can be defined through cross-functional process mapping exercises, and can be institutionalised into a facility through the use of the right documentation and training methods.

- It's also possible to standardise the core production activities, by utilising tools such as basic Standard Work, 3S, control of labour allocation, and the introduction of process controls or even end of line inspection.
- Once your activities are standardised, the ability of your team to respond to change with control and resilience will be improved.
- As part of standardising processes, it's also sensible to introduce management oversight protocols which ensure that performance is monitored, and appropriate actions are taken to respond when performance is away from standard. These management protocols include a clearly defined meeting structure, and audit processes.
- Finally, it's possible to integrate the option to choose when not to follow processes if necessary in order to deliver good customer service or support a team member effectively, or to modify them. By defining the right process owners, by defining a process for change, and by leading in the right way, it's possible to allow and celebrate choice and flexibility.

Actively
engage
everyone

8

STEP

Having made so much progress on your *Lean Foundations*™ journey, you might consider there to be little left to do which can help to build that well-performing facility that we've been seeking. Surely, with all of the activities we've completed, we must have fully fuelled the intrinsic motivators of our team, and established the foundations upon which a Lean excellence programme can now be started in earnest? Our efforts in addressing organisational health and psychological safety, in improving teamwork by modifying our organisation structure, in aligning everyone behind our Improvement Plan, in integrating empowering leadership, in managing daily change through the 'MDI' process, in developing a problem-solving mentality, and in creating stability and flexibility with our well-functioning management system; must have paid dividend, mustn't they?

And yes, of course, I'm sure they have. I'm confident that you can see a real difference in the way your facility functions and performs. And I'm hopeful that your team members are happier and more fulfilled in their work, whilst your operational performance has progressed and is more stable than before. Having completed numerous of these journeys myself, I have seen how the incremental benefits of the *Lean Foundations*™ approach can continuously feed into a factory over a protracted period of time. I know that, having completed all of the Steps up to now, progress is real and tangible; and improvement in both workplace happiness and operational performance will have been realised.

However, even at this late stage in the journey, and despite all of the effort and the improvements made, I've still found a number of people that do not feel happy and fulfilled in their role. When walking through my improved facility, I've listened to team members who, regardless of the seemingly significant progress made, expressed disappointment and frustration with the fact that things have not improved enough for them in their particular job. And, when deliberately seeking feedback, I've still found some team members who do not feel actively involved, or do not properly understand their role in the improvement journey that we are all on. I would suggest that, if you take the same walks that I have taken, and seek feedback in the same way that I did, you may well find that some of the team members in your facility feel the same way. You may still find examples of people who do not feel fulfilled, or do not feel part of the process in the way that others do. In particular, you might find that these people work on the very front-line of your processes; on your production lines making components, in your warehouse moving materials, or in your office areas processing your paperwork. Experience tells me that it's these front-line areas that can be forgotten, and it these people whose extremely valuable opinions and contributions can be overlooked. I have found that it's easy to make the mistake of driving an improvement activity only through the efforts of a small number of managers, supervisors, and engineers. And, I've been guilty myself of neglecting my most informed and experienced people, and of failing to take advantage of the wonderful opportunity that they represent as a result. Their knowledge is an invaluable resource, and their committed involvement can be a real differentiator on any improvement journey.

In trying to comprehend why these people could have fallen between the cracks, and to understand what to do about it, I continued my personal learning journey, and sought out more books, articles and knowledgeable opinions that might help. I endeavoured to understand why some people still felt on the periphery of the process, why their insight and knowledge was being left underutilised, and why they remained unfulfilled and even unhappy in their role. And that's when I learned about the concept of employee engagement. I realised that, even with all of the Steps taken to this point, there was still more that could be done to engage all of my team members throughout every layer of my organisation. I came to understand that all of my efforts to this point had, almost inadvertently, created a good level of engagement of some of my people; but that a more deliberate and focused approach to engagement could stimulate workplace happiness to even greater depth, and could permeate through my entire team. And, I concluded that truly inclusive employee engagement, which captures the ideas and capabilities of every single person, could be the final piece of the jigsaw in improving workplace happiness, operational performance, and the ability to implement Lean.

We are now nearing the end of our *Lean Foundations™* journey. We are in the final stretch, and can see the light at the end of the tunnel. The achievements to this point are considerable, and you and your team should take the time to reflect and celebrate just how far you have come. But, when we started on this path, we set out with the aim of improving workplace happiness for everyone in our team, and not just for some. We sought to improve operational performance by utilising the capabilities and knowledge of all our people, and not just those who happened to be in the right place at the right time. And, we wanted to enable our ability to utilise Lean practice in the future, which surely requires as many people as possible to be engaged and on board.

To meet our aims, therefore, it's important that we ensure that we have fully engaged every individual at every level in our team in the improvement process. We need to be confident that all our team members feel that they have a voice, and that their contributions add value and make a difference. We need to be certain that we have challenged everyone appropriately and with purpose, and that each person is able to see the impact of their involvement for themselves. And, we need to know that every person is taking a measure of enjoyment (as much as is possible) from meeting their role, with their day to day responsibilities offering them the opportunity to gain satisfaction and even pleasure from their completion. The empowerment of all of our team members, which we have been so deliberate in infusing into our facility, goes hand in hand with their engagement. It only delivers its full potential if we can truly engage every person, particularly those on the front-line, to contribute their efforts and opinions with enthusiasm. Without the full engagement of every team member, we risk missing out on valuable insights and knowledge, and potentially undermine everyone's confidence in our 'Why'. And, without the active engagement of as many of our team as possible, our hope of becoming good on the path to great is unlikely to be fully realised.

In this final Step, I'll take you through two sub-steps which can help us to address this last vital point; 'Learning to engage', and 'Engaging actively'. I hope that in sharing these sub-steps, I'm able to support you in understanding what influences employee engagement, and can help you to successfully introduce it into your facility. Good luck.

LEARNING TO ENGAGE

When learning more about employee engagement, I came to understand two key things. First, as a field of study, it appears to be relatively new; with books, articles and blogs only really exploring the concept more fully in the last 15 to 20 years. Second, whilst there is a lot of discussion, with some commonality of ideas and conclusions, there is also a fair degree of variation in the thoughts and opinions presented. As with most things, you have to work your way through until you find something that makes sense to you. In this first sub-step, I intend to present two pieces of work that I find best summarise the concept of employee engagement. In doing so, I hope that I can share an understanding of the concept, and can highlight where we have been successful in achieving it so far. It's this understanding that has influenced some of the activities already integrated into the *Lean Foundations*™ approach in earlier Steps, and which has resulted in the specific activities described in this Step. Together, I believe that they will enable us to comprehensively engage everyone in our team, and in the process will support our desire to improve workplace happiness and operational performance.

Lencioni's 'Truth'

In his thoughtful book '*The Truth About Employee Engagement*', Patrick Lencioni looks to address a life-long concern around the nature of work, and how in far too many cases it can cause misery, rather than pleasure and fulfilment. He recalls his childhood experiences of his father's unhappiness at work, and his amazement at the idea that people would spend so much time in a place that caused them to feel that way. And, he shares his own negative and unfulfilling experiences from the early part of his career, and describes the 'Sunday Blues' that preceded his dread at going back to work after a weekend. They're sentiments that, unfortunately, I'm sure we can all empathise with from our own personal circumstances; having no doubt suffered from the same 'Sunday Blues' on perhaps more than one occasion, and because of more than one job.

In response, Lencioni identifies three factors that he believes are the primary contributors to job misery; 'Anonymity', 'Irrelevance', and 'Immeasurement', and describes how resolving these three factors can bring happiness and fulfilment at work. He believes that tackling these three root causes of job misery is at the heart of effective employee engagement, and that workplace happiness is only achieved when they are properly addressed. He's also clear in his belief that addressing employee engagement effectively leads to significant organisational benefits. He describes how productivity is improved as a result of each person working with greater passion, enthusiasm, and attention to detail. He explains how employee retention improves, which reduces the costs associated with recruiting and training new people. And, he even outlines how the improvements in work culture result in a sustainable competitive advantage through improved strategic and tactical decision making. For Lencioni, employee engagement is a must have cultural differentiator. The graphic below is used by Lencioni to illustrate his idea.

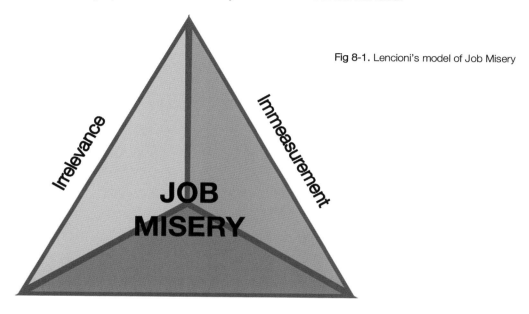

Fig 8-1. Lencioni's model of Job Misery

First, Lencioni defines 'Anonymity' as the need for all people to feel known, and to feel that they are *"...understood and appreciated for their unique qualities by someone in a position of authority..."*. He believes that without this basic recognition, no one can possibly enjoy their job. We all have a need to be recognised and appreciated for who we are, whether at work or in our personal lives. Therefore, effective employee engagement needs to recognise every person as a unique contributor, and as someone who adds value because of their individual capabilities.

Second, Lencioni describes 'Irrelevance' as the need for every person to feel that their job matters, and to feel that there is a *"... connection between the work and the satisfaction of another person or group of people..."*. He argues that without this sense of value, and the belief that their work matters to someone, no person can find fulfilment in their job. We all have a desire to add value and contribute, and to feel that we make a difference as part of our team. Therefore, effective employee engagement needs to ensure that every person feels that their efforts are relevant and important, and that their contribution is appreciated.

Third, Lencioni describes 'Immeasurement' as the need for every person to be able to understand for themselves the progress and level of contribution that they make, and not to feel that *"… their success depends on the opinions or whims of another person…"*. He argues that without this ability to measure their own impact, no individual can feel motivated in their job because they feel that their fate is out of their own hands. We all have a desire to be in control of our own destiny, and to feel that our contributions add value. Therefore, effective employee engagement needs to ensure that every person has an opportunity to be involved and make an impact, and for that impact to be measurable with evidence and data, rather than through arbitrary opinion and feelings.

Lencioni's ideas, as he openly acknowledges, are by no means radical or complicated. In fact, it's potentially their simplicity and honesty that makes them seem even more insightful. Importantly for us, they offer useful advice on how to create a sense of engagement with our team. If we can ensure that our team members feel recognised as an individual, that they feel that their contributions are relevant and appreciated, and feel that they are making an impact that is tangible; we can be successful in engaging them at work, and in helping to them to be happy in the process.

As you have no doubt noticed, much of what is described by Lencioni shares common themes with many of the ideas we have discussed previously. The concepts of psychological safety, organisational health, and empowerment, appear to support and underpin the ideas of recognition, relevance and tangible impact. As a consequence, it would suggest that many of our activities to date will have already created an improved level of engagement in our team. And, it's highly likely that this is the case. No doubt you can sense that many of your team members feel that they are recognised as individuals, that their contribution is relevant, and that their impact is clear. The introduction of tools such as the 'MDI' process, of the Improvement Plan, of our 'Golden Circle', and of 'Start of Day' meetings, will all have contributed to those feelings in your team. However, in establishing that this is not the case for all of our team members, and in particular for those in front-line roles, it seems clear that our efforts to date may not have been sufficiently inclusive, and suggests that we can utilise Lencioni's ideas to guide a more deliberate approach to the engagement of our people.

From engagement to happiness

In their article '*Positive Engagement: From Employee Engagement to Workplace Happiness*', Martin Stairs and Martin Galpin seek to better understand the concept of employee engagement, and its synergies with workplace happiness. The article provides considerable insight into the concept of engagement, and explores different definitions, ways of measurement, expected benefits, and approaches for implementation that can add value for us on our learning journey.

First of all, Stairs and Galpin offer a definition of employee engagement that I consider to be the most relevant and practical of those that I have encountered. They believe that engagement can be defined as

"... the extent to which employees thrive at work, are committed to their employer, and are motivated to do their best, for the benefit of themselves and their organisation...". For me, this definition captures the very essence of the kind of engagement that we've been, as a deliberate side-effect, hoping to achieve throughout our *Lean Foundations*™ journey to date. As part of our attempts to empower our team members, and to build a healthy and psychologically safe environment; we've been keen to encourage their commitment, their motivation, and their desire to fulfil their own potential. By building the right approach to leadership and organisational culture into our facility, we have also taken steps that have engaged at least some of our team members, realising benefits to workplace happiness and operational performance as a consequence.

Second, Stairs and Galpin summarise the work of other authors, and provide numerous statistical examples of just how much difference employee engagement can make to organisational performance. They outline how engagement drives well-being and attendance, how it positively influences retention, how it improves employee effort and performance, how it drives quality, and how it increases turnover and profit. With this data, they demonstrate how engagement really can be a driving force in improving workplace happiness and operational performance.

Third, Stairs and Galpin also define what they call a 'Model of positive engagement', which seeks to align the elements which they believe improve employee engagement, with the factors that contribute to workplace happiness. The graphic below is used by Stairs and Galpin to illustrate their idea.

Fig 8-1. Stairs and Galpin's model of employee engagement

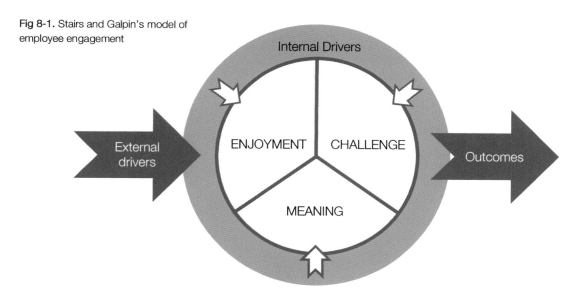

You might surmise from this model that there are many similarities with the kind of points we've discussed previously in our *Lean Foundations*™ approach, as well as with Lencioni's perspective on engagement, and you'd be correct in your conclusion. There are however, a couple of interesting additions and perspectives for us to consider.

The 'External Drivers' that the model refers to are factors related to the organisational environment, and which Stairs and Galpin believe are able to be directly influenced by an organisation in order to affect the level of engagement and happiness of each employee. They include aspects such as opportunity for personal control (autonomy and empowerment), environmental clarity (purpose and role definition), contact with others (teamwork), and achievement (success in areas of importance). These, and others that they list, bear considerable similarities to the intrinsic motivators of teamwork, purpose, autonomy and success that we have focused much of our efforts in addressing to date. They argue that by taking steps to improve these organisational factors, employee engagement and happiness will improve by default. This idea can reinforce our confidence that our activities so far will have made a real difference to our levels of engagement and workplace happiness.

The 'Internal Drivers' that Stairs and Galpin discuss initially appear to be a new factor for us to consider. They are described as the individual differences in the ability of each person to achieve engagement and happiness, based on their own personal perspectives and perceptions. Knowing how to address these 'Internal Drivers' can seem to be a challenge, with every individual likely to be uniquely different. But, Stairs and Galpin do suggest some activities that can help; such as the routine recognition and appreciation of each individual's strengths, the deliberate identification and appreciation of successful achievements, and the recognition of things for which a person is grateful. Once we understand these ideas, we can see that we have already taken some steps to positively influence them through our approach to the 'Performance Appraisal' process that we discussed back in Step 4. There, I suggested that you encourage self-reflection; with a focus on strengths, achievements, and an appreciation for what is working well.

However, it's in the central part of their model where Stairs' and Galpin's approach appears to add most value. First of all, in defining 'Enjoyment' as specific feature, they offer a different aspect of happiness and engagement than we've previously considered. It may seem obvious, but they have included the idea that achieving a feeling of pleasure from the nature of your work is likely to improve your level of happiness and engagement. This means that we can consider things such as the nature of tasks being completed, their level of repetition and automation, and their suitability for the person completing them. Secondly, they include the idea of 'Challenge' in their model, and describe that feelings of being stretched and subsequently developed by work can enhance engagement and workplace happiness. This is not a new idea for us, and has been part of our considerations when we discussed the need for driving performance and maintaining standards back in Step 3. It also bears similarities to the ideas of tangible impact described by Lencioni. Finally, they include a sense of 'Meaning' in their model, and describe how a need for purpose and contribution to serving something bigger than just ourselves, is a critical factor in our levels of engagement and happiness at work. Again, this is something we've discussed at length as one of our intrinsic motivators, and as a contributor to organisational health and psychological safety. It also aligns well with Lencioni's ideas around relevance and recognition.

Once again, it's evident that much of what is described by Stairs and Galpin shares considerable synergies with some of the concepts and ideas that we have already worked hard to introduce into our facility. Our focus on tapping into intrinsic motivators, on enhancing psychological safety and organisational health, and on challenging our team with a need to perform and deliver results, show clear alignment with Stairs' and Galpin's findings. However, as with Lencioni's ideas, Stairs and Galpin's ideas offer an informed and useful insight into the factors that influence engagement. If we can ensure that every person enjoys their work, can provide each individual with an appropriate level of challenge, and can ensure that every person derives a sense of meaning from their activities, we can perhaps be successful in achieving our aim of all-inclusive engagement.

ENGAGING ACTIVELY

It seems clear that employee engagement offers us an opportunity to lift workplace happiness and operational performance to new heights. For Lencioni, Stairs and Galpin, and the many other authors of the numerous published materials not referenced here; employee engagement is the electricity that can energise every person, and is the rocket fuel that drives an organisation to achieve even greater success. We have already introduced many initiatives that will have engaged our team members. But, it's also possible that we will not have fully engaged every single person in our facility. We're therefore failing to take advantage of the full potential of our team when working to improve operational performance, and are falling short in meeting our aspiration of improving workplace happiness for all. We have an opportunity to be more deliberate in our employee engagement efforts, and to ensure that we embrace every member of our team on our journey towards becoming a well-performing facility.

Having now understood the importance of employee engagement, and the factors which influence it, our next challenge is to determine exactly how to introduce it in such a way that it permeates through to every person in our team. By bringing together the ideas of Lencioni, with those of Stairs and Galpin, the *Lean Foundations™* approach encourages you to introduce a number of tools and activities that can hopefully provide a more thorough and all-inclusive approach to engagement than we've been achieving to date. There are obvious consistencies and synergies in the ideas that they both present, and aligning them appropriately has helped to ensure that the activities defined here are extremely effective in engaging people successfully. The approach is divided into three sub-headings, with specific activities applied within each one.

Conspicuous relevance

'Conspicuous Relevance' flips Lencioni's ideas of 'Anonymity' and 'Irrelevance' on their head, and blends them with Stairs' & Galpin's ideas on 'Meaning'. Here, the focus is on ensuring that every person feels that they have a voice, that they feel that their contributions are recognised and appreciated, and that they believe that their role is important and adds value to the organisation. The activities described all support one or more of these aims, and can be introduced at any point in the *Lean Foundations™* journey.

- *Employee Forum* – Sometimes called a Works Council, the Employee Forum serves as a routine opportunity for employees to raise issues and ideas which they believe need to be addressed by the leadership and management team. It can also serve as a communication conduit for any relevant organisational changes. The introduction of an Employee Forum can help to provide every person in your team with a voice, and with an opportunity to raise any points they feel are not being properly addressed by their supervisor or manager, or by the management systems you've introduced such as the 'Start of Day' meetings or 'MDI' process. As a consequence, your front-line team members can feel that their feelings are respected, and their sense of involvement and relevance can be enhanced. Normally, I lead monthly Employee Forum sessions myself as top-leader of my organisation, and am often supported by the HR Manager for the site. Usually, the facility is divided into clearly separated areas, with a representative for each area identified as a spokesperson. You may choose for this person to be nominated and voted for, or simply to volunteer for the responsibility. It's a good idea to ensure that this spokesperson is a front-line team member from each area, rather than a supervisor or manager, to make sure that you're engaging with people throughout all levels of your team. Prior to the Employee Forum meeting, each representative is responsible for canvassing the employees within their area for ideas and issues that they feel need to be addressed. It's a good idea to define rules around what kind of points should be included, and to encourage the Employee Forum representatives to reject any contributions that do not meet those rules before bringing them to the meeting. The meeting itself can be structured with three main agenda items. Firstly, to communicate any significant organisational news, which the representatives are asked to cascade following the meeting. Secondly, to review the status of any outstanding items raised in the previous meeting. And thirdly, to discuss and agree the actions for any new issues raised. Often, these issues can require repairs or the introduction of new equipment or facilities, so you may wish to involve your Facilities & Maintenance representative in the Forum. It's important to note that the Employee Forum process does not have to accept and act on every issue raised, but does need to provide clear and well-reasoned arguments in order to justify a rejection. I usually ensure that minutes of the meeting are taken, are documented, and are made available after the meeting in a variety of public areas. This ensures that every person has the opportunity to understand what issues have been discussed, and what actions are planned to take place to resolve them if any.

- *Health & Safety Committee* – A Health & Safety Committee can function in a very similar way to the Employee Forum, but with a specific focus on Health & Safety performance and issues, rather than a more general consideration of the needs of your facility. As a result, it can benefit engagement in the same way, encouraging your front-line team members to feel that their opinions are respected, and that their involvement in managing Health & Safety is valued and is important. As with the Employee Forum, I usually divide the facility into clearly separated areas, and seek volunteers as Health & Safety representatives for each area. You may find that some individuals have a particular interest in this subject, and your Health & Safety reps may also be First Aid and Fire Marshal trained. In the early stages of a *Lean Foundations*™ journey, I have often created two Health & Safety Committees; one populated by supervisors and managers of all relevant functions and team areas, and another populated with front-line team members from each of the segregated areas. The first of these committees is usually created to build knowledge and a sense of ownership within my supervisory and management team for Health & Safety, and takes part in the monthly Health & Safety reviews discussed back in Step 7. I utilise this forum to educate this organisational layer, and to drive in processes and procedures such as Risk Assessments, COSHH Assessments, and Accident and Incident investigation. The second of the committees is usually the more engagement focused forum, and is created in order to involve front-line team members in the identification and ongoing management of good Health & Safety practice. These committees would normally meet on a monthly or quarterly basis, and would usually be led by the Health & Safety Manager (or your equivalent), with support from yourself as top leader of your facility. Within the meeting, Health & Safety KPI's can be reviewed; such as number of accidents and incidents, number of Hazards raised, and number of Near Misses reported. And, Health & Safety representatives can be encouraged to raise any concerns that either they, or other team members from their area, feel appropriate. Actions can then be agreed, which often require equipment maintenance and repair, and therefore you may wish to include your Facilities and Maintenance representative within the committee. As with the Employee Forum, it's important that minutes of the meeting are taken, are documented, and are made available after the meeting in your public areas. I've often ensured that specific Employee Forum and Health & Safety noticeboards are located throughout my facility which include details of the relevant representatives, and are locations where meeting minutes are shared.

- *Open Forums* – Alongside these formal meeting forums, I have also found it useful to establish a more casual and open setting for people to raise any concerns or ask questions of members of the management or leadership team. You may choose to call these a 'Coffee morning', or a 'Q&A session', and can endeavour to introduce them in a way that is a little more relaxed in order to encourage a sense of trust and freedom of expression. Here, rather than inviting specific representatives, you can ask for volunteers from each of the previously identified work areas to join the meeting. In the session, people can be given the freedom to ask whatever question they may choose, or to raise any problem that they feel is not being addressed. Of course, there is a risk that you may get asked a silly question, or be presented with a problem from a very specific and perhaps personal perspective; but I have found such occurrences to be rare, and have always been able to communicate a response, or manage the question to a sensible conclusion. By introducing a forum such as this, you provide everyone in your team with an opportunity to discuss anything they feel appropriate (within reason of course), and as a consequence provide them with a loud and clear voice in their organisation. They can choose to be as conspicuous as they wish to be, and to speak up when they feel necessary.

- *Quarterly Town Hall Briefs* – As well as creating forums where you can listen to the thoughts and feelings of your team, I've also found it a good idea to establish settings that enable routine communication out to my team. We've discussed previously the use of Town Hall Briefs, and in the past, I have found it very worthwhile to utilise these on a quarterly basis in order to share key business information, and to build a sense of camaraderie and community. To complete these sessions, I would suggest that you create a standard agenda, where you can share key information about the performance and direction of your facility. I would normally start by communicating KPI's and financial performance, which can help everyone to understand how you are performing, and whether or not their contribution is making a difference to the overall direction of your plant. It's a good idea to try and relate these to your 'Golden Circle', and to the status of your improvement Plan. Of course, some organisations may feel that it's not appropriate to share too much financial performance information. After all, if the employees know that your facility makes a profit, surely, they'll ask for a pay rise, won't they? In my experience, I always prefer to be as open and honest as possible, and to trust people with information. This approach can help to build relationships and demonstrate respect. Alongside the KPI's and financial performance, you could also consider sharing information around wider business performance. You could demonstrate new products that are being introduced, inform everyone when new orders or contracts have been signed or are near to completion, or can communicate organisation structure changes. As a final item, I've also used these sessions to share information around the more social and community related aspects of my facility. Later in this sub-step, we'll discuss these in more detail, but it's here where I would choose to present any charity activities that are being completed by your team members, or could celebrate the successes of individual team members who have perhaps completed a training course, or have been recognised by their peers. By creating these forums, I have found that my team members feel a greater sense of community, and realise feelings of being part of something greater than just themselves. And, by recognising the efforts and contributions of team members who have achieved success, I have helped everyone feel relevant and appreciated for who they are.

- *Peer Recognition Schemes* – Some organisations include schemes such as 'Employee of the Month', or something similar, where particular team members are selected by managers for recognition and perhaps even reward as a result of their efforts over a previous month. Personally, I don't like to utilise such schemes. Drawing again on the ideas of Dan Pink and Alfie Kohn, I believe that they can become reward mechanisms that potentially encourage the wrong kind of behaviour, and at best only deliver short-term benefits to employee engagement and satisfaction. Instead, I prefer to introduce a peer recognition scheme, where employees are recognised and appreciated by their fellow team members and colleagues for their performance. That recognition may take the form of nothing more than a public thank you, communicated in the quarterly Town Hall Brief. Or, it could include some kind of unexpected reward, such as an extra day of holiday entitlement, or a voucher for a family meal at a local restaurant. What is important here is that the recognition is given not by someone in a position of authority, but by someone who is a peer and who is genuinely grateful for the efforts and support of the person in question. It's also important that the recognition, and any associated reward, is unexpected, so that the behaviour is given genuinely and selflessly. When establishing such schemes, I've usually provided a means for nominations to be given, perhaps into HR, and for those nominations to provide justification for the recognition. Where you have corporate values, you may choose to ask your team members to align their justification for selection with those values. Where you have numerous nominations, it may be necessary for the leadership team to select those that they feel are most worthy, or you may simply choose to recognise everyone nominated. I've found that schemes of this nature really help to build a sense of community across functions, and help individuals feel that their efforts are recognised by the people that matter to them most; their colleagues. By introducing the scheme, you're simply providing a means for people to say thank you to one another.

- *Systemised recognition* – Acts of recognition and appreciation can sometimes be a little awkward, or can be difficult to deliver with sincerity. As a consequence, some people may avoid saying 'thank you' for fear of appearing disingenuous. Obviously, this isn't going to help your level of engagement, and isn't going to make people feel that their personal contributions are appreciated and relevant. To help, I've found that it can be useful to deliberately add a need for appreciation into the agenda of every standard meeting forum in your facility. Where you have 'Start of Day' meetings, 'MDI' meetings, and your weekly and monthly tactical meetings, you could intentionally require that some aspect of the performance that has been discussed is recognised and appreciated, and that any individuals who are responsible for that performance are thanked for their involvement. This may seem a little forced, but by deliberately encouraging recognition and appreciation in this manner, I've found that it can become easier and more habitual, and can embed a genuine level of gratitude within your team. It can be a really positive way of reinforcing every person's internal drivers, and of reminding them that positive progress is being made.

- *Lean Awareness Training* – Delivering Lean Awareness training to every team member, particularly those on the front-line, can have an extremely positive impact on engagement. If you recall our discussion back in Step 4, I suggested that you deliver Lean Awareness training to support the empowerment of your team, and proposed that you complete it with all layers of your organisation structure. By taking every team member through such training, you can enhance their understanding of basic Lean principles; such as the seven wastes, single piece flow, quality first, and problem-solving. And, you can include team-building games and exercises, of which there are many to choose from (plug game, planks game), which can encourage and enhance teamwork in your facility. At the same time, by completing the training with your front-line team members, you can provide them with the skills and knowledge that they need to contribute, and can demonstrate to them that their contributions are both welcome and necessary. You can improve their sense of relevance and importance, and can share your vision for their engagement in the improvement process. This simple training programme, rolled out team by team throughout your facility, can benefit your level of engagement greatly, and I would actively encourage you to introduce your own version with help from your CI Manager.

- *Kaizen/Continuous Improvement events* – Having completed the Lean Awareness training, it's often a good idea to put it into use as quickly as possible through the completion of a Kaizen or Continuous Improvement event. You may choose to select the improvement opportunity from within your Improvement Plan, or you may simply choose to address a problem identified by the team in their Lean Awareness training session. In either case, asking a front-line team to commit time and energy to a Kaizen event, and to improve a process or resolve a problem within their specific work area, can be hugely engaging and empowering for all of the people involved. These are usually led by the CI Manager and the supervisor or manager for the functional area or cross-functional team. I've seen such events last one day, or five days; and have completed small 3S/5S activities, or have completely redesigned the layout of a production line to improve efficiency or resolve quality issues. The scale of the activity is not necessarily important, and remember you're not going to be aiming for world-class Lean processes. Instead, you're simply trying to establish the foundations of good performance, whilst engaging your people. Therefore, the involvement of front-line team members is critical, and the responsibility of supervisors and managers to support the implementation of their solutions is vital. I've found that such events often deliver very clever and cost-effective solutions, and highlight previously unknown issues and problems that deliver even greater efficiency and improvement results than expected. Importantly, they can also engage and enthuse your front-line team, can ensure that they feel that their contributions are valued and appreciated, and help them to feel that their opinions are important and relevant. To make them even more worthwhile, it's a good idea to include an end of event report out session with managers and yourself, and to create a 'Kaizen Storyboard' that can be used to communicate the before and after states of the improvement activity.

Measured challenge

Measured Challenge addresses Lencioni's idea of 'Immeasurement', and combines it with Stairs' and Galpin's ideas on 'Challenge'. Here, the focus is on ensuring that team members feel that their contributions are measured fairly and against tangible criteria that is not subject to personal interpretation, and that they feel that the requirements of their role challenge them without stretching them beyond their capabilities. Some of the activities listed have been touched on previously, and simply need to be expanded to cover engagement. Others are new and can be introduced as you see fit.

- *The right objectives* – You may remember that all the way back in Step 3, we discussed the need to define individual objectives for every person in your team. At that point, we were discussing how to cascade the detail of your Improvement Plan through your facility, and I described the use of individual objectives to help in that aim. However, they can also be used to support the engagement of each of your team members if targeted and measured correctly. By defining objectives that are clearly relevant to the overall Improvement Plan, you can enhance a person's sense that their contribution is relevant and important to your overall purpose. At the same, if those objectives are challenging in nature, and are clearly measurable with data rather than with opinion, they can address both the desire for challenge and the need for fair and tangible measurement of contribution. It's therefore important that you and your management team are very selective and careful in determining exactly what objectives should be set for each person, and how they are to be measured. In their article *'With Goals, FAST beat SMART'*, Donald and Charles Sull introduce a new anacronym to help explain how to define good goals. Instead of defining SMART goals, they suggest that 'Frequently discussed', 'Ambitious', 'Specific', and 'Transparent' (FAST) objectives are more effective for individuals. They believe that SMART goals undervalue the need for ambitious objectives that stretch a person's capabilities and development, and that they restrict company-wide visibility between peers. They propose that FAST objectives solve these problems, because they are shared openly across teams, are discussed routinely (as we discussed back in Step 4), and are intentionally challenging. They therefore offer us a means of defining goals that boost the performance of our team members, and encourage their sense of engagement.

- *The Individual Development Plan* – Alongside the definition of individual objectives, you also have the opportunity to agree and support an Individual Development Plan for every person as we discussed back in Step 4. At that point, we were discussing utilising such a plan as a means of empowering a person in the pursuit of their own development. However, Individual Development Plans can also be used to encourage the engagement of your team members, particularly if they include content which can challenge each person on their own developmental journey. If you can agree training and coaching that develops their skillset, and perhaps opens them up to new roles and opportunities within your organisation, then your team members are likely to feel both supported and challenged all at the same time. Once again, you and your management team will need to carefully agree the Individual Development Plans with each person; ensuring that they are actively involved in order to maintain their empowerment, whilst also being careful to provide them with challenge that is achievable and which supports the needs of the organisation. This can be done with front-line team members just as much as with supervisor and engineer level roles. I've found that the Skills Versatility Matrix is a really useful tool to help to identify and balance the right developmental requirements of each person with the needs of the organisation. The Skills Versatility Matrix, first discussed back in Step 2, can help you to see where a person has an opportunity to increase their skill level in their particular areas of responsibility, or can identify where organisational skills gaps can be filled with the training and development of someone new. Offering a team member the opportunity to be trained to a higher level of skill, or the opportunity to be trained in a new role elsewhere in your facility, can provide a genuine sense of challenge for some. However, you need to be careful, as some people could find the idea disturbing and uncomfortable, and you may unsettle their psychological safety. You'll need to be selective and give people choice in order to truly engage and support them. You may find that some people desire external training in professional qualifications that may allow them to progress in their career. Personally, I always endeavour to say 'yes' to such requests. I consider that it's my responsibility to support every person in my team as fully as possible, even if that means that they may leave in the future. I'm sure you've all heard the phrase *"…train them so that they can leave, treat them well so that they don't want to…"*. Well, I believe it.

- *Additional roles and responsibilities* – A feature that is sometimes surprising, but I've found to be very true, is the desire of some people to be given additional responsibilities above and beyond their normal role. This may be as a Health & Safety representative, a First Aider, a Fire Marshall, a member of the Spill Team, or as a Trainer. I've often introduced additional level responsibilities such as these into my facility specifically to encourage and challenge those people who seek them out. In each case, I would always suggest that those additional responsibilities are recognised with small incremental pay benefits. I believe that it's important to respect the people who take on those responsibilities, and not to try and take advantage of them. I've found that introducing those opportunities provides just enough additional responsibility to satisfy those who wish to be involved and be challenged, without stretching them beyond their capabilities.

- *Support personal interests* – If you take the time to inquire, you're likely to find that a number of your team members are actively involved in hobbies, societies, clubs or charity work outside of their normal daily work responsibilities. These are pursuits that they may be passionate about, or simply enjoy for relaxation and pleasure. I've found that a really good way to engage your team is to very actively support them in those activities wherever you can. Their Individual Development Plans can be utilised as a means of agreeing actions that can support their skills in areas that can support their personal life, just as much as their work life. You might consider options such as allowing people to work flexibly, or by enabling them to work with particular colleagues who share the same interests outside of work. They may even be able to set up clubs or societies in your facility. In supporting these personal interests, you can challenge your team members to add value to your entire facility through their integration into your team, or you can simply challenge them to free up their time so that they can follow their interests without disrupting their performance.

Enjoyable work

Enjoyable work addresses Stairs' and Galpin's idea on 'Enjoyment', and focuses on ensuring that all team members take some pleasure from the completion of their responsibilities, and experience positive emotions in the course of working in your facility. Here, the activities listed attempt to address the potential impact of repetitive work, and help to create a positive and supportive working environment.

- *Eliminate the terrible job* – It's likely that somewhere in your facility there is a job that absolutely no one could possibly enjoy. I've seen it more than once, and they're often the least satisfying and most boring activity that you can imagine. To give an example, I once saw a person whose job was to hold up a stop/go sign in a corridor that was too small for more than one fork-lift truck at a time. They were traffic controlling, in a facility that didn't have much traffic. If you have a job like this in your facility, I implore you to find a way to eliminate it. I suggest that you treat it like a problem-solving exercise, and try to find a way to work without it if you can. If you have a role like this in your facility, you're basically asking someone to do something that you would never choose to do yourself, and you'll undermine your other efforts to encourage and create enjoyment as a result.

- *Elevate the boring job* – Many roles in manufacturing involve a large degree of repetition. The constant loading and unloading of machines, the short cycle times that repeat every few seconds, or the continuous hum of a conveyor belt; can be somewhat mind-numbing, and not particularly pleasurable. Whilst it's not necessarily possible to eradicate these roles, and whilst some people may take a small amount of pleasure from completing a repetitious task well, it's likely that these roles are going to suffer with high turnover and low engagement. In addition, you may find that people who work in them suffer with repetitive strains and injuries caused by the overuse of certain parts of their body. It's therefore a really good idea to first of all identify these roles, and then to elevate the way that you manage them. One option is to ensure that people rotate jobs, with perhaps just two to four hours in a particular role before swapping to something different. Another option is to try and build in more interesting activities into the particular job. Perhaps the piece of machinery used in the job needs basic calibration checks or routine maintenance. Or perhaps quality checks and part inspections can be added. There are different options, but again I would suggest that you and team address each of these roles as a problem to be solved, and consider ways of improving the enjoyment potential for the people who occupy them.

- *Focus on strengths* – We are all different, and find different activities enjoyable. Some people are suited to higher levels of repetition and perhaps seek to perfect our abilities over time. Others are more suited to flexible creativity, and enjoy the challenge of responding to something new. Whatever the scenario, I've found it useful to try and match people to roles that suit their personality and preferences. If a role requires attention to detail, for example an inspection activity, I've tried to ensure that it's been allocated to someone who enjoys that kind of work. Obviously, getting to know your team members well enough can take time, and you may not always be able to be completely flexible. But, if you choose to respect your team members, take the time to understand their strengths, and then seek to align those strengths with the right kind of role and task, you can be very successful in engaging your team. This is just as applicable in front-line office-based roles as it is on the production floor or in your warehouse. Processing paperwork, filing, and computer-based data entry suits some people, and doesn't suit others. At times, even people in supervisory, engineer, and management level roles, can find themselves in a function or team that doesn't suit them. Working with them to identify the right role for them, and supporting them in their transition with training and development, can significant benefit individual and team engagement.

- *Build a sense of fun and community* – Whilst your facility is a place where work has to be completed, it's also a place where people spend a considerable amount of their time together. Building a sense of community, and encouraging fun and laughter, can help people to feel happy and enjoy the time that they spend with their colleagues at work. There are lots of options to help build that sense. For example, you can encourage your team members to start small groups, teams and societies in your facility. I've seen music clubs, soccer teams, golf societies, and social events groups that encourage people to mix from functions that do not normally work together. You can also support and promote charity activities that your team members are taking part in, both outside and inside work. I've found that another great option is to introduce an annual Family Fun day, where you provide entertainment activities for your employees and their families. This gives your team members the chance to show their family where they work, and to take pride in the facility that together you're building. You could also introduce a monthly or quarterly newsletter, which shares information about major changes and developments in your facility, perhaps with a focus on the events that most effect your people. You could welcome new starters, recognise long-service, and celebrate significant events such as birthdays, weddings, and births. You might even choose to send flowers and gifts to employees who welcome a new family member. As a final option, you might consider introducing group bonding activities that perhaps take place at the start of each working day. I've seen examples of daily huddles, or even of team 'planking' exercises. However far you choose to take these, I suggest you ensure that it's your team members that are at the forefront of the selection process, perhaps through the Employee Forum. For me, levels of laughter and amusement are a real indicator of progress.

- *Socialise* – To enhance the sense of community, it can be a good idea to organise social events that take place outside of work. Typically, these might include annual celebrations for Christmas or other such holidays. But, they could be something that you encourage to take place on a more routine basis in order to bring people together. It's during social events like these that funny or unusual incidents occur, and which then can become legendary tales that help to bond people together in friendship and camaraderie. Such stories often become the ties that keep people together for the long-term, and help them to feel comfortable and accepted in their working life. They also bring humour and laughter into your facility, and can lighten the mood when circumstances are challenging.

- *Put your people first* – Building a working environment that is genuinely positive and supportive begins by treating every single individual with respect. If each person is considered to be nothing more than a resource that can be utilised and consumed, it's going to be difficult to demonstrate a commitment to engagement and happiness. And there are many ways we can demonstrate respect. We've touched on issues around compensation and pay previously, but obviously this is a good place to start. We can offer flexible working conditions, and support people during health problems or in times of family crisis. We can lead and manage effectively, and communicate with one other in the right way. We can coach and guide in order to help people learn and develop. And we can listen and support when needed. We can ensure our facilities are fit for purpose, and our equipment reliable and safe. We've already discussed all of these points, along with many more, at length at various points in our *Lean Foundations*™ journey. I reiterate them here just to make the point, and to demonstrate how much work we have already done to engage your team successfully.

STEP 8 SUMMARY

In completing Step 8 of your *Lean Foundations*™ journey, you have hopefully taken the final step in building the well-performing manufacturing facility that it's been our aspiration to achieve from the very beginning. By embracing employee engagement as the final piece of the improvement jigsaw, and by introducing targeted activities that help to permeate engagement through to your front-line team members, you should find that you're benefiting from higher levels of enthusiasm and commitment in your team, and are identifying and solving the most relevant and performance enhancing problems in your facility.

We should remember that a great deal of our activities in the previous seven Steps will have dramatically improved employee engagement in their own right. Our efforts to define and agree a common purpose, to improve teamwork, to align with a clear plan, to empower, to lead situationally, and to provide stability and control with processes, will already have raised the level of engagement considerably. And, the use of tools such as 'Start of Day' meetings, the 'MDI' process, 'Daily audits', team based problem-solving, and A3's, will have added significant value. However, the introduction of some or all of these specific engagement activities can help to ensure that every member of your team has the opportunity to be engaged, and as a consequence is able to thrive in their role. Workplace happiness, operational performance, and your ability to implement Lean should now be good, and the opportunity to progress to great is absolutely within your grasp.

In drawing Step 8 to a close, let's take a moment to reflect on the main points...

- Whilst we have made significant progress on our *Lean Foundations™* journey, it's possible that some team members do not feel fully involved in the process, and perhaps do not feel happy in their role.
- It's possible that our efforts to date have not been sufficiently inclusive, and have missed out the extremely valuable contributions of our front-line team members.
- Employee Engagement is a concept that can help us to address this missed opportunity.
- Lencioni believes that employee job misery exists when we suffer from 'Anonymity', 'Irrelevance', and 'Immeasurement'. He believes that employee engagement has to address these three issues in order to improve workplace happiness and eradicate job misery.
- Stairs and Galpin believe that employee engagement requires the correct management of external and internal drivers, and the consideration of factors of 'Enjoyment', 'Challenge' and 'Meaning'. They believe that addressing these points enhances workplace happiness, which as a consequence positively impacts organisational performance in a variety of ways.
- For *Lean Foundations™*, we can combine these two perspectives to introduce activities that provide an all-inclusive approach to employee engagement.
- We can encourage a feeling of Conspicuous Relevance, where people feel that their contributions are relevant and valued, and that their role is important and has meaning. Activities such as the introduction of an Employee Forum, a Health & Safety committee, routine Town Hall Briefs, and Peer Recognition schemes can help to achieve this aim.
- We can encourage a sense of Measured Challenge, where people feel that their role stretches their abilities, and where their contributions are measured against tangible criteria rather than individual whim. Activities such as the use of Individual Development Plans, correctly defined personal objectives, and the opportunity to undertake additional responsibilities, can help to create this feeling in our team.
- We can create an environment of Enjoyable Work, where people take pleasure from meeting their responsibilities and completing their daily tasks, and from being at work. Activities such as building a sense of fun and community, putting our people first, and of removing or elevating repetitious tasks, can help us to meet this aim.

And in the end....

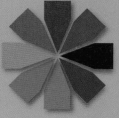

... what have we achieved?

In completing your *Lean Foundations*™ journey, I would hope that you feel that what you and your team have achieved is something quite significant. I'm confident that in having introduced some or all of the activities, processes, tools and methodologies that we've discussed, your manufacturing facility is now a far happier and more capable place than it was before. And, I'm optimistic that you're now in a much better position to begin to introduce the *Lean Basics* that can take your operational performance and workplace happiness to the levels of excellence that all but a few attain. However, I know from experience that you may well feel that not enough progress has been made, and that more improvements are possible. The urge to keep moving forward is strong, and can sometimes cause you to lose perspective. It's therefore important to take the time to reflect, and to look back at the considerable progress that you have made.

To begin with, you will have embraced organisational health and effective teamwork as the corner stone of your improvement journey. By creating and sharing your 'Golden Circle' to introduce purpose and meaning, by nurturing psychological safety to enable healthy and vital conflict, by adjusting your organisation structure to facilitate teamwork and bring the right people on-board, and by developing and cascading your Improvement Plan to provide direction and alignment; you will have brought clarity and enthusiasm into what was possibly a confused and soul-destroying situation.

Next, you will have created the environment where empowered front-line team members are actively engaged, and will have super-charged the path to improvement with the energy of everyone in your team. By embracing empowering leadership to give freedom and support to your talented team, and by actively engaging everyone through enjoyment, challenge and relevance; you will have embedded creativity and accountability in a place that may previously have been dark and indifferent.

And finally, you will have built the well-functioning management system that stabilises your capabilities, and creates the capacity for your team to really thrive. By introducing daily management that systematically supports prioritised problem-solving and performance management, by institutionalising problem-solving into your daily routines, and by standardising your activities whilst enabling choice and supporting your ability to lead; you will have cleared your path, and will have instilled a process of continuous improvement in a place that was no doubt stuck and going nowhere.

In short, you will have addressed the three common factors of a lack of organisational health and effective teamwork, of a lack of engagement of empowered front-line team members, and of a lack of a well-functioning management system. You will have achieved a level of good, and will be performing well. In the process, you will have fully enthused and engaged the intrinsic motivations of your team. Their senses of purpose and meaning, of collaboration and teamwork, of autonomy and ownership, and of success and improvement, will hopefully be enhanced to the point of happiness and fulfilment. And, all of these are likely to be completely aligned with the desire for your facility to improve, grow, and achieve excellence.

But, this is not the end. This is just the beginning of the next step in your journey. Now, you can move forward towards excellence, and can follow your desire to embrace Lean practice in the knowledge that you've establish the solid foundations on which it can flourish. Without necessarily knowing it, your team, and the culture of your facility, is now perfectly primed to actively embrace and even apply Lean philosophy in the pursuit of true operational excellence. Their mentality has been positively affected, and they now embrace a multitude of ideas that are fundamental in enabling Lean methodology to take hold. Your team completely understand the need to add value for their customer. They want to support and fully utilise the capabilities of every person. They are focused on improvement and the resolution of problems in order to reduce waste. They are not frightened by change and welcome it as the route to improvement. They desire to work in teams in the knowledge that together they are stronger. They see standardisation as the basis of improvement, and know that stability and control underpin flexibility and responsiveness. They have a desire to learn, and accept that failure and problem identification support learning. And most importantly, they're desperate to make things even better than they have already become. They want to keep moving forward for the benefit of themselves, of each other, and of the journey itself. You've instilled in them a resilience, a passion, and skillset that will bring them happiness and fulfilment, and which will add value to their lives, both personally and professionally. On their behalf, thank you.

With all of that said, there are a couple of important final comments for me to make.

First, I know that every person who reads this book will do so in their own way. Some will read it through, and may then apply each of the 8-Steps in logical sequence. Others will develop their own route from A to Z, and will simply use the book as a reference and guide. Of course, there is no right or wrong way, it's about whatever works for you.

Second, please do not be concerned if there are one or two people in your team who are still not fully engaged with the improvement journey that you are on. I know from experience that you will be successful in persuading the majority, but there will still be some who are not convinced. Give it time, know that you have done your best, and be confident that you have made a difference for most.

Third, if you have found what you have read here to be interesting, and want to get more involved, feel free to take a look at the *Lean Foundations™* website at www.leanfoundations.co.uk, or the LinkedIn page. I intend to try and share more ideas, information, and resources on this platform in order to help as many people as possible on their *Lean Foundations™* journey.

And finally, it is my sincere hope that you have enjoyed reading what is presented here, and have found it in some way useful in achieving the aspirations of enhanced workplace happiness, improved operational performance, and the ability to implement Lean. I'm a passionate believer in the *Lean Foundations™* approach, and I hope that you now are too.

References

Allan, Andie, *Employees aren't engaged in the manufacturing sector: here's what to do about it.* June 2018, https://www.staffconnectapp.com/internal-communications/employees-arent-engaged-in-the-manufacturing-sector-heres-what-to-do-about-it/

Angel, D. C., and Pritchard, C., *Where 'Six Sigma' went wrong.* Transport Topics, June 2008.

Autry, James A., *The Servant Leader: How to Build a Creative Team, Develop Great Morale, and Improve Bottom-line Performance.* New York, NY: Three Rivers Press, 2004.

Belbin, R. Meredith, *Management Teams: Why They Succeed or Fail.* Oxford, UK: Elsevier Butterworth-Heinemann, 1981.

Benbow, Donald W., and Ali Zarghami, *Introduction to 8D Problem Solving: Including Practical Applications and Examples.* Milwaukee, WI: ASQ Quality Press, 2017.

Bhasin, S., *An appropriate change strategy for Lean success.* Management Decision, 50(3), (2012).

Blanchard, Ken, Patricia Zigarmi, and Drea Zigarmi, *Leadership and the One Minute Manager.* London, UK: HarperThorsons, 2015.

Brassard, Michael, *The Problem Solving Memory Jogger.* Methuen, MA: Goal/QPC, 2016.

Byham, William C., and Jeff Cox, *Zapp! The Lightening of Empowerment.* New York, NY: Fawcett Books, 1998.

Collins, Jim, *Good to Great.* New York, NY: Harper Business, 2001.

Dennis, Pascal, *Getting the Right Things Done: A leader's guide to planning and execution.* Cambridge, MA: Lean Enterprise Institute, 2009.

Dweck, Carol S., *Mindset: How You Can Fulfil Your Potential.* New York, NY: Random House, 2006.

Edmondson, Amy C., *Psychological Safety and Learning Behaviour in Work Teams.* Administrative Science Quarterly 44.2 (1999)

Edmondson, Amy C., *The Fearless Organisation: Creating Psychological Safety in the Workplace for Learning, Innovation, and Growth.* Hoboken, NJ: John Wiley & Sons, 2018.

Gagnon, Chris, Elizabeth John and Rob Theunissen, *Organisational Health: A fast track to performance improvement.* September 2017, https://www.mckinsey.com/business-functions/organisation/our-insights/organisational-health-a-fast-track-to-performance-improvement.

Gallup, *State of the American Workplace 2017.* https://www.gallup.com/workplace/238085/state-american-workplace-report-2017.aspx

Goldratt, Eliyahu M., and Jeff Cox, *The Goal: A Process of Ongoing Improvement.* New York, NY: North River Press, 1986.

Goldratt, Eliyahu M., *What is This Thing Called the Theory of Constraints.* New York, NY: North River Press, 1990.

Goleman, Daniel, *Emotional Intelligence: Why it can matter more than IQ.* London, UK: Bloomsbury, 1996.

Goleman, Daniel, *Leadership that Gets Results.* Harvard Business Review, April 2000. https://hbr.org/2000/03/leadership-that-gets-results

Grant, Adam, *Give and Take: Why Helping Others Drives Our Success.* London, UK: Weidenfeld & Nicolson, 2013.

Greenleaf, Robert K., *The Servant as Leader.* 1970. https://www.greenleaf.org/products-page/servant-leader-download/

Heath, Chip and Dan Heath, *Switch: How to Change Things When Change is Hard.* New York, NY: Broadway Books, 2010.

Herway, Jake, *How to Create a Culture of Psychological Safety.* December 2017, https://www.gallup.com/workplace/236198/create-culture-psychological-safety.aspx.

Industry Week Magazine: *Best Plants Award 2017.* https://www.industryweek.com/operations/meet-2017-industryweek-best-plants-award-winners-exceptional-performers

Jackson, Thomas L., *Hoshin Kanri for the Lean Enterprise: Developing Competitive Capabilities and Managing Profit.* New York, NY: Productivity Press, 2008.

Kohn, Alfie, *Punished by Rewards: The Trouble with Gold Stars, Incentive Plans, A's, Praise and Other Bribes.* New York, NY: Houghton Mifflin Company, 1999.

Lencioni, Patrick, *The Five Dysfunctions of a Team.* San Francisco, CA: Jossey-Bass, 2002.

Lencioni, Patrick, *Death by Meeting.* San Francisco, CA: Jossey-Bass, 2004.

Lencioni, Patrick, *Silos, Politics and Turf Wars.* San Francisco, CA: Jossey-Bass, 2006.

Lencioni, Patrick, *The Advantage: Why Organisational Health Trumps Everything Else in Business.* San Francisco, CA: Jossey-Bass, 2012.

Lencioni, Patrick, *The Ideal Team Player: How to Recognise and Cultivate the Three Essential Virtues.* San Francisco, CA: Jossey-Bass, 2016.

Lencioni, Patrick, *The Truth About Employee Engagement.* San Francisco, CA: Jossey-Bass, 2016.

Liker, Jeffrey K., *The Toyota Way: 14 Management Principles from the World's Greatest Manufacturer.* New York, NY: McGraw Hill, 2004.

McCord, Patty, *Powerful: Building a Culture of Freedom and Responsibility.* San Francisco, CA: Silicon Guild.

Ohno, Taiichi, *Toyota Production System: Beyond Large-Scale Production.* Portland, OR: Productivity Press, 1988.

Peters, Tom J., and Robert H. Waterman, *In Search of Excellence: Lessons from America's best-run companies.* New York, NY: Harper & Row, 1982.

Pink, Dan, *Drive: The Surprising Truth About What Motivates Us.* New York, NY: Riverhead Books, 2009.

Radecki, Dan, and Leonie Hull, *Psychological Safety: The Key to Happy, High-performing People and Teams.* The Academy of Brain-based Leadership, 2018.

Rother, Mike, *Toyota Kata: Managing People for Improvement, Adaptiveness, and Superior Results.* New York, NY: McGraw Hill, 2010.

Rozovsky, Julia, *The five keys to a successful Google team.* Re: Work Blog. November 2015. https://rework.withgoogle.com/blog/five-keys-to-a-successful-google-team/.

Schein, Edgar H., *Humble Inquiry: The Art of Gentle Asking Instead of Telling.* San Francisco, CA: Berrett-Koehler Publishers, 2013.

Shook, John, *Managing to Learn: Using the A3 management process to solve problems, gain agreement, mentor, and lead.* Cambridge, MA: Lean Enterprise Institute, 2008.

Sinek, Simon, *Start with Why: How Great Leaders Inspire Everyone to Take Action.* New York, NY: Portfolio Penguin, 2009.

Sobek II, Durward K. and Art Smalley, *Understanding A3 Thinking: A Critical Component of Toyota's PDCA Management System.* New York, NY: Productivity Press, 2008.

Stairs, Martin and Martin Galpin, *Positive Engagement: From Employee Engagement to Workplace Happiness.* Published in The Oxford Handbook of Positive Psychology and Work, Oxford University Press, 2013.

Stanier, Michael Bungay, *The Coaching Habit: Say Less, Ask More and Change the Way You Lead Forever.* Toronto, ON: Box of Crayons Press, 2016.

Sull, Donald, and Charles Sull, *With Goals, FAST beats SMART.* MIT Sloan Management Review, June 2018. https://sloanreview.mit.edu/article/with-goals-fast-beats-smart/

Watanabe, Ken, *Problem Solving 101: A Simple Book for Smart People.* London, UK: Vermilion, 2009.

Womack, James P., and Daniel T. Jones. *Lean Thinking: Banish Waste and Create Wealth in Your Corporation.* New York: Simon & Schuster, 1996.

45450654R00170

Printed in Poland
by Amazon Fulfillment
Poland Sp. z o.o., Wrocław